D0913151

Civil Rights, Culture Wars

CHARLES W. EAGLES

Civil Rights, Culture Wars

The Fight over a Mississippi Textbook

The University of North Carolina Press *Chapel Hill*

This book was published with the assistance of the Fred W. Morrison Fund
of the University of North Carolina Press.

Set in Arno Pro by Westchester Publishing Services
Manufactured in the United States of America

The University of North Carolina Press has been a member of the
Green Press Initiative since 2003.

Library of Congress Cataloging-in-Publication Data
Names: Eagles, Charles W., author.
Title: Civil rights, culture wars : the fight over a Mississippi textbook /
    Charles W. Eagles.
Description: Chapel Hill : University of North Carolina Press, [2017] |
    Includes bibliographical references and index.
Identifiers: LCCN 2016021187 | ISBN 9781469631158 (cloth : alk. paper) |
    ISBN 9781469631165 (ebook)
Subjects: LCSH: History—Study and teaching (Secondary)—Mississippi. |
    Mississippi—History—Textbooks. | Civil rights—Mississippi—History.
Classification: LCC E175.8 .E24 2017 | DDC 976.2—dc23 LC record available at
    https://lccn.loc.gov/2016021187

Jacket illustration: Open book © 123RF.com/stillfx; vieux papier background
© istockphoto.com/AndreyBeka.

To George Brown Tindall
and W. F. Minor

There is nothing more important than molding the hearts and minds of children in the right direction.

—Governor Ross Barnett, 1963

Here all they learn is they're niggers, and they haven't got a chance in the world, except to serve the white man, be under him, do what he wants . . . . They don't get much out of school. Our people aren't supposed to take their education too seriously. We're supposed to do all the dirty work, and the white man is supposed to do the learning. I've seen the books they give our children in school . . . . they tell all about the white man, and they tell nothing about us, except that we're here, and we're no longer slaves. Well isn't that nice! So long as our children don't learn the truth about themselves in school, then they might as well be slaves!

—Thirty-one-year-old black mother in Clarksdale, Mississippi, in 1964

Contents

A gallery of photographs follows p. 36

Civil Rights, Culture Wars

Conflict
Combating Ignorance

In the early 1970s two young college professors in Jackson, Mississippi, led a team that wrote a boldly revisionist textbook that upset the staid field of Mississippi history and caused a major public controversy. James Loewen, a sociologist at Tougaloo College, and Charles Sallis, a historian at Millsaps College, worked with several of their students and colleagues to produce in 1974 a ninth-grade textbook, *Mississippi: Conflict and Change*.[1] The title told their story. On many levels Loewen and Sallis argued that conflict produces change, and they embraced controversial subjects related to race and class, examined unpleasant subjects such as economic depressions and violence, and included subjects neglected by other books—blacks, women, workers, and the arts. By paying attention to dissent, the revisionist writers revealed past conflicts and highlighted lost possibilities for change. Loewen and Sallis believed that writing and teaching about the potential conflicts in Mississippi's history would stimulate intellectual growth among ninth graders but also foster change in the state and among historians.

Loewen and Sallis presented a perspective that differed dramatically from previous textbooks. As Loewen would later demonstrate for American history in his best-selling *Lies My Teacher Told Me*, they wanted to correct the "lies"—the omissions, false impressions, distortions, errors—in Mississippi history textbooks.[2] Marginalized women, workers, and blacks and other minorities learned little about their own histories from their Mississippi history textbooks. More important, they gained no knowledge about challenges to the established elite and about struggles against its control, whether by slaves or farmers in the nineteenth century or more recent civil rights demonstrators. The textbooks thereby denied many Mississippians access to their own traditions of resistance and protest, their own achievements and progress, and kept them ignorant of everything but the homogenized, continuous success story of the dominant class. At the behest of the white elite, the history books preserved ignorance of past inspirational heroes and, more generally, of lost possibilities and forgotten historical opportunities. The state-sanctioned amnesia played a vital role in the perpetuation of white supremacy and racial discrimination.

Ignorance has many causes and takes many forms. Though education seeks to overcome the innocent ignorance of birth, ignorance can also result from a failure to study certain subjects, from a loss of memory, and from a suppression of information. In school textbooks, educational authorities deliberately decide what to include and what to exclude. The powerful can make decisions that actually "strive for a goal of stupidity," rather than for genuine education. Under the guise of protecting children, imposing an engineered ignorance protects the privileged by preserving the status quo and by releasing leaders from responsibility. It also reinforces orthodox values and preserves useful stereotypes. One method of constructing ignorance involves a fearful elite's actively and strategically instilling ignorance by leaving out specific information and analyses and by limiting access to dangerous knowledge. Too much knowledge could lead to troubling questions and a loss of control of the classroom, and the elite feared the unknown results. Such a constricted education preserves power arrangements. As one scholar concluded about the impact of ignorance, "We rule you, if we can fool you."[3]

Privileged whites have used historical ignorance to maintain their superiority over blacks but also over other minorities, women, and less influential whites. Through an "airbrushed white narrative," the elite denied the excluded groups' knowledge of their own past victimization by the powerful. For example, to keep blacks subservient, a purging or "management of memory" has deliberately suppressed or forgotten inspiring historical information. The manipulated official history justifies white privilege as well as black inferiority, and it also denies any need for reform. Not only do blacks lose their past, but many whites do too; nonelite whites feel their comparable powerlessness when history omits accounts of class struggles. Ignorance of historical facts can also lead to "moral ignorance": a lack of accurate information that can yield "incorrect judgments about right and wrong." Moral ignorance causes erroneous historical interpretations. As a consequence, the "mystification of the past underwrites a mystification of the present" that produces a "feel-good history for whites." It particularly makes ruling whites comfortable and confident in their status and authority while it denies the historical, and by implication the contemporary, significance of everyone else.[4] As teachers and authors Loewen and Sallis wanted their textbook to combat ignorance in textbooks.

Viewing the school as an intellectual marketplace, the authors of *Conflict and Change* sought to extend a type of conflict into the classroom where competing ideas would prompt students to consider both the state's past and its future. Unlike previous writers of Mississippi history textbooks, Loewen and Sallis did not seek to reinforce the status quo but urged students to question it and eventually, if necessary, to change it. By presenting clashing historical interpretations, *Conflict and Change* also undermined the conventional view of history as a fixed set of facts and made the study of history itself an intellectual contest full of questions rather than answers. The authors wanted to transform Mississippi history textbooks and the study of the state's past, but the introduction of *Conflict and Change* caused a controversy because of the importance of textbooks not just in Mississippi schools but in all of American education.

Before the electronic classroom, textbooks constituted the "big gun in the educational arsenal" and were often the only weapon available to teachers. Long dominating American primary and secondary education, textbooks occupied as much as three-quarters of classroom time and 90 percent of homework. By the end of a typical twelve-year educational career a student had encountered more than thirty thousand textbook pages, and often no other significant books. A textbook exerted an especially powerful educational influence because the average student "accept[ed] everything in the text as gospel." As a result of textbooks' virtual monopoly power, they not only determined what students learned, but they also played a major role in shaping students' attitudes, values, and interests. Textbooks often determined the content of what teachers taught. Diane Ravitch concluded that in history classes textbooks "*are* the curriculum" because history teachers usually have not studied history but have an education degree in social studies. In the upper grades where each teacher had many more students than in the lower grades, teachers may have especially depended on textbooks. Combined with teacher's manuals, texts also often determined how teachers presented subjects and how they tested their students.[5]

Students, the ultimate textbook consumers, played no role in selecting the books they studied. According to one industry saying, "kids don't buy books," so publishers cavalierly ignored student preferences and interests. Like students, teachers individually and collectively usually had little impact on textbook selection even though textbooks shaped their curriculum and classroom activities. Instead textbook selection involved a more centralized, politicized procedure under the authority of individual school districts or, more often, the state.[6]

By the 1970s American schools spent more than twice as much for books as for other teaching materials. With yearly sales of more than $600 million in 1975, textbooks constituted a big business, but smaller than the dog food industry. Sales of commercial fiction and nonfiction books exceeded that of textbooks and dominated the domestic book industry, but publishers depended on textbooks because their steady sales promised larger profits with smaller risks. Although one-fourth of textbooks did not make a profit, the chairman of Houghton Mifflin acknowledged, 80 percent of his company's profits came from textbooks. In the lucrative national market, publishers fought for textbook sales.[7]

After this introductory chapter, the story of *Conflict and Change* must begin with an appreciation for both the history of **textbooks** (chapter 2) in Mississippi and American education and the methods used to produce, market, and select them. Textbooks' long dominant role in education meant that they had frequently sparked controversies. For more than a century the public repeatedly debated the selection, production, and, especially, content of textbooks. The fight for textbook contracts created a competition rife with shady and even illegal sales methods, and widespread abuse led to efforts to restrict unfair practices. Publishers tried to form a monopoly to restore order by eliminating costly competition and controlling prices. On the other hand, through progressive legislation, state governments created agencies to achieve lower book prices by stopping corruption and professionalizing textbook selection; a few states tried printing their own books. Despite attempts to cleanse the textbook market, controversies frequently erupted, often at the state and local levels.

In writing *Conflict and Change*, Loewen and Sallis dissented from the predominant view of Mississippi **histories** (chapter 3) that celebrated a harmonious story from the perspective of dominant white males. According to the established interpretation, white men did everything important: they settled the state, operated the plantations, controlled the slaves, ran the government, developed the economy, and, in general, made the state's history. Conventional Mississippi history textbooks portrayed a past without disruptive events and contentious issues; the books lacked oppressed people and dramatic clashes. The white ruling class had tried to avoid the conflicts that could have produced change by coercing conformity and stifling dissent over slavery, white supremacy, violence, secession, poverty, disfranchisement, black oppression, and other divisive issues. The minimized disagreements of the past had yielded little historical change. Endorsing the view of the white elite, contemporary Mississippi history textbooks' presentation of a peaceful past compounded the problem by denying even the potential for conflicts.

The contrasts between *Conflict and Change* and older traditional Mississippi histories echoed larger debates over the contours of American history. Two interpretative traditions have prevailed in American history. One, called progressive history, originated during the progressive era and saw instability and divisions in the nation's past, just as in early twentieth-century society. It stressed conflicts and struggles between classes but also between different groups who divided along ethnic, racial, political, ideological, sectional, or religious lines. In the fights each side sought the power to control, or at least influence the direction of, change. As supporters of reform, progressive historians identified with the past forces working for a more democratic society; they supported the people against the entrenched conservative interests. Their positive portrayals of political and economic reformers in the past offered historical confirmation for their advocacy of contemporary reforms. During the first third of the twentieth century, progressive historians had great influence, and a generation later in the 1960s another group of historians called the New Left revived a revised version of the progressive interpretation. The New Leftists also saw divisions and conflict in the American past, and they too sided with the people against the interests. Unlike the progressives, however, the sixties radical historians had little optimism that reform of the political and economic system could achieve meaningful results, so they advocated more extreme change.[8] Without any declaration of allegiance, *Conflict and Change* fit in the tradition of the progressives and the radical critics of the 1960s.

Appearing between the progressive and New Left historians, a second view of American history minimized differences among Americans and emphasized the nation's persisting consensus around shared fundamental values and ideas. Though the new consensus history resembled the nationalistic celebrations by nineteenth-century histories, it developed most fully in the affluent post–World War II years marked by stability, prosperity, and conformity. Instead of stressing divisive classes, they focused on unifying American culture. Upon their closer examination, apparent conflicts in the past appeared to consensus historians as only minor disagreements occurring within a wider harmony. Without periodic clashes between various groups, the consensus interpretation of history generally told a story characterized by continuity among a homogeneous population with uniform values. Consensus history, according to historian John Higham, resulted from a "massive grading operation that smoothed and flattened" the past and eliminated serious contention and controversy. Historical change occurred when society agreed on needed modifications and the consensus gradually shifted, not as a result of any disruptive disagreement. Conservative historians approved the consensus; more liberal ones bemoaned it. Conservative forces wanted schools to teach the true facts about the past, while liberals thought schools should teach students to ask critical questions about their history.[9]

Mississippi history textbooks shared the consensus school's positive perspective, and they resembled the triumphal nineteenth-century American histories. The state histories, however, arrived at their similar interpretations for different, more parochial reasons. Like most schoolbooks, especially in the social sciences and particularly state histories, the books presented the views of the state's civic elite who ran the political system and public education. The orthodox interpretations justified the leadership's status and power, and Mississippi's elite based its authority on white supremacy and racial segregation. Working constantly to block anything that seemed to subvert the southern way of life, the white leaders' continued dominance required the unremitting suppression of African Americans. In the words of University of Mississippi historian James W. Silver, the state became a "closed society" that barred new ideas and information that could threaten the culture's values and stability.[10] By justifying white dominance, Mississippi history books played a key role in maintaining the closed society. Whites as well as blacks suffered from the suppression of subversive ideas. The traditional official consistent confirmation of the white male leaders' importance meant that when James Loewen and Charles Sallis sought to overturn the "feel-good" historical narrative they caused a controversy.[11]

To write a different version of Mississippi history, the two professors assembled a team of **writers** (chapter 4) for the Mississippi History Project. Not the experienced educators who usually wrote textbooks, the group included fledgling faculty and even undergraduate students. Coming from Tougaloo College and Millsaps College in Jackson, the assorted writers included professors and students, men and women, blacks and whites, northerners and southerners, historians and non-historians. The eight writers brought a variety of perspectives, strengths, and interests to the creation of *Conflict and Change*. Loewen and Sallis maintained overall control, coordinated the writers, and played the role of editor as they directed their unusual collection of contributors. In the entire process Jim Loewen played the driving role.

The Mississippi History **Project** (chapter 5) sought to expand in an unbiased way the state's story to include all Mississippians, even the silent, the unnamed, and the dispossessed. The radical approach began with their inspiration to write a textbook and the unique group gathered to work on the Project. The textbook's design and format also had many original features. It employed numerous maps, tables, bar graphs, pie charts, photographs, drawings, and other illustrations, and it presented extracts from primary sources along with vignettes and personal profiles. The margins also highlighted key points, posed questions, and defined terms. Loewen and Sallis also often urged the reader to compare information to material found in other places in the text; to prompt ninth graders to see relationships, for example, they suggested comparing a map showing the 1850 distribution of slaves to an earlier map of soil types. Each chapter also contained an annotated bibliography to encourage further reading, and the text itself occasionally explained the clashing interpretations of events. The textbook introduced new features not for novelty but to help ninth graders interact with history by thinking critically about new questions and by becoming active learners instead of passive memorizers of the traditional historical facts.

As their primary objective, however, Loewen and Sallis wanted to eliminate bias in Mississippi history books. Fairness had many facets. It, of course, meant giving blacks full and accurate treatment, but it also involved a more comprehensive discussion of whites, Native Americans, and women. Older history textbooks downplayed any conflict associated with the farmers' movements in the late nineteenth century, and they paid little attention to lynching and racial violence. In the view of Loewen and Sallis, dissenting whites who did not approve of white supremacy deserved inclusion, and white racists required a more forthright description.

Discriminatory treatment of blacks especially attracted Loewen and Sallis's attention. For the state with a black majority for a century after 1840, their textbook elevated and expanded the presence of blacks in the state's history. *Conflict and Change* did not flinch in its discussions of lynching, white supremacy, and Jim Crow segregation in the late nineteenth century. Its simplest but most dramatic innovation expanded coverage of recent Mississippi history and directed unprecedented attention to the civil rights movement in "The Struggle for Civil Rights," the book's longest chapter. For the first time black and white ninth graders could read about the civil rights movement in their state.

As Loewen and Sallis worked on their book, they began to worry about the **reception** (chapter 6) *Conflict and Change* would receive. Initial concerns focused on editors and publishers. They had produced their book without any professional editorial advice, whereas most textbook ideas originate with editors and publishers who direct their development to ensure eventual profitability; textbook writers, therefore, usually had a publisher even before they began writing. As a result of their unusual, naive approach, Loewen and Sallis later had to scramble to interest a publisher. A radical secondary school textbook with a market limited to one small state had little appeal because it promised negligible profits. Loewen and Sallis had the good fortune that Pantheon and Andre Schiffrin, its director, accepted their Mississippi textbook. In addition to finding a publisher, the authors had to worry about the reaction of students and teachers who tried a manuscript version in their classes and about the response of scholars and others who offered expert commentaries on the manuscript. After publication in 1974, the authors waited for the book's critical reception in the popular and professional press, mostly from outside the state. The most important response would come, of course, from the educational establishment within the state.

Controversy (chapter 7) quickly engulfed the new ninth-grade history book. The battle over the Loewen and Sallis text involved whether the state's public schools could adopt it. A local school district's purchase of textbooks depended on state funds because individual districts could not afford to buy books with their own resources. State monies could only buy books approved by the State Textbook Purchasing Board, and it relied on advice from a Rating Committee for Mississippi history textbooks. The approval process presented the question of whether professional educators, laypeople, or scholarly experts should evaluate textbooks and determine the "knowledge" that students should learn. State law posed the judgment of political appointees, who included teachers and educators, against the textbook's authors who had professional scholarly expertise. The two state groups determined, for example, if a textbook employed appropriate levels of vocabulary and analysis for its readers. Judging a history text's suitability also included deciding if its historical interpretation would become, in effect, the state's official view of its history. State-authorized books set the standard for what students would learn about many controversial subjects. Usually objections to schoolbooks came from conservatives who discerned a liberal or radical bias.

In the 1970s, decisions about Mississippi history textbooks emphasized their treatment of the Civil War, Reconstruction, race and sometimes, as in other states, communism, American presidents, the nation's capitalist economic system, religion and evolution, and patriotism. Concerns over black history and race relations dominated; the Rating Committee, basing their evaluations largely on their own opinions and experiences, accepted or rejected a textbook based on its members' approach to racial issues. When Loewen and Sallis routinely sought acceptance of their textbook for assignment in the state's schools, traditionalists opposed it. As a result, the teachers on the Rating Committee for Mississippi history books rejected the Loewen and Sallis book, and the members of the State Textbook Purchasing Board affirmed the decision. The state authorities refused to approve the revisionist *Conflict and Change* that brought blacks fully into the state's history. After the official rejection, Loewen and Sallis challenged the decision in court.

Along with a dozen other plaintiffs who included supportive public school district officials, representatives of Catholic schools, and parents of affected students, lawyers for Loewen and Sallis initiated in the U.S. District Court in Greenville a **case** (chapter 8) against the state authorities. Their federal lawsuit, entitled *Loewen v. Turnipseed* (the latter after John Turnipseed, a member of the Rating Committee), sought to force the State Textbook Purchasing Board to approve *Conflict and Change*. Melvyn Leventhal of the Jackson office of the National Association for the Advancement of Colored People's (NAACP) Legal Defense Fund (LDF) filed the suit, and, after Leventhal moved from Mississippi, Frank Parker of the Lawyers' Committee for Civil Rights Under Law's Jackson office continued the lawsuit to trial. The lawyers for Loewen and Sallis pursued a protracted effort to gain the book's acceptance. For four years the two sides filed motions, replied to written interrogatories, took oral depositions, received sworn testimony, and engaged in pretrial conferences and negotiations. The plaintiffs encountered myriad delays.

Loewen v. Turnipseed finally came to **trial** (chapter 9) near Labor Day in 1979. After four days of testimony and arguments, Judge Orma R. Smith took the case under advisement. Seven months later, on April 2, 1980, he ruled in favor of the plaintiffs and ordered the state officials to put *Conflict and Change* on their list of approved textbooks.

The victory in federal court marked significant **progress** (chapter 10) for Mississippi education and for the civil rights movement. School districts would have access to a textbook that included African Americans fully in the state's history. By also telling the history of other neglected groups such as women and workers, Loewen and Sallis presented a far broader conception of their own state's history than the state had ever known; they offered a view that dramatically diverged from what the state's students, black and white, had always learned. Coming after the civil rights movement had overturned the Mississippi way of life, *Conflict and Change* sought to instill in a school textbook the social changes brought by the freedom struggle.

In the early 1970s when Loewen and Sallis undertook their work on a Mississippi history textbook, they benefitted from a combination of their own backgrounds and timing. Each author had devoted his doctoral research to studying the state's race relations, and each in his nonacademic life worked for equal rights. More important, in addition to the cycles in textbook adoption, *Conflict and Change* grew out of the civil rights movement in Mississippi. Advances attained in the 1960s made their integrated effort possible and created, they hoped, a more hospitable environment for their pathbreaking book.

While *Conflict and Change* came partly as a result of the black freedom struggle, it also sparked a conflict that anticipated the culture wars of the 1980s and 1990s. In effect, the controversy over the ninth-grade history book bridged two major upheavals of the second half of the twentieth century: it grew out of the civil rights movement and foreshadowed the emerging culture wars. Cultural conflicts over textbooks had particular intensity not just because of the money involved in the growing textbook market but also because the issues involved what values the nation's schools and textbooks would pass on to the children of the next generation. The sides fought over how the American culture would perpetuate itself. Defending America's identity as a democratic, capitalist, Christian country gained power in a time of national uncertainty and fear. In the Depression challenges to Harold Rugg's social studies textbooks had, for example, focused on his textbooks' treatment of the New Deal and capitalism. Later during the Cold War textbook fights commonly involved discussions of communism. Intractable clashes over religion and evolution had also perennially affected textbooks. Beginning in the 1960s, Texans Mel and Norma Gabler attacked textbooks that undermined conservative Christian values by promoting moral relativism and secular humanism. A battle contemporaneous with *Conflict and Change* erupted in Kanawha County, West Virginia, over diversity but even more in defense of Christian values.[12]

For history books in the twentieth century the debates repeatedly centered on the increasing inclusion of racial and ethnic minorities and what diversity meant for national identity and patriotism. Critics of new textbooks argued that an emphasis on America's historical pluralism would necessarily focus attention on racism and prejudice and, as a result, lessen students' respect for and devotion to their country. Conservatives feared diversity would cause patriotism and loyalty to decline. Throughout the first half of the twentieth century, the solution for American history texts involved compromises that included in the books mere token representatives of minorities but without disrupting or threatening the celebratory, patriotic view of the nation's history.

After the culturally disruptive sixties challenged Americans' basic values and the fall of communism raised questions of national purpose, the culture wars, according to one historian, "were fights over how the nation's history was narrated . . . and over whether the purpose of America history was to make Americans proud of the nation's glorious past or to encourage citizens to reflect on its moral failures." In 1994 a major controversy over National History Standards focused attention on American history textbooks and teaching. In the uproar, according to another scholar, the wars "increasingly connoted battles about race, ethnicity, and patriotism."[13]

Years before the fight over National History Standards, the civil rights movement had challenged white Mississippians' vaunted southern way of life that rested on white supremacy and white control. Just as uncertainty about national identity led to the national controversies in the 1990s, unexpected changes in Mississippi during the civil rights movement meant state history textbooks suffered from similar, more parochial perils if they deviated from the established positive story of progress and if they did not support the entrenched interests' sense of their own unique collective character. *Conflict and Change* continued the movement's assault on the supposedly fixed identity of white Mississippians who had always dominated the state and its official culture. In the wake of the civil rights movement, the authors presented challenging ideas about who was a Mississippian, what it meant to be a Mississippian, and who and what should be in Mississippi history. By revealing the lack of consensus in the state's past, *Conflict and Change* prompted students to consider the state's past errors, and it questioned the standard all-white narrative. Threatened whites, who had by 1974 already lost much of their cultural and political authority, wanted to protect and preserve their place in the state's history books. Fighting a ninth-grade textbook constituted one way to resist change.

CHAPTER TWO

Textbooks

Their History, Role, and Importance

With an attack in 1960 on some schoolbooks as "subversive, un-American, [and] advocating integration of the races through communist propaganda," the Mississippi chapter of the Daughters of the American Revolution ignited a controversy. The Mississippi Education Association's response defended the books and criticized "investigations of our textbooks made by irresponsible parties." The teachers' organization also lauded the state's methods for selecting textbooks as one of the nation's best.[1] As the heated debate during the Cold War and the civil rights movement demonstrated, citizens attached great importance to the books school children studied. Periodically disagreements over textbooks roiled public life and divided white Mississippians. Controversy had erupted at the turn of the century over who would choose the books and what method they would use, and in the 1920s Governor Theodore G. Bilbo had stirred outrage over his proposal for the state to publish its own schoolbooks. The Great Depression had caused great concern over the costs of books and disagreement over the state's provision of free textbooks. Later, as the 1960 episode proved, the Cold War and the civil rights movement provoked fears of subversive textbook contents. Such controversies could only occur, of course, after the state provided for public education.

Mississippi's Reconstruction Constitution of 1869 created the state's first public education system. Before the Civil War, Mississippi had lacked any statewide public school system because a small, dispersed population made public schools impractical and the wealthy slaveholding elite had little interest in paying taxes to finance public schools for poor whites. Political rivalries and general indifference also presented obstacles to antebellum education. When the Reconstruction schools began operation in 1871, the legislature authorized each local school board to "prescribe a uniform series of text books." Concerned about dishonesty and chicanery, the legislature required that no member of the board could "act as agent for any author, publisher or bookseller" nor could a director accept "any gift, emolument or reward" for influencing the selection of books. The state mandated that schools provide books to students at cost. After the removal of the Reconstruction government and the restoration of local white rule, the legislature reestablished a free statewide public school system. Although control over school textbooks went in 1873 to each county superintendent, two years later under a new law teachers assumed the responsibility for selecting books to be used for five years. To combat malfeasance in choosing schoolbooks, the prohibition against a superintendent's acting on behalf of any book persisted and extended also to teachers.[2]

The creation of the state's public schools reflected broader national changes. In the nineteenth century, a dramatic growth in public education produced a corresponding increase in textbook demand, and more publishers entered the business. Before the Civil War small, scattered schools lacked the enrollments to support a national textbook industry, and a competitive national market in schoolbooks did not develop. Along with various primers, students in the antebellum era frequently used Noah Webster's *Blue-Backed Speller* and the *McGuffey's Eclectic Readers*; by the end of the nineteenth century, Webster and McGuffey each had sold a million copies. After the Civil War, with westward expansion and immigration from Europe, the nation grew, and public school enrollments soared. The increasing demand for schoolbooks spurred the growth of textbook publishing, and many companies began to engage in cutthroat competition in the individual state markets. Publishers and their representatives, for example, commonly bribed local and state school officials to influence their book purchases, and they offered discounts to appeal to the buyers. They also exchanged free copies of their books for their competitors' books because they hoped for later purchases.[3]

To curb uncontrolled corruption and protect profitability, publishers in the early 1870s created the Publishers' Board of Trade. When their reform efforts failed, the board dissolved in 1876. Keen, unscrupulous competition resumed, for example, nearly eighty publishers bid to sell schoolbooks to Kansas. Recalling the tactics, one publisher admitted, "Nothing short of manslaughter was excluded." To guarantee profits eighteen leading publishers in 1884 formed the School Book Publishers' Association, but it too failed to cleanse and rationalize the business. As a last resort in 1890, several major publishers formed a book trust, the American Book Company (ABC). It soon sought to ensure its dominance by buying a dozen smaller firms and becoming the world's largest producer of textbooks. Unethical business practices continued. To win book contracts, publishers' field agents continually cultivated friends in public schools, bribed school officials, secured teaching positions for supporters, installed friends on school boards, and engaged in other improper behavior. As a result, an Oregon committee of forty-one school officials formed to choose schoolbooks just happened to select

98 percent of the new books from the ABC list. In another state most county superintendents of education also worked as book salesmen for the ABC. Though payments often amounted only to one hundred dollars, a school superintendent could receive a paid vacation courtesy of a publisher. The trust even used its power to unload obsolete old books on unsophisticated frontier districts. One commentator claimed the ABC "grasp[ed] the lion's share by means fair and foul." Occasional exposures of bribes and illegal deals discredited the ABC and allowed smaller publishers to stay temporarily in business.[4]

Many observers recognized the evils of the textbook business. In 1896, according to the *Atlantic Monthly*, one school superintendent observed, "As now conducted, the school-book business is a portentous evil." The next year George A. Gates, the president of Iowa College (later Grinnell) told the Iowa Teachers' Association that the book trust's evils included bribery, threats to employment, electoral support for candidates, and undue influence of local newspapers. It had, said Gates, "used all the wiles of the devil." With muckraking journalist Henry Demerest Lloyd, he published his charges in a Christian socialist newspaper, and the ABC responded with a lawsuit. Though it never went to trial, the intimidating response demonstrated the trust's confidence in its position. With the trust controlling about 90 percent of the textbook business, one educator declared, "Even the notorious Standard Oil Company has no such monopoly as this." The book trust's extensive power meant that it effectively determined what schools taught and what students learned. A four-hundred-page ABC sociology book, for example, mentioned monopolies, combinations, and trusts three times, and in each case excused or defended them. While ABC sold many fine textbooks, it also, according to Gates, peddled "some of the most disgraceful trash."[5]

In Mississippi the Constitution of 1890 continued the "uniform system of free public schools" and required racial segregation, but it also responded to the industry's cutthroat tactics and to attempts to restrict competition by one dominant company. Anticipating the American Book Company's control of the nation's textbook market, Mississippi reformed its method for choosing schoolbooks. It still called for uniform textbooks in a district, but, in a move toward centralization, a committee, not all made up exclusively of teachers, would make the decisions. The local school board would name five teachers of "recognized ability," and the superintendent would appoint two more. The committee could select only one book per subject in each grade.[6]

In response to mounting concerns about graft, Mississippi lawmakers in 1904 enacted a drastic reform. A comprehensive law curtailed the number of people involved in deciding which books students would use. Instead of hundreds of individuals on scores of local committees, the new plan called for one commission for the entire state. The governor appointed eight educators of "known character and ability," with no more than one coming from each congressional district; the state superintendent of education served as an ex officio member. Repeatedly and explicitly, the legislators revealed their fears of malfeasance and their intent to purify the process. One of the law's lengthy sections directed that each commissioner swear to have "no interest, direct or indirect, in any contract that may be made hereunder; that he will receive no personal benefit of profit there from; that he is not in any manner interested in any books or publishing concern publishing any books of the kind contemplated for use in the public schools of this state or any state." In providing for punishment of a fine up to $1,000 and two years in prison, the law restated and extended the prohibited conflicts of interest: "It shall be clearly unlawful for any member of the school books commission during the term of his appointment to office to accept or receive from any school book company, firm, corporation, or agent, any employment, retainer, compensation, reward, emolument, gift, or donation, directly or indirectly." The reform also required a commissioner to abstain from voting if "any person *related within the third degree by blood or marriage* to any member of the school book commission, or is associated in any business or partnership with any member of said commission, shall be employed in good faith by any school book company, firm, corporation or agent in connection with the adoption of school books in this state."[7]

The 1904 reform also specified how the commission operated. To avoid inside deals, the commission advertised for sealed bids, required a deposit from every bidder, and opened the bids in an executive session. By law the commission notified the chosen publishers by registered mail. The recipient of a contract had to post a $10,000 bond, and it had to maintain in a state warehouse sufficient copies of the book. Except for foreign language course books, the legislation required that every book had to be in English and mandated that no book could "contain anything of a partisan or sectarian character." Though the law expected the commissioners to "use their discretion and judgment," it specifically directed them to consider the book's physical characteristics such as binding and durability, the appropriateness of the content, and the price that had to equal the lowest price offered to any other state. The commission had the authority to reject all bids and reopen the search. To prevent fraud after letting a contract, the law stipulated that the books delivered had to be exactly like the sample approved by the commission.

Contracts extended up to five years during which no other books could be used as textbooks.[8]

The law creating Mississippi's textbook selection commission relied on a centralized group of education experts instead of multiple politically unpredictable and vulnerable groups of local teachers and citizens. By directing the selection of textbooks, the state's leaders also took control of the content of textbooks to protect students from objectionable ideas. Over the years, the reform effort itself needed refinement as the lawmakers tried to balance the competing demands of democracy and efficiency, popular will and central control. In 1912, to increase stability, the legislature withheld from the commission the authority to change more than 25 percent of the books in a year. Four years later the legislature required each county to set up a committee of five teachers to recommend to the district board and superintendent books for use in the agricultural high schools; except for bypassing the state commission, the new provisions closely followed the earlier ones. Further adjustment came when the 1918 legislature repealed the limitation on the percentage of books that could change at any adoption.[9]

Mississippi's reforms resembled the efforts of many states between 1890 and 1920 to combat the widespread corruption and the resulting unnecessarily high cost of textbooks. As progressive innovations, state textbook commissions resembled other reforms to regulate business by giving state governments greater authority. Viewing the state positively, reformers believed it could and should provide more public services. To avoid scandals, state legislatures increasingly gave more centralized regulatory power to administrative bureaucracies staffed by experts, not politicians. In effect, state textbook commissions represented a shift in power away from dispersed local lay authorities susceptible to payoffs and bribes. Contrary to popular democratic influences, the commissions tried to "remov[e] politically volatile elements from possibly exercising power." Instead more closely monitored state educational experts would make efficient, professional, if perhaps paternalistic, decisions regarding textbooks. As a result leaders would maintain protective control over the content of textbooks. Southern and western states found the textbook commission especially appealing.[10]

Adopting books statewide had several advantages. By negotiating for a larger market, reformers hoped for the lowest prices and for an end to costly bribes and corruption. Use of the same books would promote a standard statewide curriculum. A state commission could also exert greater control over textbook quality by taking the decision out of the hands of sometimes naive and incompetent local citizens and teachers. With an increasingly mobile population, uniform textbooks would lower costs for parents who would not have to buy different books when they moved within the state. The textbook commissions themselves varied in size, organization, scope, and responsibilities. The people or the legislature elected commissioners, or state officials such as the governor or superintendent of education appointed them. The commissions ranged from three to fifteen members, and their terms from one to six years. Though designed to increase expertise in choosing books, most had a combination of lay and professional educator members.[11]

Some commissions had control over books for only the first eight grades, while others chose books for the high schools too. The adoption periods extended from one year to six years, with the percentage of books that could change in one year often limited. Perhaps the most important variation involved the number of books chosen by the commission. Some states permitted selection of only a single book per subject for each grade, so schools had to use the only title available. Other commissions had the authority to approve multiple titles, so an individual school district could choose. In open adoption states, the commissions applied only basic criteria to make available virtually all the appropriate textbooks, and as a result the local authorities exercised almost complete control over the commissions' selections. Not all legislatures assigned responsibility for choosing schoolbooks to a new state textbook commission. An almost equal number of state boards of education assumed most of the responsibility for deciding which textbooks to adopt. In half of the states, counties or local districts largely retained control over the books used in their schools. Each state system had distinctive characteristics, and some states allowed a combination of authorities.[12]

Pressured by reforms that included not just textbook commissions but also antitrust laws, the American Book Company in 1908 reorganized under New York law and sold many of its subsidiaries. Soon it broadened its business by entering the high school textbook market and in the 1920s by beginning a college text division. As the nation's public education system grew, in part due to continued population growth and spreading compulsory attendance laws, the textbook market also increased. The ABC remained the major force in the industry. A Chicago newspaper charged as late as 1923 that the ABC was "honey-combed with crime, and its continued power is a menace to the public good." Its unsavory methods pervaded the industry. With other companies joining the competition, ABC's market share declined to perhaps 60 percent. In the rivalries, publishers employed more than financial incentives. To obtain an adoption, a publisher might attack the contents of a competitor's book and engage in libelous assault on its author's character.[13]

In the early 1920s Upton Sinclair investigated the American education system, and in *The Goslings: A Study of the American Schools* he cataloged the corruption he discovered in the textbook industry. The muckraker exposed it as "a battle-ground of graft and favoritism." The publishers' agents routinely used cash to pay local school superintendents or state commissioners for adopting their books; the payments sometimes reached thousands of dollars. According to Sinclair, with more subtle and indirect tactics, publishers provided financial support for friendly candidates campaigning for school boards and superintendents, and they opposed uncooperative elected officials. The resulting school leadership would ensure the selection of the companies' textbooks, and they might additionally reward the publishers' friends with teaching jobs. Book company representatives also attended professional conventions to support their allies, and they lobbied legislators for desired laws. Many politicians expected the payoffs and bribes. Of course, as historian Howard Beale suggested in a study prepared for the American Historical Association, school officials and politicians were "often not unreceptive to 'favors' from publishers"; the ethics of the textbook industry could, therefore, sink no lower than the morals of educational and political leaders.[14]

In Mississippi demagogic politician Theodore G. Bilbo advocated a different method to fight corruption and high prices in the textbook industry: he wanted the state to publish its own textbooks. Representing white small farmers who constantly faced economic distress, Bilbo sought to extend state government to provide aid to the "rednecks." In his first term as governor, his 1918 and 1920 proposals called for a state printing plant. Both attempts died in the legislature. Bilbo renewed his call in the 1923 gubernatorial campaign when he made a state printing plant a major platform plank. A state printer could, he argued, save citizens money by providing textbooks at cost, and it could also protect children by keeping Darwinism out of the state's schoolbooks. The latter claim appealed to his rural, fundamentalist supporters. After his defeat, Bilbo pursued his interest in state printing by investigating similar programs in California and Kansas. He corresponded with leaders and later visited the two states to inspect their printing operations. What he learned further convinced him of the wisdom and practicality of a state printer.[15]

Proponents of state publishing argued that it would not only end corruption but also would reduce costs of textbooks by eliminating publisher's field agents, making advertising unnecessary, and erasing corporate profits. The nonprofit government enterprise either could select authors to write books published by the state or it could rent the printing plates for an existing text and use them to produce the books. California was the first state to adopt state printing of schoolbooks. In 1884 a California constitutional amendment authorized the adoption of books edited by the state's board of education and printed at a state plant. Students would buy the books at cost. The state's teachers had opposed the plan as "inexpedient and impractical" because they thought the books would cost too much and would suffer from inferior quality. California educators never endorsed the program. At first the state actually printed few books, but in 1888 the legislature required state publication of all textbooks. Twenty-five years later the California legislature expanded the experiment by requiring not only that all schools purchase books printed by the state but also that the schools provide the texts free to all public school students.[16]

Many other states considered state publication of textbooks. In the 1890s four states authorized state printing, though Georgia and Louisiana never followed through by printing books and Indiana tried some state publication only to abandon the project after a few years. Florida pursued a hybrid plan that also called for state authorship, but it never succeeded. In 1905 Kansas built its own printing plant, and in 1913 its legislature approved an expansion of the plant and state production of elementary school textbooks. Kansas soon added high school books. The *Nation* found in 1915, however, no significant movement for state publication. Other states from Alabama to Oregon to Michigan considered state textbook publication, but every one decided against the idea. Colorado, Illinois, and West Virginia voted specifically against state publication.[17]

State printing projects provoked sharp disagreements over the programs' desirability, quality, and effectiveness. Proponents claimed state printing would lower costs to parents of school children and, according to a member of the former Kansas state textbook commission, "free the state from one of the most corrupting influences in our political life." Countless school officials would no longer face the corrupting influence of publishers' bribes and payoffs. Critics of state textbook publication denied that the new system would eliminate dishonesty and charged that it would instead "become an open road to inefficiency and graft." Publishers would still try to influence the state printer to gain contracts for their books, even if the state did the actual printing. The state system would also "become dependent upon political ambition or caprice or emergency." More important, opponents challenged the quality of state-produced textbooks.[18]

In 1915 *School and Society*, published by the Society for the Advancement of Education, presented an exchange between a New York City educator and a former Kansas state printer on state publication of schoolbooks. John Franklin Brown, an experienced educator with a doctorate from Cornell University and the author of *The American High School* (1909), claimed that the Kansas system produced books inferior in printing, paper, and binding. Though perhaps compromised by his position as education editor for Macmillan publishers, Brown made more damning allegations about the books' content. When cost became a major concern, he believed, educational "quality must yield" and the books would be pedagogically "inferior." Professional experts in an academic discipline would have little interest in writing for a limited state market, and one state would seldom have a sufficient supply of qualified writers to produce all the necessary textbooks. By providing only one book for each grade and subject, a state printer would prevent any choice. The state printer's investment in a book would also make changing texts difficult, even switching to a superior book. Finally, Brown concluded, the Kansas printer did not save the public any money.[19]

A reply to Brown came from T. A. McNeal, who had served six years as state printer for Kansas. After conceding initial delays in Kansas's textbook publishing, McNeal defended his state and claimed that many of Brown's charges derived from a Wichita newspaper editorial prepared by a disgruntled commercial publisher. McNeal claimed that educators disagreed on many of the often technical points presented by Brown. Though the first Kansas textbooks had typographical errors, McNeal maintained "the books printed by the state will average better in both quality of material and workmanship than the books put out by the school-book publishing houses." Not only did the state printing of textbooks save Kansans $200,000 each year, it freed the state of the "most flagrant and persistent" and "corrupting influences in our political life": book publishers' representatives.[20]

Knowledgeable about the Kansas operation, Bilbo made a state printer central to his 1927 gubernatorial platform. On the stump he claimed that California and Kansas produced textbooks at half the cost of Mississippi's schoolbooks and that a Mississippi printshop could yield similar savings. After his election, the new governor continued making a state-owned printer a key proposal in his inaugural address. He pledged it would save "hundreds of thousands of dollars" because it would pay no taxes, require no insurance, engage in no advertising, and employ no salesmen. Warning against the "most insidious propaganda" coming from opponents, Governor Bilbo denied that his ultimate objectives involved providing free textbooks for black children. He simply wanted to save taxpayers and parents money by printing and selling schoolbooks at cost.[21]

Once again, despite immediate and intense opposition, Bilbo pushed for a state printer. He convinced the Mississippi Educational Association to back his idea and received support from the state affiliate of the American Federation of Labor. At Bilbo's urging a former governor of California explained to the legislature the advantages of state printing. The state senate passed the bill, but the house refused to act. In response Bilbo called a special legislative session for October 1928. The senate again backed the proposal. In a ninety-minute address to the House of Representatives the governor declared, "I am ready to get down on my bended knees if necessary, and appeal to you on behalf of this measure for the poor people of Mississippi who are unable to pay the excessive price for school books." Despite his appeal, Bilbo's plan for a state printer suffered a second setback. In the regular session in 1930, Bilbo again lost in the House of Representatives.[22]

Some legislators opposed spending five hundred thousand dollars on such a questionable venture, while the plan struck others as socialistic and made them wonder what the state would produce next after it started printing books. Of course, the commercial textbook publishers, especially the still-powerful American Book Company, resisted Bilbo's proposal because it would deprive them of profitable sales. The Mississippi Press Association (MPA) offered the strongest, most organized, and loudest opposition.[23]

To explain its position and to stir up additional opposition, the MPA prepared and circulated several pamphlets. One claimed to provide "authentic figures" on the expenditures and costs of the California and Kansas programs and concluded that "in neither state has the State Printing Plant either been self-supporting or printed any considerable proportion of the books used." Another brochure offered more detailed "facts and figures" against the proposed state printing plant. An even longer pamphlet reprinted a statement prepared by the MPA's Press Committee and a score of editorials from the state's press. "What the Papers Say" included negative commentaries from the major newspapers in Jackson, Columbus, and Gulfport as well as hostile comments from small-town weeklies in Woodville, Crystal Springs, Hernando, and Ruleville. The state's press association itself called Bilbo's plan "un-American, un-democratic and unfair" because "[f]undamentally we are opposed to a State or Government engaging in business against its citizens and tax payers." Even as a business venture, the press group concluded, "It would be impossible for the state to supply first class school books at the same price" as commercial publishers. Before the special session of 1928, Bilbo had presented his own 110-point "Catechism on the State Printing Plant

Bill," and the MPA distributed a twenty-three-page point-by-point rebuttal to Bilbo's arguments.[24]

In the debate over Bilbo's plan, two groups bolstered the opposition. First, the governor's legislative political enemies worked to defeat nearly all of his proposals. Second, the printers in the state press association feared that a state facility would, in addition to publishing schoolbooks, take away all the printing business they provided to state, county, and local governments. Without the government printing jobs, the local printers could not survive. Bilbo's opponents won, and Mississippi would never publish schoolbooks.

While Bilbo advocated a state printer, the textbook commission continued to adopt books for the state's schools. In a wholesale reorganization the 1924 legislature created a new textbook commission. The governor appointed eight teachers with at least five years teaching experience: at least one teacher from the elementary grades, one from the secondary grades, and one from each congressional district. Unlike under previous programs, schools used the new uniform set of books for five years. The law's other requirements regarding bids, bonds, and book depositories resembled earlier legislation. On one point the new law differed considerably in language and tone if not in intent. It too prohibited conflicts of interest by the commissions and disqualified any commissioner "related within the third degree by blood or marriage" to anyone involved in the book business, but in general the law dealing with conflicts of interest employed far less impassioned language than earlier legislation. By the mid-1920s the power of the book trust had waned, and as it did concern over corruption ebbed.[25]

Legislators increasingly focused on the school system itself, rather than graft. In 1926 the general assembly created a separate high school textbook commission with three members from separate school districts, three from consolidated school districts, and one from agricultural high schools, plus the state supervisor of high schools. Other provisions for the high school textbook commission followed the standards set for the lower grades. In its greater attention to educational matters, two days before it set up the high school textbook commission, the legislature had decreed that no school supported by state funds could "teach that mankind ascended or descended from a lower order of animals" and that no textbook could teach the doctrine of human evolution.[26]

By the late 1920s Mississippi had two state textbook commissions with established procedures and policies governing their operations. When the Great Depression hit the state, a new controversy erupted over school textbook adoptions. A lawsuit brought by Adams County residents challenged the elementary textbook commission's requirement that the public schools adopt all new textbooks, even in the midst of the economic crisis. As the case developed in the summer of 1930, the *Jackson Clarion-Ledger* declared, "Never before has the state been so wrought up over any public question."[27]

The textbook commission in December 1929 had called for all new textbooks in the elementary schools at an added cost of several hundred thousand dollars for parents. Scheming secretly with the governor, the commission also solicited bids for printing plates and manuscripts for the textbooks. Bilbo's enemies suspected that he and his appointees on the commission sought to use the expensive new adoptions to make a state printing plant look like an economical alternative. Immediate objections greeted the commission. The Mississippi Education Association and the Mississippi Press Association protested the solicitation for anything other than books. Paul B. Johnson, a former congressman and Hattiesburg attorney who represented the MPA before the textbook commission, persuaded the commission to withdraw its request for plates and manuscripts because the action lacked any legal authority, but the criticism continued. W. F. Bond, the state superintendent of education, decried the decision to change all the textbooks as "unnecessary and unwise." To prevent the costly effects of the commission's action, Representative Lawrence T. Kennedy of Natchez and Speaker Thomas L. Bailey proposed legislation to allow school boards to disregard the new adoptions; as the speaker explained, "I feel we owe it to the people of the state to save this money for them."[28]

The dispute intensified when Bilbo again proposed a state printing plant. The resulting political warfare included charges of dishonesty and waste on all sides, suggestions of socialism, claims of Bilbo's political ambition, and allegations of his desperate grab for patronage. J. O. Emmerich, editor of the McComb *Enterprise Journal*, declared that Bilbo "is intoxicated with power; drunk on personal ambition; unconcerned regarding the public welfare; obstinate; unyielding; poisoned on mankind; bankrupted in good intentions; lousy with selfishness and political greed." The *Vicksburg Herald* damned the proposal as a "socialistic and impractical scheme." According to one observer, however, "derision, more than fright" greeted the printing plant proposal. After the senate approved Bilbo's plan, the house for the fourth time rejected a state printing plant.[29] The new textbook adoptions, however, remained in force, and Bilbo's opponents decided to continue their fight in a different forum.

Facing the required purchase of new textbooks, Warren Trimble and seven other Adams County parents sued in June 1930 to block enforcement of the state textbook law. Two legislative opponents of Governor Bilbo, Lawrence T. Kennedy and John Culkin, represented the plaintiffs. Defendants included the John C. Winston Company, seven other textbook publishers, and the county and state school superintendents. The attorney general represented the public officials, while a major Jackson law firm represented the publishers. In chancery court the plaintiffs challenged the qualifications of several textbook commissioners and claimed that the commission did not follow the legally required procedures. As a result of multiple errors, the plaintiffs argued, the resulting contracts were "null and void and unenforceable." Trimble and his cohorts claimed that the contracts would "cause great confusion, the discard and abandonment of text books now owned . . . , and the purchase of new books at exorbitant and unreasonable prices." Estimating the switch would cost the state's parents more than eight hundred thousand dollars, the plaintiffs called on the chancery court to cancel the book contracts.[30]

In the midst of complex legal maneuvers, parents all over the state worried about which books their children should have when schools opened in a few weeks. The state superintendent of education acknowledged the confusion and recognized that, whatever the outcome of the lawsuit, the losing side would appeal and further delay a conclusive decision on the textbooks. Critical of the commission and the governor, Superintendent Bond in late July ignored the attorney general's endorsement of the book contracts and proposed his own solution: "In case the books are bought now and the courts decided the recent adoption was illegal, the new books may be used anyway because each school could use whatever books it desired. Likewise, a school using old books could continue to use them." The *Jackson Daily News* damned the advice as "absurd" and "ill-timed" and a conspiracy to "evade or violate the law."[31]

The day before the lawsuit went before chancery court in August 1930, a judge on the U.S. Fifth Circuit Court of Appeals took the extraordinary step of intervening at the publishers' request even though no lower federal court had heard the case. The judge found the actions of the textbook commission "regular, legal and binding" and ordered the state's elementary schools to use only the books adopted by the commission. When the Natchez chancery court convened, however, Chancellor R. W. Cutrer refused the publishers' request to dismiss the lawsuits because of the federal court's prior action. After hearing testimony and arguments, Cutrer ruled that the textbook commission had not followed the statutory procedures, so the adoption had been illegal. The textbook companies then removed the case to the U.S. District Court, where another federal judge affirmed the legality of the 1930 adoptions. The Adams County parents next appealed to the U.S. Court of Appeals for the Fifth Circuit. In February 1932, the court denied federal jurisdiction and sent the case back to the state court, where the chancery court had originally ruled in favor of the parents and voided the textbook adoption. The decision left the state without required textbooks until a new commission acted.[32]

Though the drawn-out legal fight over the 1929 textbook adoption involved other issues, the prices parents paid for schoolbooks remained the central concern for many politicians, educators, and parents. In the 1920s and 1930s the idea that the state should provide free textbooks for school children occasionally surfaced. During the controversy over the 1929 adoption two representatives introduced a bill to provide free textbooks in all of the state's schools, but the proposal received little attention. Many states offered free textbooks. Philadelphia, Pennsylvania, had offered free textbooks as early as 1818, and other eastern cities had followed. In 1884 Massachusetts became the first state to provide free schoolbooks. When an 1891 study concluded that nationwide the parents of perhaps one student in five could not afford to buy needed textbooks, many realized that genuinely free public education required free textbooks. Provision of free textbooks spread in the early twentieth century, especially for indigent students. By the 1920s many states provided free books for all secondary school students, and thirty-nine states made them available to all elementary school children. Various funding methods tapped state, county, and district sources.[33]

Across the nation proponents of free textbooks emphasized their equality, efficiency, and uniformity. More important, state provision of books meant parents would save money, especially if their children used the books for only one year and could not resell them. Providing free books to the indigent would also encourage their attendance and eliminate any unpleasant economic distinctions. Opponents claimed that free texts would be unsanitary when used by many students, that students would not care for them, and that state-purchased books would be used until worn out and outdated. Objections also included the higher state taxes necessary to pay for the books and the greater burden placed on teachers who had to administer the system.[34] In Mississippi the argument over free textbooks took on other more volatile issues.

In 1939 Paul Johnson, who had advocated free textbooks for more than two decades, made them the key to his successful gubernatorial campaign. In his inaugural address, the attorney and former judge and congressman recognized that seventy-five thousand schoolchildren lacked textbooks and reiterated his commitment to the "doctrine of free text books" that was "close to my heart." Claiming an election mandate, in January 1940 Johnson called on the new legislature to make free textbooks a top priority. State school officials and the Mississippi Education Association endorsed the idea, and bills began to make their ways through the house and the senate.[35]

With observers predicting easy passage, the legislature immediately considered proposals. Suggested provisions called for a textbook rating and purchasing board made up of the governor, the superintendent of education, and three gubernatorial appointees to provide free books. An unexpected "avalanche" from "orators who are, if not masterly, at least energetic" soon greeted the bills in the house. Legislative opponents protested the governor's proposed power to appoint board members, and they complained about the legislative rush to pass a bill without adequate deliberation, even though the bill ran to fewer than four pages. Critics such as Walter Sillers, a representative from the black-majority Delta, charged the state could not afford free books for all students. Outnumbering whites by perhaps fifty thousand, blacks would account for most of the expense, and free textbooks would only encourage more of them to go to school. Sillers preferred providing books only to the truly needy and suggested that local officials (white) determine which students should receive free books. Amendments also called for separate boards to adopt and to purchase books, for buying books in some subjects but not all, and also for providing books to parochial school students. Concerns over white supremacy emerged in attempts to prevent a white and a black child from using the same actual book in successive terms and to require civics books for blacks that did not undermine white supremacy by teaching blacks about voting rights. After rejecting what one Jackson newspaper called the "emasculating amendments," the house passed the bill.[36]

Outside the legislature the proposal provoked other opponents. The Mississippi Education Association's executive secretary damned the specific bill as "wholly unsatisfactory," because it allowed changing texts only when 15 percent of the teachers objected, and the number could include Negroes. He also insisted on a commission of professional educators, and he wanted to allow each teacher to choose among several approved texts. The Mississippi bishop of the Episcopal church also questioned any attempt to "deprive the pupils of the negro race of instruction in the fundamental principle of civil rights and duties and responsibilities of citizens." The American Civil Liberties Union in New York agreed and threatened a legal challenge to special civics books for blacks.[37]

The senate education committee held a hearing on the free textbook bill, but no witness appeared in opposition. Several school superintendents did ask unsuccessfully that the textbook board approve more than one book per subject in each grade. In the senate, the bill's supporters "zealously, intelligently, and courageously beat down, exposed, and defeated" all amendments except for two calling for a separate civics book for blacks and for segregated storage of white and black texts between terms. Senators still expressed concern over the governor's control of the board, and the provision of only one textbook per course disappointed some educators and worried some senators. The bill nonetheless easily passed the senate in what the *Jackson Clarion-Ledger* called a "glorious climax." A house-senate conference committee to reconcile the two bills deleted the amendments related to race but recognized the commission's broad authority to deal with similar issues. The compromise bill also dropped the provision that allowed only teachers to call for a new adoption.[38]

On February 15, 1940, each house of the legislature considered the compromise version of the bill. During the senate debate, the *Jackson Clarion-Ledger* reported "[s]cenes never seen in a Mississippi legislative hall within this generation." Tactics used by the bill's desperate opponents included "dragging in the race issue in their last-ditch fight to defeat the bill." Senator Albert Lake of Greenville asked all women to leave the chamber before he read several letters northerners had sent to his colleague H. L. Davis of Oxford. According to one newspaper, the letters were "unprintable" and "threatened the veteran Oxford senator with dire peril, both here and hereafter." One letter called Davis "diabolical scum . . . . Who should be hanged by the neck until dead, a fate you and your kind have visited upon so many men of the black race." The chairman of the senate education committee accused Lake of trying to use "a little bit of negroism" to block the bill, but he told the senators that they "are not going to be swept off your feet by the nigger issue." Not immune to racial appeals, the bill's defenders took comfort in the fact that the "sons and grandsons of Confederate veterans are going to enforce this law." After what the *Clarion-Ledger* called "a most vicious, dangerous and wholly unjustified appeal to racial prejudice," the senate passed the bill. On the same day the house "quietly, and without hysterics," defeated all proposed amendments and also passed the bill.[39]

The next day opponents took a "final stab" at the textbook bill. Senator Lake called the bill "the most shameful act a Mississippi legislature ever performed," and from the Delta Rosedale's elderly senator W. B. Roberts, a veteran of the 1890 constitutional convention, led the assault. Resenting the northerners' letters, Roberts wanted reconsideration of the textbook measure to "proclaim to the world that in Mississippi the white race is still paramount." Specifically he called for reviving provision for storing separately the textbooks used by whites and by blacks. Senator Lake endorsed Roberts's position as the only "manly answer" to Yankee critics. Their racial appeals failed and the senate rejected the attempt to reconsider the bill.[40]

As he signed the bill into law, Governor Johnson called the occasion "the happiest moment of my public life." After years of advocacy, he declared his satisfaction with the legislation and his belief in its constitutionality. At the "triumphant end of the long fight," the *Clarion-Ledger* hailed the textbook bill as "an action creating joy in the hearts of thousands of Mississippians" who had struggled, sometimes in vain, to provide schoolbooks for their children. It savored "the first moment of a new day, a literal new day, dawning in Mississippi, a day of wider educational opportunities for all our children."[41]

The free textbook program did not escape legal challenge. Months after the legislature provided for free textbooks for elementary schools, W. M. Chance and other Forrest County citizens sued the State Textbook Rating and Purchasing Board in chancery court. According to the plaintiffs, the board violated the state constitution when it used citizens' tax dollars to distribute the free textbooks to thirteen private religious elementary schools. The state constitution, they argued, prohibited the use of state funds to support any religious group. After the chancellor denied the plaintiffs an injunction, they appealed to the Mississippi Supreme Court. In February 1941 the court warned, "Calm reason must not be stampeded by random cries of church or state or sectarian control, or by the din from the conflict of catechism and dogmatism. A wholesale sanity must keep us immune to the disabling ptomaine of prejudice." Upholding the law, the court ruled that provision of free textbooks to students in private schools did not constitute state support of sectarian schools because the "books belong to, and are controlled by, the state [and] . . . are merely loaned to the individual pupil." The loan did not amount to aid, "direct or indirect," to the religious schools. The next year the legislature extended free textbooks to all high school students.[42]

By the post–World War II period, Mississippi had joined most states in having uniform state adoptions and in providing free textbooks. Though a majority of American students received free textbooks, the programs varied widely. For example, they included both single and multiple textbooks for each subject. Free textbooks in some states depended on state moneys while others required local communities to pay for the books. Rules also frequently applied differently to elementary grades and to high schools. Mississippi's textbook program, though typical in most respects, had the unusual features of paying for textbooks in private as well as public schools and of using only state funds.[43]

With the procedures for selecting and purchasing textbooks largely set-tled, disagreements in Mississippi and across the nation increasingly involved only the textbooks' content. In late nineteenth century disputes, northerners and southerners each had wanted textbooks that reflected their views of the Civil War. Intense concern over schoolbooks began after World War I with charges that texts did not display sufficient patriotism and more specifically portrayed the British too sympathetically. In the 1920s, the American Le-gion's new National Americanization Committee, the Ku Klux Klan, and the Knights of Columbus targeted various unacceptable books, while oppo-nents of Darwin and evolution fought such repugnant ideas in schoolbooks. A New York City committee issued a Report on Investigation of Pro-British History Textbooks in Use in the Public Schools in 1923, and at the same time the state of New York had a Joint Legislative Committee Investigating Sedi-tious Activities in the Schools. In 1928 the American Federation of Labor re-ceived a report on questionable social science textbooks, and the Federal Trade Commission investigated the utility industry's efforts to spread propa-ganda through textbooks. Seeking reelection support from German and Irish immigrants, the mayor of Chicago attacked history textbooks as pro-British. Mississippi stayed largely unaffected by the national uproar, except for its 1926 prohibition of evolution.[44]

As concerns over content escalated, national conservative forces focused on Harold G. Rugg of Teachers College, Columbia University. In the 1920s, professor Rugg had begun a series of social studies textbooks that annually sold three hundred thousand copies in more than four thousand school dis-tricts, by 1940 a total of more than five million books. Critics in the late 1930s alleged that Rugg's texts' support for the New Deal amounted to communist propaganda. The Advertising Federation of America in 1939 denounced his unflattering portrayal of the advertising industry. Soon B. C. Forbes used his *Forbes* magazine to attack Rugg's depiction of capitalism, and the *American Legion Magazine*'s "Treason in the Textbooks" joined the assault. Officials in Binghamton, New York, yanked Rugg's books from the schools, while protes-tors in Ohio burned his books. A professor hired by the National Association of Manufacturers reported antibusiness attitudes and socialistic ideas in

Rugg's books. In 1940 the Daughters of the American Revolution demanded suppression of Rugg's books. The witch hunt worked, and by 1945 sales had sunk to twenty thousand copies a year.[45]

After World War II, with fears of communist infiltration intensifying, conservative critics found a new target in communist influences within schoolbooks. They attacked textbooks that they believed approved the welfare state, supported socialism, and failed to appreciate individualism and private enterprise. After failing to gain nationwide support, their early Cold War campaign took root primarily in the South where it converged with growing racial fears tied to the civil rights movement. Many southern states sought to secure schools from subversion. In 1958 *Brainwashing in the High Schools* by E. Merrill Root, a professor at Earlham College, concentrated worries on textbooks. Though a Quaker, pacifist, and conscientious objector in World War I, Root wrote the bible for right-wing critics of public education. Root castigated eleven high school American history textbooks for failing to teach American values of democracy, individualism, private initiative, freedom, and patriotism; instead they emphasized the "historical nonsense," the "seamy side of American history" of class conflict, xenophobia, corruption, imperialism, state centralization. Especially significant for Root, "every attempt of the American people to meet infiltration and subversion by the Communist conspiracy is misinterpreted, attacked, ridiculed—or ignored" by the textbooks. According to Root, the textbooks' failures left soldiers captured during the Korean War unprepared to withstand brainwashing, and he claimed the same would apply to American citizens during the Cold War.[46]

Critics and publishers rejected Root's methods and arguments. Root had measured subversion by counting index entries, and Ginn and Company demonstrated his error by applying the same technique to Root's own books. Root had cited freedom twice but collectivism eighteen times and the American way of life once but communism eighteen times. A review in *Social Education* by an education professor labeled *Brainwashing in the High Schools* "a phony" that itself uses "the techniques of totalitarian brainwashers." Root took statements out of context and misrepresented them to reach "his irresponsible conclusions." According to the reviewer, instead of a scholarly analysis, Root presented "a diatribe against government regulation, the welfare state, foreign aid, and any interference with what Root called the free-enterprise system." Other critics pointed out that Root had no scholarly credentials, except an undergraduate degree from Amherst College, that qualified him to write his book. An education scholar concluded, "The kindest view of

Mr. Root in this matter is that he had ventured where he is *unfamiliar* with either the facts or their meaning."[47]

One observer accurately predicted that Root would "give comfort to others who share his anxieties, not to say neuroses." Soon after Root stirred fears of subversion, a report by the Daughters of the American Revolution (DAR) confirmed his findings by condemning 170 textbooks in biology, music, math, literature, and geography, as well as history. In its nationally distributed *Textbook Study*, which had its largest effect in the South, the DAR objected to books that treated "our Christian heritage warily," referred to the government as a democracy rather than a republic, stressed the Bill of Rights more than the Constitution, highlighted a "pattern of 'economic determinism,'" included too much "realistic literature," and did not warn against government assistance programs. At the same time an organization called America's Future, Inc., began providing reviews of textbooks. Root, the DAR, and America's Future "quickly became the dominant forces in the fight to censor school books." As a result of their activities, textbook controversies erupted in the 1950s from New York to California, from Michigan to Texas, but especially in the South.[48]

An important crisis occurred in Mississippi. In the summer of 1959, the Mississippi DAR announced that forty-four textbooks used in the state's schools appeared on the national DAR's list of unsatisfactory books. Accepting the DAR report, the state's American Legion convention unanimously condemned textbooks that taught the un-American, subversive philosophies of communism and socialism and that advocated "integration and amalgamation of the races and the destruction of the sovereignty of the state of Mississippi." As a partial solution, the DAR proposed including parents and other lay people on the textbook rating committees. Textbook critics tied the battle against subversives to the fight for white supremacy and racial integrity.[49]

The concerns of the DAR and the American Legion affected the 1959 campaign for state superintendent of education. In an indication of the textbook issue's importance, the candidates' newspaper advertisements stressed their commitment to loyalty in schoolbooks. Challenger George L. Tutor promised to "carefully screen the Mississippi textbooks before adoption" and charged that "under the present administration 17 subversive textbooks have been adopted." Incumbent J. M. Tubb claimed the textbook program, "recognized as one of the best in the nation," had "been administered strictly according to law" and had not been criticized before the political campaign. Tubb charged that his opponent had only served briefly on textbook committees in Adams and Simpson counties "without voicing any criticism of a single textbook." Tubb won reelection easily.[50]

A month after the DAR leveled its charges, the Mississippi Association of School Administrators (MASA) fought back when it "repudiate[d]" the DAR report and "deplore[d]" the American Legion's charges. Questioning the DAR's "professional competence," the school leaders called its charges "so vague and general as to be unanswerable from the standpoint of logic and realistic analysis." To reassure Mississippians, the MASA declared that "there are not any Communists, Socialists, agnostics, infidels, or atheists teaching alien ideologies in Mississippi schools" and that no schoolbooks "advocate an alien ideology." The administrators compared the DAR and Legion tactics to the methods of Hitler, Mussolini, and Stalin and blasted "witchhunt tactics and irresponsible attempts to undermine the people's trust in their schools, teachers, and textbooks."[51]

Although Hodding Carter, the Pulitzer Prize–winning liberal editor of the Greenville newspaper, praised the MASA stand as "courageous" and "correct," the search for communist influences gained momentum. On November 18, the General Legislative Investigating Committee (GLIC), which acted for the legislature between sessions, held a two-day public hearing on un-American activities. The main witness, J. B. Matthews, a former employee of the House Un-American Activities Committee and assistant to Senator Joseph R. McCarthy, testified that "the full force of the Communist organization is being brought on integration," not to change race relations but to disrupt southern society. Communists, according to Matthews, had infiltrated the state's schools, churches, and social activities, and he named a dozen individuals linked to groups influenced by communists. The NAACP, according to Matthews, had been "infiltrated with Communists and Communist sympathizers [more] than any other organization I know of." Similar testimony came from a retired FBI agent and an investigator for the State Sovereignty Commission, the state agency created in 1956 to resist the civil rights movement and defend segregation. GLIC's report to the governor and the legislature recommended requiring all state employees to file an affidavit listing all dues-paying memberships and having the legislature study further legislation to prevent "un-American activities" and "agitation of unrest, conflict between, and turmoil between the races." The American Legion and the state senate each unanimously commended GLIC for its important work.[52]

Coinciding with the protests against some textbooks, the hearing reinforced popular concerns about subversion. More important, it occurred at the same time that GLIC employed Merrill Root as a special consultant to study subversive influences in twenty-seven state textbooks. GLIC had heard criticism of the textbooks but recognized its lack of expertise, so it turned to "an expert in the field of public school textbooks and subversive writing." Root accepted the assignment because he believed that "superficial or false textbooks are the greatest danger to America"; he argued that whatever "weakens our wills and confuses our minds will overthrow us more surely than the tanks that roll or the bombs that fall." Subversive textbooks left Americans "impotent" against the communists' "clever, cynical brainwashing." Root approved history books that did not use "imperialism" to describe the United States, displayed genuine patriotism, and mentioned Cold War spies Alger Hiss and the Rosenbergs. Unsatisfactory texts gave a "misleading" view of the Russian revolution and ignored internal subversion, in addition to overemphasizing reform. Root rejected a literary anthology because it contained "too much" Arthur Miller, Lincoln Steffens, and Carl Sandburg but nothing from Thornton Wilder, Ayn Rand, and Robert Nathan. After receiving Root's report early in January 1960, GLIC recommended that the State Textbook Purchasing Board stop using a dozen of the textbooks unless further study proved them acceptable.[53]

Root's work sparked further wrangling. The *Jackson Clarion-Ledger* helped stir a "stormy debate" by publishing his report as a series of articles and by running many letters to the editor. It also reported the Jackson schools used five of the books Root rated unsatisfactory, but mostly for what it termed "aesthetic values" not "subversion." While the state DAR commended GLIC and Root, a spokesman for the State Textbook Commission maintained that teachers and the board had already carefully screened the books for "objectionable" material and doubted that further study would reveal anything new. Publishers and their representatives defended their books. For example, T. N. Touchstone, a Jackson representative for D. C. Heath publisher and a former longtime educator in the state, supported one textbook and criticized Root. His detailed rebuttal charged that Root lacked qualifications for the work, had taken words out of context, distorted the authors' meaning, and made false statements. Touchstone trusted qualified teachers to evaluate books, and his ultimate solution to the controversy was "building better schools for Mississippi children." In the heated controversy, even Carl Walters, a *Clarion-Ledger* sports writer, devoted an entire column to defending Touchstone and flaying Root, but a letter to the editor from the GLIC chairman objected to Walters's "vicious attack" on Root and the committee.[54]

While the legislature met early in 1960, the hot debate over textbooks continued. At the late February state DAR convention in Jackson, the women displayed in the King Edward Hotel's lobby some books that their organization labeled as disloyal, communist influenced, and integrationist. Publishers' representatives picketed the display and discouraged observers from paying attention to the DAR's propaganda. When the book display moved to the state library, the picketing continued. During the DAR meeting, the local YWCA sponsored a panel on "The Textbook Controversy." In response a month later, the Mississippi Education Association convention formally denounced reckless allegations against schoolbooks and suggestions to ban some books. The teachers took such criticism as an attack on their professionalism and patriotism. The convention praised "the Mississippi plan of textbook adoption as one of the best."[55]

The legislature also began to act on textbooks. As adjournment approached, the house education committee approved two bills sought by Governor Ross Barnett, who had run for governor in 1959 as a committed opponent of integration. In the battle to gain control over the Textbook Purchasing Board and the individual rating committees, the governor and his friends sought to control what students learned in school; they wanted to protect young people from unsafe ideas that would undermine the authority of white segregationists. Barnett's allies included the DAR and the Citizens' Council, a private segregationist organization started in Mississippi in 1954 and dedicated to resisting the *Brown* decision. One bill expanded the three-member board (all appointees of moderate former governor J. P. Coleman) to seven members, with Barnett to name the four new ones, two of whom had to be laymen. The other bill authorized the governor to appoint four members to each rating committee. Barnett told the state Parent Teacher Association (PTA) meeting, "I don't know if there is any subversive teaching in our schools, but you owe a vote of thanks to our lawmakers who are trying to end left-wing doctrine teaching." The PTA board instead recommended that the Textbook Purchasing Board and the rating committees "should not in any way be altered or changed." In the PTA's opinion, the groups had acted "on the highest plane of integrity and there has never been a single indication of the slightest fraud or failure to serve in the best interests of our children." To some Mississippians, however, the PTA had "knowingly or unknowingly endors[ed] the teaching of subversion, racial integration, evolution, and one-worldism." In an apocalyptic view of the textbook battle, critics charged that following the PTA would mean "Communism will overthrow your government, slavery will overtake your children, and death will come to your nation."[56]

The house engaged in "a long and bitter fight" over the textbook bills. Former governor Coleman, serving as a representative, angrily defended the work of the State Textbook Commission and opposed the proposed changes. In the debate one representative even recalled Bilbo's idea for a state printing plant and argued that enacting Bilbo's plan would have avoided the controversy entirely. By a narrow margin the house agreed to call for an entirely new Textbook Purchasing Board named by Barnett. When the senate took up the bills, the options multiplied. The governor could gain control over both the commission and the committees by expanding each of them, or he could gain control of one but not both, or he could gain control by naming all new members to either or both. According to a "blistering attack" by Hayden Campbell, a senator and Citizens' councilor from Jackson, "If these bills are passed, it will immediately throw this commission into politics and could ultimately bring about a textbook scandal." The DAR, the American Legion, the Farm Bureau, and the Citizens' Council, however, continued to lobby for reform, while the Mississippi Education Association opposed any change. Educators especially opposed involving laymen: as one Greenville English teacher asked, "What would a layman know about the books we need in the classroom?" In the legislative maneuvering, Governor Barnett's role remained unclear as he appeared variously uninvolved, willing to compromise, and committed to one or both bills.[57]

As a result of intense negotiating and parliamentary fighting, the senate killed expansion of the Textbook Purchasing Board and approved other changes that the house accepted. It enlarged the rating committees by giving the state superintendent power to name three educators to each rating committee and the governor authority to name four individuals to each committee. The superintendent and education professionals retained power over the State Textbook Purchasing Board, but the governor gained possible control over the rating committees.[58]

In September 1960, the governor and the superintendent of education announced their rating committee appointments. Barnett's thirty-two appointees included the president of the Mississippi Farm Bureau, a leader of the DAR, a segregationist historian at Mississippi College, and an advocate for veterans. His other appointments usually were either former teachers or had connections to education. Of course, the head of the state department of education named twenty-four teachers to the rating committees. Two years later, in the spring of 1962, Barnett announced three new members of the Textbook Purchasing Board, and each was an experienced educator. When the newly appointed board then voted to retain the same books for another year, reporter John Herbers observed that Barnett's "interest in reorganizing the board, it now appears, was purely a matter of patronage and had little to do with what was in the textbooks." If the impact of the changes proved unremarkable, they dissatisfied the hardcore opponents who feared subversion in the textbooks. For several years they continued to lobby for banning un-American schoolbooks and for reforming the textbook selection process, especially every four years when the governor made appointments, but their efforts had little effect.[59] As the Cold War's anti-communist hysteria faded and massive resistance to integration eased, popular concern about textbooks also lessened. The battles of 1959–60 proved, however, that schoolbooks could provoke intense disagreement and controversy in Mississippi, as one would again in the 1970s.

Front cover of *Mississippi: Conflict and Change*

James Loewen

Charles Sallis

John Bettersworth

Charles Sallis, David Sansing, and Ray Skates

Dixiecrat Walkout

This was the first of many times since World War II that the Mississippi Democratic Party has withdrawn from the national Democratic Party. Skim ahead to Chapters 15 and 17 or do outside reading to find out about the state Democratic Party. What have been the Mississippi party's reasons for leaving the national party? Have Mississippi Democrats become Republicans? Independents? If so, why? Why not? What do you see in the future for the Mississippi Democratic Party?

Black Mississippians Demand Change

The day is past and forever gone when white men can go behind closed doors and work out all the Negro's problems and bring them to him on a platter. As long as this is done there is going to be misunderstanding and terrible blunders are going to be made.

With these words, Dr. T. R. M. Howard of Mound Bayou opened the first annual meeting of the Mississippi Regional Council of Negro Leadership in 1952.

Black political leaders in Mississippi were realizing that the Democratic Party, federal government, and other national forces had become resources which they might use to get change in their home state. In 1950 the NAACP asked the Supreme Court to declare the "separate-but-equal" doctrine illegal. While the Supreme Court was considering what to do, black Mississippians pressed for the improvement of their schools.

Before 1954 the Regional Council didn't ask for integrated rest rooms; it simply wanted rest rooms at a time when many stations had them only for whites.

248

"Equalization"

Aware of black Mississippians' concern, Governor Hugh White in 1953 proposed a school "equalization" program. Designed to keep the schools separated by race, this program provided $50,000,000 to make black schools equal to white schools. An increase in black teachers' salaries was the first step of the two-year program.

Table 5. White Schools, Black Schools, 1952

	white	black
Money spent per student	$117.43	$35.87
Length of school year	167 days	158 days
Average college education of teachers	3.7 yrs.	1.9 yrs.
Teacher salaries	$1,981	$1,019

"Equal Education" Revisited

Table 5 compares white and black schools in 1952, just before Governor White proposed to "equalize" them. Compare the statistics to those in Table 4 on page 213. Was Mississippi making progress in closing the over-all gap between white and black schools?

White hoped that blacks would be content with a promise to upgrade the schools while keeping them separate. Some black Mississippians would have been satisfied if the schools had honestly been made equal. But in a letter to the governor, the Mississippi Teachers Association emphasized that if equalization were adopted, blacks must have equal power, including supervisory positions at the state level. Most black leaders felt that segregation was a white tool for regulating and controlling the blacks' behavior.

Some white Mississippians recognized that the belief in human rights for all could not include segregation. Many

The MTA was then all black.

Even restrooms were segregated; these photos were taken in a downtown Jackson restaurant in 1973.

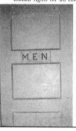

Pages 246–47 from *Conflict and Change*

CHAPTER THREE

Histories

Earlier Mississippi History Textbooks

History textbooks, according to Frances Fitzgerald, "tell children what their elders want them to know about their country," and "the texts contain the truths selected for posterity." They sometimes result from debates, "battles, and compromises" over what will constitute the "official knowledge" that the schools will teach. Each history book necessarily includes and emphasizes some subjects while it excludes and dismisses others; the texts establish historical reality as defined, selected, and organized by the people who control the schools. What students learn about their history affects their values and beliefs not just about the past but about their contemporary society and about future possibilities. History as taught in the schools, therefore, has greater ideological weight and political importance than does instruction in arithmetic, grammar, or science. Mississippi's legislators in the late nineteenth century would have agreed with George Orwell's later argument, "Who controls the past controls the future: who controls the present controls the past." In addition to establishing a process for selecting schoolbooks, therefore, the Mississippi general assembly periodically exerted authority over the history curriculum in the state's public schools and over the contents of the history textbooks studied.[1]

Concern focused especially on Mississippi history schoolbooks. In history courses teachers relied on "the textbook as the source of knowledge," and the textbook often served as "the central instrument of instruction."[2] In the case of their state's history, Mississippians considered themselves experts able confidently to judge the merits of books. The personal immediacy of state history gave it great potential for transmitting the particular values and ideas of Mississippians. As a separate school subject, however, Mississippi history gained official importance only in the late nineteenth century when it became part of the required state curriculum.

During Reconstruction the Mississippi state government, imposed by federal authority, mandated teaching the "history of the United States," the side that won the Civil War, but not the history of Mississippi, which was on the losing side. After local whites regained control and "redeemed" state government, the state legislature in 1878 dropped the U.S. history requirement. A dozen years later, just a quarter century after the Civil War's end but at a time of stress in race relations, the general assembly in 1890 showed heightened concern over what the state's schools taught about the war. At the same time that white leaders used the new Constitution of 1890 to disfranchise blacks and protect white domination, the state legislators feared an influx of threatening northern values, so they resolved that school officials "exercise the utmost care in the selection and introduction of school histories." Worried about "biased, prejudiced, and unfair textbooks," the legislature directed the governor, attorney general, and state superintendent of education to examine and recommend books that met their approval. In condemning "books that suppress full, free and candid presentations of questions and principles upon which American people have been honestly divided, and in the maintenance of which they have acted according to the promptings of courage and honor," the legislature implicitly called for books that defended Mississippi, white supremacy, and the Confederacy. Two years later, to ensure students learned the proper interpretation of their state's history, the legislature required that the schools teach Mississippi history.[3]

When the 1904 legislature established a state textbook commission, it also created a uniform curriculum that included its versions of both United States history and Mississippi history. Displaying an awareness of history's influence, the law defended the state's past by requiring that "no history in relation to the late civil war between the states shall be used in the schools of this state unless it be fair and impartial." Of course, only Confederate veterans and their sons would determine which textbooks embodied fairness. The law also prohibited from textbooks "anything of a partisan or sectarian nature," that is, anything that did not support loyal Democrats and white supremacy. Twenty years later legislation that reorganized the textbook commission repeated the demands for fairness and for teaching state history. The Mississippi history requirements remained unchanged for fifty years.[4]

The legislature's concerns for historical interpretation reflected larger trends across the South around the turn of the century. New laws regarding history teaching sought to perpetuate the southern white elite's leadership position when it faced challenges from inside and outside the South. To protect their status, powerful southern whites resisted a historical vision that criticized their culture and their dominance in it. Northern writers and publishers promulgated historical accounts that southern patricians considered offensive and slanderous because of their criticisms of antebellum southern planters and slave owners, their denunciation of slavery, and their rejection of southern views of the Constitution. In effect, the northern writers claimed moral superiority in advocating a more egalitarian society instead of the hierarchical southern society controlled by a few whites.[5]

At the same time, the southern elite worried about internal challenges to their traditional authority. Agrarian protestors in the Grange, the Farmers' Alliances, and the Populist Party expressed dissatisfaction with the southern order dominated by the white upper class. In potent organized challenges to the whites in control, ordinary southern farmers, black and white, sought political power and advocated economic change that imperiled the patricians' place at the top. While northern historians posed a moral and intellectual threat to the white elite, lower-class southerners presented a more immediate challenge to the social order.[6]

The white leadership defended itself in many ways. It not only disfranchised many poorer citizens, black and white, who posed a potential threat, but the patricians fought for the loyalty of all white southerners, present and future, through a purging of unacceptable textbooks. Campaigns for "unbiased" schoolbooks in the 1890s preoccupied the United Confederate Veterans (UCV), the United Daughters of the Confederacy (UDC), and the Sons of Confederate Veterans (SCV). The southern patriotic organizations sought to protect children by purging their textbooks of any dangerous northern ideas. In 1895, for example, Stephen D. Lee, a former Confederate general and the founding president of Mississippi Agricultural and Mechanical College (now Mississippi State University), claimed that northern histories contained "many errors and false indictments against the South," including their claim that the Civil War involved any "high moral purpose of the North to destroy slavery." He advocated "banishing from the schools any books which teach false lessons, either of fact or sentiment." Lee and other white leaders claimed to defend their region and its values, but they also wanted to shore up their own authority by teaching southern whites the value of the "southern aristocratic orthodoxy."[7]

In addition to eliminating dangerous history textbooks coming from the North, the campaign for supposedly unbiased history books involved legitimizing and promoting "objective" histories written by reliable southerners. Despite claims to objectivity, the confederate organizations' preferred history presented a romantic view of antebellum plantation life and defended slavery as necessary for blacks whom they considered inferior. It also justified secession as a patriotic defense of the Constitution and denounced Reconstruction corruption. In a clear argument for the rightful authority of the elite's persisting postwar power, the southern patriotic history celebrated the leaders who redeemed the South from northern control during Reconstruction.

Their southern history, therefore, justified rule by heroic, principled, natural aristocrats who defended white supremacy.[8]

When the Mississippi legislators in the 1890s called for unbiased school histories, they participated in the regional effort and responded in particular to the concerns of the state's active Confederate patriotic groups. Worried about blasphemous history textbooks, the UCV in 1892 created a Historical Committee to promote its interpretation of historical reality. The committee's leader lashed out at writers "who endeavor to undermine the faith of the Southern youth in their ancestors" and called them "the real enemies of the republic." One speaker at a Mississippi UDC convention urged the group "to collect, preserve and transmit, as a precious heritage," their region's "glorious history" and to correct the "errors of prejudiced writers." Referring to the "hallowed memories we preserve," she demanded that books preserve the historical truth. The state UDC's historian called for "truthful history" by "loyal Southerners" because their books would "cancel the false impressions" created by northern historians.[9]

The Mississippi legislature's call for unbiased and fair history textbooks targeted the same Yankee books denounced by the UCV and the UDC. After the law's enactment, the UDC made the requirement more explicit when it declared that the state could not adopt a textbook that "will inculcate false ideas as to the issue of that struggle, as to the motives which prompted our people, or as to the merits of the controversy which result in the war." It even objected to books that included Lincoln's speeches and preferred books that did not employ the term "civil war." More pointedly, the Meridian UDC opposed histories that "either openly attack, covertly misrepresent, or insolently ignore the achievements of Southern statesmen and soldiery." When lawmakers established a uniform statewide curriculum with the state textbook commission, the UDC endorsed the action because "every history used in our schools which deals with the great struggle between the two parts of our country should be impartial and untinged with local coloring." Defending its version of history, the UDC assumed the virtues of its views—objectivity, fairness, impartiality—and failed to acknowledge, and even understand, the polemical nature of its defense of slavery, secession, white supremacy, and aristocratic power.[10]

Requiring a course in Mississippi history, as the legislature did in 1904, also satisfied UDC concerns. The women regretted the "lack of knowledge of state and . . . local history," and they hoped that studying state history, more than national history, would provide students with a true understanding of the past. According to the UDC, state history would "touch the popular heart" and "kindle a flame which will not burn out with the life of our generation." The UCV also advocated courses in state history. Good state histories could protect and preserve the traditional values cherished by the UDC, the UCV, and other Mississippi patriots.[11]

The state mandate for teaching seventh-grade Mississippi history created a continuous demand for textbooks. Between 1890 and 1970, fewer than a dozen Mississippi history books dominated the schools. An examination of the books reveals how the initial interpretations satisfied the demands of the patriotic organizations and how, despite gradual change over the decades, some of the textbooks' worst flaws persisted.

Two Mississippi history textbooks quickly gained acceptance and dominated the market in the 1890s. According to one later assessment, the "textbooks constituted a series of historical polemics stressing the virtues of aristocratic society, the venality of the Negro race, and the villainy of the Yankee nation." Defending antebellum white Mississippians, the books justified slavery and denounced antislavery efforts. They also, of course, supported southern secession, denounced the Union army's invasion, and condemned the postwar occupation during Reconstruction. Explicitly pro-southern in outlook, the books met the legislature's call for unbiased and unprejudiced schoolbooks, and they satisfied the patriotic societies' demands for eliminating all northern influences from history textbooks.[12] Despite their similarities, important differences between the early texts did exist, and they illustrate Mississippi history's significant development as a field.

Mary V. Duval's *History of Mississippi and Civil Government* appeared in 1892. Though born in Georgia, Duval moved to Mississippi as a very young girl. An experienced teacher in Sardis but an untrained historian, she had earlier written a *Students' History of Mississippi*, the first history of the state. Responding directly to the 1892 requirement for state history, Duval's new textbook carried endorsements by the state superintendent of education, who found "the narrative entertaining" and judged the text "invaluable." Duval's Panola County superintendent praised it "without qualification" and "earnestly recommend[ed] its adoption" by other districts. In forty-seven brief chapters Duval recounted Mississippi's history from De Soto to the 1890 Constitution. A half dozen chapters surveyed the eighteenth century, and a similar number focused on the Confederacy. Relentlessly political and positive in approach, Duval scarcely mentioned slavery except as a political issue, but she referred to the North's "insidious attacks" on southern institutions and called John Brown's raid at Harper's Ferry an "atrocious outrage." She seemed to share Mississippians' "intense excitement and enthusiasm" for secession.

Duval lauded the "unflinching courage" and gallantry of the state's patriotic soldiers. She also praised not only the civilians' "almost superhuman efforts" on the home front but also the contented slaves' "fidelity" to their owners: "All honor to the memory of the slavery of the olden times!" Ever optimistic, Duval vaguely claimed that the abolition of slavery actually benefitted the state and that devastation made Mississippi "more prosperous and self-reliant through the enforced discipline of poverty and self-denial."[13]

During Reconstruction, according to Duval, racial conflicts often resulted in "bloodshed and death," and "the inhabitants of the State were compelled to submit to the armed bodies of negroes, commanded by officers of their own color, of the most dangerous and turbulent type." Whites thought Republicans leaders' "inflammatory speeches and incendiary teachings" promoted the "barbarity"; "menaced by armed bodies" of blacks, whites "recoiled in horror." With the breaking of Reconstruction's "yoke of misrule and oppression," the intelligent and wise whites regained power. In 1890 a constitutional convention considered how to deal with "the race question" that "had assumed colossal proportions." Though a copy of the 1890 Constitution appeared as an appendix, Duval did not mention disfranchisement and alluded only to the convention's "securing of a more enlightened elective franchise, without race discriminations or injustice." She mentioned the People's or Populist Party only in passing but had previously called the Farmers' Alliance a "large and respectable association" and farmers "the very bone and sinew" of the state. Her ostensibly unbiased and unprejudiced story that ended in 1892 must have pleased the women of the UDC and other southern patriots.[14]

A textbook by Robert Lowry and William H. McCardle differed little in point of view from Duval's history. Lowry and McCardle each had attained great prominence in the state. A lawyer by training, Lowry served in the Confederate army, suffered wounds at Shiloh, and rose to the rank of general in 1865. After the war he served a term in the legislature and two terms as governor (1882–90), and for seven years early in the twentieth century he commanded the state UCV. McCardle, a controversial Vicksburg newspaper editor, gained fame as the plaintiff in the Reconstruction challenge to habeas corpus in the U.S. Supreme Court case *Ex parte McCardle.* He and Lowry had previously written a popular state history, but they maintained the new textbook was "an entirely different book." They thought that the state's history, "brilliant with the illustrious names and heroic deeds of her gallant sons," should "thrill [students] with pride and patriotism" and "inspire" them "to sustain the honor . . . and add to the fame" of their state. Hailing the new textbook, the *Jackson Clarion* claimed "no history of our State . . . is so full of information, so entirely comprehensive in its details" and found the work "scrupulously accurate."[15]

In a much more dispassionate narrative account than Duval's, Lowry and McCardle concentrated on state politics and government, often governor by governor with chapters entitled "The Administration of...." Though they mentioned the creation of nearly every county and of every Indian treaty, the authors paid scant attention to slavery and made no racial distinctions when they reported the state's population. They discussed national politics only as it impinged on Mississippi. In regard to John Brown, for example, they merely commented, "The whole story is fully told in the histories of the United States, and its only effect in Mississippi was to increase the apprehension felt by the people concerning that protection which the Constitution of the United State had guaranteed." Coverage of wartime courage and heroism, however, extended far beyond the state. For Lowry and McCardle, Mississippi's devotion to constitutional principles explained secession. During the war slaves completely sympathized with whites and "rejoiced with them in their victories and mourned with them over their defeats"; the Emancipation Proclamation, mentioned almost as an aside, "made no difference in their conduct." After the war, prejudiced Freemen's Bureau workers disrupted the "best feeling" that had prevailed between the races, and the Reconstruction government brought only "seven years of misrule, outrage, and robbery" by Carpetbaggers, "characterless adventurers," "aliens and strangers." Lowry and McCardle cursorily covered the post-Reconstruction period, which included Lowry's two terms as governor. Though they reprinted the Constitution of 1890 in an appendix, they ignored disfranchisement except to comment that the constitution's most significant part "concerned the elective franchise."[16]

As lawyer and journalist, Lowry and McCardle avoided in their account Mary Duval's rhetorical excesses, but they shared her sympathies. They told history from the powerful elite's perspective and ignored much of what happened away from the seats of power. On the central issues of the Civil War and Reconstruction, however, Lowry and McCardle displayed their Confederate loyalties. Though Lowry died months before publication of their textbook, *A History of Mississippi* did not disappoint legislators or former Confederates.[17]

A third textbook prompted by the legislative requirement came later from a professional historian, Franklin L. Riley. Born after the Civil War to an old southern Mississippi family and educated at Mississippi College (A.B., 1889; A.M., 1891), Riley received his doctorate in 1893 from John Hopkins University, where he trained in the research methods of modern scientific history with the great Herbert Baxter Adams. He returned to Mississippi in 1897 to become the University of Mississippi's first professor of history. During the seventeen years before he left the university for Washington and Lee College, he published his own research and directed fifteen master's theses. An energetic Riley also led a "historical renaissance" in the state by resuscitating the Mississippi Historical Society, starting and editing the society's annual scholarly publication, and helping found the state's Department of Archives and History. In 1900 he wrote *A School History of Mississippi*. With Stephen D. Lee's help on the Civil War chapters and with James W. Garner's contributions on Reconstruction, Riley wrote his textbook in seven months. Quickly adopted by two-thirds of the counties and most city districts, Riley's textbook dominated the market for thirty years until 1930.[18] Much more than its competitors by Duval and by Lowry and McCardle, Riley's book resembled the prevailing interpretations by the nation's professional historians.

Historians later hailed it as "wholly admirable" and "an important milestone in the writing of Mississippi's history." Riley's work, the first scholarly Mississippi history textbook, rested on research in primary sources and contained footnote references. It also reproduced a variety of illustrations and detailed maps, and it included an alphabetical index. Chapters did not include study questions, as did the Duval and Lowry-McCardle volumes, because Riley wanted students "to think more about the principal points in their lesson rather than the answer to be given to such questions"; he stressed analysis and comparisons in addition to, perhaps more than, the traditional teaching of cultural and moral values. Though at the outset Riley conceded that he devoted too little attention to "religious, social, economic, educational, and literary" topics, he included much more than had either Duval or Lowry and McCardle. Twelve strong chapters covered Mississippi under colonial rule, while one chapter dealt with its American territorial status. With a political structure, the book's forty chapters divided the state's history according to eras under the state's three constitutions of 1817, 1832, and 1890.[19] Riley's history far surpassed its predecessors in scope and quality.

A School History of Mississippi's more thorough narrative discussed schools and colleges, transportation, churches, and daily life of whites, but it also explicitly considered slavery (the index contains nearly thirty entries under "slavery"). From the first slave's arrival in 1707, Riley traced the growing slave population and devoted paragraphs to slavery in each time period. Riley's treatment of the cotton gin told how one skilled slave mechanic created a gin based on a rough drawing of Eli Whitney's invention. On the early nineteenth century, separate sections pertained to the "legal rights of slaves," "slave laws," "free negroes," and "the true condition of slaves." Regarding the last, Riley maintained that most slave masters, out of their own economic interest but also due to public pressure, treated their slaves humanely, but he also acknowledged variations that included inhumane treatment. In the antebellum chapter that described slaves' quarters, food, and religion, Riley portrayed the slaves as "simple minded, music-loving people" who lived peacefully on a kindly plantation. The white patriarch and his family slept "in perfect tranquility, without locking a door." At the same time, however, Riley recognized abolitionist agitation of the slavery question, white fears of slave insurrection, and the legally sanctioned use of "whipping and branding." Compared to the earlier historians, Riley's professional dispassion appeared most clearly in his description of John Brown's raid at Harper's Ferry as "a desperate, though unsuccessful, attempt" to promote an insurrection."[20]

Under Garner's influence, Riley's handling of the Civil War and Reconstruction, while partisan, lacked Duval's excited rhetoric; it more closely resembled the tone of Lowry and McCardle. In his discussion of the war, Riley mentioned almost in passing the Confederates' gallantry and endurance, and from the southern perspective he pointed to the "superior forces of the enemy." "When the war closed," Riley calmly commented, "slavery was dead," but the demoralized state had suffered destruction, "despair," "terrible desolation," and "impoverishment." In his portrayal of 1865, "colored troops, who were under little or no discipline . . . plundered and even murdered inoffensive white citizens" because northerners had poisoned their relationship with their former masters. Riley (Garner) downplayed the Ku Klux Klan "troubles" by claiming its "hideous disguises and mysterious proceedings were well calculated to strike terror" but usually amounted only to "a single warning delivered in a pompous manner" against a "superstitious" freedman. Violence in the form of riots and other racial disturbances resulted instead from the work of carpetbaggers.[21]

Though Riley appreciated the Reconstruction government's creation of a public school system and the development of higher education for blacks, he deplored the financial excesses. He reported the "wastefulness" and "extravagance" of "political adventurers" in state government. Local government also often suffered from "incompetent and corrupt" leaders. As a result Riley applauded the 1875 end of the "corrupt rule of the carpet-bagger." Though a few carpetbaggers had "good character," Riley described most as "destitute of principle" and committed to the "spoils of office, regardless of the results" for the state.[22]

More than the texts by Duval and Lowry-McCardle, Riley paid attention to late nineteenth-century financial improvements, yellow fever epidemics, industrial development, and educational progress. Like the others, Riley ignored the Farmers' Alliance and Populist Party and devoted many more words to the 1878 yellow fever outbreak and to the 1889 death of Jefferson Davis. On the Constitution of 1890, he also ignored disfranchisement of blacks. Only blandly did he mention provisions "related to the requirements for voting" and then referred students to the constitution in the appendix.[23] As a professional historian, however, he had presented a more comprehensive, balanced, and readable account of the state's past.

After 1930 new textbooks displaced Riley's book in the schools. Two professional historians produced a survey of the state's history in 1930; a school teacher wrote another in 1935 (revised in 1952). In 1945, a history professor and his historian wife published a textbook, and fourteen years later a Mississippi State College scholar penned yet another. The first by Charles S. Sydnor and Claude Bennett represented a return to the "neo-Confederate apologetics" of the Lowry-McCardle and Duval books. Sydnor, a Georgia native, had received his doctorate in 1923 from Johns Hopkins University. After teaching for two years at his alma mater, Hampden-Sydney College, he joined the University of Mississippi faculty. In 1935 he would leave Oxford for Duke University and a distinguished career that included the presidency of the Southern Historical Association and the Harmsworth Professorship at Oxford University. In the late 1920s, while still in Mississippi's Oxford, Sydnor teamed with Claude Bennett to write *Mississippi History* for secondary school students. Bennett too had a distinguished career. From rural Mississippi, he attended Mississippi College before graduating from Duke University. In 1925 he earned a master's degree from Peabody College. Bennett spent much of his career in public education as teacher, principal, superintendent, and high school supervisor for the education department. While working with Sydnor, Bennett served as president of Mississippi Teachers College. The two combined historical expertise with clout in the state's education circles.[24]

Sydnor and Bennett hoped that knowledge of the state's past "struggles, successes, and failures" would prepare students for citizenship and give "them an ambition to make Mississippi rank still higher among the great industrialized states of the Union." With an unusual stress on "the economic and industrial development of the state," the authors explained the importance of steamboats, railroads, sawmills, cotton mills, and banks. Though less celebratory and defensive of an agrarian life than earlier historians, they did not neglect agriculture. Their initial discussion of the cotton gin and cotton production did not mention slaves. Later Sydnor and Bennett recognized the slaves' work picking cotton and the planters' great wealth that derived from the slaves' labor, and the authors analyzed social classes among whites with a careful explanation of the distribution of slaves among white masters and across the state. Their discussion of "slavery in Mississippi," however, came exclusively from the point of view of the white owners. In a specific section on "how slaves were treated," Sydnor and Bennett admitted that "[m]uch good and bad might be said about slavery," but the two white authors concluded that "the life of a slave [was] pleasant" and "[u]sually the negroes were well cared for, given enough food and clothing, and not required to do more than a reasonable amount of work." Though some "owners were cruel men," they generally provided for their slaves because each "was worth a great deal of money." Ill treatment could have resulted in financial loss.[25]

Two of forty chapters addressed the Civil War. Using calm language Sydnor and Bennett stressed the centrality of slavery to the North-South dispute. They described how (white) southerners thought northerners mistreated them and explained that constitutional beliefs justified secession. In assessing the war's impact, the authors accentuated the destruction of fields, homes, railroads, factories, towns, governments: "The ruin was complete." Without even mentioning the Emancipation Proclamation, Sydnor and Bennett acknowledged the war's effects on slavery. Though "some of the slaves were loyal and stayed to help and care for the families of their masters, many were not." The latter either refused to work or fled to help the Union army against their former masters.[26]

In two chapters on Reconstruction, Sydnor and Bennett's strident tone and harsh language resembled Mary Duval's work. Suggesting that Mississippi "suffered more from Reconstruction than from the war," they excused the Black Code of 1865 as necessary to control the former slaves who refused to work and wandered the countryside. The freemen begged and robbed and generally "did not know how to behave." The "state suffered greatly at the hands of selfish and ignorant men who were in power," blacks and whites, scalawags and carpetbaggers. They stirred disorder and lawlessness that led to race riots. Sydnor and Bennett conceded that "the negroes were on the whole more honest than the white men who held office during this time." Without effective government protection, whites resorted to the Ku Klux Klan to protect them and reestablish some order; the authors justified KKK behavior "on the grounds of grim necessity." Only when whites regained control did Reconstruction end, though Sydnor and Bennett suggested the actual rebuilding of the state took many more years.[27]

Writing in the late 1920s, Sydnor and Bennett put a new emphasis on the half century since Reconstruction. Their book's thirteen chapters covered progress in education for whites and blacks, in agriculture, in industry, in highways and railroads, and in health. Regarding race relations, the authors claimed that the former slaves returned to work under their former masters and that "soon the negroes and white people were on good terms and as friendly as ever . . . just the same as before they were free." They also explicitly declared that the "most important feature" of the 1890 Constitution was a literacy or understanding clause to prevent "ignorant people" (*not* specifically blacks) from voting and controlling the government "as was done in carpetbag days." After disfranchisement, blacks scarcely received any attention. Sydnor and Bennett's textbook, though it had a broader coverage, still represented a throwback to the Confederate orthodoxy of Lowry-McCardle and Duval.[28]

Five years after publication of Sydnor and Bennett's book, Pearl V. Guyton wrote *The History of Mississippi*. Educated at Blue Mountain College, she graduated from the University of Mississippi in 1917 and did graduate work at the University of Chicago and Columbia University before teaching in the public schools of Eupora, Laurel, and Natchez. Her *History of Mississippi* showed the practical effects of her experience. In addition to keys for pronouncing names, each chapter had a preview and a concluding summary, and it presented problems to consider and projects to carry out, along with a bibliography. If Sydnor and Bennett, despite their modulated tone and modified views, returned to interpretations found in the 1890s, Guyton displayed even more retrogression. The worst appeared in the introduction by her relative, David E. Guyton, a Blue Mountain College historian. Celebrating the state's "purest Anglo-Saxon stock," he boasted that "Mississippi merits the love, the loyalty, and the deep devotion of her sons and daughters," and he bragged that "Mississippi has marched steadily, proudly, and majestically onward and upward." Noting the population divided almost equally between whites and blacks, David Guyton claimed that the races dwell "together in mutual good will, sympathetic understanding, and readiness to render a helping hand in solving the many-sided problems of the State."[29]

Pearl Guyton justified Mississippi slavery as "a very old custom" practiced by ancient peoples, and she pointed out that northerners also had held slaves. Slavery, she suggested, might have died out except that the invention of the cotton gin made practical the development of plantation slavery. She offered little information about slave life except to acknowledge that in the Delta slaves worked in unhealthy areas where whites refused to live. In assessing the coming of the Civil War, Guyton omitted any reference to John Brown and proposed that differences over the expansion of slavery into western territories divided the North and South and led to war. After the election of 1860, according to the author, whites feared that they "were about to be robbed of their slaves and cheated of their liberty." In discussing Mississippi's "most important part" in the war, she occasionally referred to the heroism of Confederate soldiers; for example, "Pemberton and his men fought bravely and desperately, but they were far outnumbered." Though the author largely ignored the wartime home front, she did claim that most slaves "were loyal to their masters' families and continued to serve them," despite the Emancipation Proclamation.[30]

In one of her longer chapters, Guyton explained "the first ten years of peace were worse in many ways than the years of war." With their state devastated by war, whites had to contend with irresponsible and incapable former slaves. The Black Code gave blacks many rights but also sought to control them and force them to work. Northerners "who knew little about the negroes" tried to help them with the Freedmen's Bureau. Guyton contended, however, that the Bureau "caused much hard feeling in the South" because its agents tried to turn blacks against southern whites. Reconstruction transferred "power from the hands of able [white] men and put it in the hands of [black] people who were incompetent and uneducated." Swarms of "unscrupulous" carpetbaggers and scalawags influenced the freedmen. According to Guyton, the resulting "evils" included "misgovernment" and "lawlessness and rioting" that threatened whites and their property. In reaction whites formed the Ku Klux Klan to protect the "weak, innocent, and defenseless" whites from scalawags, carpetbaggers, and freedmen. The KKK also sought to restore "educated and responsible white men" to power. And by 1875 the white elite had regained control. In explaining that the Constitution of 1890 protected the power of "men of intelligence and thrift" by limiting voting to taxpayers who could read or understand the constitution and who met basic residency requirements, Guyton ignored racial concerns as an impetus for the suffrage restrictions. Except for the new constitution, Guyton, like other textbook writers, covered the post-Reconstruction years topically and failed to include blacks.[31]

In 1945, a decade after Guyton's text, Richard Aubrey McLemore and Nannie Pitts McLemore produced another comprehensive historical survey. Each taught in the public schools before doing graduate work at Peabody College where they met. After receiving his doctorate from Vanderbilt in 1933, he served briefly as dean and she taught history at Jones Junior College before they moved to Mississippi Southern College in Hattiesburg. Together in 1941 they wrote an "Outline of Mississippi History" and soon followed with their textbook. They continued to write together as Aubrey McLemore rose to become dean at Mississippi Southern, president of Mississippi College, and finally director of the Mississippi Department of Archives and History. Each of the McLemores would serve as president of the Mississippi Historical Society.[32]

The McLemores' *Mississippi Through Four Centuries* featured many maps and illustrations and boasted eight modern full-color pictures. Its remarkably traditional contents, however, would have pleased the UDC and the UCV. Unmentioned in the first third of the book, blacks initially appeared in chapter 11, "Cotton Is King." The cotton gin made slave labor important. Though the McLemores declared that slave labor was "essential to cotton culture," their extended discussion of planting, hoeing, picking, and ginning cotton did not mention slaves. "The slave trade," they admitted, "was one of the worst features of the slave system," but white planters often built "a close relationship" with longtime workers and took good care of elderly slaves. Because a "healthy and contented slave meant a better worker and greater profits," slaves received good treatment of daily food rations and even "[l]uxuries" such as coffee and sugar, clothing "of good quality," "the best medical service available," and "special gifts" at Christmas. Overseers managed the slaves with the help of "Negro leaders, known as drivers," but the authors omitted any discussion of slave discipline. In fact, they portrayed slavery as benign and "much better than" life in Africa.[33]

Eight of the McLemores' thirty chapters covered events from the 1850s through Reconstruction. In discussing the approach of the Civil War, they blamed northern opponents of slavery, who, though honest, "did not know anything about the conditions in the South," and their "ignorance caused them to make false statements about the treatment of the slaves." The authors called John Brown's raid a "dreadful incident" and Brown "a dangerous criminal." In recounting the state's secession and the wartime fighting in the state, the McLemores avoided paeans to courage and bravery in retelling the events. On the homefront, they blamed a food shortage on poorly working slaves and on the Union army for taking slaves from their owners. The McLemores apparently could not appreciate that blacks wanted to flee slavery.[34]

In a devastated postwar Mississippi, whites employed the Black Code to combat the "evils" of the freedmen's laziness and petty criminality. Even the Freedmen's Bureau failed to protect the ex-slave from his own "weaknesses." When Republicans gained control, they engaged in financial "extravagance" and willingly put "untrained people in important places." The inexperienced freedman "was easily fooled and many people took advantage of him." The Ku Klux Klan, however, provided needed help "in a difficult time" by frightening, beating, and even killing troublesome blacks. Critical of blacks in government as "the worst type" and "under the influence of dishonest white people," the authors conceded the honesty of some freedmen and explained that "they made mistakes because of lack of experience" in government.[35]

Following a chapter on the restoration of white rule, the McLemores' coverage of the Constitution of 1890 described how "native whites" regained control and used the new constitution to secure their hold on power. Unlike earlier textbook authors, the McLemores unequivocally approved the constitutional convention that sought "to insure the control of the state by the white man" by "prevent[ing] the Negro from voting." To avoid a violation of the federal Constitution, the new state constitution copied from other states nonracial means that exploited the "weaknesses and habits" of blacks. With home rule secured, the McLemores' text quickly lapsed into a pedestrian series of topical chapters ranging from agriculture to culture, from industry to education. It often resembled a civics textbook.[36] By stressing the beneficence of slavery, the necessity of the Civil War, the horrors of Reconstruction, and importance of white supremacy, Aubrey and Nannie Pitts McLemore deviated little from the interpretation approved by the Confederate patriotic organizations. The view established around the turn of the century persisted in their text into the post–World War II era.

The textbooks by Sydnor and Bennett, by Guyton, and by the McLemores competed for adoptions by the state's schools. When the state legislature in 1940 passed a law to provide free textbooks, it also created the State Textbook Purchasing Board to approve every textbook purchased by the state. If a local district wanted to use other textbooks, it had to buy them with local funds, but few did. In its first months of operation the board approved Charles Sydnor and Claude Bennett's *Mississippi History* for continued use by seventh graders in the state's schools, and a later edition gained acceptance in 1944. New textbooks continued to seek the board's approval. In 1945 the board discussed with Aubrey McLemore his planned textbook, but it could not act without the published book. As during wartime, the board for financial reasons in 1947 delayed buying new books and extended the 1944 adoptions for one year, so the McLemores' 1945 book had to wait. The commission in 1949 did endorse the McLemores' *Mississippi Through Four Centuries* but rejected Pearl Guyton's manuscript version of her revised textbook.[37]

Like many textbooks that went through multiple editions, which seldom involved any significant changes in organization, tone, or analysis, Guyton's textbook appeared in 1952 as a new version. Her limited revisions did not improve her history. In discussing class divisions in antebellum Mississippi, she observed that "more than half of the people of Mississippi belong to families which owned no slaves," when she must have meant half of the "white" people. She began the next paragraph with the almost dismissive, "Then, of course, there were the slaves." Changes in structure, more than revisions in historical content, improved Guyton's new volume. Even more than her earlier book, *Our Mississippi* showed the practical influence of her nearly fifty years' experience teaching in the public schools with helpful lists of vocabulary, places, people, and dates. The most visible innovation came in the book's format. For easier reading Guyton's textbook also had a larger format more appropriate for a textbook (6" × 9" instead of its predecessors' 5" × 7½"). Despite the book's modern features, the writer largely repeated the interpretation found in her book of seventeen years earlier. The new form could not disguise the old content.[38]

When the State Textbook Purchasing Board decided to approve multiple textbooks for the same course, Pearl Guyton's revamped textbook *Our Mississippi* gained the commission's endorsement in 1952. To avoid further major expenditures by delaying an adoption cycle, the board extended the contract on the McLemores' textbook and even purchased additional copies of the popular book in 1956.[39]

In the 1950s, during the tensions of the Cold War and the domestic Red Scare, the Textbook Purchasing Board felt pressure from politicians and patriotic groups to avoid subversive textbooks and safeguard established values. State superintendent of education J. M. Tubb in 1952 directed the board and its committees to "[l]ook closely for any expressed or implied statement suggestive of subversive principles, Communistic propaganda or any ideas that connote alien ideologies antagonistic to the basic principles of our political faith or way of life." Repeating his warning about alien ideologies two years later, Tubb hoped to avoid the "scandals connected with book adoptions in some other states." He urged the educators not "to aid and abet the enemy by being careless in the evaluation" of textbooks. To avoid "any material that might advocate a departure from the true and tried American way," Tubb in 1960 asked them to exercise "care and caution."[40] In Mississippi, as the civil rights movement began, the way of life needed defense against the alien ideas of not just communists but also integrationists. For white Mississippians, the two threats had in the 1950s merged into one huge, indistinct menace.

While public officials often warned of internal threats to security, the state legislature also acted to preserve American ideals and Mississippi's way of life. In 1953, for example, it required that every school display during daylight hours the United States flag (later extended to include the state flag) and that students daily pledge allegiance to the American flag. A few years later the legislature also created an official pledge to the Mississippi flag that stressed the state's sovereignty and "pride in her history and achievements." To ensure students learned the state's history and its way of life, lawmakers early in 1958 expanded the required curriculum to include a course on Mississippi for high school students, in addition to the existing course for elementary pupils.[41]

The legislature's curricular mandate caused the Textbook Purchasing Board to find Mississippi history books for the new high school course. To avoid hasty action and to wait for a Department of Education report on the social studies, the board deferred action on Mississippi history books, both elementary and high school, until its March 1959 meeting. The board did adopt for elementary students the McLemores' *Mississippi Story* and Pearl Guyton's *Our Mississippi*. For high school courses, the board accepted the only book nominated, John K. Bettersworth's *Mississippi: A History*, and for the next generation it dominated high school courses in Mississippi history.[42]

Except for wartime service as a Navy navigation instructor, John Knox Bettersworth had taught in the history department at Mississippi State University since 1937. Born in Jackson in 1909, Bettersworth graduated from Millsaps College in 1929 and then for several years taught Spanish and later history at his alma mater, Jackson's Central High School. In 1937 he received a doctorate in history from Duke University where he studied with William K. Boyd and Charles S. Sydnor. Over his several decades at Mississippi State, he scaled the bureaucracy as chairman of his department, chairman of the Social Science Research Center, associate dean for liberal arts, and, in 1961, vice president. In 1948 at Mississippi State, Bettersworth founded the *Mississippi Quarterly*, a journal of the humanities and social sciences related to the South, and he edited it for its first nine years. Beyond the Starkville campus he engaged in extensive public and professional service as a member of the Mississippi Historical Commission starting in 1948, as a trustee of the Department of Archives and History after 1955, and as a longtime member and leader of the Mississippi Historical Society and in 1962 as its president.[43]

An active scholar, Bettersworth early published articles in many scholarly journals including the *Journal of Mississippi History* and the *Journal of Southern History*. His revised dissertation appeared in 1943 as *Confederate Mississippi: The People and Policies of a Cotton State in Wartime*, followed a decade later by his *People's College: A History of Mississippi State*. His writings revealed both his prose talent and his views on southern and Mississippi history. *Confederate Mississippi* described the secessionists as having that "tenacious, self-immolating, half-mad style of leadership that . . . was the stuff of Abolitionism," and Bettersworth argued that they sought preservation of the economic system of slavery, "evil as it was," not some defense of constitutional principle. Far from a defender of secession and the Old South, he wrote of the "secession psychosis." Non–slave-owning whites supported the war in hopes that they too could become wealthy slave owners. Though Bettersworth concluded that "slaves, even on masterless plantations, were far more docile" than he might have expected, he also acknowledged among slaves cases of "insubordination, rebellion, and desertion of their owners during the war." With apparent approval, Bettersworth quoted a Presbyterian wartime report that a slave must be thought of "as a *man*" and only slavery that benefitted both masters and slaves could be at all justified.[44] His unorthodox views about secession and slavery differed greatly from the state's textbook writers, even Riley, and would have concerned SCV and UDC members if they had known about his scholarship. Mississippians also undoubtedly missed Bettersworth's views as they appeared occasionally in his work that reached a far larger audience than his academic articles and books.

Unusual for a history professor in Mississippi, Bettersworth's most distinctive writings appeared in the *New York Times Book Review*. Beginning in 1951, he wrote more than thirty reviews, and his essays gained him far more national attention than did his traditional scholarship. Bettersworth's connection to the *New York Times* ran back through Jackson. At Central High School, Bettersworth's fellow students included Nash K. Burger and Eudora Welty, and the latter two had been friends all through childhood. After college, when Bettersworth returned to Central High as a teacher, one of his fellow instructors was Burger, who by then had an undergraduate degree from the University of the South and a master's in English from the University of Virginia. They became good friends during the years of teaching together. While Bettersworth went to graduate school and then became a college professor, Burger worked a variety of jobs that by wartime included editing the Ingalls Shipbuilding Company's newspaper and teaching again at Central High. By 1944 Nash's friend Eudora Welty had taken a job with the *New York Times Book Review*, and she persuaded her editor to let Burger review books. The aspiring writer's first review so impressed the New York editor that it appeared on the *Review*'s front page. Soon the editor offered Burger a full-time job with the *Book Review*. He started in New York in 1945 and for the next thirty years reviewed hundreds of books, edited others' reviews, and wrote miscellaneous essays for the *Times*. By 1951 Burger had recruited his old Central High colleague Bettersworth into the *Book Review*'s stable of regular reviewers.[45]

Though Bettersworth had no choice in the books assigned to him, he often contributed reviews on books about the South and the Civil War era. At the particularly perilous time, the gathering momentum of the civil rights movement forced the nation to confront volatile racial questions, and the controversial Civil War centennial approached. Even if reviews by the southern-born and -educated professor might have offended orthodox defenders of the southern way of life, they must have satisfied his editors and readers, because reviews by the comparatively unknown Mississippi State professor continued to appear in the *Book Review* alongside essays by some of the nation's most renowned historians—Henry Steele Commager, David Donald, Oscar Handlin, T. Harry Williams, Bell I. Wiley, and C. Vann Woodward. Though he sometimes commented on histories for children and on histories for a popular audience, Bettersworth also reviewed scholarly works by Commager, Wiley, Clement Eaton, Charles Sellers, Kenneth Stampp, and Frank E. Vandiver. Without being pedantic or precious, Bettersworth's pithy commentary and epigrammatic phrasing made entertaining, memorable reviews. Lamenting historians who "take the color out" of history, he did his best not to join them.[46]

In his most important review, Bettersworth in September 1956 appraised Kenneth M. Stampp's pathbreaking *The Peculiar Institution: Slavery in the Ante-Bellum South*. "The literature of slavery has resounded with the criticism of critics and the apologies of apologists, while the plain truth about the 'peculiar' institution has gone begging," began Bettersworth. Stampp avoided the "verbal wars" and "eschew[ed] the errors of slavery's enemies no less than those of its eulogists"; instead he provided the "definitive word on slavery" by marshaling facts and by letting "slavery, not its partisans, speak." Quibbling with the title, Bettersworth proposed slavery "was hardly peculiar" but instead "the invention of man. Not all good or all bad." The book, according to the reviewer, concluded that "a well-managed plantation was an economically sound operation that hardly violated good business sense, even if it offended moral sense." Bettersworth then decided that slavery "could hardly have come to the bankrupt end to which certain of its contemporaries and many latter-day prophets condemned it." In Bettersworth's opinion, *The Peculiar Institution* "pursues the slave and slavery all the way from 'day clear to first dark.'" As a result, the native-born white Mississippian hailed Stampp's work as "American scholarship at its lucid best."[47] His glowing appreciation of the revisionist interpretation of slavery would have appalled the descendants of Mississippi planters.

In generous reviews of Civil War books, Bettersworth did not argue with authors, whether over the roles of railroads and industry in the South's defeat or over the significance of the Atlanta campaign, but he did applaud straight-forward dramatic writing and what he considered objective history. In a review of two books on Atlanta, for example, he concluded, "These two volumes are full of compassion indeed; but not of passion. No hatchets are buried; but neither are any axes ground." Of an edited volume, he applauded "the compiler [who] wisely refuses to interpret or moralize." He deplored writers with old-fashioned views of the South and the war. In a review of a book on southern thought, he disapproved of interpretations in the "Civil War and Reconstruction chapters . . . [that] can pass muster with any unreconstructed Rebel." Alert to biases, he also pointed out unfortunate cases of "unreconstructed Yankees." The Mississippian expressed dissatisfaction with portrayals of a "mythical" Jefferson Davis created "to suit the fears and aspirations of the people who dreamed them up." About one partisan southern biography of Davis, he suggested, "Perhaps in rescuing the bones of the Confederate President from the [Yankee] infidels he may, indeed, be guilty of an indefensible defensiveness." Pointing to the "vast literature of apology that has grown out of the South's defeat," Bettersworth regretted that "it has been the South's fate to undergo a veritable Hundred Years' War of verbal charge and counter-charge" over the causes of its defeat. "The Lost Cause," he commented, "was a long time a-losing."[48] Celebrants of the Lost Cause back in Mississippi would not have shared Bettersworth's evaluations.

If old arguments bored Bettersworth, new approaches appealed to him. In advance of what would later be known as the new social history, he saluted accounts of the Civil War that went beyond the usual emphasis on planters and politicians. Regarding one military history he commended the author who "never fails to see the men for the battles. One relives the adventure with all its sights, sounds and smells, as . . . men swear, sweat and swagger." Conventional Civil War history had told its story through generals, not guerrillas. "At long last," according to Bettersworth, "we are beginning to see the Civil War from the underneath, where the seams and the people show, not from the fancy outside of the garment." With new attention to the "private, the shavetail and the ranger," the reviewer proclaimed, "[h]istory will never be the same."[49]

Bettersworth also welcomed revisionist views of Reconstruction. If "carpetbagger" had "always been a dirty word" for white southerners, a biography of one carpetbagger presented carpetbaggers as, in Bettersworth's words, "civilians of fortune who interrupted the prevailing westward trend of frontiersmanship to 'go South' after the Civil War." He readily accepted the more benign reinterpretation of a traditional southern nemesis as "simply a Southern name for a national phenomenon." When a study of the Reconstruction Ku Klux Klan emphasized that it functioned as a social fraternity until it realized the frightening effects its hoods and robes had on freedmen, the appreciative professor parenthetically opined, "This was not the first time a fraternity went bad."[50]

Writing about the South and the Civil War era, Bettersworth acknowledged many contemporary relevancies. A 1959 review of a "timely" book on the historical background of southern thought demonstrated his awareness of controversies over segregation. The book's historical approach made sense to Bettersworth because he believed that the "present-day South has been made, sometimes even done in, by its history" and that few on either side understood that history. He regretted that the "current war of words between the North and South has reduced communications between the embattled sections" and hoped that the book wanted to explain the South to both sides. He did not question the contention that a distinctive "Southernism" was "approaching extinction," except for its racial problem, and he agreed that "the race problem is national, not merely Southern." In a rare long quotation he seemed to side with the author who said, "It would help if non-Southerners more fully realized the truth of the observation that, whereas the South formalized segregation but never completely practiced it, the North formalized social integration but never completely practiced it." If somewhat defensive for the South, Bettersworth also criticized southerners who "poorly comprehended" their own region and its past. Once again he showed frustration with the ignorant "unreconstructed Rebel." A few years later Bettersworth declared, "Time eventually sweetens the old bitterness. Northerners and Southerners have long since begun to outgrow their inherited Civil War hatreds, even if only to find contemporaneous issues to hate about." He lamented the reappearance of such sectional ill will.[51]

While writing for the *New York Times Book Review*, Bettersworth continued climbing the administrative ladder at Mississippi State while editing *Mississippi Quarterly* and directing the university's Social Science Research Center. His developing career pulled him away from primary research and scholarly publication. At the same time his reviews for the *New York Times* introduced him to writing for a larger public, and his friendship with Nash Burger led to his further reorientation toward a broader popular and profitable audience.[52]

When a publisher asked Burger to write a book on Confederate leaders after the Civil War, he declined but suggested Bettersworth as an alternative. The publisher insisted on Burger, and as a result the two old Central High

teachers teamed to write *South of Appomattox.* In lively writing that the journalist Burger credited to his historian friend, ten biographical portraits told
the story of Reconstruction. In an appreciative argument for continuity in
southern history, Burger and Bettersworth contended that the wartime generals had greater influence in postwar peacetime because they redeemed the
South from "carpetbag and Negro rule" under which the "social and economic system of the South had received a wound more lethal than any it had
suffered during the war." The Redeemers connected the Old South to the
New South and preserved the former's conservative, traditional values of the
"ancient social order." According to the respectful authors, "The war did not
create a new Southern heritage. It sustained an old one, now called Confederate, and now gave it renewed life." The South that the generals had "shaped
and reshaped . . . still lives and asserts itself in the region's concern for the
past and the traditional values, its attachment to the land, its opposition to
outside interference, and its insistence upon a caste system that manifests
itself in racial apartness." Blithely characterizing the oppression of contemporary racial segregation as *apartness* allowed Burger and Bettersworth to
celebrate the Redeemers' persisting influence.[53]

The book received generally favorable reviews, though a few scholars
balked. T. Harry Williams lauded its "charm of style and felicity of fact" but
saw a "basic defect in the book['s] . . . old and inadequate analysis" of fifty
years earlier that pitted "literally the good guys against the bad guys, and with
a big dose of sentimentality about the poor South." Another academic historian appreciated "sentences that move the reader easily and swiftly through
colorful decades, emotional times, and dramatic action," but he also scolded
the authors for neglecting "complex economic and social problems" in an
"oversimplified story of the thoughts and actions of a few men." In a rather
gentle review in the *New York Times Book Review,* C. Vann Woodward demurred that the sample of ten left "the whole minority race unaccounted for."
He also found "much jobbery and chicanery" in the Compromise of 1877 and
argued that the "redemption" of 1877 that led to the return of white rule left
the reputations of many of the ten "badly splattered." While Woodward appreciated any attempt to "raise a cheer for a good loser," he hoped the writers
had not aimed their book at "beleaguered South[erners] who are presently in
quest for models from the past and guidance in present quandaries of a Second Reconstruction." When even a skeptical editor had questioned Burger
and Bettersworth about their interpretation by asking them if their subjects
ever did anything wrong, they had told her, "No, they never did." Despite its

"lack of attention to [recent] scholarship," *South of Appomattox* satisfied the authors and their editors by selling perhaps twenty-five thousand copies.[54]

The old fashioned interpretations in *South of Appomattox* diverged from some of Bettersworth's more modern views expressed in the *New York Times Book Review*. In writing for wider audiences, Bettersworth understood the marketplace and the differences between the Civil War enthusiasts, likely mostly southerners, who would read *South of Appomattox*, and the much more northern and urbane readers of his book reviews, and he savvily crafted his works for their particular audiences. Published in the same year as *South of Appomattox*, his textbook in Mississippi history took the author even further afield from traditional academic scholarship and to a very different and more narrow popular audience, but he had learned how to conform to the expectations of its secondary school audience consisting of the state's Textbook Purchasing Board and its history teachers. Bettersworth presented in *Mississippi: A History* a conventional prerevisionist interpretation of the state's past. For the next quarter century, most public schools adopted *Mississippi: A History*, and as a result Bettersworth became well known. He worked with school teachers and became a popular public speaker, particularly for high school graduations. As his university's president later noted, "For a generation of Mississippians, the name John K. Bettersworth became a household word."[55]

Bettersworth subsequently recalled that the president of a Texas publishing company came to his office and first suggested that he write a Mississippi history textbook, but representatives from the Textbook Purchasing Board may have also encouraged him. Rumors have persisted that the board may have postponed its decision to allow Bettersworth to complete his textbook. Rumors also continue that Mississippi segregationists put Bettersworth up to writing the book. No evidence confirming the rumors can be found. Whatever its origin, he must have written his massive six-hundred-page textbook very quickly. In the summer of 1957 he expressed embarrassment that "Mississippi still has no up-to-date definitive account of its historical development" because no historian "can afford the time necessary for the self-sacrificing effort that would be involved in a mature and exhaustive study of Mississippi history." Less than a year later the legislature mandated a high school course in Mississippi history, which required a suitable textbook, and in March 1959 the State Textbook Purchasing Board adopted his *Mississippi: A History* for use in the high schools. The prospect of profits must have made the "self-sacrificing effort" worthwhile.[56]

Written during white Mississippi's frenzied response to *Brown v. Board of Education*'s call to end racial segregation, *Mississippi: A History* could not succeed if it deviated from the prevailing racial orthodoxy. Demands on textbooks for conformity escalated in such times of crisis or upheaval when the established elite faced challenges to its authority. During the civil rights movement, the segregationists and white supremacists in the legislature, the Citizens' Council, and the State Sovereignty Commission, more than the UDC or the UCV, increasingly set the standards of acceptability in schoolbooks. While Bettersworth's textbook necessarily defended the southern way of life, it also had to advocate traditional American values. To do otherwise during the Red Scare would have courted accusations of disloyalty, investigations by the legislature, and, more important, rejection by the Textbook Purchasing Board. As an experienced writer with multiple audiences and as an author who wanted to sell books, he produced a book that annually sold thousands of copies; a later version in the late 1960s and early 1970s sold as many as 10,000 copies annually. Bettersworth wrote a Mississippi history textbook successful for his time and place.[57]

In discussing slavery, *Mississippi: A History* resembled many secondary school American history textbooks of the 1950s. It conceded "some incidents involving the abuse of slaves" but reported that "prevailing sentiment was inclined toward lenient treatment of slaves." The law and public sentiment "assured the slave of good treatment." The planter "minister[ed] to both their physical and spiritual needs" and "assumed the responsibility for the souls of his Negroes." When attacked by the abolitionists' "violent propaganda," white Mississippians remained "calm and reasonable." Despite "rumors of insurrection," Mississippi stayed "relatively free of trouble" with its slaves. Secession had an "economic basis" with "bread and butter arguments" to protect slavery. After the war, according to Bettersworth, "reconstruction was a worse battle than the war ever was." To describe the waste and corruption of Reconstruction, Bettersworth resorted to quoting at length from James W. Garner's long-outdated 1901 study *Reconstruction in Mississippi*. With redemption, the state returned to "the control of the white people" and "it was Mississippi for the [white?] Mississippians from now on." In a cheery view Bettersworth said that "white and black could now set about the task of getting along together in the 'New South' as they had in the 'Old.'" In discussing the 1890 Constitution, unlike earlier textbooks, *Mississippi: A History* boldly stated that "Negro suffrage" was the major issue because whites could not control the black vote, and Bettersworth described how whites used voting requirement to disqualify blacks.[58]

Bettersworth's coverage of the twentieth century surpassed all prior textbooks, yet he too largely ignored blacks after disfranchisement. Without mentioning the civil rights movement, he said, "In the fifties, as the integration campaign of the federal government threatened the white Democracy in Mississippi, vigorous measures were taken to preserve the established social and political order." The State Sovereignty Commission, for example, "was expected to devise ways and means of resisting federal encroachments on state sovereignty." To explain the creation of the Citizens' Council movement, he referred to its purposes as found in Council literature on the importance of the Constitution, law, and order. With apparent regret Bettersworth declared that the 1954 Supreme Court decision, which he never dignified with a name, interrupted the state's efforts to equalize schools, "a situation [that] had been accepted in good spirit by all concerned." Except for mentioning author Richard Wright and soprano Leontyne Price, Bettersworth said little else about blacks or their push for racial equality.[59]

Under the repressive conditions of Mississippi in the 1950s, Bettersworth produced a traditional textbook much like earlier ones by the McLemores, Pearl Guyton, and Mary Duval. The state's schoolchildren, white and black, suffered the effects of its defects and distortions; they learned only the white supremacist history that the entrenched whites wanted them to know, a history that supported the status quo. They would have to wait another generation for a radical change in a textbook that offered a truly modern, progressive, inclusive coverage of their state's history.[60]

CHAPTER FOUR

Writers

Jim Loewen, Charles Sallis, and Their Team

More than a decade after the first publication of Bettersworth's book, James Loewen and Charles Sallis's partnership on *Mississippi: Conflict and Change* overturned the traditional approach and conventional interpretation found in Bettersworth's volume and its predecessors. Using the scholarly findings of modern historical research, they challenged the established understanding of the state's past. Their innovations extended beyond their historical analyses. In their boldest move Loewen and Sallis worked with a group of undergraduate students and faculty colleagues to write the textbook. The writers included blacks and whites, northerners and southerners, men and women, and representatives from several academic disciplines (history, sociology, political science, and education), and they came from both Millsaps and Tougaloo colleges. Work on *Conflict and Change* built upon both the longer informal relationship between the two institutions and each college's experiences with race. The institutions' histories helped make possible the collaboration.

Though located just a few miles apart near North State Street in Jackson, the two schools actually existed far from each other in the divided, racially segregated world of Mississippi.[1] Beginning before World War II but expanding in the postwar years, contact between the black and white colleges developed, initially almost surreptitiously and later both more publicly and more controversially. Ernst Borinski, a pioneering Tougaloo professor, proved a key figure in drawing the faculty and students at the colleges into closer interracial contact and in providing the foundation for cooperation between Loewen and Sallis. The professor's often unobtrusive, usually hidden, sometimes dangerous work sought to overcome racial separation at the very time that white supremacists tried to enforce it by retaliating against transgressors.

In 1947, Ernst Borinski arrived at Tougaloo College and began thirty-five years on the black college's faculty. The émigré professor and the small, isolated Mississippi college made a special combination. Borinski set for himself a bold mission to expand the education of blacks living in the repressive, segregated state and to help them subvert the entire system of white supremacy. He believed the academic study of the social sciences could promote activism in the community as students began to understand social problems and their responsibility, and ability, to bring about change. Optimistic in outlook and with the perspective of a non-southerner, even non-American, he wanted to break the bonds of the postwar "closed society." One former student concluded that "Borinski's greatest legacy was the production of students trained to question and challenge the society in which they lived." His impact extended beyond the Tougaloo campus to the Jackson community and particularly to nearby Millsaps College, a white Methodist school. Usually Borinski operated behind the scenes out of the view of white supremacists, but occasionally he dared to speak and act publicly.[2]

Born in the Silesia region of Poland in 1901, Borinski graduated from college in Germany and received a doctorate in law from the University of Berlin in 1928. For a decade in Germany he served as a judge, practiced law, worked on labor law at an optical company, and was a teacher. In 1938 Borinski, a secular Jew, fled Nazi Germany and the impending Holocaust for the United States. While working in retail stores and at a Bausch and Lomb factory in Rochester, New York, he became a naturalized citizen in 1942, and soon thereafter he was drafted and served as an interpreter with Army intelligence in North Africa and later at a prisoner-of-war camp at Fort Dix, New Jersey. After receiving an honorable discharge, he used the GI bill to earn a master's degree in sociology at the University of Chicago in 1946. Through black students at Chicago, he learned of the American Missionary Association's (AMA) schools in the South, and he soon accepted a position at the AMA's Tougaloo College. After joining Tougaloo as its sole sociology professor, Borinski continued his graduate education and received another doctorate from the University of Pittsburgh in 1954; reflecting his German legal background and his Mississippi experiences with racial segregation, his dissertation examined the sociology of the judiciary in civil rights cases. A consummate intellectual and teacher, Borinski developed the sociology program at Tougaloo and taught more than twenty students who later received doctorates in sociology or social work. During summers he taught at other universities, including Duke, Vanderbilt, and the University of North Carolina. As a promoter of social inquiry and activism, especially in race relations, Borinski had a profound impact on the Tougaloo College community.[3]

Tougaloo College started in 1869 as Tougaloo University on five hundred acres of a former plantation seven miles north of downtown Jackson. Though former abolitionists in the American Missionary Association founded the school to educate freed slaves primarily to be teachers, the school worked with students at all stages of academic development. Funding for the new college came initially from the Reconstruction state legislature and the Freedmen's

Bureau; state support ended in 1892. Northern whites served as teachers and administrators. In many ways like a secondary or manual training school, Tougaloo offered its first college-level course in 1897 and awarded its first undergraduate degree in 1901. Historian Vernon Wharton praised the Tougaloo of the late nineteenth century "as the one institution where the young Negroes of Mississippi might obtain competent training." In 1916 its name changed to Tougaloo College. The college's high school gained regional and state accreditation in 1931, as did the college soon thereafter. In the 1940s and 1950s financial difficulties and low faculty salaries plagued the college and threatened its accreditation. With recruitment and retention of faculty with advanced degrees a priority, Ernst Borinski offered needed help to the college.[4]

Historic ties to the AMA and abolitionism gave Tougaloo a tradition dedicated to racial equality. At the same time the AMA, its northern trustees, and other northern philanthropists afforded the college remarkable independence from Mississippi revenue sources. Much more than state-sponsored colleges, Tougaloo operated outside the direct control of the state's segregationist politicians. Unlike other black colleges, such as the private Rust College in Holly Springs, Tougaloo occupied a central position in the state near the capital, yet its rural location kept it isolated from downtown.

After arriving in Jackson, Borinski witnessed racial oppression. Appreciating Tougaloo's potential for fomenting change, the professor decided to do what he could to undermine the system of white supremacy. His legal training and his familiarity with Nazi Germany gave him a special understanding of his new environment, though as a Jew in Mississippi he was in many eyes neither white nor black.

In addition to his European and American degrees, the dynamic five-foot-four German refugee brought a cosmopolitan tone, a varied academic background, and intellectual strength to the campus. According to one colleague, Borinski became "the most important personality at Tougaloo College." Without any family, he lived alone in campus housing and devoted his abundant energy almost exclusively to the college and his students.[5]

At first Borinski taught all of Tougaloo's sociology classes, with the exceptions of rural sociology and race relations, which a sociologist from Millsaps covered, and a course on the family, which a local minister taught. In 1948 Borinski expanded his teaching opportunities by creating a Social Science Laboratory in the large basement room of an abandoned academic building. He described it as "a plain spacious classroom that combines the features of an office, of a round-table conference hall, and a reading, study, and guidance center." Shelves lining the walls contained all kinds of publications related to the social sciences and contemporary society that students could use in the lab during its long hours from early morning to late at night. The lab also featured a variety of maps, charts, posters, and other information sources, and Borinski made available works by African-American scholars and writers, especially about black history and Africa. As a teacher, Borinski made sure that the materials represented a wide range of ideological and political views. He hoped the lab would help students understand how to apply their social science education to contemporary social problems. To broaden his students' perspectives even further, Borinski, who could speak five languages, also provided some foreign language periodicals. Four large tables with numerous chairs allowed classes to meet in the lab. From an adjoining office equipped with a small kitchen, Borinski supervised the lab, which under his direction became a popular campus gathering place.[6]

At Borinski's initiative, the Social Science Lab in the early 1950s regularly hosted guest speakers. In 1954 the Field Foundation provided funding for the series. With support also from the college, he organized the Social Science Forum on a bimonthly basis with meetings on alternate Wednesday evenings. Starting with a dinner for small integrated groups that included Tougaloo students, the Forum presented outside speakers to larger integrated groups of students, faculty, visitors from Millsaps College, and townspeople. The integrated informal social gatherings offered rare opportunities in Mississippi's closed society for blacks and whites to share a meal and exchange ideas in open, frank discussions. One early speaker was Percy Greene, black editor of the *Jackson Advocate*; and others in the 1950s who also usually came from the area included state NAACP head Medgar Evers, writer Eudora Welty, journalists Bill Minor and Hodding Carter, Rabbi Perry Nussbaum, and Roman Catholic Bishop Joseph Brunini. Each spoke on a contemporary topic that typically featured a racial component. Subjects ranged from integration and the church to the NAACP and the role of the press. In the 1960s, after the Forum's reputation for welcoming civil rights activists had spread, students could meet visiting movement leaders. Lecturers also included sociologist David Riesman, movement lawyer William Kuntsler, writer James Baldwin, socialist Michael Harrington, Harvard economist John Kenneth Galbraith, singer Pete Seeger, and American diplomat Ralph Bunche. By subverting segregation, reinforcing dissenters, and encouraging his students, the Forum series furthered Borinski's campaign to break open Mississippi society.[7]

After the 1954 *Brown* decision on school integration, Borinski proclaimed privately to his campus colleagues that "Tougaloo has ceased to be a Negro college" and "white and Negro students will soon live and study together."

The Social Science Forum served "as a vivid rebuke of the absurd assumption that the integrated education does not work," and Borinski's Social Science Division continued to promote desegregation. Encouraged by the court decision, he called on Tougaloo to "assume the role of leadership in educational integration in our state." The college, he believed, had "the full responsibility for rejecting accommodation to the traditional pattern of segregation and humiliation."[8]

As with his statement to his fellow professors, Borinski mostly served behind the scenes as an adviser and facilitator of activism. Occasionally he spoke publicly, and his stands sometimes provoked threatening responses from segregationists. In letters to local newspapers he poked holes in the segregationist position. For example, a December 1955 letter to the *Jackson Clarion-Ledger* respectfully but logically pointed out the error in a Citizens' Council's argument. At a recent meeting the Council had reiterated its advocacy of using legal means to support segregation and had disavowed responsibility for violence against blacks. Former lawyer Borinski reminded the "honorable citizens of the Citizens Councils" that "in light of the very recent decisions of the Federal Courts and many State Courts segregation just cannot be maintained any more by legal means." They could, therefore, defend segregation only by "illegal means" that violated the law and the Constitution. By advocating illegal acts, he proposed, the Councils "share the responsibility for the acts of violence" against blacks and whites because of their racial views. He urged the Citizens' Councils to "arrive at a constructive and positive approach to the race question."[9]

Borinski irritated segregationists. Tom Ethridge, a *Clarion-Ledger* political columnist, deflected Borinski's charges against the Citizens' Council and responded that the professor "preaches law obedience for whites but neglects to emphasize its need among blacks." Turning the argument on Borinski, Ethridge claimed that black leaders had to accept "a share of responsibility for Negro crimes." He further suggested that Borinski could "perform a public service" by conducting his "missionary work" preaching the same sermon to blacks.[10]

A few years later, in March 1958, at a Millsaps College lecture series on "Christianity and Race Relations," Borinski became embroiled in another controversy when he spoke in favor of integration. He declared that racial segregation violated Christian principles. In response the *Clarion-Ledger* called Borinski's statement an "asinine argument that real Christians do not believe in segregation." Aroused state legislators unanimously demanded an investigation of the NAACP and Professor Borinski, who had been identified as an NAACP member. Conflict continued later in the week because Borinski had scheduled a Social Science Forum panel on race relations, but in the wake of Borinski's comments all the panelists withdrew except for George Maddox, a Millsaps sociologist, and Millsaps and Tougaloo student panelists. About thirty Millsaps students and twenty Tougaloo students attended the forum and participated in the discussion of racial differences and perceptions. From the segregationists' perspective, the Forum breached the walls of segregation by "aggravat[ing] the already explosive subject of race mixing," and the uproar led to calls for ouster of the "imported pink intellectual." By 1958 his activities attracted the attention of State Sovereignty Commission investigators.[11]

Others at Tougaloo shared Borinski's inclinations. Along with Borinski in the late 1940s, the Reverend William Bender, the college chaplain and a Tougaloo alumnus, and August Meier, a white history professor in the late 1940s, belonged to the NAACP. In 1943 the Reverend Bender had served as president of the Jackson branch of the NAACP, and three years later he tried unsuccessfully to vote in the Madison County Democratic primary. As the civil rights movement gained momentum, Tougaloo's president, Samuel Kincheloe, came to the defense of civil rights participants. Trained in the sociology of religion at the University of Chicago, Kincheloe told the Tougaloo board of trustees in 1957, "We do not dare let it be assumed that we accept the proposition of white supremacy and of racial inferiority." With the trustees he declared, "We think of the work of our college as liberal and liberating." Two years later at the height of Mississippi's massive resistance to the *Brown* decision, the board endorsed academic freedom for Borinski and others: "The teacher in Tougaloo is entitled to full academic freedom—a principle which rests in the philosophy and tradition of the college."[12]

With Borinski playing the key role, the Tougaloo campus became "an oasis of freedom" in Mississippi. In 1959 the Reverend John Mangum, Bender's successor as chaplain and another NAACP member, had worked with Medgar Evers to help students form a Tougaloo branch of the NAACP. In 1960, with new president Adam D. Beittel, who backed student and faculty involvement in the movement, Tougaloo engaged in what one historian has termed "a full frontal assault on white supremacy." In the spring of 1961 nine Tougaloo students, advised by Mangum and Evers, staged Jackson's first sit-in at the segregated public library; most of the demonstrators had often attended the Social Science Forum. Soon after the sit-in, the college welcomed interracial groups of Freedom Riders to the state by providing them safe housing on campus. At the same time Beittel announced that he belonged to the NAACP, and he refused to stop Tougaloo students from participating in boycotts and protests in Jackson, including attempts to integrate white churches. He also helped organize the Mississippi Council on Human Relations and participated in Medgar Evers's funeral. In 1963 Borinski's protest against segregation at the annual meeting of sociologists in the state led to an agreement to integrate the organization and to hold its first integrated meeting at Tougaloo the next year.[13]

Segregationists sought methods to stop the civil rights activities at Tougaloo. Legislators considered revoking the college's charter and denying it accreditation, and the State Sovereignty Commission even elicited a court order to enjoin the Tougaloo trustees and president from "engaging in, sponsoring, inciting or encouraging demonstrations." Unwilling to allow the college to continue to foment dangerous civil rights activity, the Sovereignty Commission continued to harass the college and focused pressure on its board of trustees. The board worried about the college's financial stability and the bad publicity caused by the movement activism. Fears about the college's finances had prompted the college, in conjunction with Brown University, to apply for a major Ford Foundation grant. The president of Brown convinced the Tougaloo trustees that the turbulence at the college would not please officials at the Ford Foundation, and the college's board capitulated to pressure from its own members and to perceived demands by the Ford Foundation. As a result, Beittel resigned, the Ford Foundation made a major grant to Tougaloo, and the college established a formal partnership with Brown University. After 1964, under a new president, civil rights protesting and organizing moderated until the Sovereignty Commission could report in 1968 that the new president "had not allowed the campus to be used by subversive groups, in sharp contrast to the Beittel regime."[14]

While activism at Tougaloo subsided after 1964, Millsaps College in 1965 became the first Mississippi college to integrate voluntarily. As a white college, Millsaps had an extremely different history with race. Mississippi Methodists seeking to provide a Christian college education for young men received a charter from the state in 1890, and the college opened two years later. The founders included men with progressive racial views. Major R. W. Millsaps, the original benefactor, had served in the Confederate Army but during Reconstruction had supported Republicans because of his Christian concern for helping blacks and because of his interest in promoting business. White supremacists attacked another Millsaps founder, Bishop Charles B. Galloway, after he gave the 1904 commencement sermon at Alabama's Tuskegee Institute. One politician damned the bishop as "a greater traitor to the South than Benedict Arnold was to the Colonies." Unyielding, Galloway responded, "If it is treason to teach the gospel to Negroes, then I am a traitor and not ashamed of it." The young college also benefitted from briefly having Jackson College, a black institution, as a next-door neighbor along North State Street. When after just a few years Jackson College moved in 1902, Major Millsaps bought the college property and gave it to Millsaps College.[15]

In the early twentieth century Millsaps College did not contest the prevailing racial segregation, but it did establish a reputation for excellence and enlightenment. It gained accreditation in 1913, and a state study of higher education reported in 1926, "The students [at Millsaps] rank higher in ability than do students at any other Mississippi college or university." When the state outlawed the teaching of evolution in state schools, Millsaps stood for academic freedom. Speaking on the campus, a representative of the Methodist church declared, "Millsaps as a Church College says that science is no enemy of religion, and there is no conflict between the two when properly understood and taught. The apparent conflict is in the minds of the third-rate scientists and shallow religionists."[16]

Tolerance at Millsaps extended beyond the conflict between science and religion. In the late 1930s, as Congress considered legislation against lynching, the International Relations Club, a student group, wrote Mississippi's representatives and senators in support of federal anti-lynching laws. An outraged Senator Theodore G. Bilbo tried to bully the college by holding public hearings into what he labeled "communist doctrine" at Millsaps. The senator advocated "a complete overhaul" of the college. Boldly defending the students' rights and academic freedom in general, President David M. Key of Millsaps explained that a "college worthy of the name is an educational institution and not an organ of propaganda. Its function is to teach how to think and not what to think." The college would not force on its students and faculty segregated Mississippi's oppressive values. Academic freedom and inquiry at Millsaps even included questions about race. Everyone at Millsaps was not, of course, enlightened or progressive about race, or even about lynching. In the 1920s some Millsaps students had joined a mob intent on lynching a black man accused of murder; only losing the suspect had averted a disaster.[17]

Though Millsaps had a relatively open-minded attitude, officially it practiced complete segregation. As a result, relations between Millsaps and Tougaloo developed slowly, cautiously, and unofficially. Significant interaction may have begun with the exchange of professors, with Millsaps professors usually teaching at Tougaloo for no pay. In the 1930s Millsaps hired Mabel

Cobb, the Tougaloo academic dean's wife and a white woman, to teach foreign languages. In the 1940s Vernon Lane Wharton, the chairman of the Millsaps sociology department, taught rural sociology and race relations at Tougaloo. Wharton, a Mississippi native and Millsaps graduate, had earned a doctorate in American history and written the path breaking *The Negro in Mississippi, 1865–1890* (1947). James Ferguson, another Millsaps historian, also taught at Tougaloo. Many of the Tougaloo classes taught by Millsaps faculty met in the evenings. Traveling in the opposite direction, Ernst Borinski in 1957 taught Millsaps students German and Russian. Though the shared professors did not include black Tougaloo faculty in Millsaps's classrooms, Borinski's students did temporarily desegregate the white college when they went to Millsaps for his language classes.[18]

More informal contact between the two colleges' faculty and students had occurred since the 1930s. Millsaps YMCA students had participated in meetings and discussions at Tougaloo as early as 1935. Often the visits to Tougaloo afforded white students their first opportunity to encounter educated black contemporaries. Interracial meetings also took place in private homes and on the Millsaps campus, but after the *Brown* decision in 1954 participants in similar gatherings had to exercise more discretion to avoid investigations by the Sovereignty Commission and attacks from the Citizens' Council. In the postwar years Millsaps students also participated in integrated intercollegiate meetings at Tougaloo.[19]

Public interaction most frequently occurred at Borinski's Wednesday evening Social Science Forums. Along with Tougaloo students and professors, liberal Millsaps faculty and students attended, as did like-minded people from the community. The suppers followed by a lecture and discussion sometimes featured Millsaps faculty such as historian James Ferguson, sociologist Harry Dillingham, and political scientist Gordon Henderson. The occasions proved important for introducing people across racial lines and for breaking down barriers against interracial meals, discussions, and general social interaction.[20]

Violations of segregation's racial etiquette always endangered the college and risked retaliation, as Borinski's lecture at Millsaps and Maddox's appearance at the Social Science Forum in 1958 proved. In the uproar that followed, the Citizens' Council questioned Millsaps's commitment to racial segregation and racial integrity. A letter to the editor reminded the college's president, Ellis Fenger, of the "life and death struggle for our very existence" and accused the college of "undermining everything we are fighting for." A Council official warned, "I tell you frankly and without rancor that the time has come for a showdown. . . . Either you and your faculty are for segregation, or you are for integration." President Fenger had to respond. In a public statement espousing academic freedom, he declared, "Every thoughtful person needs carefully to consider that if freedom is attacked at one college, it will eventually be attacked at all educational institutions. Moreover, every pulpit, every newspaper, every individual could be pressured. Differences of opinion are to be welcomed. The only alternative is dreaded thought control. Millsaps College joins with the entire Christian Church, of which it is an integral part, in pledging to its constituents its devotion to preserving a climate where freedom may prosper and where intimidation, fear and bondage are doomed." At the same time, Fenger reminded his professors of the volatility surrounding racial segregation and asked them to exercise discretion. Though the Millsaps trustees endorsed Fenger's stand for academic freedom, they also repeated the college's official commitment to segregation.[21]

In the years following the Borinski-Maddox controversies, Millsaps, its president, and its activist faculty experienced various forms of retaliation ranging from social ostracism to threats. The college tried awkwardly both to defend academic freedom and to adhere to racial segregation. While participation in Borinski's Social Science Forums continued, Millsaps faculty took care to avoid public controversy. In the fall of 1962, after James Meredith desegregated the University of Mississippi, however, Marguerite Goodman, a Millsaps professor of English, presented her colleagues with a simple question: "[S]houldn't we be the first white Christian college of Mississippi to open our doors to a limited number of Negro students who can meet scholastic and character standards?" She then proposed, "Such an offer from us *might* ease some of the tension in Mississippi and the South."[22]

Tougaloo and Millsaps faculty and students soon supported Professor Goodman's proposal. In the spring of 1963 interracial groups pushed for integration by trying six times to integrate audiences at public events on the Millsaps campus. In four instances, police escorted the mixed groups away. Also that spring the Millsaps chapter of the American Association of University Professors asked that the college reconsider its segregation policy and begin accepting black students. Later in 1963 the Millsaps board of trustees decided to permit integrated groups to attend public events on campus. Three major breaks came the next year. The Civil Rights Act of 1964 prohibited racial discrimination by institutions receiving federal funds, the college president announced his departure to become a bishop in the Methodist church; and the Jackson public schools began desegregation under freedom of choice. Early in 1965 a new president came to Millsaps, and the college announced that it would follow an open admissions policy that would admit qualified blacks. Though hardly pioneering, integration occurred without incident.[23]

While the college received considerable criticism for its new position on race and suffered declines in the number of students and in donations, it also received recognition for its voluntary integration. Hodding Carter praised it. The editor of the Greenville *Delta Democrat Times* called the college "perhaps the most courageous institution in the nation because it has a tradition of relative liberalism. It lets the students and professors speak their minds." According to Carter, the small Methodist school "attracted the best student body in Mississippi. It has a higher percentage of what I would consider the right people than probably any other school in the South. . . . They go because Millsaps challenges their souls." The outspoken editor, whose editorials on intolerance had won a Pulitzer prize in 1946, concluded, "There is not an institution in the country that cannot learn something from this little school in Mississippi . . . it is a candle burning in the darkness."[24]

Interaction between Millsaps and Tougaloo increased. In 1967 students from the two colleges met several times to plan a weekend symposium to bring together students from Jackson colleges. Three years later the colleges' deans held a luncheon at Millsaps to discuss greater intercollegiate cooperation. As a result, a visiting professor from Ghana taught an anthropology course that met at Tougaloo on Tuesday and at Millsaps on Thursday. Three Tougaloo students also took a French literature course at Millsaps. Mickey Clampit, chairman of the Millsaps sociology department, taught a course on sociology and evolution at Tougaloo. In the fall of 1970, an excited Ernst Borinski reported that a mixed class in criminology from the two colleges along with other Millsaps students in a social problems course visited the Jackson police station. According to Borinski, "It was a great experience for the students and a still greater experience for the whole personnel in the Police Department. It was so new for them that they could hardly hide their amazement about this event." One officer told the students that they had, in Borinski's words, "made a tremendous impact on the whole" police force.[25]

The light that Hodding Carter saw at Millsaps also included increased civil rights activism. With the help of supportive faculty, integration proceeded. Activist professors backed the creation of a Black Student Association at Millsaps in 1968. The college faculty passed a resolution condemning the assassination of Martin Luther King Jr., and a year later they openly endorsed public school integration in Mississippi. In 1970 three faculty ushered in further major changes. Ten days after law enforcement personnel killed four Kent State University students protesting the war in Vietnam, a clash between Jackson State College students and police and National Guardsmen left two black students dead. Millsaps students and three of their professors marched in protest to the governor's mansion. Later the college faculty passed a resolution condemning "the use of excessive force" that resulted in the deaths on the Jackson State campus. One professor who marched with students to the governor's mansion and who wrote the resolution protesting the violence on the nearby campus was Charles Sallis, a professor of history.[26]

Charles Sallis had not always been so enlightened about race. Later Sallis recognized that he grew up in Mississippi as a "benign bigot. In other words, I honestly believed blacks were inferior . . . but I wasn't about it." Born in 1934 in northeastern Mississippi's Itawamba County, as a boy he lived in several small towns across the state. His father, with degrees in the sciences from Mississippi State and the University of Alabama, taught school in Kingston, near Natchez, and served as an elementary school principal in Scott County before joining the U.S. Department of Agriculture. Between the ages of three and thirteen, Charles Sallis lived in the Noxubee County seat of Macon. After his father taught for a year at a junior college in Raymond, outside Jackson, he rejoined the USDA, and the family moved to Greenville. As a teenager in the Delta town, Sallis went to school with Jewish and Chinese-American children, but he had few interactions with the majority black population. Sallis did not recognize the system of Jim Crow as different or discriminatory because it seemed a natural part of his world. His future wife, Harrylyn Graves, also lived in Greenville where her father was president of one of the South's larger stockyards.[27]

After high school, Sallis attended his father's alma mater, Mississippi State where he was active in student government, participated in ROTC, and served as president of his fraternity. Influenced by impressive instructors, Sallis switched his major from economics to history. Lectures in European and medieval history by Harold Snellgrove, a native of Meridian, especially attracted him. He also studied with Glover Moore, a specialist in the Old South, and John K. Bettersworth, who taught Mississippi history and chaired the department. Halfway through his fourth year, Sallis had completed all the requirements for a bachelor's degree but still needed one semester of ROTC to receive his commission as a second lieutenant, so he stayed the extra semester and began taking graduate courses. Before long he earned a master's degree. For his master's thesis written under the direction of Glover Moore, Sallis chose to work on LeRoy Percy (1860–1929), a well-educated, wealthy lawyer, planter, and politician from Sallis's hometown of Greenville. The Sallis family had lived just around the corner from the Percys' family home, though he had not known them well.[28]

Born in the Mississippi Delta months before the outbreak of the Civil War, Percy offered Sallis an opportunity to use his life to examine state politics, and in the process the young scholar revealed his own historical views on race. Sallis described "black slaves who had deserted in a frenzy when they learned of the Emancipation Proclamation." According to Sallis, the "days of Reconstruction were equally as terrible as those of war" and "ignorance and corruption reigned supreme." After "the carpetbaggers grew fattest and richest" in the black belt, white redemption in Greenville's Washington County "marked the end of waste and robbery." Whites had, in Sallis's view, learned that "freedom could not, in a moment transform an ignorant, immoral, and degraded slave into a good citizen." Percy played a major role in the restoration of white rule that "resorted to various expedients. Election victories were gained by intimidation and force, disfranchising black voters, ostracism, vote buying, and ballot box stuffing. It was dirty, heartbreaking work, but it was considered necessary." In telling Percy's story, Sallis entered no dissent. Later, on James K. Vardaman's politics in the 1880s, Sallis reported that the politician believed the black man "was a curse to the country and especially to the South . . . a social scab; a lazy, lustful animal who could never be trained to be a useful animal. His nature resembled the hog's." Only about Vardaman's belief that the "Negro's lust for white women" that could be controlled only with violence did Sallis demur that "Vardaman exaggerated."[29]

When Sallis had nearly finished his thesis, Glover Moore thought to recommend Vernon Wharton's boldly revisionist *The Negro in Mississippi, 1865–1890*. It came to Sallis too late to have much effect on his thesis, so he cited it only a few times in discussing the politics of white supremacy. The professor and his student never discussed the book, just as they never talked about race. Whatever Moore's intention, Wharton's book, Sallis later recalled, changed his life and his view of southern history. It gave him a new perspective on Reconstruction that did not involve evil carpetbaggers and incompetent blacks, with heroic whites coming to the rescue of the prostrate South. Wharton's complex, expanded assessment of blacks examined religion, family life, education, nonagricultural labor, legal status, migration, and other aspects of their complicated lives. The book began to break down Sallis's benign bigotry.[30]

The reorientation of Sallis's racial ideas continued after he received his master's degree. Before he joined the military in 1957, Sallis had spent his entire life in small Mississippi towns, most in areas with large black majorities. His family never had black help around their home, and they did not discuss race. In the 1940s and 1950s, before the civil rights movement, the Sallises, like most southern whites, accepted without question the prevailing Jim

Crow system. As his friends and neighbors did, Sallis simply conformed to racial segregation. Except for a few trips to Alabama, Louisiana, and Memphis, and for ROTC summer camp at Georgia's Fort Benning, he had not traveled outside Mississippi to places where he might have seen other patterns of race relations.[31]

Active duty in the Army offered further challenges to his racial assumptions. With an armor assignment to Fort Knox in Kentucky, Sallis ventured for the first time out of the deep South. Jim Crow did not prevail at Fort Knox as it did in Mississippi. More important, he came into contact with many other Army officers, some of whom were black. For the first time he had as equals black classmates and colleagues. One captain, an instructor in tank gunnery, had graduated from West Point and was black. Sallis found, of course, that he had to salute the black captain and acknowledge his superior rank. The twenty-three-year-old white Mississippian definitely noticed his new relationship with blacks but also realized that he had adjusted to it painlessly.[32]

After eighteen months in the Army, Sallis taught math for a year in Elizabethtown, Kentucky, before pursuing graduate work in history at the University of Kentucky. In Lexington he studied in the new doctoral program with four southern history specialists, Thomas D. Clark, Clement Eaton, Holman Hamilton, and Albert Kirwan. Clark, the department chairman, directed Sallis's dissertation. In 1960 Sallis and his wife left Lexington for Athens, Tennessee, where he taught history and she taught music at Tennessee Wesleyan College. While continuing to serve in the Army Reserve, he taught a variety of courses, chaired the department, led the college's chapter of American Association of University Professors, and started a family. He also worked on his dissertation, which he completed in 1967.[33]

Though in ways a refinement and expansion of his master's thesis, Sallis's dissertation on "The Color Line in Mississippi Politics, 1865–1915" demonstrated his growing understanding of historical revisionism and his maturing appreciation for blacks as historical actors. His dissertation also revealed his developing awareness of race and his increasing consciousness of the contemporary civil rights movement. From the outset, Sallis rejected the traditional view that blamed the freed slaves and carpetbaggers for everything bad and that exonerated southern whites. Seeing the story from multiple perspectives, he empathized with blacks and whites. "As Mississippi Negroes had never been free," he observed, "they naturally had an imperfect understanding of the duties and responsibilities of 'liberty.'" The ex-slaves, therefore, while moving "to get the 'feel' for freedom," committed fewer major crimes "than the whites committed against them." In considering the postwar labor system, Sallis conceded that blacks "performed less efficiently than in slavery days" but pointed out the ex-slaves "knew nothing of work without supervision." Like whites, blacks also did not understand labor negotiations. Though critical of the Black Code as "unwise" and "oppressive," Sallis explained its basis in white fears and recognized that the Black Code "carried the implication that the Negro was unfit for freedom." With compassion and regret he concluded, "To provide for the equality of white and black was beyond [whites'] imaginations; perhaps it is unreasonable to have expected more of them at that time. The suppression of prejudices was not easier then than it is a century later." Whites were "emotionally unready" to allow blacks political rights. The "attitude of white Mississippians toward the Negro had not changed with the cessation of war."[34]

In assessing Reconstruction, Sallis denied any "such thing as 'Negro domination.'" Blaming any excesses of the time on white manipulation of black voters, he acknowledged the Ku Klux Klan as "a profound intimidation device" to maintain the "Southern way of life." The bold revisionist declared, "Defeat was a psychological blow and [white] southerners suffered the psychosis of defeat" and could not realize that "the South was more leniently treated than any other defeated power in history, that military rule was neither unbearable nor unreasonably long. They forgot the lasting achievements of Reconstruction regimes." With resignation, he decided that "historical revisionism and re-evaluation cannot alter folklore; stereotypes have persisted to this day." Later in the disfranchisement movement and clash over Populism, according to Sallis, "the poor Negro, dragged once again into a white man's fight (after they had been told to stay out) became the scapegoat." Whites repeatedly used "the racial theme to get votes," even when blacks posed no substantive political threat.[35]

Writing in the mid-1960s, Sallis suggested, "In many respects the race problem today is the same as it was a century and a half ago. One hears the same arguments, reads the same slogans from an unforgotten past. The South has not solved the Negro problem; it was, and still is, a riddle." He saw whites' ideas about black inferiority deeply set in "the mores of the South," even though "white Mississippians have thought more about the Negro than any other single subject ... [and] the Negro influenced behavior, morals, habits and philosophy of whites." With despair, Sallis argued, "The tragedy of Mississippi is that racism has adulterated the energies of its leaders" and every other aspect of life. Quoting historian U. B. Phillips, who identified the central theme of southern history as "a people with a common resolve indomitably maintained—that it shall be and remain white man's country," Sallis ended his dissertation, "This was certainly true of Mississippi in the first half century after Appomattox." Fifty years later, in the midst of the civil rights movement, it still seemed true.[36]

"The Color Line in Mississippi Politics" demonstrated Sallis's development as a historian and observer of Mississippi. His views had changed dramatically from the ones the Mississippi State graduate student held a decade earlier. Life outside the South, Army service, further historical study, and contemporary events had caused the changes. His new ideas would become very significant when he returned to his home state.

With family still in Mississippi, the Sallises wanted to go back home. On a visit in 1967 Sallis talked with Millsaps College about his interest in coming back to the state, so when an opening appeared in 1968, he left Tennessee Wesleyan. Starting in the fall of 1968, Sallis and his wife quickly made friends with the liberals on the Millsaps faculty and their wives. He developed particularly close ties with three ordained Methodist ministers in the Millsaps religion department—Robert Bergmark, T. W. Lewis, and Lee Reiff. The couples, along with Tougaloo chaplain Ed King and his wife, regularly socialized. In addition, Sallis met Ernst Borinski and attended the Social Science Forums at Tougaloo.[37]

While teaching, Sallis also became active in the small liberal community in Jackson. Soon after joining Galloway United Methodist Church, he proposed that the downtown church create a child care program. With many of its potential clients in the nearby black community, the church rejected the idea. Sallis also participated in the Alliance Against Racism. Affiliated with the Jackson Council on Human Relations, it gathered information to help promote anti-racist public policies. In 1970 Sallis led the Alliance's effort to encourage the local Boys' Club to accept black members. He and another member met with leaders of the Jackson organization to discuss integration, but they failed to persuade the club to desegregate. With children in the public schools, Sallis also worked with Jacksonians for Public Education and represented the group on a committee to establish a Community Coalition for Public Schools. Far from a benign bigot, Sallis actively sought to promote interracial progress.[38]

As a Millsaps professor, Sallis continued to teach southern history while furthering his research and broadening his expertise to include Mississippi history and black history. He participated in a nine-week National Endowment for the Humanities (NEH) seminar at the University of Washington. In the summer of 1969 he went to Columbia University for six weeks in the

Harvard-Yale-Columbia Intensive Summer Studies Program, where he studied with Charles V. Hamilton, James Henry Clarke, James Shenton, and others in African-American history. After the Columbia program, Sallis started teaching perhaps the earliest course in African-American history at a traditionally white Mississippi college. For 1970–71 Sallis received a year-long NEH fellowship.[39]

In Sallis's second year at Millsaps, Robert Bruce Adams took his Mississippi history course. The senior history major from the Gulf coast appreciated Sallis's comment that no good Mississippi history textbook existed. When Adams decided not to go to law school immediately after graduation, he approached his professor with the idea of taking a year off and writing a Mississippi history textbook. Though Sallis acknowledged the need, he expressed reservations about the ambitious project and wished his student good luck.[40] Adams and Sallis were not the only persons thinking about a new textbook for high school Mississippi history classes.

Mary Frances Derfner, the wife of an attorney representing the Lawyers Committee for Civil Rights Under Law in Jackson, had also grown frustrated with the Mississippi history textbooks. Independently she investigated the books approved for use in the elementary grades, Richard A. and Nannie P. McLemore's *The Mississippi Story* (1964), and, in the secondary grades, John K. Bettersworth's *Mississippi Yesterday and Today* (1967). Derfner entitled her nearly thirty-page analysis "Perpetuation of a Myth: The Nature of State History as Taught in Mississippi Schools." The textbooks did not contest the prevailing ideology of segregation and black inferiority but actually "buttress these distortions." In required Mississippi history courses students could not "avoid a rather intensive proselytization" of a "contorted view of the history of their state." Derfner concluded, "The most outstanding feature that both texts share is not their blatant racism or their misstatement of fact to conform to the southern ideology but rather their omissions." Blacks' contributions did not appear, and neither did the white leaders' excesses. Both texts also "gloss over the subject of desegregation or race relations since the turn of the century." In Derfner's view, a new textbook "could play a major role in the social changes now sweeping the state." An improved textbook would address the activities of blacks, not assume their passivity, and would help white students understand the changing Mississippi society. Black students and white students would each gain "a heritage to believe in and heroes with whom to identify."[41] When circulated among some Millsaps faculty, her analysis further piqued Sallis's interest.

Coincidentally, a few miles north at Tougaloo, James Loewen had also become annoyed by the sorry state of Mississippi history textbooks. A professor of sociology, Loewen in 1969 asked students in a freshman social science seminar what they knew about Reconstruction, and their responses shocked him. His black students repeated the unrevised, old-fashioned view of Reconstruction found in their Mississippi history textbooks—one that would have made the women of the United Daughters of the Confederacy proud. The only exception came from a Gary, Indiana, student. When Loewen later visited public school classrooms, he observed that black teachers taught the textbook and nothing more and challenged their students only with such rote tasks as memorizing the state's counties and county seats. The black students' ideas about Reconstruction came straight from their old-fashioned textbook. Realizing the central role played by the textbook, Loewen knew immediately that the students deserved a better book. Later in the fall of 1969, Loewen made a short presentation to the Tougaloo College social science faculty to interest the historians in creating a new textbook. He informed them that the Southern Education Foundation had announced its interest in "projects which accelerate the pace of racial integration," including "more balanced textbooks." Even though Loewen thought the foundation might fund such a project, none of his colleagues expressed any interest.[42]

In the winter of 1969–70, therefore, four separate individuals simultaneously realized the need for a new textbook. Loewen knew the Derfners, and Bruce Adams had taken classes with both Sallis and Loewen. Sallis knew Borinski because he had frequently attended meetings of the Social Science Forum, and Loewen taught in Borinski's department. Sallis and Loewen may have encountered one another at Social Science Forums, but they did not remember each other. As a result of their personal connections, probably through their mutual student, Bruce Adams, Loewen and Sallis met in 1970 and began discussions about writing a textbook. Four years later *Mississippi: Conflict and Change*, a ninth-grade history book, resulted from their association.[43]

Jim Loewen and Charles Sallis made an odd combination. In contrast to the Mississippi-born and southern-educated historian, Loewen had a northern background and had studied sociology at prestigious northern schools. Eight years younger than Sallis, Loewen was born and raised in Decatur, a typical American small town, near the geographic center of Illinois. His father, a Minnesota native, grew up in a Mennonite community before going to Carleton College and medical school at the University of Minnesota. His mother was from the Washington, D. C., area and had grown up in New Jersey. She had graduated from the University of Michigan. Each of Loewen's parents had contracted tuberculosis, and they met at a New York hospital where she went for treatment and he worked as a physician. Later in Decatur,

Dr. Loewen practiced at the county tuberculosis sanitarium, while his wife worked as a school librarian. The small industrial city of Decatur had an ethnically varied population. Jim Loewen, who had a sister three years younger, attended the integrated public schools, belonged to Boy Scouts, participated in Junior Achievement, and worked summers at a Wisconsin Boy Scout camp.[44]

Growing up, Loewen developed a sense of social justice. Part of it came from his mother's religion, originally Presbyterian but later Unitarian. Though no longer Mennonite, his father's commitment to public service medicine instead of a more lucrative private practice conveyed to his son a similar dedication to the community. Living in Decatur also encouraged Loewen's social conscience because he saw how the city's strong labor movement protected the social and political status of workers. Decatur's unions nurtured a sense of social justice that crossed class and ethnic lines. In school and in extracurricular activities, Loewen, a doctor's son, interacted equally with children of factory workers.[45]

As a National Merit Scholar, Loewen decided to follow his father's path to Carleton College. In the liberal arts curriculum, his numerous history courses included a seminar taken during the Civil War centennial on the effects of the Civil War in 1863 and 1963. Majoring in sociology he read John Dollard's classic *Caste and Class in a Southern Town* (1937) on Indianola, Mississippi, and the book increased his interest in the southern state. More than most midwestern college students he already had a concern for Mississippi because his uncle Peter F. Loewen taught English at Mississippi State University. In Loewen's junior year, he decided to spend the winter term away from Carleton, but instead of choosing to go to Europe or some other popular destination, Loewen decided to visit a different region of the United States. In the aftermath of James Meredith's integration of the University of Mississippi, Loewen chose the Magnolia State. His plan included auditing classes at his uncle's university and traveling to confer with nearby sociologists as part of an independent study program for Carleton credit.[46]

At Mississippi State, Loewen sat in on a number of classes. Glover Moore's course on American history appealed to him most because of the way Moore integrated into his lectures compelling stories from primary sources. Rather than stay in town with his uncle's family, the visiting sociology student lived in a college dorm, where he befriended a number of students of Chinese background from the Mississippi Delta. On trips to the state capital he met Tougaloo sociologist Ernst Borinski and conferred with sociologist Charles Gomillion at Tuskegee Institute in Alabama. His field work involved visits to the Delta to meet black civil rights leaders Charles Evers in Mound Bayou and Aaron Henry in Clarksdale. In addition to allowing him to complete three Carleton courses for credit, Loewen's Mississippi experiences proved valuable in his development as a sociologist.[47]

After graduating from Carleton in 1964, he entered graduate school in sociology at Harvard where his professors included luminaries Barrington Moore, Talcott Parsons, Thomas F. Pettigrew, Eric Vogel, and Harrison White. After his first year of graduate work, Loewen went back to Mississippi in the summer of 1965 to work as an assistant to Ernst Borinski in the Touga-loo Social Science Lab. During the summer he learned from working with Borinski and interacted with the Tougaloo community. He also encountered members of the Mississippi Freedom Democratic Party and deepened his in-terest in Mississippi. When he returned to Harvard, Loewen considered dis-sertation topics on the lack of southern industry up to 1920 and on the Chinese community in Mississippi. His experiences with Mississippi Chi-nese students in the Mississippi State University dormitory had, of course, introduced him to the general subject, and his uncle Peter had told him about the Chinese living in the Delta. Continuing to read about Mississippi and be-ginning to identify with the state, he decided to pursue a study of the Delta Chinese. Eric Vogel, a social scientist specializing in East Asian studies, liked the topic and agreed to direct his dissertation, even though it had only a pe-ripheral relationship to his own scholarship on Japan and China. On two field trips to Mississippi in January and February and from May to September in 1967, Loewen conducted his dissertation research. A year later he successfully defended his dissertation and received his doctorate.[48]

While at Harvard, Loewen gained teaching experience in the Department of Social Relations. In the summer of 1966 he taught urban sociology and field research methods, and for the following two years as a resident tutor he taught a sophomore seminar on social relations. He also helped create a graduate course on teaching the social sciences. At Borinski's invitation, Loewen in 1968 accepted a position in Tougaloo's sociology department where he taught a class in research methods and statistics and a freshman so-cial science seminar. After three years he won the college's Distinguished Teacher Award.[49]

Outside the classroom, Loewen joined Jackson's small activist commu-nity. He helped start the Mississippi chapter of the American Civil Liberties Union, attended the Unitarian church, and participated in the Madison County chapter of the Mississippi Loyalist Democratic Party. In addition to serving as an expert witness in legal proceedings, his professional activities included memberships in the Southern Sociological Society and the Mississippi

Historical Society. He also took his Tougaloo students outside the classroom on projects usually supported by external grants. For an experimental course, he involved students in field research related to local community organizations. In another project aided by funds from the Ford Foundation, Loewen's students conducted an in-depth assessment of "Caste, Class, and Commerce in Mound Bayou, Mississippi," the all-black community in the Delta 130 miles north of Jackson. In preparation for a lawsuit, Loewen supervised Tougaloo and Millsaps students in gathering information on Jackson municipal services. And after *Alexander v. Holmes* (1969) ordered school desegregation, Loewen devised a "School Desegregation Project," later renamed "School Involvement Project," that for three years used grant money from the Southern Regional Council to get Tougaloo students involved in their hometown's integrated schools during the college's short January term.[50] The special projects and his teaching methods revealed the importance of social activism to Loewen's view of sociology.

In a 1969–70 exchange with Philip M. Hauser in *Sociological Inquiry*, Loewen's activist view of sociology appeared more clearly. By the late 1960s organized radical movements had appeared in many professions and academic disciplines. Growing out of the antiwar movement and the civil rights movement, the radicalism questioned symbols of authority and their conservative support for the prevailing corporate capitalism. The critics protested the hierarchical leadership in professional organizations and contended that conservative elites did not use their expertise to address important human and social problems. In the American Sociological Association, a group of younger sociologists had mounted a challenge to the entrenched leaders. Contemporary sociology struck the radicals as sterile, boring, and irrelevant to the larger society, especially questions of inequality; while it claimed to be value-free, traditional sociology actually defended and protected the social status quo. Radical sociologists wanted to engage with society, not stand removed from it. Similar dissident movements occurred among lawyers, doctors, ministers, and other academics, including historians. While Loewen did not participate in the radical movement in his profession, he shared many of its professional values and perspectives.[51]

Philip Hauser, a University of Chicago demographer and former president of the American Sociological Association, criticized "marginal sociologists" committed to an "actionist ideology" that he saw as "incompatible with the role of sociologists as scientists." Where activist sociologists took "positions on social, economic, or political issues," Hauser argued for sociology as "a science, not a vehicle for social action." Social scientists "should not yield to the temptation to turn activist" and should "avoid direct participation of any kind in the general political arena." Probably feeling besieged by a younger generation of radical sociologists, the sixty-year-old Hauser contended that sociologists could best participate "indirectly" in the "elimination of evils which beset man and society" through their "contribution to the funding of knowledge." The journal's editor invited Loewen to respond, and in the journal's next issue he did.[52]

Charging Hauser at the outset with "profound" "errors" and "vicious" "distortions," an unyielding Loewen asserted, "Morality requires public action, directed toward social inequities, and it involves political opposition to misguided public and private policies." Hauser opted, according to Loewen, for an "*amoral*" sociology removed from direct involvement with social problems, and he reserved activism for the sociologist's private, nonprofessional life. Using race relations as an example, Loewen pointed out how sociologists conducted little research on race before 1960 and studied race largely in response to "forces acting upon sociology. . . . Societal pressures wag sociology." In a more personal response, Loewen said that Hauser supported the "small elite, a social elite," that dominated the sociological profession and that tried to suppress "ideas that do not fit the prevailing political consciousness." Loewen suggested the "oppression of free discourse might be termed liberal fascism." Rebelling against the older elite's attitudes, Loewen declared that "we cannot relegate our moral activities to 'after hours,' Sunday mornings, or charitable donations." Sociology was "far too important to remain cooped up inside amoral uninvolved scientists." Loewen boldly called for "new kinds of sociologists" who would engage in activism.

Responding to what he termed Loewen's "polemic," Hauser damned the younger sociologist as "someone on a continuum between a social reformer and a revolutionary in the disguise of a sociologist."[53] But Loewen wore no disguise. As did many younger sociologists, he did not try to hide his activism. If activism characterized Loewen's sociology, so did a historical perspective. As an undergraduate he had enjoyed both sociology and history, and later as a sociologist he combined the two disciplines because he found them complementary, not competing. For Loewen, the best sociology employed a historical approach, and the best history used sociological methods. The revised version of his dissertation, published in 1971 by Harvard University Press, demonstrated his commitment to historical analysis. *The Mississippi Chinese: Between Black and White*, a volume in the Harvard East Asian Studies Series, examined the twelve hundred Chinese in the Mississippi Delta by reaching back into the late nineteenth century to the arrival of the first Chinese immigrants in 1870. In addition to over three hundred interviews and other standard methods of sociological fieldwork, Loewen used nineteenth-century newspapers, court cases, census data, and other historical sources to explore the development of the Chinese in Mississippi. With a historical perspective, Loewen devoted three of eight chapters to the Mississippi Chinese before 1940.[54]

"Originally classed with blacks," observed Loewen, "they are now viewed as essentially 'white.'" Loewen explained the historical developments that caused the change in status. Sought at first after the Civil War as replacements for black labor, the Chinese lived between black and white. Described by Loewen as "sojourners" instead of "immigrants," the Chinese aimed for economic success. Unsatisfied with and unsuited for docile agricultural labor, they found a gap between the two races and by 1872 began their move into the grocery business. Soon they nearly monopolized the business for black customers; more than 90 percent of the Chinese operated grocery stores. As the prospering Chinese gradually changed from sojourners to immigrants, according to Loewen, they also began to escape their inferior status and to join white society. He marked the historic change around 1940 and "rank[ed] economic success as the most important basic cause of the upward racial mobility of the Chinese." More specifically, he concluded, "Image change was in fact the key to the process." The Chinese worked hard to change their image so that whites would not class them with blacks.[55]

Loewen devoted one chapter to an analysis of the opponents of the Chinese transition. Though both lower-class and upper-class whites discriminated against the Chinese, Loewen attributed most of the opposition to the upper class. The "effective opposition . . . is mobilized only by the upper class." When the white lower class did act against the Chinese, it did so under the influence of and with the approval of their social and economic superiors. "In short, in a cultural sense, racism originates in the upper class," he concluded. Loewen believed that his analysis of the opposition to the Chinese advancement constituted his study's "most important single contribution to the theory of race relations."[56]

Throughout *The Mississippi Chinese*, Loewen referred to white-black relations and racial segregation. He used his study of the small Chinese minority "between black and white" to illuminate the larger relations between Delta blacks and whites. Understanding the larger "polarized segregation system" formed Loewen's larger purpose. He contrasted, for example, the successful mobility of the Chinese with the failure of blacks, and he compared the attitudes of whites toward Chinese with their prejudice against blacks. Attentive to the special status and role of Chinese in the Delta, Loewen concluded that the successful transition of the Chinese "offers little hope for Negro replication." Despite its title and subject, Loewen's book revealed his ultimate concern with black-white relations, as his subtitle suggested.[57]

Jim Loewen the sociologist brought many of the same concerns to the Mississippi history textbook project. Sociological questions dealing with race, social structure, and class made a unique contribution to a state history text. As a northerner, he offered a distinctive outsider's view of the Deep South state, a rare perspective for any state history. After publishing his dissertation, he also had experience working with editors. Obtaining financial support for his work gave him skill at securing outside funding. In addition, Loewen's dedication to scholarly social activism would influence the textbook.

Though he had tried to persuade others at Tougaloo to take on the project, once he decided to do it himself, Loewen had the great luck to find Charles Sallis already sharing his thinking about the need for a modern Mississippi history textbook. In important but different ways, Sallis also made essential contributions to their project. As a native Mississippian and a college professor, Sallis had credentials that other Mississippi whites could respect. He also supplied deep knowledge about his state and expertise in its history. From his experiences teaching Mississippi history, he especially appreciated the deficiencies in earlier treatments and recognized the need for a new textbook, and his academic background in history prepared him to understand the changing historiography and to bring the textbook into line with current scholarship.

The partners also complemented each other in more personal ways. The high-energy, assertive, and intense Loewen had great passion for the work and expected others to share his commitment. Direct and demanding, Loewen could strike people as abrupt and headstrong, even rude, but he supplied the organizational force behind the project. Willing and able to work long hours, he closely supervised much of the work conducted by others. With a calmer demeanor, Sallis did not lack enthusiasm, and he shared much of Loewen's progressivism, though he pursued their common goals differently. Always a polite and modest gentleman, Sallis provided a steadier, patient presence on the project and helped it proceed smoothly.

When the sociologist and the historian first started discussing the possibility of cooperating in writing a textbook, they realized the enormity of the task. As a partial solution, Loewen suggested bringing students into the project. He had confidence that the undergraduates, with guidance from him and Sallis, could do the work. As he had done in fieldwork exercises for his students,

Loewen believed involvement would benefit the students by providing an original, valuable learning experience. Including students, black and white, male and female, would also make the project unique and add important perspectives to the effort. Bruce Adams of Millsaps came first to the minds of his two professors. Originally from Pass Christian, Mississippi, Adams was a quiet, reserved student little involved in campus social life. The senior history major worked on the student yearbook and participated in Phi Alpha Theta, the history honorary association, but largely kept to himself in his off-campus apartment. Adams had once discussed with Sallis his idea of writing a textbook himself, so he readily agreed to join the endeavor. Though he graduated in the spring of 1970, Adams stayed in Jackson and joined the project later in the summer.[58]

Bruce Adams interested his fellow student Jeanne Middleton in the enterprise. A native of Jackson and the daughter of an Episcopal priest and Army chaplain and the granddaughter and great granddaughter of earlier Episcopal priests, Middleton grew up in a prosperous and educated family. A graduate of Jim Hill High School and a National Merit Scholar, Middleton was the eighth African American to attend Millsaps and the only black female entering in 1967. As the only black woman in her dormitory, she felt alone, and she experienced subtle racism. In the difficult learning environment, she did encounter supportive faculty, including Charles Sallis, but she also found a refuge at Tougaloo where she had friends and her brother was a teacher. With an excellent academic record, Middleton participated in 1969 and 1970 in Harvard University's Intensive Summer Studies Program. With other black Millsaps students, she helped organize the Black Student Association on campus. Though a political science major, she took many history classes and belonged to Phi Alpha Theta, and in her senior year she served as its president. Through her classes and in Phi Alpha Theta, Middleton knew Professor Sallis and Bruce Adams.[59]

Jim Loewen recruited three people from Tougaloo to work on the project. Two other white Tougaloo faculty also agreed to contribute to the textbook. In 1966, James A. Brown had joined the faculty as an assistant professor of history. Born in Philadelphia in 1943, Brown graduated from Temple University where he ran the mile for the track team, and at Tougaloo he also coached the cross country and track teams. In addition to his interest in sports, Brown's multidisciplinary interests included music, and he traveled widely. As a graduate student at Memphis State University, Brown participated slightly in the civil rights movement and even joined the last day of the 1966 Meredith march from Memphis to Jackson. With a master's degree from

Memphis State he taught courses on the Holocaust and Eastern Europe, but not American history. The second Tougaloo colleague was Stephen C. Immer, an instructor in history. In Portland, Oregon, Immer grew up as a liberal Republican and earned his history undergraduate degree at Whitman College in 1964. After serving two years in the Coast Guard, he earned a master's degree from the University of Oregon in British history. After one year teaching at North Carolina A&T College, he started at Tougaloo in the fall of 1969 and worked on the textbook team during the academic year 1970–71. Immer and Loewen recruited Olivia Jones, probably Immer's best student, to work on the textbook project. A history major, she started to work with Loewen and Sallis in September 1970 and worked all during her senior year.[60]

Loewen and Sallis recruited two other whites who were not students or faculty at Millsaps or Tougaloo. William R. Ferris, born in 1942 in Vicksburg, had studied at Davidson College, Northwestern University, and Dublin's Trinity College before receiving a doctorate in folklore from the University of Pennsylvania with a concentration in black folklore and culture. Starting in the fall of 1970, he returned to his home state to teach in the English department at Jackson State College, a historically black institution. Ferris added expertise in black music, especially the blues. The last member of the team was Maryellen Haines Clampit. A native of New York City and a graduate of Brooklyn College, Clampit had a graduate degree from Bowling Green College where she specialized in children's literature. She taught at Western Michigan University for four years until she married Mickey Clampit and moved to Jackson. Mickey Clampit, a friend of Jim Loewen from their days as graduate students at Harvard received his doctorate in sociology a year after Loewen did. In 1970 he joined the sociology department at Millsaps. Maryellen Clampit brought nonhistorical writing and reading skills to the project. Acting as a consultant more than a writer, she used her knowledge about written communications for children to work with the actual authors on adapting their work for young readers.[61]

In the summer of 1970, led by Loewen and Sallis, the unusual group of nine students and faculty, plus one contributing consultant, came together to work on a ninth-grade textbook in Mississippi history. In the state history project, collaboration between Tougaloo and Millsaps colleges reached a new professional, personal, and academic level. By the fall of 1974 the unique joint venture had produced *Mississippi: Conflict and Change*, a boldly revisionist history of the state and a landmark innovative school textbook.

CHAPTER FIVE

Project
Development and Writing of Conflict and Change

From the outset, James Loewen and Charles Sallis wanted to "turn every received answer in Mississippi history upside down, examine its underside, and make our own decision as to the proper interpretation." They would write "a new textbook in Mississippi history . . . the first 'revisionist' state history ever written in the South, perhaps in the nation." It would supplant John K. Bettersworth's *Mississippi: Yesterday and Today*, which they considered "antiquated historically, biased racially, inadequate in its treatment of the recent past, and unimpressive pedagogically." In seeking to overturn the conventional interpretation, Loewen and Sallis reflected their times. They objected to the historical status quo in ways that resembled contemporary radicals in sociology. Like their sociological colleagues, radical historians beginning in the late 1960s wanted their scholarship to challenge established authorities, defend the marginalized, recognize class conflict, and promote significant social change. For a variety of reasons Loewen and Sallis shared many of the radicals' concerns. They too felt the effects of the civil rights and antiwar protests of the 1960s. In addition, Loewen's background in sociology allowed him to combine a theoretical perspective and a base of concrete historical knowledge with his progressive political views to write radical history. On the other hand, Sallis's historical revisionism grew out of his knowledge of southern and Mississippi history and his lifelong experience with race; his more intuitive liberal social ideas also propelled his commitment to a revisionist Mississippi history.[1]

The Loewen and Sallis textbook would appear at an opportune time. The Bettersworth text served the interests of whites in segregated schools, while it ignored the invisible blacks. In 1969, however, for the first time, the U.S. Supreme Court had mandated an immediate end to school segregation. The Court refused to tolerate continued delays in the implementation of the 1954 *Brown* decision. As result of *Alexander v. Holmes County Board of Education*, which originated in Mississippi, widespread school integration began for the first time in the state, as in most of the South. Integrated schools would need an integrated Mississippi history that included blacks just as the classrooms would.[2]

In addition to its substantive distinctiveness, the Loewen and Sallis Project, formally named the Mississippi History Project (MHP), boasted other original features. Its creative process brought together students and faculty as writers in a joint scholarly effort, and it marked an important advancement in cooperation between two Jackson colleges, Millsaps and Tougaloo. In a way unusually significant for Mississippi, the textbook combined the efforts of blacks and whites. The MHP originally encompassed more than a ninth-grade textbook. The plan called for writing the customary teacher's manual to the textbook and for distilling a fifth-grade text from the high school version; it also proposed creating an innovative kit of supplemental materials to accompany the text and for holding unusual teachers institutes or workshops to assist teachers using the new book. As the Project developed, constraints of time and money caused Loewen and Sallis to scale back their ambitious objectives to only the high school book and the teacher's guide. The State Textbook Purchasing Board's 1974 adoption deadline only increased the pressures on the Project. Developing *Mississippi: Conflict and Change* required Loewen, Sallis, and their colleagues to overcome many obstacles and solve many problems.

The most immediate worry concerned money. Neither Tougaloo nor Millsaps could support such a costly undertaking, so the Project required external funding. In addition to stipends for the scholars and the students, the Project's costs would include considerable travel, research materials, and office expenses. In the late 1960s Ernst Borinski had received funding from the Southern Education Foundation (SEF) to promote cooperation between Tougaloo and Millsaps, and he helped Loewen and Sallis approach the Atlanta organization. Consisting of four funds—Peabody, Slater, Jeannes, and Virginia Randolph—the SEF traced its history to the post–Civil War era. According to SEF's stated purpose, it sought to "assist Negroes in 13 Southern States to gain equal access to quality educational opportunity." It supported "administrator and teacher training, colleges which serve Negroes, curriculum and materials Projects, and student and community sponsored programs of educational improvement." To Loewen and Sallis, the textbook Project seemed to fit "exactly the stated aim" of the SEF.[3]

On May 22, 1970, Loewen and Sallis sent John A. Griffin, the SEF's executive director, a request for $9,450, half of the projected costs. Loewen had previously met Griffin at the Tougaloo Social Science Lab and hoped that Griffin remembered. The grant application stressed the Project's revisionist impulse, its timeliness in the wake of the *Alexander* decision, its involvement of undergraduates, and its combination of efforts by black and white colleges. According to the proposal, the textbook's avoidance of racist history would test the authors' belief that "attitudes of racial prejudice and stereotype can be decreased indirectly by the presentation of unbiased historical materials." Beyond enlightened racial views, the book would offer ingenious, experimental approaches that would "force involvement in issues rather than reception of answers." The unique participation of undergraduates as writers would bring a "freshness of view" to the textbook, but it would also benefit the students themselves. By working closely with faculty, they would experience a "new combination of intellectual growth, meaningful research, and intellectual and ideological change," even as they learned much about the "problems and challenges in the educational process." In a separate letter to Griffin a few days later, Ernst Borinski endorsed the proposal as important in increasing Millsaps-Tougaloo cooperation. He hailed it as "original, very promising," and he praised his colleague Loewen who "masterminded the whole project" for his "spirit, enthusiasm, and stamina."[4]

One month later, after reviewing the request, Griffin telephoned Loewen to show SEF's real interest in the proposal, and they talked again a week later. Immediately after the second call, Griffin notified Loewen that with "considerable enthusiasm" SEF would provide funding for work on the Project that summer. Starting July 1, SEF gave $1,400 for two months, and Griffin promised to seek additional support from other sources. Within a few weeks Griffin had persuaded the Louis W. and Maud Hill Family Foundation to contribute $13,240 through SEF. The St. Paul, Minnesota, foundation directed its money to Tougaloo's library to strengthen its holdings, especially in history and the social sciences, and to a "library based project in Mississippi history." With significant support secured, Loewen persisted in seeking outside funding. Later in 1970 he applied for a grant from the U.S. Office of Education under its basic research in education program. With help from Hodding Carter, the Greenville *Delta Democrat Times* editor who served on the Twentieth Century Fund's board, Loewen hastily applied to the fund. Carter, son of the editor reviled by the state's segregationists as a racial liberal, thought the textbook project "the best idea to come along in a decade." When neither appeal proved productive, Loewen appealed to SEF for an additional $8,000 to complete the Project, and SEF agreed to the additional funding.[5] With the Project's financial viability assured by the summer of 1970, the Loewen and Sallis team could concentrate on planning and producing their textbook.

The Mississippi History Project developed in reaction to the perceived faults in John Bettersworth's *Our Mississippi*, but Loewen and Sallis, inexperienced with textbooks, especially for secondary school students, did not know that Bettersworth's book in many ways typified state histories. Focused on Mississippi history books, Loewen and Sallis failed to realize that they had not made the first negative assessment of state history books. They apparently missed the extensive previous analyses and critiques of state history and textbooks. In a similar way, they recognized and condemned the racial biases in Bettersworth but did not realize others had for years made much the same complaint about history books in general. Not only Mississippi's but other states' textbooks needed creative changes to overcome inherent weaknesses in state history, and U.S. history books suffered from similar liabilities.

Offered in nearly every state in seventh, eighth, or ninth grade, state history had great potential. It could refine and clarify historical generalizations made at the national level; it could personalize history by paying attention to individuals who had direct effects on the states and communities where students lived. Through more localized study, state history could explain and demonstrate in tangible ways how a democratic society functioned. But one analyst of state history courses instead described them as "intellectually sterile" and rife with problems. A debilitating provincialism too often advanced romanticized and distorted visions of a state's historical importance, and an ethnocentrism promoted each state's supposed superiority. By boosting local loyalty, state history discounted obvious interstate dependence, alienated natives of other states, encouraged unwanted "state consciousness and state pride," and undermined national unity by creating "a sense of separation from national life." Usually state history also stressed the "unique, bizarre, and traditional" while it neglected contemporary social problems. Supportive of and promoted by genealogical and patriotic groups, state history tended "to glorify the past" instead of addressing problems in the past such as economic depressions, political immorality, and poverty. It avoided controversial issues and discouraged critical thinking, while frequently treating "myths as though they were facts." Considered "sacrosanct" by many, state history resisted change.[6]

State history also had more practical problems. "History is the most poorly taught of all academic subjects in today's high school," one study concluded, and state history would have offered no exception. In fact, state history may have been the worst. Of all the social studies, state history had long suffered neglect and had become for many "a pseudo-academic subject" that resulted more from political demands than from academic objectives. As a result, teaching and studying state history had lower professional status than other fields. State history also may have attracted inferior teachers because its narrow focus worked against a cosmopolitan historical preference for generalizing, comparing, and finding the typical. Often seeming to have no purpose except to make students learn a series of facts (dates, counties, governors), teaching state histories lacked a consensus on topics, methods, and analysis. The field actually consisted of fifty disparate fields, not one. State history also contained far more "apologies" than theories. The absence of a professional literature that addressed the special issues in teaching state history proved that practitioners and scholars had neglected the field. Within each state, a lack of competition also hurt state history. The economics of the textbook market caused many publishers to decline to produce textbooks, especially in the smaller states. The dearth of competition led to generally poor quality among state history textbooks.[7]

Reacting to Bettersworth, Loewen and Sallis intuitively understood many of the problems with state history and wanted to improve the field, but they were not the first. Earlier Mississippi writers had advocated teaching state history and proposed ways to improve teaching Mississippi history. Their suggestions proved the paucity of ideas about state history. As early as 1911, Franklin Riley defended state history by quoting Herbert Baxter Adams, "History, like charity, begins at home," and Riley believed state history would foster a valuable love of the state. In the mid-1940s slightly more substantive thoughts about teaching state history appeared in the state teachers' magazine, *Mississippi Educational Advance*. Richard A. and Nannie Pitts McLemore, who would later write a fifth-grade state history book, offered their "suggestions for the teaching of Mississippi history." In a frank concession, the McLemores declared, "The best textbooks are uninspiring unless properly used," and they emphasized supplementing the textbook with school library materials, current newspaper articles with a historical angle, maps, easily available picture postcards, the stories of public buildings, local industries, and even family Bibles. The McLemores especially stressed the value of the "historical tour." Without addressing the question of cost, they suggested taking students to the state capitol and the governor's mansion, to Natchez, and to the Vicksburg and Shiloh battlefields.[8]

A decade later in the 1950s, Charlotte Capers, a Department of Archives and History employee, wrote a series of articles pointing to the "highlights" of the state's history that students needed to learn. In the *Mississippi Educational Advance*, she stressed her state's beauty and pride, its progress and development. Her seven articles emphasized "thrilling events, intrigues, battles, and achievements," but she barely mentioned slavery and virtually ignored blacks. Her suggestions stopped before the end of the nineteenth century. At the same time, when John Bettersworth commented on "Mississippi historiography," he paid no attention to interpretation and could only suggest that the state's history needed a new textbook. Finally, "Tips on Teaching Mississippi History" summarized a session at the 1959 meeting of the Mississippi Education Association. A panel of teachers that included Bettersworth offered an unremarkable set of ideas: make history "interesting," follow chronological order, give due credit to individuals, "teach as a story," emphasize "adventure and romance," and "teach with pride in the state."[9] The paucity of new insights from expert scholars and teachers only confirmed the unimaginative and traditional characteristics of Mississippi history. Their comments proved the need for the MHP. It would take the state's history in an entirely different direction from previous textbooks and would counter the state history's dominant characteristics.

To reorient the field with a distinctively new type of history textbook, Loewen and Sallis set four large goals. First, they wanted their book to reflect recent trends of American historical interpretation, where Bettersworth's conformed to the outdated historiographical patterns of an earlier generation. Second, they aimed to balance the chronological coverage by paying comparatively less attention to the "distant past." Bettersworth used four chapters to cover the explorers and settlers in the years before 1812 and a similar number to discuss the entire century since Reconstruction. As a consequence, Loewen and Sallis wanted to give more attention to the twentieth century, particularly the years since World War II that appeared in only one chaotic chapter in Bettersworth's volume. Third, the MHP sought a textbook that would involve students in actively thinking about historical issues, not merely memorizing information. The text would present questions as well as information. Fourth, Loewen and Sallis insisted on correcting the racial bias in Mississippi history textbooks by presenting blacks fairly and accurately and by making the same correction for the whites who did not support white supremacy and racial segregation. In their opinion, Bettersworth seemed "bent on denying not only that blacks were occasionally heroic in Mississippi history, but almost that they were participants."[10]

Preoccupied with identifying and correcting the racial bias in Bettersworth's textbook, Loewen and Sallis may have missed a larger, extensive discussion of racism in American textbooks that had concerned scholars for two decades. A June 1970 *New York Times* article by Fred Hechinger attracted Loewen's interest because it described how textbooks evaded or downplayed the mistreatment of blacks under slavery. In support of the MHP, Loewen recommended the article to SEF's Griffin and suggested that at the "state level, the situation would be far worse." Two years later Jeanne Middleton explained that a 1970 essay by Mark Krug in *School Review* on racial equality in textbooks "got me to thinking." That Hechinger's and Krug's assessments of racism in schoolbooks impressed Loewen and Middleton suggested their unawareness of the ongoing discussion among professional historians. Once again, the MHP had not discovered an issue but had actually come to it after others had studied it; the MHP joined a growing national trend instead of starting one.[11]

Even before the civil rights movement heightened racial awareness in the 1950s and 1960s, sensitive observers had pointed to textbooks' limited, prejudiced coverage of blacks. In 1932 the NAACP's Committee on Public School Textbooks protested textbooks' prejudiced treatment of blacks and called for the unbiased inclusion of blacks. Seven years later the committee issued *Anti-Negro Propaganda in School Textbooks* to help its members identify and object to offensive schoolbooks. Confirming the NAACP's position, a 1934 survey of American history textbooks used in the South consistently found a pro-Southern bias and an "altogether unfavorable" depiction of blacks. Lawrence D. Reddick, a black historian, concluded that history books "generally defend the attitudes and action of the [white] South toward the Negro." To promote an unprejudiced black history, Carter G. Woodson, the nation's leading black historian, had in 1926 started Negro History Week. In the interwar years, Woodson and others despaired of equal treatment in textbooks and instead increasingly advocated separate books and courses on black history. Many southern black schools, even in Mississippi, began offering courses in black history. Conservative southern whites, of course, complained about the anti-white southerner bias in textbooks published in the North, and they pushed publishers to follow the Confederate orthodoxy. By the end of the 1930s, reformers had made little progress. As one scholar later concluded, at the start of World War II "anti-black errors and stereotypes continued to mar nearly every American history text."[12]

Scholars and educators continued to identify racial bias in history textbooks. As early as 1940 a Columbia dissertation that examined "the treatment of Negroes in American History textbooks" compared the content of the books to the latest historical scholarship and found the texts deficient. A 1949 American Council on Education report criticized history books for portraying slaves as "well treated, contented, and happy"; for describing Reconstruction governments as characterized by "[e]xtravagance, corruption, social crudity, and incompetence"; for perpetuating the stereotypes of "happy-go-lucky irresponsibility" and "comic ridiculousness and mental inferiority"; and for having a "narrow and limited" view of black accomplishments. The typically limited treatments of blacks after Reconstruction failed to explore the great migration north or to mention segregation. The textbooks usually left "the student with the belief that all is well" in race relations and offered no suggestions for further reading on black life.[13]

In the 1960s, as the civil rights movement gained strength and attention, the textbook coverage of blacks received repeated scrutiny as more than a dozen analysts damned the books. One concluded that the findings of the 1949 American Council on Education's report remained in 1960 "equally valid," and another convicted historians of indoctrinating students with "the three D's: distortion, deletion, and denial" in their historical treatments of blacks. Popular magazines also raised questions about the portrayal of blacks in books. A 1965 *Saturday Review* article discussed "The All-WHITE World of Children's Books," which did not specifically address textbooks but did discuss the issue more broadly. In *Ebony*, Lerone Bennett, a well-known black historian, argued that racism, the fourth R along with the traditional "reading, 'riting, 'rithmetic," "permeate[d] the whole curriculum." He disparaged textbooks as "still white, middle-class and antiseptically unreal" because they "defame or ignore black people and other minorities." In textbooks, according to Bennett, "Black people have been made Orwellian non-persons" through "omissions, distortions, and paternalistic put-downs." The "white oriented texts," he charged, "tend to innoculate white Americans with the virus of racism," while having a "devastatingly traumatic" effect on blacks. In 1966 an ad hoc committee of the House of Representatives even held hearings on the treatment of blacks in schoolbooks. Chaired by Rep. Adam Clayton Powell of New York, the committee sought to "destroy the invisibility of one-tenth of America's population" in textbooks. One witness lamented that the "historically dishonest" and "downright derogatory" depiction of blacks in textbooks was partly "responsible for the warped attitudes rampant in our society."[14]

Publishers, pressured by civil rights activists and by some northern urban school districts, began in the 1960s to create integrated or multi-ethnic textbooks. Doubleday's president acknowledged that the omission of blacks "reinforces feelings of personal insignificance and inadequacy. It also gives whites a false sense of superiority." As a corrective, publishers started to include illustrations of blacks and whites playing together, selections by black writers, and stories about black historical figures. Southern segregationists, however, retaliated against integrated books. One publisher assumed it had lost Mississippi's high school literature contract because it included an essay by black writer James Baldwin. In response to the white southerners' demands, publishers frequently prepared two textbooks, one all-white for the South and a second integrated for the rest of the nation. For example, Scott Foresman appealed to white southerners by replacing a story of black astronomer Benjamin Banneker with a biography of Paul Revere. With changes in textbooks occurring slowly and unevenly, southern blacks continued to use all-white schoolbooks selected by white education officials.[15]

Between 1964 and 1971 professional historians published three major assessments of blacks in history textbooks. A group of University of California historians—Kenneth M. Stampp, Winthrop D. Jordan, Lawrence W. Levine, Robert L. Middlekauf, Charles G. Sellers, and George W. Stocking Jr.—reviewed history books used in California's schools in grades five through eight. In most books the scholars discovered "views on racial and sectional themes that have been rejected or drastically modified by the best of current scholarship." According to the eminent historians, the books "help perpetuate and intensify the pattern of racial discrimination" in the nation through "a bad history that reinforces notions among white people of their superiority and among Negroes of their inferiority." They concluded, however, that "the greatest defect in the textbooks we have examined is the virtual omission of the Negro." Six years after the California study, Mark Krug's examination of five high school history books revealed persisting clichés, myths, and misinterpretations. Pointing to the "new and rich harvest of historical research" in black history, Krug found "little excuse" for the omissions and inaccuracies.[16]

Even more detailed analyses of racism in schoolbooks appeared as the Mississippi History Project got underway. *Phylon*, a journal devoted to racial topics edited at Atlanta University, published the most significant assessment by University of South Alabama historian Melton McLaurin. In a study of the "image of the Negro in Deep South public school state history texts," McLaurin found that "formal education perpetuates the traditional image of the Negro" as "docile, trusting, lazy, emotional, childlike." McLaurin concluded that in the state history books "the Negro is never treated as an actor; rather he is always acted upon, always described as a passive agent." As one of his examples, McLaurin evaluated Bettersworth's Mississippi textbook and found it typically dominated by these sorts of outmoded myths. McLaurin's work could only have confirmed and encouraged Loewen and Sallis when they read it in 1971.[17]

Within Mississippi the post–World War II black freedom struggle had produced two other unusual histories that fully incorporated African Americans in Mississippi history, but curiously each remained unknown and unacknowledged by the authors of *Conflict and Change*.[18] In 1950, Jessie B. Mosley wrote *The Negro in Mississippi History*. Born in Texas in 1904, she moved to Edwards, Mississippi, with her husband, Charles C. Mosley, when he became dean at Southern Christian Institute where she taught social studies. Nine years later, when he joined the Jackson State College faculty, they moved to Jackson. Published the year before the Mosleys moved to Jackson, her 150-page paperback built largely on published sources and sought not "to incite conflict over already existing problems" but to explain "the contributions and achievements of the Negro." The state's textbooks taught "little of value . . . concerning the Negro" and instead spread "a misconception of the Negro's ability and accomplishments." Her preface claimed that blacks "shared the dreams and aspirations" of whites, and she acknowledged that "somewhere something happened" to the dream and called for a renewal of "the aspirations and hopes of our forefathers." To educate whites and blacks, she quoted the "great [white] statesman" L. Q. C. Lamar: "My Countrymen! Know one another and you will love one another!"[19]

In the book's first sixty pages Mosley presented a largely positive view of black life in Mississippi history. After describing race relations in the territorial period as "harmonious," she stressed the importance of free blacks during slavery and contended that slaves' great loyalty to whites during the Civil War was "beyond comparison." Calling Reconstruction "a dark period," Mosley optimistically reported that all "would rather forget those things that are unpleasant and continue to strive to build a new world on an entirely new foundation." She lauded "Negro Statesmen" John R. Lynch, Blanche K. Bruce, and Hiram Revels and also other "able bodied and well trained Negroes" who served the state. According to Mosley, the "period from 1865–1890 could well be called the 'Golden Era' for Negroes in politics in Mississippi." After praising blacks' accomplishments in all areas from literature to the law, Mosley heralded "a new day dawning for the Negro in Mississippi" and pointed to "citizens quietly working always for the better of the South and race relations" through organizations such as the Southern Regional Council.[20]

Like the authors of the other Mississippi history textbooks, the researchers for *Conflict and Change* apparently did not use Mosley's work. Though they may have simply missed it, they more likely dismissed it because of its saccharine tone and because Hederman Brothers published it (the Hederman family also controlled the notoriously racist *Jackson Clarion-Ledger*). The Loewen and Sallis team could have assumed Mosley's book had little accuracy and integrity. In her text, however, Mosley subtly buried her revisionist views. In addition to claiming that slave owners exploited slave women and that mistreatment of slaves "caused unrest among the slaves," Mosley argued that disputes over freedom for slaves led to the Civil War. After the war and up to 1950, the "masses" of whites refused to adjust to the existence of free blacks. During Reconstruction whites tried to "terrorize" blacks, but despite the abuse "the Negro served creditably in most cases while in office." In a notable achievement the Reconstruction government finally established a public school system in the state, though the Ku Klux Klan attacked teachers and burned many schools. Throughout, Mosley wrote approvingly about black voting. Referring to the years after the Civil War, she reminded readers that "there was a day in our State when the law granted to all its citizens equal rights and privileges." She stressed that the Mississippi Democrats Association supported the right of blacks to register and vote and the Southern Regional Council endorsed blacks' right to vote. In an appendix Mosley compiled a list of state laws affecting blacks and reproduced relevant sections of the state constitution, which included the disfranchisement provision in the Constitution of 1890. Intending a clearly subversive comparison, she followed it with the contrasting Thirteenth, Fourteenth, and Fifteenth Amendments to the U.S. Constitution.[21]

If Jessie Mosley in 1950 offered a quiet corrective to Mississippi history textbooks by white writers, fourteen years later civil rights activists in the Summer Project presented a more direct challenge to the traditional white histories. Later referred to as Freedom Summer, the Mississippi Summer Project in 1964 brought college students to challenge white supremacy, particularly in the Democratic Party. In addition to establishing community centers and encouraging voter registration, volunteers established Freedom Schools as a summer antidote to the public schools' malignant impact on black students. With a curriculum designed by whites, the public schools reinforced the southern way of life and left black children "at best invisible and at worst humiliated." As Charles Cobb, the originator of the Freedom Schools, explained, the "ideas, thought, and creativity among black people [were] ruthlessly suppressed" in the white-controlled schools. Freedom Schools wanted to transform passive students who merely observed their communities into active learners who could actively work to improve society. To prepare black students for political participation and leadership, the Freedom Schools fought a "war against academic poverty"; they encouraged self-expression, countered white historical myths, and taught blacks their own culture.[22]

Black history formed a main component of the "Citizenship Curriculum." As designed by Yale historian Staughton Lynd, the *Guide to Negro History* promoted a desegregated history by providing the "previously untold stories of [black] resistance, accomplishment, and heroism." Classes in black history taught about the origins of prejudice, slave life, black resistance, white myths about the Old South and Reconstruction, and the beginning of segregation.

Accurate historical knowledge enabled black students to understand their contemporary situation and prepare to shape their future. If the public schools were, according to one Freedom School teacher, "geared and oiled to operate efficiently for the status quo," the Freedom Schools also had a political motive to equip students to transform Mississippi.[23] With the end of Freedom Summer and the closing of the schools, little remained of the movement's revisionist view of black history, except for fugitive documents produced by Lynd and other activists. The revisionist effort quickly disappeared. The Freedom Schools' black history curriculum had negligible impact on history as taught in the Mississippi public schools. The traditional "bleached" history preferred by whites continued uncontested.[24]

Loewen and Sallis's enthusiasm and zeal to correct the faults of Bettersworth's book far outweighed any knowledge of larger scholarly trends in social studies education and earlier attempts to include blacks in Mississippi's history. Their lack of unawareness may have actually benefitted the MHP by fueling their effort with an independent, even innocent, evangelical air. More important, unlike the many critics who remained largely unknown to them, Loewen and Sallis set out to do something unprecedented to correct the problem—write the revisionist textbook that others had only called for.

When the MHP began in the summer of 1970, Loewen and Sallis first had to devise a tentative table of contents and then distribute assignments among the expected writers. As the overall coordinators, Loewen and Sallis envisioned eighteen chapters. The first would introduce ninth graders to "the uses of history," the second would provide a description of the land, and the last would challenge them to take an unusual look into their state's future. In-between, the text would offer balanced coverage with five chapters before the Civil War, two on the Civil War and Reconstruction, and eight from Reconstruction to the present. Loewen assumed responsibility for the opening chapters on the idea of history and the land and for the concluding chapter on the future. Sallis wanted to write in the areas of his specialty, Reconstruction and the late nineteenth century.

A five-page preface opened with a conventional map of the counties and towns and with the state's basic demographics. It boasted of the many "firsts" accomplished in Mississippi and bragged about its famous writers and musicians. With remarkable candor, however, it also recognized that "Mississippi has been a land of slavery and segregation, of hopelessness and hope" and then quoted "perhaps the most moving description of Mississippi." Written by James Meredith, it spoke of the joy and hope and love he felt in his state but also described his "sadness. Sadness because I am immediately aware of the special subhuman role that I must play, because I am a Negro, or die . . . ."[25] The textbook's beginning marked it immediately as distinctive.

The first chapter continued the different approach. Treating ninth graders as capable of serious thinking, Loewen proposed four reasons students should study history. First, "We were formed by the past." Two maps showing the similarity between slaveholding in 1850 and the 1954 vote for segregationist James O. Eastland demonstrated "how a pattern from the past can linger on" and suggested that "to understand an event . . . we must start far back in history." Second, the past provided "models" of "Mississippians of all races [who] have acted with courage and dignity for the progress of the state and the good of its people." It discussed biographies and suggested students try creating a historical biography. Third, it proposed that "we can learn from past errors so that in the future we can make Mississippi a better society." As a failure, it mentioned the exodus of Mississippians since 1920 and explained that leaders "afraid of new ideas, afraid of change, afraid of 'outsiders' . . . . fail to understand that a state that does not attract other people may also not be attractive to its own residents." Fourth, it argued that knowing history can empower people to protect themselves from others who want to distort history for their own selfish purposes, to defend and explain their own status. Knowledgeable students would not readily accept "myths" about Reconstruction, the Old South, slave loyalty, white supremacy, and progress in the New South. Understanding history "affects our understanding of the present."[26]

An insert in the first chapter encouraged students to separate "truth from falsehood" and offered questions they should ask of historical sources, even of their textbook. It suggested readers should learn as much as they could about the author's background and intentions because "an author's ideology influences what he writes." Even more significant, the textbook called for ninth graders to ask about the author's "basic assumptions" and values. It challenged readers to think whether the writer offered facts to support conclusions, how the conclusions compare to what the student found in other books, and if they "seem to be true from your own experience." The imaginative Mississippi history textbook not only aimed to promote critical thinking rather than rote learning of discrete facts, but by urging students to question the authority of their textbook it also implicitly suggested the general need to question authority.[27]

Loewen extended his unorthodox approach in the second chapter where he directly challenged the customary consensus in state histories by exposing conflict within Mississippi. In discussing the state's geography and topography, he provocatively explained that the "deepest split in Mississippi politics is between the Delta and 'the hills,'" and he attributed it to "the development of two very different kinds of societies. In the Delta, a few white plantation owners controlled the labor of hundreds of black farm workers and became quite wealthy" by growing cotton. "In the hills, farm families worked their own land, usually making enough to support themselves." In state politics, the Delta's "domination only increased the hostility between the hills and the Delta." He used maps to show the similar patterns of black population and of cotton production.[28]

Just as Loewen's opening chapters presented a unique introduction to Mississippi history, Charles Sallis's treatment of Reconstruction proved the textbook's dramatically revisionist views. After decrying federal abuses of white Mississippi's leaders and criticizing state government under Reconstruction, traditional accounts celebrated the restoration of conservative whites' power. *Conflict and Change*, reflecting a modern revisionist view of Reconstruction, offered a sympathetic assessment of whites but also a positive analysis of the Freedmen's Bureau and the state government under congressional Reconstruction. The authors also boldly described the Ku Klux Klan and racial violence during Reconstruction and criticized the return of white supremacy.

Sallis rejected as myths the idea "of a helpless South suffering under unbearable military rule for a decade," the claim that "all Reconstruction governments in the South were corrupt," and the belief that blacks dominated state government. Acknowledging the war's destructive effects on white landowners, Sallis also made the former slaves central to the story when he described the postwar years as "a time of great suffering for black people. Food and clothing were hard to get. Medical care, always scarce, was now almost nonexistent." Some whites "blamed blacks for the troubled times," and the freedmen "became the symbol of the defeat of the Confederacy." Despite the Freedmen's Bureau's good efforts to help blacks, the federal government failed them by neglecting to provide land, and "[w]ithout land, black farmers had no economic power" and were "at the mercy of their former owners." The Black Codes passed by the white legislature "made sure that blacks were kept down, socially and economically." According to Sallis, under the state government established by congressional Reconstruction, "many of the Republicans were honorable men doing what they felt to be right," and "Mississippi was especially fortunate to have capable black leaders during these years." To regain control of state government, whites engaged in a "reign of terror" against blacks and used other illegal methods to achieve success in what they saw as a "moral crusade." Calling Reconstruction a "failure," Sallis concluded, "The black man in the South was abandoned to the mercy of his former owners. The dream of the freedmen was dead . . . the tragedy of Reconstruction is not that it brought suffering to the South, but that it failed to bring equality to the black citizens of this nation."[29]

In Sallis's sweeping revisionist view, he argued that the late nineteenth century "had more lasting effects upon Mississippi than Reconstruction." Small government and low taxes "favored the rich more than the poor." Cuts in educational funding failed to address illiteracy. Elections always involved "fraud and violence." The national government failed in "its responsibility to guarantee civil rights." Blacks migrated out of the state. In an "absence of respect for law and order and a great fear of the black man on the part of whites," whites used lynching as the "ultimate weapon to keep blacks under control." By century's end, "segregation [had] replaced slavery as the means of maintaining white control," and an "elaborate racial etiquette was developed." Sallis did not dodge or ignore the central issues, however unpleasant. In addition to statistics on lynching, for example, the chapter clearly presented lynchings and even included a photograph of "a Mississippi lynching." Sallis also candidly explained that the white fear of mythical "Negro domination" led to the disfranchisement of blacks under the Constitution of 1890. After the debate over disfranchisement, the text specified the restrictions placed on voting and how they functioned. Even in discussing the low point for blacks, *Conflict and Change* devoted one page to the complex life of Isaiah T. Montgomery, the only black delegate to the constitutional convention, and his efforts to establish the all-black town of Mound Bayou.[30]

After Loewen and Sallis assumed responsibility for writing their chapters, they discussed the remaining chapters and distributed them among their MHP colleagues. In addition to chapters on Indians and explorers, Bruce Adams accepted responsibility for Mississippi's period as a U.S. territory and for the Civil War. The antebellum chapters fell to Olivia Jones, and Jeanne Middleton took the two chapters on the early twentieth century. Loewen's Tougaloo colleagues Jim Brown and Stephen Immer took assignments, respectively, for the civil rights movement and recent Mississippi. Jackson State professor William Ferris agreed to contribute a chapter on literature and folklore, while Loewen handled mid-twentieth-century cultural changes.

Research and writing presented formidable challenges, especially for the three recent graduates. Their assignments required not just original research in primary sources but also extensive reading in the secondary literature. Though Sallis's research and teaching gave him expertise in the state's history and William Ferris had studied folklore and folk music, the others lacked any extensive background and had to master a portion of Mississippi's history quickly. The three students also had to develop their writing skills because creating a secondary school textbook required them as well as the college professors to learn to write for a new, younger audience. The team also had to figure out the details of how to maintain a consistent style making their textbook revisionist in content and innovative in form. Coordinating the work of half a dozen contributors, particularly several students, presented challenges for persons accustomed to working individually.

In July 1970 the Mississippi History Project first hired Bruce Adams, but financial limitations and administrative difficulties prevented the planned employment of a female Tougaloo student. While creating a list of articles and monographs relevant to his early period, Adams immediately set about processing grant proposals and handling routine office work. He also compiled a list of dissertations on Mississippi history in the state archive and, after reviewing more than seventy, ordered six on microfilm for the Project. No longer enrolled as a student, Adams owed the Project forty hours of work each week. As it would for later contributors, especially paid non-faculty, the MHP expected from Adams a typed weekly progress report that explained how much time he had worked, what he had done, any problems he had experienced, and what he expected to do next.[31]

Loewen stressed to Adams the importance of maintaining organized and readable research notes, along with a clear record of sources consulted that proved to be of no help. In his initial work, Adams also had responsibility for accumulating outside his assigned areas bibliographic references to sources that might help others on their topics, and Loewen urged him to "[b]e vastly creative" in pursuing them. One week Adams reported reviewing thirty-eight books, about one-third of them primary sources. He also read the Bettersworth and McLemore textbooks' coverage of the pre-statehood era. Along the way, Adams encountered unexpected but not unusual personal problems. He lost his apartment and spent more than a week searching for a place to live. An automobile accident and "talking with judge about my tickets" consumed more time.[32]

Late in the summer, after consulting with Loewen and Sallis and with former professors at Millsaps, Adams corresponded with authorities on the state's geography and its Native Americans to obtain advice and recommendations. As a result, he spent a day in Starkville consulting with Mississippi State University archaeologists John Peterson and Richard Marshall and with historian Glover Moore, and he learned about resources available in the university's library. Throughout the fall and winter, Adams continued reading, researching, outlining, and writing, often more than ten hours a day. On one occasion he reported having to quit work "because my eyes hurt." He did manage, however, to produce a draft chapter on Indians. In response, Loewen offered a negative assessment. Adams's reference to "a fair policy of Indian removal" struck Loewen as similar to "a fair policy of Jewish genocide," and he asked, "In what sense?" More generally, he suggested that Adams "forgot the ninth-grader" who would read the text. With other specific directions from Peterson, Marshall, and Loewen, Adams began his revisions on perhaps the most difficult part of the state's history. Later, after reading the revisions, Peterson, an expert on Indians, observed that it showed "little improvement . . . over the existing 9th grade text on Mississippi history in terms of general scope"; Adams had apparently implemented none of Peterson and Marshall's advice. Peterson also found "many minor errors of fact," and he judged Adams's chapter "unpublishable, both being bad history and bad pedagogically." Loewen agreed with much of Peterson's critique, and later he revised Adams's chapters accordingly.[33]

Conflict and Change's coverage of the conventional story of white settlement involved two chapters, one focused on the "Indian civilizations" followed by a second on white "explorers and settlers." The discussion of Indians acknowledged that most information came from whites "who did not understand what they saw." Allowing for the biased sources, the first chapter presented an unusually positive and empathetic treatment of Indians. By referring to Indian *civilizations*, the Adams-Loewen text rejected the prevailing textbook conception of Indians as primitive and offered tentative descriptions of Indian life within "stable cultures, social structures, and governments that met their needs." In recognition of the complexity of Indian civilizations, it explored religions, examined Indians and slavery, and explained the "differences" among the Choctaws, the Natchez, and the Chickasaws. A four-paragraph discussion of "women in Indian societies" sought to avoid gender bias. Respectful of Indian strategic thinking, a one-page insert reproduced an 1811 debate between Indian leaders Tecumseh and Pushmataha over going to war against the United States, and another digression provided a biography of an Indian leader. Instead of describing the whites' impact as benign, it recounted that, fifty years after the arrival of whites, "European technology, religion, politics, diseases, and wars had caused major changes in these cultures. Within a century, the Indian civilizations were almost destroyed."[34]

Despite their loyalty to the United States and treaty guarantees, whites engaged in the "destruction of the Indians' independence" and pushed them off the land. Though some whites supported the Indians, "Many whites felt that Indians were an inferior race of people, people who could never be 'civilized.'

They viewed Indians as something in the way, like tree stumps, to be cleared out before the land could be settled." The federal government supported the whites by using "bribery, threats, and blackmail to make Indians give up their land." In treating the nineteenth-century Indian removal, the text offered an extended follow-up discussion of "Mississippi Indians in Oklahoma." In the following much shorter chapter on the explorers, a provocative sidebar challenged students, "These pages retell the events of Chapter 3 [on Indians]. Try to coordinate the two accounts."[35]

In a revisionist Civil War chapter, Adams (also with Loewen's later assistance) pointed out conflicts within the state. White Mississippians, "not solidly behind secession," divided along geographic and class lines. In addition to describing the state's wartime strategic importance, the chapter discussed "opposition to the Confederacy"; according to one historian quoted, "In no other state, except possibly East Tennessee, was the war within more active or more violent." Mississippi's own Jefferson Davis "denounced states' rights as destructive to the Confederate cause." Adams also described how food shortages, monetary problems, and broken railroads made wartime daily life difficult. Stressing the war's impact on blacks, the new assessment explained that seventeen thousand "participated in freeing themselves" by serving with the Union army and that they made difficult any notion of returning them to a second-class citizenship, much less to slavery. "The arming of black soldiers had deep meaning for race relations" and caused whites "on both sides . . . to change their opinions about blacks to fit the new circumstances." One section of the chapter focused on Davis Bend where freedmen received land to farm. Though considered "an astounding success," the experiment ended when federal authorities allowed plantation owners to reclaim their lands. "If the Davis Bend experiment had been allowed to continue," the text argued, "it might have offered a real solution to the problem of securing political and economic rights for the newly freed black Mississippians."[36]

Perhaps the MHP's second most demanding assignment fell to Olivia Jones, a senior history major at Tougaloo. After joining the undertaking in September 1970, Jones worked until the following summer, two months after she graduated. She had to study to gain control of the complex and controversial subjects of antebellum slavery and the approach of the Civil War. For background she read critically the existing textbooks and concluded that "Bettersworth is more vile, McLemore more evasive." To build on her undergraduate history background, Jones labored through many standard works on slavery, including Charles Sydnor's *Slavery in Mississippi*, Kenneth Stampp's *The Peculiar Institution*, Herbert Aptheker's *Negro Slave Revolts*, and

Allen Weinstein and Frank Otto Gatell's collection of historiographical essays in *American Negro Slavery*. To gain insights into "those things that are general concerning slavery," she also read *The Masters and the Slaves* on Brazilian slavery. She also mined microfilmed dissertations and statistical data on slavery. For her chapter on antebellum society and the approach of the Civil War, weeks went into books ranging from Joseph G. Baldwin's *The Flush Times of Alabama and Mississippi* to Percy Lee Rainwater's *Mississippi: Storm Center of Secession, 1856–1861*.[37]

In one chapter, Jones analyzed the antebellum slave system and the approach to war. Older histories' discussions of slavery stressed the white slave owners' beneficence and presented nothing significant about slave life, slave resistance, or critics of human bondage. Instead of treating slaves merely as objects owned by whites, *Conflict and Change* portrayed the complexity of slavery under topics ranging from food to religion, but also slave discipline and slave resistance. The text also frankly discussed defenses of slavery as a "positive good" and a "necessary evil," as well as the arguments for abolition.[38] Its full coverage of blacks during the Civil War mentioned not just emancipation but also white fears of slave revolts and black participation with the Union and Confederate armies.

"Under the slave system," Jones explained, "social distinctions were clear-cut," and she carefully distinguished among white planters, yeoman farmers, and poor whites, but also among field slaves, house slaves, town slaves, and free blacks. While most whites owned no slaves, planters dominated politics and society. In her dispassionate description of "discipline" under slavery, Jones wrote, "Slavery took away a person's desire to work. There was little incentive to work from sunup to sundown without pay." Masters, therefore, devised a system of rewards and punishments to encourage or force the slave to work hard. Whipping "accustomed the slaves to discipline, it required them to be submissive, it made them fear white men, and it attempted to make them feel that whites were 'naturally' superior to blacks." Owners "rarely killed" their slaves because the slaves "were too valuable." Declaring that "very few [slaves] were content," Jones explored assertive slave resistance in the forms of "careless work, theft, or deliberate destruction of their master's property," but also running away from owners. She also identified slave work songs and church services as secretive, coded forms of resistance whose "double meanings deceived the enemy. At the same time, Jones observed that whites "had deep-rooted fears of mass rebellion" among their slaves.[39]

Jones also undermined many myths about whites in the Old South. For white women, "a life of ease . . . was the exception, not the rule." Even on some plantations, farm life required hard work by men and women. Few whites had plantations with hundreds of slaves and mansions for the owners; in fact, "even wealthy planters lived in log houses." Though whites had initially considered slavery a "necessary evil," higher cotton prices and more available land caused the demand for slaves to increase, and slavery soon changed to a "positive good." Using religion and the Bible to justify slavery, whites considered blacks as inferior beings and slavery as "a blessing for black people" because whites would care for them. By 1840 blacks outnumbered whites, and controls over slaves intensified as their majority grew. The abolitionists' "persistent criticism of slavery" put the white South on the defensive, and the protection of slavery took precedence over all other issues. Internal improvements, the national bank, and the tariff yielded in importance to slavery as Mississippi and the nation moved toward civil war. States' rights became a principle only when the South became a minority in the national government. Jones's interpretation contradicted the view found in other Mississippi history textbooks.[40]

By early 1971 Jones had outlined her two chapters and written partial rough drafts, all while a college senior. As expected by the MHP, Jones also edited two chapters by Bruce Adams and commented on Loewen's concluding "Into the Future" chapter. By the end of the summer of 1971, Jones married, moved from Jackson, and left her job with the Project, but she kept in touch with Loewen and Sallis and the MHP. While employed by the Social Security Administration in Tennessee and Alabama, she continued to revise her contributions and to comment on the emerging larger manuscript.[41]

Jeanne Middleton, the third student working on the textbook, also joined the Project in September 1970 and worked throughout her senior year at Millsaps. Though an excellent student, Middleton had to read widely to prepare her chapters on the twentieth century. For discussions of demagogues, the Mississippi flood, sharecropping, and the Dixiecrats, she read, for example, works by V. O. Key, John Hope Franklin, T. J. Woofter, Richard Bardolph, Hodding Carter, Richard Wright, David Cohn, Langston Hughes, and Congressman Frank Smith. After a few weeks of research, she reported that she had examined "about half of the books in the Millsaps library on blacks, looking for *anything* about Mississippi! Found a few paragraphs here and there out of about 135 books . . . . HELP!!!" In addition to examining the *Jackson Clarion-Ledger*, Middleton scoured the *Journal of Mississippi History*, the index to the *New York Times*, and *Reader's Guide to Periodical Literature*. Like the others, at the weekly meetings of the MHP group, she exchanged ideas with her coworkers and received advice, encouragement, and suggestions from Loewen and Sallis. She also edited drafts by Stephen Immer and others.[42]

By early February 1971, Middleton happily declared, "First chapter delivered. Amen!" Later in February, her schedule intensified when she began practice teaching. When her progress flagged, Loewen urged her, "It is now time to forego such pleasantries as working for Millsaps grades, eating meals, etc. And I'm not entirely facetious," Loewen added. Middleton continued working, but as she wrote drafts, she discovered problems and gaps. A few weeks later in May, Loewen demanded, "The project, as a job and as a moral and scientific enterprise, must take priority often over personal and other activities." Soon Middleton responded, "I have begun to sleep, eat, and breathe Miss history. My family thinks I have gone mad." Satisfied with her progress, the MHP renewed her contract for the summer. After a year, Middleton had written a complete draft of one chapter and completed research and a partial draft of a second, and Loewen preliminarily judged them "very well written." In the fall she began graduate work in education on a Danforth Fellowship at Harvard University, but she continued her affiliation with the Project for three more years.[43]

Middleton's chapter on the interwar era confronted the problems facing the state in low cotton prices, tenantry, sharecropping, out-migration, and lack of industry. She declared, for example, that after World War I "cotton prices crashed to frightening lows" and caused two disastrous decades for farmers. Under the tenant system that also trapped many landless whites, blacks remained in "economic bondage," but migration to the North "provided the main outlet for black frustration and protest." Calling public education "inadequate," the chapter presented a table for 1940 showing the great racial disparities in expenditures per student, length of school year, average college education for teachers, and teacher salaries. Text accompanying the data directed students, "Read the Fourteenth Amendment to the Constitution. Were these schools constitutional?" (Thirty-four pages later, another table provided similar data for 1946 and asked if the state had made progress.) Perhaps at its most daring, the chapter suggested, for further reading, "*Black Boy* is a searing autobiography of Richard Wright's coming of age in Mississippi."[44]

When Middleton addressed politics in the period between the world wars, she highlighted black activism in the Republican Party and the NAACP, and she reported white women's organizing to oppose lynching. After explaining that a demagogue "avoids the real issues and makes emotional promises to win votes," Middleton presented a balanced view of demagogue Theodore Bilbo. She acknowledged his achievements as governor—school consolidation, creation of a state tuberculosis hospital, start of a state commission for the blind—and credited him later in the U.S. Senate with supporting New

Deal measures to deal with the Depression, but he "spent much of his energy preaching race hatred and white supremacy. For the post–World War II period, Middleton described both black voter registration efforts and the white Mississippi opponents of equality who walked out of the Democratic convention to protest President Harry Truman's civil rights proposals. Black mobilization continued with the Regional Council of Negro Leadership's formation in 1952. The textbook included a photograph of a 1954 bumper sticker commanding, "Don't Buy GAS Where You Can't Use THE REST ROOM." Middleton's retrieval of early black activism made her chapters unusual.[45]

In addition to bringing blacks into the state's story, Loewen and Sallis wanted to present history in a compelling way, and helping the contributors craft well-written chapters challenged the MHP's leaders. Adams, Jones, and Middleton especially needed assistance. When they joined the Project, each met with Loewen and Sallis for an hour to receive guidelines for their work. Loewen generally supervised Middleton, while Sallis directed Jones; the two professors shared oversight of Adams. The entire staff met weekly, usually for an hour and a half, and Loewen and Sallis led discussions about proper and effective writing. Everyone on the Project commented freely on chapter drafts as they emerged. To help the students with their writing, the professors recommended several basic books and ordered several copies of each. Their suggestions, indicating the writing problems they encountered, included William Strunk and E. B. White's *Elements of Style*, Jacques Barzun and Henry F. Graff's *The Modern Researcher*, and Kate L. Turabian's *A Manual for Writers*. In commenting on a draft, Loewen instructed Middleton to *read*, underlined three times, Strunk and White. Loewen also circulated among the MHP staff a detailed guide to the proper form for an annotated bibliographic entry. In addition to the customary data for standard works, he requested "everything you can think of" for odd or fugitive sources, and he wanted descriptive and evaluative annotations.[46]

In much of the students' writing, critics found too many difficult words, complicated sentences, and poorly organized paragraphs for their ninth-grade audience. On each chapter draft the Project insisted on improvement, and Loewen often offered blunt, even scathing commentaries, or what he referred to as "straightforward criticism without sugar coating." In addition to the usual comments about "vague" and "awkward" writing and directions to reorganize, he told Middleton that her "writing style has been screwed up, perhaps by four years of college." He found "clumsy or unstrung constructions" and problems with verb tenses, while another reviewer identified "unfair generalizations," "too many dates," and undeveloped points. "For God's sake," another critic erupted at Middleton, "don't call [Sen. James O.] Eastland 'prominent.'" Recommendations included the use of active verbs, construction of relatively simple sentences, and avoidance of words beyond a ninth-grader's vocabulary. Loewen encouraged Middleton to "STAND BACK FROM YOUR CREATION AND JUNK IT IN THOSE AREAS WHERE IT MUST BE JUNKED."[47]

After reading Bruce Adams's draft first chapter, Loewen lashed out that "its beginning is terrible!" He charged that Adams assumed too much knowledge by the ninth-grade reader, and he directed him to reorganize his material and rewrite his chapter. In Olivia Jones's work, critics identified unclear quotations, a lack of a "main point," passive writing, and pronouns with vague antecedents. More seriously, Jones "perpetuate[d] the myth that the South was prosperous under slavery." Loewen's work also came under the same scrutiny. With equal vigor, another MHP member nailed one of his chapters for vagueness, repetitive word choices, and poor organization.[48]

Expert help and advice on writing appropriate for ninth graders came from Maryellen Hains Clampit. As a children's literature specialist, Clampit brought to the MHP valuable knowledge about writing and books that appealed to children. She joined the Project in the fall of 1970 and worked through the following summer. As her first assignment, Clampit collected examples of what Loewen described as "groovy writing" for ninth graders in social studies books. She also scouted out examples of exemplary writing or presentation in state history and general American history textbooks. By early 1971 she had focused increasingly on textbook design, and when she discovered something imaginative, she recommended it to the MHP.[49]

Corresponding with designers in book publishing and conferring with a Bowling Green colleague with similar interests, Clampit obtained and reviewed a variety of textbooks. One in a series that offered surveys of the social sciences for several grades especially appealed to her. She told Loewen, "Visually the book is quite exciting." Not only did it use color extensively with colored paper, colored lines, and colored type, it featured wide margins that contained notes, definitions, and questions. A multitude of graphs, maps, and pictures of varying sizes appeared either partially or entirely in the wide margins, and often their color tied them to similarly colored material in the text. A note in the margin also sometimes referred the reader to an earlier or later illustration or discussion in the text. Clampit paid close attention to features that kept the reader "visually on your toes"; she noted, for example, double columns, bold type, and different ways of presenting quotations, definitions, and illustrations. Books in the series also differed in size and shape. Though the subject had no direct relevance to a Mississippi history textbook, the unusual design characteristics proved provocative for the MHP.[50]

With Clampit's help, Loewen also devoted considerable thought to the textbook's format and style. He studied the books that she brought to his attention and examined any others that he happened to see. Two books particularly appealed to him. Kevin Lynch's *The Image of the City* (1960) presented its many maps, figures, and photographs in a distinctive design. The study of the urban landscape and urban planning gave Loewen the idea of variable margin widths and how to use them effectively. With a text that had a consistently wide margin on the page's outside edge, the subheadings ran beyond the text into the margins. Sketches, pictures, and drawings often appeared either completely in the margins or ran over into the margins. Notes in the margins referred to illustrations appearing elsewhere. The design techniques in Lynch's book reduced dependence on awkward boxes inserted in the text. Marginal notes could also highlight the text by indicating the main points and new topics. Many of the features used by Lynch would later appear in the Mississippi history textbook. For example, in discussing the civil rights movement, the margin of one page not only defined interposition but also asked, "What does 'all deliberate speed' mean?" As a result of the information in the margins, Loewen hoped, a student would "skim through the text one time, 'reading' the margins" and then the "reader will be seduced into thinking, and perhaps even seduced into reading the main body of the text."[51]

In an entirely different way, a new series of history textbooks published in 1970 "impressed greatly" Loewen and gave him ideas for the Mississippi history textbook. Called the "American Adventures Program," the four-volume survey of American history resembled the MHP in its emphasis on recent history, its focus on social history, and its claims to forthrightness. Though designed for fifth and sixth graders, volume two, *Old Hate—New Hate*, according to Loewen, provided "an appropriate model for our own work in general. Motivated by the text, Loewen wanted his colleagues to read it as soon as they could. The series aimed at students "who have had learning problems," and Loewen believed that by national standards Mississippi students would also "be termed educationally disadvantaged." When he recommended *Old Hate—New Hate* to his Project colleagues, Loewen pointed out the text's effective use of an "excellent vignette" on Mississippian Blanch K. Bruce and the "gripping" writing that appeared in "exciting" chapters. For example, in comparison, he noted that the MHP's discussion of slavery did not "make the student feel the issues and their importance. He urged his fellows "to work on making our chapters exciting and great like" *Old Hate—New Hate*. It inspired

Loewen at the same time it "depressed" him because it demonstrated how far their Mississippi book had to go.[52]

Though Clampit had helped identify useful models for the MHP, by the late spring of 1971, Loewen had begun to have doubts about her commitment and asked her if she intended to continue. Her dissolving marriage sent Clampit back to her previous job at Western Michigan and prevented her from working much on the Project, but she did want to get back to Jackson and work on the Project before starting to teach at Western Michigan University in the fall. As Bruce Adams told her, "We can really use you this summer because none of us know how to write for ninth graders." As the only Project member with experience in children's books, Clampit helped sensitize the writers to the special needs of ninth-grade readers and to strategies to address them. In her editing that summer, Clampit watched for sentences that "can intimidate slow students" or "threaten the poorer student." She pointed out "vague" questions, "very plodding and dull" prose, mechanical lists, "stiff diction," wordiness, lack of transitions, and "fragmented" structure. Regarding Immer's chapter on modern Mississippi, for example, she cautioned that one sentence was "a bear. It is difficult to follow because the subject and verb are so far apart." Another sentence "leads to some confusion" because it contained two unparallel parts, one in active voice and one in passive voice. In July and August, Clampit's editing made a valuable contribution as did her work on the textbook's design. After the summer, however, she worked only informally and intermittently with the MHP.[53]

Concerned that the team produce a text of uniformly good quality, Loewen devised a list of "questions to ask of each chapter" about writing, research, and content. Though posed as a series of queries, it served as a set of directions. Regarding writing, it stressed transitions between chapters and encouraged explicit references to earlier and later chapters; the referrals applied to charts and maps, as well as text. Contributors also had to make sure "each paragraph flow[ed] well internally and develop[ed] a major point." Loewen wanted authors to decide if each chapter had sufficient and appropriate subheadings and illustrations. Writers and critics needed to identify deficiencies in research, evidence, or bibliographical references and suggest corrections. Directions about content started with identifying each chapter's teaching objectives and judging if the chapter achieved them. More generally, Loewen asked how the chapter's themes fit the book's themes such as race and racism, extralegal violence, gender, poverty, the arts, state's rights, industry, and civil rights. If the chapter contained material relevant to the larger concepts, he wanted revisions to ensure that "these themes are brought out more clearly." Pursuing inclusivity, the list urged writers to pay due attention to all pertinent groups, such as Native Americans, other ethnic groups, young people, small farmers, workers, and the poor.[54]

Loewen and Sallis took great care to treat all groups fairly because they wanted their book to provide a stunning contrast to the white and male biases of Bettersworth's *Our Mississippi*. To set the standard for the MHP, each contributor received a copy of a nine-page mimeographed guide on "How to Evaluate Textbooks for Sex and Ethnic Biases." The document had a three-stage analytical process followed by a more general assessment. First, it called for counting the appearances of various ethnic groups and each gender. The tabulations applied to the entire work but also to the individual chapters, and not only to the text but also to the book's other elements, such as photographs and bibliographies. The data would reveal imbalances and inconsistencies. Second, the evaluation would inspect the behaviors and roles of the ethnic groups and genders to guard against a bias for or against anyone. The writers should judge the images presented as positive (e.g., competent or creative) or negative (e.g., stupid or incapable). Third, to ensure balance and fairness, the analysis would consider occupations (e.g., scientific, artistic, or manual), social roles performed (e.g., nurturer, victim, hero, oppressor, or oppressed), and level of activity (e.g., leader or follower, active or passive, independent or dependent). The intended result would be a fairer treatment of each group.[55]

The evaluation for bias would also identify examples of paternalism in which the text talked down to a group and portrayed them as childlike and needy; paternalism could also portray the superiors (whites) as "self-sufficient and generous." The text also needed searching for examples of romanticism where the writer indulged a "[t]endency to glorify unjust situations and ignore realities" such as "slavery and poverty." A romantic view of black history denied students the chance to understand the realities of black experiences and to appreciate the historical roots of contemporary racial problems. The test for bias also warned against ignoring minority living conditions and "sidestepping the issue of white participation in creating those conditions." Slavery, for example, could not be considered benign simply because it resulted from economic demands, and white pioneers' need for land did not justify taking land away from Indians, who could not be presented as savages. Authors and editors should not hesitate "to identify bigots and bigotry and to show the extreme measures by which some white Americans made life miserable for some minority people." Loewen and Sallis urged their colleagues to apply the criteria to their work and the work that they edited for the MHP.[56]

While the writing guide and the tests for bias helped make the Loewen and Sallis textbook distinct from its predecessors and different from other textbooks, thirty-two maps, eleven figures, and six tables enhanced the text, as did scores of pictures. Original questions and projects for the students' consideration appeared in the margins and at the end of chapters. Two typical facing pages in the chapter on the state around 1900 included a three-hundred-word description of influential Senator James Z. George, marginal definitions of "apportionment" and "illiterate," an explanation that the 1890 constitution still governed the state, and a question in the margin that asked students to connect the description of black voting restrictions to a subsequent section on black education. A later discussion of the post–World War II economy asked, "As industry grows, is pollution growing? What can be done about it?" and "Why is Mississippi such a poor state? Discuss in class the historical reasons for this poverty, and refer to previous chapters to back up your analysis."[57]

Numerous biographical sketches and extracts from novels, newspapers, songs, diaries, letters, and other contemporary sources enlivened the text. A new appreciation for Indians appeared in references to Indian civilizations and discussions of their lives. The text also devoted rare attention to the role of women in the state's history. Women received their own index entry that referred to women in the colonial era and the Confederacy, Indian and slave women, women's rights and roles, and women writers. Women pictured included the famous Ida Wells Barnett, Leontyne Price, Eudora Welty, and Fannie Lou Hamer, but also women teachers of the freedmen, textile workers, civil rights demonstrators, and cheerleaders. By including previously ignored subjects, the MHP aimed to have students think about history in different ways, not just as the story of powerful white male politicians, generals, landowners, and business leaders.

In an even more dramatic innovation involving historical interpretations, Loewen and Sallis introduced ninth graders to historians' clashing assessments. At the end of the chapter on Reconstruction, for example, an unprecedented discussion of historiography appeared under "How Mississippians Still Disagree." Sallis directed the ninth graders to short selections on Reconstruction by John Bettersworth, Mississippi editor Hodding Carter, and black historian Lerone Bennett; he further suggested readers consult works by Vernon Wharton, James W. Garner, and Milton Meltzer. The textbook also asked students to pose the questions Loewen had provided to examine historical sources. The one-page section on historiography concluded, "Which of the books seems most accurate? Which is most biased? Back up your answers with evidence." In a bold break from earlier textbooks, Sallis wanted ninth-grade students to go beyond memorization toward more sophisticated analysis of interpretations.[58]

The textbook's presentation of new subjects, approaches, formats, and designs necessitated careful coordination and editing by Loewen and Sallis to tie it all together into a book rather than a collection of essays. Though their colleagues helped, the two main authors had to maintain consistency of usage, balance of coverage, and distribution of topics and techniques within and among chapters coming from the seven writers. In addition to the typical editing, Loewen and Sallis had to ensure the book did not use too many boxes or vignettes, for instance, because an excess would disrupt the larger narrative, and they had to prevent two chapters from covering the same topic.[59]

Even with all the challenges, work on the textbook progressed in 1970 and 1971. In December 1970, a confident Jim Loewen reported to John Griffin of the Southern Education Foundation that he expected each contributor to the MHP soon to submit an outline and partial draft of one chapter. He believed the Project was moving ahead at "a rapid pace." The schedule called for a first draft by the end of January, followed a week later by an editor's comments; one week after receiving the editorial appraisal, the writer should have submitted a second draft. Loewen hoped to get the drafts to Maryellen Clampit in the spring, and she would review the appropriateness of the writing for their ninth-grade audience. In the middle of January, Loewen believed the group was ahead of schedule. By the end of March, however, work had slowed and worries increased. Distressed by a lack of production, Loewen chastised Jeanne Middleton for falling behind. He told her that "urgently I need your chapters. Where are they?" He implored her, "Please phone me to let me know its status, and please get in at least a chapter immediately." Two months later a frustrated Loewen warned Middleton and others that their tardiness imperiled their summer employment with the Project. As a result he put her on "probation" until she submitted more drafts, and she responded with more work. He issued a similar warning to Clampit.[60]

The major production problems, however, did not involve Middleton or Jones. Though Bruce Adams had once hoped to write a textbook by himself, after several months with the MHP he realized that "I'm afraid research is not my bag. It's really bad." By early 1971, his weekly reports had become vague with just a list of hours and no substantive activities. In the spring, Adams admitted to Maryellen Clampit that his efforts for the Project "don't seem to be working out. I may be expecting too much or the wrong things, but they seem to be going almost opposite" what he had expected. He decided to head

for law school in Denver and admitted, "I'd go tomorrow if I could." More immediately, Adams wanted "to go home to a six-pack of beer." At the end of his
draft of chapter three, Adams typed, "AT THIS POINT I RAN OUT OF
TIME AND DECIDED TO SUBMIT WHAT I HAVE DONE. GOD HELP
ME." When he did finally depart, Adams had contributed drafts of two chapters and parts of two others, but much work remained on each of them. The
Mississippi History Project's first employee had not quite worked out as all
had hoped.[61]

Three faculty who had agreed to work on the MHP also presented unexpected problems. Stephen Immer, a historian and Tougaloo colleague of
Loewen, also fell behind. Assigned the chapter on post–World War II, Immer
simply failed to finish it to the satisfaction of Loewen and Sallis. His deficient
work caused a reduction in his summer stipend. By the end of the summer, he
had left Jackson. A few weeks later an embarrassed Immer confessed to Loewen,
"Sorry I wasn't able to deliver the goods in my chapter. Scholarly pursuits,
research, and academe in general are obviously not my bags." A couple of years
later he more bluntly admitted, "I viewed my research and writing as pretty
piss-poor and something in my life I prefer not to remember. A big goose-egg
on the scoreboard." By then he found his work for the Equal Employment
Opportunity Commission "exciting, challenging, and more rewarding practically every day." Loewen eventually finished Immer's chapter.[62]

The other Tougaloo historian, James Brown, encountered difficulties with
his chapter on the civil rights movement. Initial readings of his draft prompted
serious criticism for its lack of analysis and its excessive detail, what one critic
called "one damn thing after another." Brown devoted too much attention, for
example, to the Child Development Group of Mississippi and the Mississippi
Action for Progress, rival anti-poverty programs, without addressing their effectiveness. Loewen did not call for more information about the two organizations, but for less, and for a more interpretive overview of the larger
movement. In a similar way, Brown named several groups involved in legal
actions, and Loewen responded early in 1972 by reminding Brown that "some
poor kid in Scooba is going to have to 'verify' and memorize their organizations." Though Loewen told Brown the chapter was "obviously on the right
track" factually, it needed "added work to become good history." Saying that
he would finish the chapter if Brown did not, Loewen emphasized that "the
chapter is *crucial* . . . our book will sink or swim according to how well this
chapter works." When Brown did not follow through with a reorganized revision, Loewen proceeded on his own to redraft and finish what Brown had
started.[63]

The traditional texts seldom included blacks, particularly as independent historical actors, and usually passed over the civil rights movement as quickly as possible. In *Conflict and Change* the movement began with the *Brown* decision but focused primarily on movement activism from voter registration in McComb to James Meredith's 1962 integration of the University of Mississippi to 1964 Freedom Summer. In the coverage of widespread "violence against blacks," the well-known Emmett Till case received only a marginal mention; the murder of movement leader Medgar Evers garnered a full page. A long insert in the narrative recounted Fannie Lou Hamer's appearance at the 1964 Democratic national convention, and another described James Meredith's 1966 attempt to march from Memphis to Jackson. *Conflict and Change* carefully assessed the impact of Freedom Summer and explained both black and white views of the movement. Not simply black history, it described changes among whites, and, along with opposition to the movement by whites in the Citizens' Council and on the State Sovereignty Commission, the textbook recognized diversity among whites by revealing white critics of segregation.[64]

The situation involving the third professor had many more complicating factors than either Immer or Brown. William Ferris had agreed to write the chapter on folklore and literature, and in late July 1971, just before he left for a vacation, he submitted a completed draft of his chapter. Loewen, however, considered it incomplete because it did not connect the sections on literature and folklore, failed to balance the vignette of Jimmie Rodgers with one of a black figure, did not contain two necessary maps, and omitted discussions of Parchman prison, the blues, and work songs. While Ferris was away, others on the MHP made editorial changes and additions to Ferris's contribution. Based on Ferris's limited contribution, they also decided to reduce his remuneration that they considered excessive compared to what others received. When Ferris returned in late September, he came to Loewen's office to object to the "unfair" cut in salary but even more to protest what he considered extensive editorial revisions "in both style and content." After earlier producing three successive drafts in response to criticism and suggestions, Ferris thought the additional changes "unnecessary." Disillusioned with the Project and with Loewen, Ferris decided to withdraw his contribution and return his pay.[65]

Because the "differences seem[ed] irreconcilable," the MHP decided to produce a completely new chapter on folklore and literature. Over the winter of 1972, Loewen studied to produce the replacement featuring a new organization "not polarized by race"; it brought white and black folklore, and similarly literature, together in "a unified treatment." To prevent problems regarding any claim of plagiarism, Loewen sent his chapter to Ferris for review of some phrases used from his earlier draft. Ferris acknowledged that one phrase repeated in both versions actually came from a hymnal, and he agreed that the other "passages are not mine." Later in the summer of 1972, Loewen sent a final version of the chapter for Ferris's review and for any other suggestions. Writing from his new position at Yale University, Ferris said, "The chapter you sent me looks fine and I don't feel it overlaps my own work." Ferris wished the Project success because it "is an important work and I am sure it will provide much-needed guidance to high school students of history." With the clash between Loewen and Ferris, the two young, strong-willed, and ambitious academics, finally settled on a cordial basis, Loewen and Sallis continued their editorial work.[66]

By the fall of 1971, Loewen and Sallis worked nearly alone. Ferris had quit, Brown had lost interest, Immer had moved, Middleton had gone off to graduate school, Jones had married and moved, Adams had left Jackson, and Maryellen Clampit was teaching in Michigan. Middleton, Jones, and Clampit still contributed occasionally to the Project in various ways but not on a daily basis. The job of pulling the textbook together rested with the two original collaborators. In July 1971, Loewen reported that "a tremendous amount of work" remained on the textbook. For the next two years they edited the draft submissions. To make the textbook's language, organization, and themes consistent and appropriate for their future high school audience, they eliminated difficult words, simplified sentences, and reorganized paragraphs and chapters. Working steadily, they rewrote entire sections, completed chapters, and composed vignettes, biographical sketches, and other supplementary material. In one significant revision, Loewen and Sallis decided on a more logical organization of Olivia Jones's two antebellum chapters. The final removal of Indians instead of the 1832 constitution would provide the break point between the chapters, and as a result the discussion of slavery would move to the later chapter of "the road to conflict." Though they consulted Jones, they proceeded to make the changes.[67]

To spend more time on the Project, Loewen arranged, partly with a supplemental grant from the Southern Education Foundation, to take a leave from Tougaloo in the spring of 1972. He wanted to devote more time to several projects that included the community study of Mound Bayou, data collection for a lawsuit dealing with municipal services in Jackson, and completion of a "radical" introductory text in sociology, but the state history textbook took precedence. His commitment to the MHP remained undiminished. As he explained to the SEF's Griffin, "I think it has the greatest possibility for causing social and cultural change."[68]

While busy writing and designing their textbook, Loewen and Sallis thought increasingly about how the various publics would receive the textbook. Even more than students and teachers, more than reviewers, more even than the State Textbook Purchasing Board, possible publishers concerned them. The authors realized that finding a receptive publisher for any secondary school textbook with sales limited to one small state would present special difficulties.

CHAPTER SIX

Reception

Reviews and Reactions

From the beginning of the Mississippi History Project (MHP), Jim Loewen and Charles Sallis knew that writing a revisionist history of Mississippi would have no impact unless they could find a receptive publisher. Within a year of the Project's start, they began to worry that they might have trouble securing a home for their unusual book. With Loewen in charge, they explored multiple publishing options, and by early 1972 they had secured a contract with a major commercial publisher. Two years later when *Conflict and Change* appeared, the authors waited for reactions to their work. Book reviewers rarely have any interest in textbooks, so even the limited notice given to Loewen and Sallis's book amounted to remarkable attention. Far greater recognition came in 1975, when the textbook won a significant book award. In 1971, however, Loewen and Sallis could not have foreseen the public reception of their work.

Though Harvard University Press published Loewen's revised dissertation on the Mississippi Chinese in 1971, Loewen had no experience in the worlds of textbooks and commercial publishing, and neither he nor Sallis could predict editors' responses. By May 1971, long before they had a finished manuscript, they identified nearly a dozen publishers they hoped to interest in the book; the possibilities ranged from standard textbook producers Scott Foresman and Prentice-Hall to more commercial companies like Doubleday and Houghton Mifflin. Their initial overture explained four "path-breaking" features of *Mississippi: Conflict and Change*, as they named their incipient textbook, and provided information about the market for a state history. First, they stressed the book's diverse historical content. Referring to two recent articles in the *New York Times* about textbooks' unfair treatment of minorities, they argued that "we give full consideration to all ethnic groups in the state" and hoped that it would "be a real 'first' in its treatment of ethnic minorities." Second, their state history would incorporate the latest historical revisionism that had "yet to penetrate the state history level," and as the best example the authors pointed to its treatment of Reconstruction. They believed *Conflict and Change* could serve as "a model for scholars in other states and regions." The third point involved pedagogy. By including myriad illustrations and original sources, the book would stimulate the ninth grader "to think critically and analytically, rather than forcefeeding him dates and names." Finally, Loewen and Sallis took pride in the "unique" last chapter entitled "Mississippi 1967–2000" that asked students to think about their state's future.[1]

In a more practical presentation, Loewen surveyed the Mississippi market for state history texts. Assuming 35,000 ninth-grade students in public and parochial schools, the book could sell that many copies if the state approved it and rejected Bettersworth's book. School teachers, administrators, and staff members might need another 8,000 copies, and the writers speculated that in subsequent years schools would purchase an additional 15,000 as replacements. If the state approved both *Conflict and Change* and Bettersworth's textbook, they guessed that their new book would garner 20–30 percent of sales, or about 11,000 copies in the first year. A further attempt to build their case pointed out the absence of a comparable college-level textbook and implied that college classes in the state's history, required for teacher certification, might also adopt their book, even though they had designed it for ninth graders. Finally, they estimated another 5,000 initial purchases within the state and one or two thousand library sales.[2]

Though Loewen and Sallis made a strong case for the book, they may not have realized just how much the Mississippi History Project did not fit publishers' expectations. Instead of appearing provocative and appealing, the rationale for *Conflict and Change* may have seemed puzzling and strange to editors because it violated so many norms. Major publishers had little experience with state history textbooks, because they sought a far greater sales potential, especially one larger than the small Mississippi market. The MHP even had an unusual origin. Trade book editors, one observer noted, often acted as "midwives" who helped authors, while textbook editors served as "progenitors" who selected appropriate authors. Textbook authors, especially for secondary schoolbooks, rarely approached publishers with a completed manuscript. Instead usually the idea started with an editor who had begun as a teacher and worked as a salesman before becoming an editor. When a textbook editor saw a market opportunity, he planned a book for it and then recruited an experienced teacher with some writing ability. An editor seldom could persuade a talented teacher to work on a textbook because the effort lacked creativity and excitement; in addition, a committee of editors, not the ostensible author, often did most of the actual work. One critic described the creation of a textbook as "less a writing process than an assembling of pieces, much like putting together a Tinker Toy." As bright and capable authors seeking a publisher for their nearly completed manuscript, Loewen and Sallis had unknowingly gone directly counter to established practice. Their innocent but brash approach undoubtedly confounded some editors.[3]

An editor who read the book proposal would have found the promise of a "path-breaking" textbook troubling, exactly opposite what Loewen and Sallis intended. While they took pride in their innovative approach, their unconventionality did not fit comfortably with the typical editor's view of the market. Accustomed to working in a national economy, the editor naturally wanted a book with wide appeal, and to satisfy many markets a book had to avoid controversial subjects and idiosyncratic approaches. Making a book palatable to various audiences required compromises that resulted in a conservative approach to textbook publishing. The American Association of Publishers admitted that the state adoption system "discourages experimentation, individualism, and innovation." Even though *Conflict and Change* sought only one state market, it encountered equivalent editorial expectations.[4]

With writing that engaged the student reader, Loewen and Sallis also broke with custom. One commentator concluded that typical textbook "prose is vague, characterless at best, cluttered with chatty avoidance of the issue." William Jovanovich of Harcourt, Brace and World lamented the "bad writing" in textbooks that contained "so much syntactically careless, inflated, jargon-ridden, grotesque writing." To appeal to readers *Conflict and Change* sought lively, clear, well-organized prose. The authors further wanted students to experience history and called on them to ask questions about the past and about the authors themselves. Editors, however, balked at "anything that smacks of personal communication from writer to reader."[5]

Loewen and Sallis even violated history textbook norms. According to one assessment, "the nation's history is still basically presented reverently, as a sort of graven image in print." Standard histories presented success and achievement in "a general spinning of a seemingly endless web of progress. The seams and rents in the changing social and political fabric of the nation appear less frequently." Loewen and Sallis, by paying attention to the seams and rents, the failures and frustrations, placed their textbook far outside the mainstream expected by editors.

Their introduction of historiographical interpretations also sought to break with convention and to stimulate debate. Editors, however, did not want to disturb the "smooth surface of textbook publishing" or to upset the peace of the classroom. In its own way *Conflict and Change* wanted to introduce a new way of thinking about history that involved conflicting and changing interpretations, while editors preferred to follow the established patterns and to avoid innovation.[6]

Though most publishers initially offered little encouragement in response to the MHP's May 1971 inquiry, a few showed interest. Individualized Learning Systems of California responded enthusiastically, and Loewen went to San Francisco to meet with company representatives. He quickly discovered that the company faced retrenchment and reorganization and would not soon take on a new project. Large trade publishers like Doubleday expressed no interest; for the big publishing houses the small Mississippi market offered little profit potential. The book's radical perspective and the possibility that state adoption might, as the authors suggested, require a lawsuit also discouraged publishers. Despite a passionate moral commitment to their textbook, Loewen and Sallis could not convince any major editors to take on their book. "It's not a question of morality," one expert pointed out about book publishing, "it's simply a matter of economics." Within a few weeks, however, several other publishers did express interest, and the MHP aggressively courted them and others. The tenacious Loewen even inquired about any interest at Steck-Vaughan in Austin, Texas, the publisher of Bettersworth's textbook. By the fall of 1971, parts of the manuscript had gone out to Harcourt, Houghton-Mifflin, and Scott Foresman. Rejections from the major publishers continued. As Houghton-Mifflin's editor-in-chief for the social sciences explained, his company did not publish state texts in social studies.[7] Undaunted, Loewen persisted.

With the search ongoing, the MHP continued on two other fronts. The book's contributors concentrated on writing and editing the emerging manuscript. At the same time Loewen and Sallis began efforts to solicit reactions to the book and to build support for its eventual acceptance in the schools. In the fall of 1971, the Canton public schools and the state's Catholic schools expressed interest. St. Joseph's High School in Greenville agreed to cooperate with a pilot study, and in the spring of 1972 Jean Banchetti's ninth grade Mississippi history class used lithographed copies of the textbook. As a mathematics teacher assigned to teach a Mississippi history class, she may have especially appreciated the new textbook's help. Her thirty-one ninth graders, including one black child, used Loewen and Sallis's book in conjunction with several editions of Bettersworth's history. Toward the end of the semester Loewen and Sallis surveyed Banchetti's class. They asked each student which chapter in *Conflict and Change* they liked best and which they liked least, and why. They also asked the students to choose among eight modifiers (interesting, boring, accurate, biased, too hard, too easy, too long, and too short) to apply to the MHP text and to the Bettersworth's text. Finally, the survey asked each student to compare the textbooks and answer, "Which would you choose for ninth-graders to study? Why?"[8]

As their favorite chapter the students selected the one on Reconstruction. They also liked the chapters on the civil rights movement, folklore and literature, and the Civil War. The authors noticed that "the four chapters that dealt most fully with black-white relations ... did not seem to offend this overwhelmingly white class." In fact, the chapters dealing with race "were more popular than other chapters." The students' quite favorable response to the book's last three chapters demonstrated also their appreciation for Loewen and Sallis's stress on recent history. The least popular chapter examined the era from World War I to 1950, and no other chapter displeased nearly as many. As a result, the textbook writers decided to reduce the interwar chapter by eliminating many names and dates and by including more interesting illustrations. According to Loewen and Sallis, the other less popular chapters resembled "the 'names and dates' chapters that predominate in other books," and they tended to have a political focus. The students opinions "convinced [the authors] that students were hungry for more than a bare 'names and dates' approach to their heritage."[9]

To describe the competing textbooks, the students at St. Joseph's overwhelmingly chose "interesting" for Loewen and Sallis and "boring" for Bettersworth. They also labeled *Conflict and Change* "accurate" and *Mississippi, Yesterday and Today* "biased" and "too hard." In response to the question about which they would select for ninth graders to study, twenty-eight chose Loewen and Sallis, one picked Bettersworth, and one opted for both. Though the circumstances of the survey may have lacked scrupulous scientific objectivity, students who considered both textbooks overwhelmingly chose Loewen and Sallis; that the students were white and in the conservative Delta heartened the authors even more. In a reasonable test, they believed, *Conflict and Change* would prevail.[10]

Loewen and Sallis concentrated even more on the Jackson public schools, because of their proximity but also because success in the capital and largest city's schools could prove vital to achieving state approval. The district initially agreed to test the book in classes in the spring of 1972. Early in the fall of 1971, Loewen, Sallis, James Brown, and Melvyn Leventhal, lawyer for the MHP, met with Brandon Sparkman, the local school superintendent, and his staff. The superintendent had charged a special biracial committee with reading the book and offering criticisms and suggestions. Even before hearing from the committee, the officials told the authors that the manuscript needed revising. They based their opinion on an internal report on *Conflict and Change* by Paul McArdle, the district's social studies coordinator.[11]

McArdle made a thorough assessment of the manuscript textbook along with chapter-by-chapter analyses. In "A Review of *Mississippi Conflict and Change*," he contended that the book, "written from the perspective of the civil rights movement," focused on the "development of crises throughout the state's history." Calling for a broader scope and greater variety of examples, his report pointed to several places that needed to be "reconstructed," and each involved race relations. To balance an opening quotation from James Meredith, for example, he suggested the "various perspectives" of William Faulkner, Eudora Welty, and Margaret Walker. Instead of stressing what McArdle referred to as the "negative concept—that of school integration"—in "The Uses of History," he wanted other reasons for studying history. In addition to blacks' positive contributions and whites' negative roles, he called, rather awkwardly, for examples of "blacks who might have contributed in a negative way to the progress of Mississippi history" and for whites who made positive contributions.[12]

Early chapters impressed McArdle as "very acceptable," "good," "of much interest and important," and "of little controversy." He particularly liked the report that the French first brought slaves to what became Mississippi so that Americans were "not totally responsible" for later racial problems. His major complaint on the coverage of slavery involved its neglect of the "life-style of the average white Mississippian." On the Civil War's background, he objected to its overemphasis on the causal role of slavery that only "incidentally" treated other economic and diplomatic factors, but the chapter on Reconstruction impressed him as "a very balanced presentation." He described succeeding chapters as "a fair representation" and "generally acceptable." In commenting on the coverage of folklore and literature, McArdle objected to the "non-blending of [black and white] cultures" because they did not exist separately and influenced each other. In the twentieth century, McArdle applauded the chapter on civil rights as "a good presentation" but complained that it ignored people working "quietly" outside "the limelight." He also questioned the authors' apparent impatience with the pace of change in race relations.[13]

In his conclusion, acknowledging that Mississippi history "has been taught from a white perspective," McArdle called for a balanced and "blended" history and suggested that "a book that stresses the development of Civil Rights is not necessarily the answer." He especially believed that "the tone of the book should not indicate to the reader that it is a defense of the black man's role." On pedagogical grounds, he claimed *Conflict and Change* failed to consider "the various learning needs of students," their "learning difficulties," and "different learning styles other than reading." He decided that the textbook failed to "meet *all* the students' learning needs on the ninth grade level."[14] Though ultimately negative, the review avoided the venomous and vitriolic tone that might have been expected from a white supremacist only a decade earlier. McArdle's moderate assessment did not completely foreclose all use of *Conflict and Change* in the Jackson schools. A biracial board had apparently advised the superintendent on the textbook's acceptability.

Based on McArdle's report, Loewen and Sallis continued their textbook revisions and renewed their request to test the book in a ninth-grade class. Negotiations with the city schools continued into the spring of 1972, with each side blaming the other for failing to reach an agreement. Superintendent Sparkman expressed his staff's willingness to meet with the authors, but he claimed Loewen and Sallis refused to accept criticism. With irritation he also reported that one of the authors had threatened legal action to force the district to accept the current version of the textbook. Loewen and Sallis denied threatening to sue the city schools and conceded they lacked any grounds for such a lawsuit. "We are seeking your cooperation and consideration," the authors told Sparkman; "we were not threatening you to get it!" They did admit telling McArdle that they would sue the *state* if the book did not gain acceptance by the State Textbook Purchasing Board. To understand the specific complaints they repeated their request for the biracial committee's report, so they could pursue the necessary revisions.[15]

Melvyn Leventhal, an NAACP Legal Defense Fund lawyer in Jackson who represented the MHP, pointed out to Superintendent Sparkman the school system's "untenable" position. Although the school district argued that *Mississippi Conflict and Change* presented an unacceptable biased view that reversed the racial bias in Bettersworth's book, the district had "accepted Bettersworth without complaint." According to Leventhal, the Jackson officials demanded "perfection in the new but continues to use the clearly imperfect old." The lawyer reminded the superintendent "that we have not taken a single step forward in race relations during the entire history of public education in Jackson without the compulsion of politics of integration."[16]

After prolonged negotiations and further revisions, the city agreed to allow one class to test the Loewen and Sallis book. In the spring semester of 1973, Mary Kyle used twenty copies of the draft text in her integrated Bailey Middle School class. Located almost directly across State Street from Millsaps College, the school was just a few blocks from Charles Sallis's home, and his children had attended Bailey and had Kyle as a teacher. The early version of *Conflict and Change* supplemented Bettersworth's book and, for Kyle's students who struggled with reading, the McLemore fifth-grade history. When her students finished their assignments, she encouraged them to look at the Loewen and Sallis book, but fewer than a dozen would even pick it up. According to Kyle, they did respond enthusiastically when she read "Song of Jubilee," reproduced in the chapter on the Civil War. Slaves sang the song as their master ran away and they celebrated emancipation, "the year of jubilee." Otherwise, her students unanimously found the textbook too difficult to read and refused to return to it as she suggested.[17] Though the result of the Bailey Middle School test disappointed Loewen and Sallis, they could still point to the more rigorous other pilot study in Greenville.

Beginning in late 1971, the MHP also sought to obtain feedback and to build support by asking various individuals to comment on parts of the manuscript as it emerged. The always audacious Loewen solicited leading scholars, but Kenneth Stampp, August Meier, and John Hope Franklin demurred, claiming insufficient time. Helpful readers ranged from Lawrence Goodwyn of Duke University to Jackson journalist W. F. (Bill) Minor, from New York writer Milton Meltzer to Brother Egan Hunter of Biloxi's Notre Dame High School. They and others offered sometimes extensive critiques.[18]

Lawrence Goodwyn, a history professor and activist former editor of *The Texas Observer*, hailed *Conflict and Change* as "an extraordinary achievement." Though he appreciated the book's treatment of Reconstruction and other specific events, Goodwyn liked even more the effort to "cause students to think about the causes and meaning of events." He reserved his greatest praise for "the way the book plays the past against the present" by showing parallels, similarities, and continuities over time. Goodwyn specifically mentioned the text's suggestion that students think about their society by comparing Senator James O. Eastland's pro-segregation argument in the 1950s to the effects of the 1927 Mississippi River flood. Goodwyn considered it "a deft way to address the task all good teachers of history are involved in: inducing their students to probe the meaning of their own past." The Duke historian claimed Loewen and Sallis had written by far "the best history of an American state I have ever seen."[19]

Other reviewers offered similarly positive but less extensive comments. After reading only the MHP prospectus, C. Vann Woodward, perhaps perfunctorily, praised it as "an eloquent and persuasive case for a new textbook." Milton Meltzer, author of many historical works for children and young adults, told Loewen that the textbook "could make a superb model for state histories." As relayed by Phillip Martin, the Tribal Chief of the Mississippi Band of Choctaw Indians, a University of Georgia anthropologist called a draft chapter "a great improvement" over the usual textbook coverage, and another expert on Indian history described it as "a vast improvement over present treatments of Mississippi Indians."[20]

All responses to early drafts were not nearly so laudatory. In comments on the first nine chapters, Walter Hurn and Robert Walker, two historians at Jackson State, expressed dissatisfaction with the book's coverage of black history. They wanted more individual blacks in the opening chapter on the uses of history, thought the treatment of Indians no better than Bettersworth's, and objected to the omission of the Indians' slave codes. Hurn and Walker also recommended more coverage of free blacks, slave revolts, and the Mississippi Colonization Society. In the Reconstruction chapter, the Jackson State scholars called for greater attention to black participation in politics and government.[21] When combined with the objections from the Jackson public school officials, the criticisms must have frustrated Loewen and Sallis; their revisionism could not satisfy everyone. Displeasing local black academics must, however, have especially disappointed the authors.

A more balanced yet critical appraisal that also focused on racial topics came from Loewen's Tougaloo colleague John Dittmer, later a major scholar of the Mississippi civil rights movement. Though he approved of the preface and the quotation from James Meredith, Dittmer wisely warned, "But once his name goes into print there you are stuck with it, and I have a hunch that within the next year or so Meredith will stick his foot in his mouth so many times that he will detract from the credibility he obviously shows here." After his initial cautionary comment, Dittmer lauded the first chapter on "The Uses of History" as "refreshing, candid, probably unique. I like your tone." He continued, "You don't patronize the student, but treat him like a person with a brain." According to the worried Dittmer, the first chapter paid unnecessary attention to race, and its excessive, dominating material on race "blotted out the importance of the Why Study History question." While he agreed with everything said in the chapter, Dittmer questioned "whether it needs to be said here" and argued that it made the chapter into a "polemic" and opened Loewen "to the charge of lack of objectivity here." In just the first chapter Loewen appeared to want to correct everything about Bettersworth, and Dittmer suggested removing many of the racial examples from the chapter and spreading them throughout the text. On the later chapter on the civil rights movement, he similarly warned Loewen to make sure that discussion of racial violence "does not run away with the chapter."[22]

In other areas of the text Dittmer also questioned the stress on race. He compared the book's relentless focus on race to what people often said about the demagogue James K. Vardaman that no matter the time, place, or subject, Vardaman always got around to "the nigger question." "So with you," Dittmer told Loewen about an early chapter. In the chapter on the land, for example, he recommended excluding racial material unless it uniquely pertained to a particular section and unless it could not appear elsewhere in the book. To moderate the book's tone, Dittmer also suggested letting racist whites speak for themselves, without the authors "getting editorially (or emotionally) involved." Despite his reservations about parts of the draft, Dittmer thought Loewen and Sallis "may have done the near impossible: Written a readable, truthful high school history text."[23]

A far more stinging attack came from Ken Lawrence, a Mississippi civil rights activist and organizer from Chicago. Though the MHP shared the manuscript with Lawrence but without asking for his comments, he offered his unsolicited evaluation from his avowed Marxist perspective. Lawrence bristled at the text's idea that students ask, "In what region of the country did the author live?" "I can't imagine anything better calculated to reinforce the reactionary xenophobia so prevalent among white Mississippians," fumed Lawrence. It seemed to suggest that someone not from the state could not understand it. After the text encouraged students to be critical of sources, Lawrence protested the hypocrisy of using anonymous sources such as "a" civil rights worker, "a Mississippi writer," or "an" observer. In his most biting comment, he asked, "Or is that the price they have to pay to get your book past the textbook board?" Lawrence also complained that in the text "'Americans,' 'Mississippians,' 'Southerners,' and 'people' are implicitly white, most often male. This can only serve to strengthen white supremacist (and male supremacist) attitudes of your white (and male) readers." In a more general criticism, Lawrence objected to Loewen's "sociological bias, the emphasis on counting people, and things." More references to blacks or women did not make the textbook better than Bettersworth's simply because qualitative differences outweighed quantitative ones. By setting out to write "history as the activities of great men," Lawrence suggested, Loewen and Sallis would not discover many women subjects. He accused them of having a "male supremacist ideology." As examples, he pointed out that the text told whom Eliza Jane Poitevant and Ida Wells Barnett married but did not name the wives of men. He also objected to the omission of Ellen Woodward and Belle Kearney.[24]

Lawrence also identified flaws related to more specific topics. The discussion of slave overseers and drivers, according to Lawrence, had "slaves collaborating in their own oppression." At the same time, the text identified abolitionism and the end of slavery with the North. He argued, "Some of us believe that the massive resistance of the slaves forced the war." Regarding the Civil War, Lawrence disagreed with its characterization as the nation's "most destructive war" and pointed to Hiroshima, Nagasaki, and Vietnam. Disputing the contention that "poor whites [chose] to stay politically powerless rather than ally with blacks" in the late nineteenth century, he reminded Loewen that poor whites did not choose powerlessness but were disfranchised. In the mid-twentieth century, Lawrence claimed that the pulpwood workers' strike in 1971 was a greater turning point than the Neshoba County murders in the summer of 1964. Finally, he complained of "Highbrow biases" in the treatment of the culture and the arts in omitting the Jimmie Rodgers Festival, the State Fair, and the Neshoba County Fair.[25]

In a gracious response, Jim Loewen apologized for not asking for Lawrence's comments and thanked him for his letter. He promised the MHP would consider all of his points. He agreed, for example, to insert "white" as an appropriate modifier, and he accepted the criticism on abolitionists and would address the objections about slave resistance. Though Loewen did not rise to the bait and argue with Lawrence on every point, he did offer some rebuttal. On quantitative measures, Loewen simply disagreed. On the inclusion of women Loewen thought Belle Kearney's "career did kind of deadend into a rather unimportant brand of temperance," and he did not find Woodward sufficiently "compelling" to include. Most defensively, he called Lawrence "unfair" regarding the book's coverage of culture, and he referred to a map that included both Leontyne Price and Howlin' Wolf. He dismissed the Jimmie Rodgers Festival as only a paper organization, the State Fair as about as much a cultural event as a Holiday Inn sign, and the Neshoba County Fair as not as lowbrow as the Mississippi Arts Festival.[26]

Benefitting from the comments of Lawrence, Dittmer, and others, Loewen and Sallis continued to edit and revise their manuscript. While also teaching, they reorganized chapters, added vignettes, and polished prose. After their MHP colleagues departed, Loewen and Sallis assumed the burden of preparing the manuscript for publication, and Loewen continued to spearhead the search for a publisher. At the same time Loewen engaged two other historical causes related to the MHP, and they demonstrated his abundant energy, interest in Mississippi history, and passion for activism. In each he briefly protested actions of the Mississippi Department of Archives and History. Just as the textbook challenged Mississippi's orthodox history, Loewen wanted to widen the crusade against the state's historical establishment.

In 1971, he objected to an article in the *Journal of Mississippi History*, published by the Department of Archives and History and the Mississippi Historical Society. Eugene R. Mechelke, a Minnesota high school teacher, offered "observations on Mississippi's Reconstruction historiography" by examining the traditional interpretation and more recent revisionist views. Loewen found appalling Mechelke's "absurdly and arbitrarily limited" coverage that ignored scholarship since 1965 and failed to consider earlier major revisionist studies by W. E. B. Du Bois, Howard K. Beale, and James McPherson and the work of Vernon Lane Wharton. When Mechelke initially appeared to favor a compromised middle ground between the traditionalists and the revisionists, Loewen denied they were "polar extremes straddling 'the truth'" because the traditionalists engaged in "outright distortion," "innuendo," inadequate research, and "emotional pandering" not found among the revisionists. Mechelke's use of quotation marks around "carpetbagger" and "scalawag" also annoyed Loewen as "negatively-charged nouns of disapproval." Finally, Loewen found "incredible that charges of financial misdealing [by the Reconstruction government] should still be taken seriously." According to Loewen, "The 'failure' of Negroes during Reconstruction has been used to keep blacks passive and whites self-righteous in their maintenance of white supremacy and segregation." He saw Mechelke's essay as largely contributing to the old fashioned view, even if in the end it accepted revisionism.[27]

Loewen submitted to the *Journal of Mississippi History* a reply to Mechelke's article. As a matter of practice, the journal did not accept letters, so the editor, John Gonzales, a professor at the University of Southern Mississippi, suggested that the journal would consider an article by Loewen on the Reconstruction literature. Loewen never wrote such a formal rejoinder. He had plenty to do with his own work and the textbook. He may also have changed his mind after his zeal subsided. A calm, careful rereading of Mechelke's essay might have revealed numerous citations to Du Bois, Beale, and Wharton, might have noticed that quotation marks surrounded "carpetbagger" and "scalawag" only at the start of the article, and might have recognized Mechelke's data-driven, balanced analysis of Reconstruction. Furthermore, the article's first note acknowledged, "This article is concerned with Reconstruction historiography to 1965. Studies since that date are not included."[28]

A second campaign involved the Mississippi Hall of Fame in the Old State Capitol. Operated since 1961 by the Department of Archives and History as a museum, the Old Capitol attracted many school groups every year, and *Conflict and Change* planned to recommend the Old Capitol as an important historic site. The museum's Hall of Fame honored seventy-five Mississippians; it featured plaster busts of many of them. After Bruce Adams helped compile a list of the honorees, Loewen realized that they included no blacks, and he considered the omission a "travesty." Only "blatant racial discrimination" could have excluded U.S. senators Blanche K. Bruce and Hiram Revels, congressman John R. Lynch, and novelist Richard Wright. Though Loewen conceded it was a "minor" issue, he also knew that the neglect "influenced" school children and others "to believe that Mississippi Negroes have never amounted to enough of anything to merit inclusion." To desegregate the Hall of Fame, Loewen proposed a "nuisance lawsuit" against the state, but he soon abandoned the idea.[29]

While considering a lawsuit, Loewen and Sallis continued the search for a publisher. By sending the manuscript to so many scholars and experts, they hoped to elicit leads on publishers in addition to critical comments on the text. The strategy succeeded. Early in the fall of 1971 Loewen sent two chapters on the civil rights movement to Pat Watters and asked for his reactions. During the 1950s and early 1960s, Watters had written extensively about the civil rights movement as a reporter, editor, and columnist for the *Atlanta Journal*, and in 1963 he began a dozen years as director of information for the Southern Regional Council while he continued to travel the South and write on the movement. With Reese Cleghorn, Watters wrote *Climbing Jacob's Ladder: The Arrival of Negroes in Southern Politics* in 1967, and four years later Watters offered his own "reflections on the southern civil rights movement" in *Down to Now*. After reading the two chapters, Watters declared them "excellent—a balanced and fair presentation interestingly presented." Others at SRC had a copy of the full manuscript that Watters also reviewed. Based on his readings, Watters called Verne Moberg, an editor at Pantheon Books who had helped him with *Down to Now*, and urged her to contact Loewen and look at the manuscript. Moberg wrote Loewen that "if you're looking for a publisher, we'd be delighted to consider the book." Loewen immediately sent it to Pantheon.[30]

The head of Pantheon Books, Andre Schiffrin, showed great interest in the textbook, but Pantheon since 1962 was just a small part of Random House. Others within Random House strongly objected—Schiffrin later recalled that they had "violently objected"—to accepting the Mississippi history book because Random House's textbook division, Singer Books, regularly did a strong business in Mississippi. Earlier Singer had rejected the history book because it did not want to offend Mississippi officials by publishing such a controversial, radical book; if state officials did not see the connection, Singer editors believed that their competitors would definitely point it out. Schiffrin especially wanted to publish the textbook, so he appealed to Random House president Robert Bernstein to resolve the differing judgments. At one point

Schiffrin joked with Bernstein that they could issue the book under "Pantheon Books, a Division of D. C. Heath," a major rival in the textbook business. Bernstein received encouragement from his son Peter who was home for the holidays. While a student at Brown University, Peter Bernstein had as part of the Brown-Tougaloo exchange program spent a semester at Tougaloo, where he had taken a class with Jim Loewen. When Robert Bernstein mentioned having a manuscript from someone at Tougaloo, his son praised Loewen and urged his father to publish it. Robert Bernstein, a human rights advocate and publisher of Soviet dissidents, had no doubt about what to do. When Loewen went to New York to participate in the negotiations, he met Schiffrin, Bernstein, and others at Random House-Pantheon. By the end of December 1971, Schiffrin and Pantheon had agreed to publish the book, despite the potentially significant risks to its Mississippi textbook business.[31]

In Andre Schiffrin, the Mississippi History Project had found a remarkably appropriate editor. Born in 1936 in France, Schiffrin had a French mother and Russian father. Secular Jews, they fled the Nazis in 1941 and went to greater New York. In Europe, Schiffrin's father had worked in publishing, and in 1944 he joined New York's Pantheon Books. The family moved into Manhattan, where after 1945 the younger Schiffrin grew up. A socialist and a supporter of Norman Thomas's 1948 presidential candidacy, Andre Schiffrin kept secret his French citizenship because he feared that he might be deported as a radical. After high school Schiffrin entered Yale University, where as a socialist he felt "like a missionary among heathens." When he turned eighteen, he became a naturalized citizen and more comfortably entered student politics. At Yale he helped start a chapter of the Student League for Industrial Democracy (SLID), forerunner of Students for a Democratic Society. Heavily involved in the leftist student group, Schiffrin became in the mid-1950s president of the national organization, which had fewer than one hundred members. He later recalled SLID as a "training ground for marginality." After graduating from Yale with honors in 1957, he attended Cambridge University on a two-year scholarship. In 1959 he enrolled in graduate school at Columbia University and three years later joined Pantheon as an editor.[32]

In 1941 Kurt and Helen Wolff had begun Pantheon Books in their Washington Square apartment in New York City. Kurt Wolff had been a distinguished publisher in Germany before fleeing to the United States. As intellectuals, the Wolffs sought and published serious works, many by European intellectuals. Pantheon published Jacob Burkhardt's late-nineteenth-century lectures at the University of Basel as *Force and Freedom: An Interpretation of History* (1943), Zoe Oldenbourg's historical novel *The World Is Not Enough*

(1948), *The I Ching: Or, Book of Changes* (1950), translated by Richard Wilhelm and Cary F. Baynes, and Boris Pasternak's *Dr. Zhivago* (1957). According to one assessment of its initial eight years, Pantheon had "not issued a single trivial or merely popular title, nor a book chosen primarily because of its income-producing possibilities." Each book on the list was "of unquestionable cultural value, or of decided artistic significance, or a genuine attempt to contribute to the solution of the intellectual and spiritual dilemmas of those early years." Schiffrin's father worked at Pantheon until 1962, when his son joined the prestigious imprint and attempted to continue the tradition established by the Wolffs and his father.[33]

As an editor Andre Schiffrin pursued his long interest in history and began Pantheon's commitment to leftist scholarship, especially radical history. "I started a series of 'anti-textbooks' that brought together the young dissidents in various fields," he later remembered. In 1964 he brought out the first American edition of E. P. Thompson's *The Making of the English Working Class*, a classic in social history, and books by Eric Hobsbawm, Christopher Hill, and George Rude soon followed. In 1965, "based solely on my own reactions and instincts," Schiffrin published Eugene Genovese's Marxist *The Political Economy of Slavery* even though many academic publishers had rejected it. Schiffrin worked also with Staughton Lynd on *Intellectual Origins of American Radicalism* (1968) and with Frances Piven Fox and Richard Cloward on *Regulating the Poor* (1971). At the same time Pantheon's list included many books by Michel Foucault and Noam Chomsky.[34] Publishing radical scholarship gave the editor great pleasure.

Schiffrin took special pride in helping to develop new fields such as black history. In addition to Genovese's work on southern slavery and planters, Schiffrin recruited James McPherson to edit *The Negro's Civil War* (1965). Other books on race and the law published by Schiffrin included Loren Miller's *The Petitioners: The Story of the Supreme Court of the United States and the Negro* (1965) and Leon Friedman's anthology *Southern Justice* on "what happens to the law when it becomes the instrument of only one segment of the society." Under Schiffrin's editorship, Pantheon also gave voice to southern liberals such as Pat Watters and later Leslie Dunbar, the one-time head of the Southern Regional Council.[35]

Schiffrin's political ideology, his concern for dissident historical works and his company's dedication to serious, radical scholarship combined to give *Mississippi: Conflict and Change* a positive reception. Though Pantheon had never published a textbook, Loewen and Sallis's volume seemed entirely compatible with Schiffrin's concept of "anti-textbooks," and he thought its importance demanded publication. As Loewen remembered a few years later, "There seemed to be a real affinity for the book at Pantheon, and more than that, for the nature of the enterprise—a willingness to publish it even if it lost money, because it was a book which needed to be published." After securing a publisher, Loewen and Sallis had to finish the manuscript and work with Pantheon to prepare it for publication. Schiffrin turned the responsibilities for the actual editing of the textbook over to one of his assistants, Milly Daniel.[36]

For the Mississippi History Project, Loewen handled relations with Daniel and Pantheon. Negotiations first concerned details of the contract, such as changing "authors" to "editors." Months later, in September 1972, after receiving advice from Pantheon's legal department, Daniel accepted all Loewen's proposed changes but reported that Pantheon could not supply five hundred free promotional copies and that Loewen and Sallis would have to submit the textbook to the Textbook Purchasing Board because Pantheon would not. At the same time, Daniel finally replied to Loewen's request the previous spring for Daniel's help in cutting the text by 5 to 15 percent to match Bettersworth. Reviewing the revised chapters as they arrived at Pantheon, Daniel offered no suggestions but instead saw places for expansion; she and Schiffrin left cuts to Loewen and Sallis who knew Mississippi history and ninth graders better than the editors did.[37]

Loewen and Daniel also tussled over photographs. To avoid the typical portraits of famous figures, *Conflict and Change* sought many imaginative illustrations. The MHP could not afford to pay for more than 150, and Loewen asked for Pantheon's assistance because he had heard from photo agencies that publishers had a picture budget. Daniel pointed out that the contract did not provide for pictures and that it would not have even if Loewen and Sallis had requested it earlier, and that she could not amend the contract. Though Loewen maintained that cutting back on photographs "would do a disservice to our book's readers," he and Sallis had to decide on pictures "not on the basis of quality or importance but price."[38]

Finishing copyediting, Daniel in late August 1973 questioned grammatical inconsistencies she found in the book and suggested reviewers for the state could use them as an excuse to reject the book. She also expressed her concern about failures to provide sources for quotations that looked "suspicious" and suggested "you made it up" or "you have something to hide." After raising the issues, she left the matters to Loewen and Sallis. Bristling at her allegations, Loewen explained the awkwardness of some citations and the need to suppress others "because they would cause more trouble than they are worth."

Agreeing that others were "too cryptic," he submitted some changes and "absolutely guarantee[d] that we made up *no* quotes!"[39]

After telling Loewen a year earlier that she saw no places to cut, Daniel a few days later called without explanation for a major reduction in the manuscript. The author-editor relationship exploded. Loewen charged that she had "goofed radically on the page count." Claiming that "I am only an author and I'm from pore ole Mississippi but I can count," he provided a detailed analysis of characters per page and total characters both in Bettersworth and in Loewen and Sallis. Daniel, however, had already dismissed any calculations that he might make as amateurish and irrelevant. A frustrated Loewen told her, "Great! I am left with a mandate to cut 200 pages ... and not only will you not hear my counterargument, you won't even share with me the reasoning behind your mandate!" He concluded that he "won't do it" and called the treatment "inhumane." He believed that Pantheon's numbers that called for a one-third reduction were "grotesquely wrong."[40]

In exasperation, Loewen took the dispute to Schiffrin. He complained about "troubles I have relating to Milly." She struck him as "extremely cold" with "a kind of urban arrogance that puts me down and makes me feel I must prove over and over again that I'm not incompetent." Her recent direction to cut the manuscript would produce a book too short for the state to adopt. He reminded Schiffrin that he had repeatedly asked Daniel for advice about cuts and deletions. Now two years after Pantheon received virtually the complete manuscript and after copyediting, she asked for the major cut. And the authors had to complete the new revisions by December 1 for the project to stay on schedule. The "timing of this request," declared Loewen, "shows incompetence." Though he did not want to jeopardize Daniel's job, he asked Schiffrin to "get Milly to read my calculations (and to do so *with the assumption that perhaps I'm not an idiot*)." After November 2 when Daniel left Pantheon and Allen Graubard took over responsibility for *Conflict and Change*, Loewen's fractious relationship with Pantheon settled down. Graubard may have taken special interest in the textbook because he had participated in Mississippi's Freedom Summer.[41]

The MHP met a December 1 deadline for a finished manuscript, but Loewen still pressed about the required cuts. Admitting that some of them "resulted in a stronger, more compact manuscript," he wanted to restore other small bits of text, maps, and illustrations if a new page count revealed room. The top priorities remained producing their revisionist textbook and meeting the Textbook Purchasing Board's deadline. Graubard understood the objectives and told Loewen, "We want to present the whole project in terms of an attempt to break into the textbook 'orthodoxy' that is characteristic of practically all states." As publication, marketing, and publicity became central, Graubard requested a list of places committed to using the book and of prominent people who supported the project. Loewen provided a list of names but admitted that he could not predict sales. With a paperback edition that cost five dollars, he guessed that the state's Catholic schools would use it to teach Mississippi history to 740 students a year and that some public schools would use it. As for college enrollments in Mississippi history courses, he seemed confident of adoptions at Tougaloo College, Millsaps College, Alcorn A&M University, and Jackson State University for a total of 370. He expected serious interest in the book at the University of Mississippi, Mississippi Valley State University, the University of Southern Mississippi, Rust College, and Belhaven College, with total enrollments in Mississippi history of 590, but not at Mississippi State University where Bettersworth taught. Greatly reduced from the unrealistic claims in the book proposal, the numbers would help Pantheon plan the size of the first printing, which the company expected would lose money.[42]

When page proofs arrived in the spring of 1974, Loewen and Sallis spotted in the complex text numerous errors involving typeface, page width, marginal notes, factual errors, and omitted lines. "I realize that these resettings will cost money," Loewen told Graubard, "but surely there is no alternative." With the exceptions of the width of text on several pages, Pantheon corrected the errors. Later, when the final proofs arrived, they found remaining errors but only two that Loewen considered "terrible." One presented in different forms three maps that the textbook wanted students to compare. The textbook also mislabeled photographs of the state's three black congressmen during Reconstruction: "I wish that this had happened to any other batch of photos but this one!" said an embarrassed Loewen. The dust jacket also disappointed the authors. The cover featured seven photographs that all portrayed an old Mississippi tied to a cotton economy and that did not indicate any of the "change" included in the book's title. Loewen found the images "a 'yankee' stereotype" of the state.[43] With everything set for publication in September, Loewen, Sallis, and the MHP could only wait for public reactions to their book.

In the interval Loewen persisted in his bold effort to change Mississippi history. As he anticipated reviews of his own *Conflict and Change*, he attacked a reviewer of another Mississippi history published in 1973. In two volumes of over fifteen hundred pages, *A History of Mississippi* promised comprehensive coverage without attempting to be a textbook. Richard Aubrey McLemore edited the books' topical essays by forty-one authors. Financed partly by the state of Mississippi, edited by the director of the Mississippi Department of Archives and History, and published by the University and College Press of Mississippi, it gave the official, orthodox history. A mature, adult version of Bettersworth's textbook, it presented the closed society's view of the state's history. The prestigious *American Historical Review* asked Harvard University history professor David Herbert Donald to review the books. Donald, a native of Goodman, Mississippi, had graduated from Millsaps College and had won a Pulitzer Prize.[44]

Donald's review appeared in the journal's December 1973 issue. Referring to the "highly factual essays" as "a reference tool" not "an interpretive history," Donald told the *AHR*'s audience that the volumes probably "offer most readers all the information they ever need to know about Mississippi." In Donald's judgment the essays proved "remarkably objective," without excessive state pride, and they testified to the "healthy state of historical scholarship in Mississippi." The first volume up to 1900 impressed Donald as "sounder and more informative" than its successor, even with the "enormous variation in the quality of the chapters." He excoriated J. P. Coleman's account of the 1890 constitutional convention because it "shows how little a former governor and present judge of the United States Circuit Court of Appeals understands either about his state or about history." Donald praised William K. Scarborough's "thoughtful account of Mississippi slavery" and Neil R. McMillen's "admirable account" of the civil rights era.[45]

After acknowledging the McLemore volumes would "be, at least for a generation, a standard work," Donald pointed to three significant flaws. First, they were "essentially a history of white Mississippians." Though "not a racist work" with "slurs upon Negroes," the history contained few references to the black half of the population and little discussion of interracial relations. Donald noted, for example, that neither volume had an index entry for "lynching." Second, he argued that the volumes' narrow internal perspective "neglects the connections between the state and the rest of the nation." Third, according to Donald, the McLemore books failed to explain "what has made Mississippi such a distinctive and peculiar place."[46]

The long review prompted a fierce rejoinder from Loewen. In a letter to the Harvard professor, and in a later shorter one to the journal's editor, Loewen denounced the book as a "disaster . . . vitiated by traditional white racism." As an "outrageous" example, he decried the all-white cast of contributors when good black historians taught within the state and others from the state lived elsewhere. He also castigated Donald's apparent suggestion that a mere omission of slurs against blacks freed the book of racism. Although he agreed with Donald that Judge Coleman had written the worst essay, Loewen argued that McLemore's chapter on higher education came in second. It "ignore[d] almost every major issue, particularly of the past twenty years," for instance racial segregation and academic freedom. "This kind of theft of the past for cover-up or public relations reasons," charged Loewen, "is a crime" because it "denies to all Mississippians a resource for understanding the present." Another "bland" form of racism appeared in McMillen's chapter, which Donald had praised. Though ostensibly on the civil rights movement, it really discussed only "the white reaction to that struggle"; as a result, according to Loewen, "blacks do not act" in McMillen's essay. The chapters on Reconstruction were "similarly disappointing." In a scathing assessment, Loewen said the two chapters on insurance and banking "do not merit comment . . . since it is a disgrace to the historical profession that they exist." For "its white establishment perspective" generally and for specific chapters' "white segregationist perspective," Loewen dismissed the McLemore history.[47]

In his personal letter to Donald, Loewen suggested that the Harvard historian may have joined other "Harvard ideologues . . . as spokesmen of racist reaction." Mischaracterizing the review as "glowing," the sociologist damned it as "a travesty of scholarship." In conclusion he told Donald, "I am sorry that you stooped to such depths as this review." Donald replied to neither the personal letter nor the letter in the *American Historical Review*. But Loewen had made his point. The review proved to Loewen "that we simply cannot expect historical scholarship about Mississippi from older white Mississippians."[48] Respectable scholarship would have to come from blacks or younger people, even one from the North, and even in the form of a ninth-grade history textbook.

When finally published in late September 1974, *Mississippi: Conflict and Change* received a muted public reception, but textbooks rarely garner any attention. Only sales matter. If few took notice, the authors undoubtedly took pride and pleasure in the 368-page book that appeared four and half years after Loewen and Sallis first took on the challenge. A few local bookstores began to sell the book, and a month later friends and supporters staged a book party at the Tougaloo College library. Major national book reviewing forums such as the *New York Times Book Review*, the *Washington Post Book World*, the *New York Review of Books*, and popular magazines ignored the textbook, just as they would any other textbook, especially one designed for the secondary schools in one small state. The book nevertheless received a remarkable number of reviews. The first review appeared in the *New Orleans Times-Picayune*, which had a large circulation in southern Mississippi. Calling it a "splendidly written, handsomely illustrated" book, the review described *Conflict and Change* as "like no other textbook used in American schools today." The reviewer hoped that as "a model of its kind" it would "inspire similar revisions of other state histories" because Loewen and Sallis told things "like they were—and like they are."[49]

In Jackson, a writer for the *Clarion-Ledger* reviewed the book in late October. Bob Casey praised the book's "excellent balance and perspective" and its "highly readable style." With appreciation he noted the "frequent notes and interesting, in-depth sidebars interspersed throughout" the book and the way the writers "build a dialogue with the reader and envelope him in Mississippi's past." In addition to providing an "excellent" and "comprehensive chronicle of events," Loewen and Sallis explained "the social forces that shaped them." Casey also reported that the new revisionist textbook "helps destroy some of the popular myths about Mississippi—'the noble savage,' 'slave loyalty,' 'white supremacy,' and 'New South progress.' It does so," he noted, "by carefully explaining how each myth developed and why it was perpetuated." It also discussed lynching, Jim Crow, attacks by Vardaman and Bilbo, the Citizens' Council, and the Ku Klux Klan. "Page by page," according to the review, "the sorry side of Mississippi's history unfolds." Casey approved how *Conflict and Change* "described the entire tumultuous struggle of an entire race to achieve some semblance of equal rights and opportunities." He carefully noted that, "as ugly as this chapter is to many Mississippians—black and white—today, the editors point out that 'the conflict in the 1960s made possible the changes leading into the 1970s.'"[50] Though not acknowledged by the reviewer, one of the major changes allowed the very positive review of a radical textbook to appear in a newspaper that had just a decade earlier staunchly defended segregation and advocated massive resistance.

Seven months after the book's publication, the *Nation* ran a review by Jason Berry, a white New Orleans political reporter who had served as press secretary to Charles Evers, the brother of slain NAACP leader Medgar Evers, when he ran for governor in 1971. Berry had told the story in *Amazing Grace: With Charles Evers in Mississippi*. After describing Bettersworth's textbook as "an antiquated text that casts black people as happy darkies in a society of benevolent whites," Berry declared that *Conflict and Change* "effectively destroys traditional misrepresentations of history." Calling the narrative "temperate, simple, persuasive," Berry pointed out that the textbook portrayed blacks "less as victims of white people than of a historical tradition, of a mythology that produced fear and violence." The review stressed, "It doesn't gloss over inconsistencies and the things that are wrong, but examines them in a rational way." Berry concluded that Loewen and Sallis had produced "a model of what a state history should be."[51]

Few other reviews of the Loewen and Sallis book appeared. Even scholarly publications paid little attention. The *American Historical Review* ignored it as it did all textbooks, and the *Journal of American History* merely listed it among new books received. In a small unsigned note, the *Journal of Southern History* did recognize it as "a very different type of high school history textbook" because "it presents a very fresh picture of the state's shortcomings as well as its advances." The short description also pointed out its "biracial approach" and "profuse illustrations." A very brief review in *Equity & Excellence in Education* called *Conflict and Change* "a book about real people, past and present," and praised its "uncompromising refusal either to create new myths to replace the old ones or to write off the entire past as mere ancient darkness." Calling the textbook "exciting," the review ended with a question and answer: "But why should the kids have all the fun? Buy a copy and enjoy it yourself."[52]

The *Harvard Education Review* published the most extensive review in a professional journal. Written by Bill Minor, the veteran Mississippi correspondent for the *New Orleans Times-Picayune*, the review declared that "Loewen and Sallis have produced a book of protest. It is a protest against the accumulated indignities to which the Blacks of Mississippi have been subjected by being taught state history which reflected the view that their ancestors were nonpersons. The book is also," Minor continued, "a protest against blandness and sterility in the state's educational system." He applauded the clarification of "the myths of Reconstruction," the exposure of slavery's "horrors," the presentation of "the case of racial demagoguery against the [Ross] Barnetts, [Theodore] Bilbos and [James K.] Vardamans." Minor also appreciated the warranted attention to black leaders and black contributions to the arts, and he saluted its coverage of the civil rights movement. Though the longtime reporter criticized omission of the coastal area's fishing industry and shipyards and of the NASA facility, he liked the book's "interesting, provocative questions posed to students." In a "valuable contribution," according to Minor, Loewen and Sallis had produced "a fresh, new history book that forces public awareness of the white bias that has permeated the teaching materials used in Mississippi's public system."[53]

More than a year later a long and sophisticated review by Robert Coles appeared in the *Virginia Quarterly Review*. Trained as a child psychiatrist, Coles served in the late 1950s at Keesler Air Force base in Biloxi and later lived in

New Orleans before becoming a professor at Harvard University. His books and articles included many on southern race relations and the civil rights movement, and he received a Pulitzer Prize in 1973 for his *Children of Crisis*, a series on how children cope with change. In Coles's view, Loewen and Sallis wrote "as populist revisionists with a strong sociological bias" and sought to be "unquestionably provocative" with their "blunt cultural and economic analysis." The authors wanted "their young readers to become critical, skeptical, and it can be said, class-conscious." For Coles, *Conflict and Change* produced "a sense of sadness that so many have been hurt, betrayed, excluded, for so long in the interests of (really) a handful." Tax policies, according to Loewen and Sallis, "favored the rich more than the poor. Care for the poor, the sick, and the blind was maintained at very low levels." As a result, reading the book produced for Robert Coles "a growing spirit of indignation."[54]

Coles argued that Loewen and Sallis's "account becomes even more pointed, lucid and sometimes unnerving" as it approached the present. The textbook's discussion of Fannie Lou Hamer, Robert Moses, and Richard Wright would, Coles predicted, have a profound effect on student readers who "are going to be stirred up alright, and maybe made rather suspicious of and angry at . . . people who consider things as they are just fine." And he included white students "who have been lied to, cheated of an honest inquiry into their own past." The Harvard professor saw the textbook as "a vigorous attempt (done without condescension or vengefulness, but with considerable insistence) to encourage a new way of thinking" among students. "Beyond any doubt," he concluded, "the book is disruptive; it will cause pain, sorrow, anger, and shame" among the state's white leaders. As a result of the textbook, Coles predicted, the next generation would be "less gullible" and "not readily conned by the old rhetoric." He endorsed Loewen and Sallis's "candid, undisguised, and unremitting assault" on established "authority and interests."[55]

Three professional historians also reviewed the book, one in an obscure newsletter, one in an activist publication, and one in a minor scholarly journal. John Anthony Scott taught half-time at both the Ethical Culture School in New York City and at Rutgers University law school. In the December 1974 newsletter of the Committee on History in the Classroom, Scott called *Conflict and Change*'s interdisciplinary approach a "pioneer contribution to American Studies." He wrote, "It is precisely the humanity of its contents that enables it to appeal to young people in general and to transcend the conventional pedagogical boxes." According to Scott, Loewen and Sallis had effectively used Mississippi "as a microcosm which reveals, in its own inimitable way, the essence of national experience." Their textbook provided a "model that points toward new ways of turning history to the service of the people."[56]

The longest, most thorough assessment of *Conflict and Change* appeared in a 1977 review published by the Racism/Sexism Resource Center in New York. In the form of a study guide or lesson plan, Robert B. Moore directly compared the textbook to Bettersworth's *Your Mississippi* in ten pages of narrative analysis, followed by eight pages of sixteen pairs of quotations presented in parallel columns. The last and shortest compared the texts' treatments of the integration of the Mississippi Highway Patrol. Bettersworth said, "[William] Waller was the first governor since Reconstruction to make it a practice to appoint blacks to office. One of his first moves was to desegregate the Highway Patrol." Loewen and Sallis, said, "Owing to a 1971 court order, the highway patrol finally hired three blacks as patrolmen. Similar lawsuits hung over the Jackson fire department and several other state and local agencies." Moore asked, "What information does each quote present? Leave out? What differing impressions result?"[57]

Moore compared the two books' language, format, and illustrations; their coverages of many subjects involving race and gender; and their treatments of particular time periods. In every instance *Conflict and Change* surpassed *Your Mississippi*. For example, while Bettersworth's discussion of native Americans used "Stereotypes, Eurocentric viewpoints and loaded, racist language," Moore found that *Conflict and Change* "gives a fuller description of Native American societies, attempts to present them as 'legitimate' on their own—rather than European—terms, and more honestly portrays the 'destruction' caused by European invaders." Loewen and Sallis also presented a "diversity of white Mississippians" while, according to Moore, Bettersworth's "white people are for the most part a generalized mass." *Conflict and Change's* plentiful illustrations "greatly add to the readers [*sic*] understanding and appreciation," while Bettersworth's illustrations tended "to view Mississippi through white eyes, wearing rose-colored glasses."[58]

Aware of the controversy over *Conflict and Change*, Moore highlighted its strengths while denigrating Bettersworth's book. *Your Mississippi*, according to Moore, "overtly and covertly reinforces white chauvinism and racism through omission, distortion and falsification of reality." He said it would be a useful supplementary text in Mississippi history "just as *Mein Kampf* would be useful in a course on German history." He called it "mythologized history." On the other hand, *Conflict and Change* provided "an analysis of and abundant information about a complex and varied region of the U.S." Calling it a "progressive" textbook, Moore hailed its presentation of "multiracial/multicultural concerns and experiences and its honest description of white racism." Its "positive and, in many ways, unique characteristics" made Loewen and Sallis's book "an advanced model" textbook for writers and publishers to "emulate." Moore declared it "far superior in format and content to all history textbooks we have seen."[59]

Two years after Moore's extended analysis and more than four years after the book's publication, another professional historian, Jimmie Lee Franklin, offered his assessment of *Conflict and Change* in the *Red River Valley Historical Review*. Franklin, a graduate of Jackson State University who taught at Eastern Illinois University, agreed with others that it "could serve as a model for the writing of state history texts." Franklin recognized that it "displays an informed scholarship and a sensitivity to the real meaning of cultural pluralism which critics of American history texts have demanded for over a decade." He judged it "not ideologically obtuse" or "overbearing" but persuasive because the textbook's "singular mission is to impart knowledge and to foster critical thought, not the promotion of blind acceptance of tradition or easy acquiescence to any grand utopian scheme." Though "not excessively preoccupied with racial conflict," it did record the "hideousness of those brutal acts which accompanied social and political changes." The Moscow, Mississippi, native conceded that Loewen and Sallis did "not present a beautiful or humane picture" of "a political system [that] must be sustained through murder." In its coverage of recent events Franklin found "scholarly craftsmanship and judiciousness which are the hallmarks of the profession."[60]

The positive reception of *Conflict and Change* reached a high point in January 1976 when the Southern Regional Council presented the textbook its Lillian Smith award. Started in 1968 two years after Smith's death, the award commemorated the controversial writer and social critic's advocacy of racial equality and social justice. The honor recognized books of literary merit, moral vision, and honesty in addressing the people, problems, and promise of the South. Previous winners for non-fiction included prominent scholars George B. Tindall, Dan T. Carter, Paul M. Gaston, Robert Coles, and C. Vann Woodward. For the 1976 award, prime contenders included Theodore Rosengarten's *All God's Dangers: The Life of Nate Shaw* and Eugene D. Genovese's *Roll, Jordan, Roll: The World the Slaves Made*. Each of them received major front-page reviews in the *New York Times Book Review* and extensive attention in the popular press. In *All God's Dangers* Rosengarten recorded Nate Shaw's reminiscences as a black sharecropper in Alabama. Calling it an autobiography of "unsurpassing greatness," the *New York Times* compared it to the work of William Faulkner and to Homer's *Odysseus. Roll, Jordan, Roll*, also published by Pantheon, addressed all aspects of antebellum slavery, especially slave culture. Reviewers hailed Genovese's study of slavery as "monumental" and "without modern peer" as a narrative and analysis of the African-American community.[61]

Despite the prominence of the competition, judges for the Southern Regional Council chose *Conflict and Change* because it "best express[ed] the ideals, spirit and realistic faith in the region for which Ms. Smith stood." Paul Gaston, historian at the University of Virginia and an early reader and supporter of the textbook, served as chairman of the selection committee. In making the presentation at an SRC meeting in Atlanta early in 1976, Gaston's description of it as "a subversive book" highlighted the textbook's activist appeal that resembled Lillian Smith's own writing.[62]

However gratifying Jim Loewen and Charles Sallis may have found the positive reviews and the recognition brought by the Lillian Smith Award, everyone connected to the Mississippi History Project understood that the only reception that really mattered would come from the State Textbook Purchasing Board. Its decision would determine if districts could adopt, teachers use, and students read the book in the state's high school classrooms. For *Conflict and Change* to have a "subversive" effect, Loewen and Sallis next sought to gain the board's essential approval.

CHAPTER SEVEN

Controversy

Rejection by the Textbook Purchasing Board

"Good news," Jim Loewen proclaimed to Pantheon in September 1974. "Our rating committee looks OK. It includes two black males, whom we hope we can count on, and a white female whom Dr. Sallis knows personally and who read and used our book two years ago." With just two books seeking approval, he knew that *Mississippi: Conflict and Change* needed only a majority to give it an acceptable rating, even if the rating committee gave its top ranking to Bettersworth's textbook. "I honestly think we'll probably get a majority giving us a *first*, over Bettersworth," he predicted. Though the Textbook Purchasing Board would make the final decision and had the authority to reject their book despite the committee's recommendations, Loewen assumed the board "may rubber-stamp" the committee's recommendation. In any case, he believed that the board would "more likely" approve the adoption than reject it. The success of Loewen and Sallis's efforts—working with students and colleagues on the textbook, obtaining grant support from the Southern Education Foundation, and finding their publisher in Pantheon—all of it depended on the decisions by the rating committee and the State Textbook Purchasing Board. After interviewing Sallis, the Millsaps student newspaper predicted the textbook would "pass the test with relative ease."[1] Loewen and Sallis did not anticipate the impending controversy.

To win the state's approval, *Conflict and Change* had to endure the State Textbook Purchasing Board's well-developed and straightforward process for evaluating textbooks. Without the board's acceptance, individual school districts could not use state funds to purchase the book, and few, if any, had sufficient local funds to spend on a ninth-grade history book. The board, created by legislation in 1940, consisted of the governor, the state superintendent of education, and one gubernatorial appointee from each of the state's three supreme court electoral districts. Rating committees in the various subject areas advised the board. Legislation in 1959 provided that the state superintendent of education appoint three members and the governor name four to each rating committee. In 1974 Governor William Waller and Superintendent Garvin H. Johnston handled the appointive responsibilities. According to the law, a superintendent's appointee had to "be a competent teacher or supervisor of instruction professionally trained" in the field, while the governor's only had to be an individual "he deems competent to participate in the appraisal of books." Each year in a three-year cycle, the board, with the advice of the rating committees, adopted one-third of the state's schoolbooks. Not only Mississippi history textbooks came up for consideration and approval in 1974. Eight separate rating committees examined books pertaining to art; business education; homemaking; music; social studies, writing, career awareness, and humanities (grades 1–6); social studies, career awareness, and humanities (grades 7–9); social studies and humanities (grades 10–12); and special education (ages 8–21). The rating committees would examine 1,129 books for 130 different courses.[2]

The board and its rating committees followed a strict schedule. In July the board advertised for proposals and bids in the relevant fields, and interested publishers submitted their proposals by August 16. The governor and superintendent appointed the rating committees before August 28 when they had their first and only meeting, which the board and the publishers' representatives also attended. The 1974 meeting took place at ten o'clock Tuesday morning in the Woolfolk State Office Building auditorium across from the state capitol in downtown Jackson.[3]

After an opening invocation, four uniformed Boy Scouts presented national and state flags, a men's chorus sang the national anthem, and scouts led the Pledge of Allegiance. The secretary of state then administered the oath of office to all the rating committees. In a surprise appearance, Governor Waller addressed the group. Two years before he had told the rating committees, "You were not selected to speak for a tradition of 20 years ago." Encouraging the rating committees, Waller declared, "You are not required to follow anything done in the past." After the superintendent spoke briefly, he introduced individually each member of the rating committees. The publishers' representatives were introduced as a group. At the end of the meeting, the committee members divided into three geographical groups to schedule meetings with the publishers.[4]

To guard against fraud, the board required each publisher to submit a signed statement certifying the physical qualities of each book. The document detailed the weight of the paper used in the book and the sizes of the pages and the length of the book. A publisher also had to guarantee the quality of the book's binding, whether sewn, stitched, or bound with wire. For hardcover texts, the company had to warrant the cover's thickness and material, and it had to describe the cover's illustrations (e.g., preprinted, stamped, or lithographed). The publisher also had to guarantee that the actual books supplied to the state under a contract would meet the state's demands just as the submitted samples did.[5]

Promptly after the August 28 meeting, each publisher sent a sample copy of its proposed textbooks to every member of the relevant rating committee and to each member of the board, plus three to the board's executive secretary. Six weeks later the publishers had to submit their final formal bids to the board. A publisher's bid to the board also had to meet exact specifications. In addition to a certified or cashier's check for two hundred dollars as a deposit, each bid had to provide the lowest net wholesale price and guarantee books conformed to the board's "Minimum Manufacturing Standards and Specifications." Between the August meeting and the submission of bids, one of a publisher's two allowed representatives could visit each individual rating committee member, but the board strictly regulated the meetings. A publisher's emissary could telephone a rating committee member to arrange a meeting, but the call could not exceed ten minutes. The one and only meeting could last no more than twenty minutes, unless the publisher had more than one book before the rating committee, but in no case could the meeting go beyond fifty minutes.[6]

To make the preliminary decision regarding Mississippi history textbooks, the governor and superintendent of education named a diverse rating committee of four men and three women, two blacks and five whites. Their residences spanned the state from Senatobia in the north to Ocean Springs on the coast and from Greenville in the Delta along the Mississippi River to Hattiesburg in the Piney Woods. Three came from the middle of the state in Jackson and Forest. They had undergraduate degrees from six Mississippi colleges and several junior colleges. Each had worked for years in the state's public schools, and combined they had taught in more than a dozen widely dispersed school districts.

The three white female members, all born in the 1920s, brought the most educational experience to the rating committee. Fifty-four-year-old Virginia Wilkins McElhaney, though a native of Ellisville, had grown up in Jackson where she attended Central High School. With undergraduate and master's degrees in education from the University of Southern Mississippi, she had taught at Sacred Heart Catholic School in Hattiesburg and for nearly twenty years in the Hattiesburg public schools. For nine of the years she had taught Mississippi history. In the mid-1960s McElhaney had served on the rating committee for writing and social studies at the elementary level.[7]

The next oldest and most experienced teacher on the rating committee, Mary M. Kyle, was born in Georgetown in 1921 and had more than thirty years of classroom experience. With a bachelor's degree in social studies and a master's degree in history from George Peabody College, Kyle had done additional graduate work at the University of Mississippi, Mississippi State University, and Mississippi College. In 1941 she started her teaching career in Lawrence County, later worked for Copiah-Lincoln Junior College, and taught in public schools in Winona and Hazlehurst before beginning twenty-four years at Jackson's Bailey Junior High School, interrupted only by a brief stint at Rowan Junior High School as a result of school desegregation. She had often taught Mississippi history and had used the McLemores' two texts in the seventh- and ninth-grade courses. In 1973 Kyle had also had her ninth-grade students try a preliminary version of *Conflict and Change*.[8]

Evelyn Harvey Wilder started teaching in 1950 at Newton High School. After short stints in Silver, Grenada, and Greenville, she moved to Jackson in the late 1950s. She taught in two Jackson public high schools before founding the English department at Jackson Preparatory School in 1970. Even though the private segregationist school did not receive state-owned textbooks, Wilder agreed to serve on the rating committee for the state's schools. In 1972 she had served on a rating committee in language arts for the high school. Except for a few years that included classes in speech and Spanish, Wilder had always taught high school English, never history.[9]

Typical of the era, the two white men on the committee had administrative experience in addition to classroom experience. Forty-two-year-old John Marion Turnipseed had earned his undergraduate degree in elementary education from Delta State College. In Missouri from 1956 to 1965, he taught fourth and fifth grades and special education before returning to Mississippi. Two years later Turnipseed received a master's degree in elementary administration. For nine years he had served in several Delta school districts (Sunflower, Clarksdale, Shaw, and Drew) as a principal and coordinator for Title I under the Elementary and Secondary School Act. In 1974 he worked as an elementary school principal in Greenville. Turnipseed had taught sixth-grade Mississippi history for one year in the Sunflower schools.[10]

Since 1963, Howard E. Railes had worked as teacher, coach, and guidance counselor in the Coldwater and Senatobia public schools in northwest Mississippi's Tate County. He earned an undergraduate social studies degree and later received a master's in education in guidance and counseling, both from the University of Southern Mississippi. After 1970 he served as supervisor of instruction for Tate County. Although Railes had taught Mississippi history during his nine weeks of practice teaching, he never taught it as a full-time teacher.[11]

The rating committee's two youngest members were black men, James E. Wash and Benjamin Berry Burney Jr. A social studies graduate from Alcorn A&M College, Wash had pursued some graduate study. He had always lived in Forest, but he taught in the Union public schools in adjacent Newton County. For two years Wash had also worked in school administration. Born in 1943, Benjamin Burney was the youngest committee member. After earning a bachelor's degree in education from Jackson State College, he went to work on the Gulf coast in the Jackson County's Davis Chapel Elementary School and later at East Central High School. He taught physical education, social studies, and world history. He had never taught Mississippi history and preferred to teach U.S. history. With only nine years of teaching experience, Burney had the least classroom experience of the rating committee members.[12]

W. A. Matthews, the executive secretary of the Textbook Purchasing Board, directed the rating committees. After graduating from high school in Meridian in 1946, Matthews attended Anderson College, a Church of God school in Anderson, Indiana. In 1950 he received his undergraduate degree in social studies. After three years as a social studies teacher at Stringer High School in Jasper County, Matthews moved to Jackson's Central High School to teach social studies. In 1955 he earned a master's degree in secondary education and later completed studies to qualify for a license in counseling and school administration. At Central High he served five years as a counselor and four years as an assistant principal. Matthews was principal of Pass Christian High School on the Gulf Coast before the Textbook Purchasing Board, on the recommendation of Governor William Waller, hired him in 1972 as its executive secretary. As one of his main responsibilities he coordinated the yearly evaluation and adoption of textbooks.[13]

Though called a rating "committee," the seven individuals never functioned as a unit. They never convened as a committee, and they did not have a leader or chair. They did not discuss the textbooks or debate their strengths and weaknesses, and they did not communicate with each other. They did not even know each other. Operating as an isolated expert adviser to the Textbook Purchasing Board, each received books from publishers and met alone with publishers' representatives. Individually they made their evaluations and submitted their assessments.[14]

The seven members of the rating committee charged with choosing books for ninth-grade Mississippi history also had to select texts for seventh-grade world history; for eighth-grade U.S. history; for ninth-grade classes in civics, Mississippi government, and career exploration; and for humanities courses for each of the three junior high grades. Their enormous assignments involved scores of textbooks with thousands of pages. To guide all of their work, the Textbook Purchasing Board supplied general "Suggested Criteria for Textbook Selection" and more specific criteria for the rating committee considering junior high school social studies and humanities books, including Mississippi history books. Matthews, the board's executive secretary, drew on other states' ideas in preparing the recommendations, and he provided them to the publishers as well as to the rating committees. Though he considered them suggestive and not binding, inexperienced committee members facing piles of books undoubtedly relied heavily on Matthews's proposals for guidance.[15]

Matthews began with a grand declaration that textbooks "should arouse curiosity and interest, should stimulate thinking, should promote the exercise of independent judgment," but he offered no rubric for measuring the characteristics or for comparing books. Sixteen more specific suggested criteria ranged from the author's qualifications of "training and experience in the field" to the book's format by "size of type, spacing, and margins." Any approved book, of course, had to meet the basic manufacturing standards and the state's statutory requirements for textbooks. One suggestion called attention to the suitability of vocabulary and sentence structure without any standards for measurement. Another expressed the need for the customary table of contents, preface, glossary, bibliography, and index. Raters should also consider the functions of maps, photographs, graphs, charts, and other illustrative materials. In a more difficult challenge for a secondary school teacher, the criteria called for "accurate, valid, and up-to-date content" presented in a way "consistent with the valid findings of recent research," and for study questions that would "stimulate original thinking." At the same time, religion should be presented "objectively and forthrightly," and "all ethnic groups at different socioeconomic levels [should] receive their fair and equitable treatment." Finally, the suggestions declared, "When more than one text is recommended for adoption in a curricular area, different approaches to content, different sequences of content, and different reading levels should be considered with a view toward adopting textbooks for students with varying abilities."[16]

As Matthews did for every course, he adapted the broad criteria to five specifically for Mississippi history textbooks. According to the board secretary, the rating committee should make sure the textbooks understood the special "geographic, social, political and cultural development of Mississippi and its people." A "topical approach," Matthews believed, would best convey to the student the "rich inheritance from the past and the need for participation in the present." With a list of the broad topics, Matthews explained that a textbook in Mississippi history should cover the state's geography, the colonial era, state governmental development, the state's economic institutions and growth, Mississippi's "social development and cultural institutions," and the state's people and their "contributions to America." The preferred "major emphases" lacked the specificity of the more general criteria for all books in that they did not mention ethnic groups or socioeconomic classes. After reminding the rating committee that the book aimed at a ninth-grade audience, Matthews declared a publisher had to make available a free "hard back" teacher's manual for each twenty-five books sold.[17]

When the State Textbook Purchasing Board sent rating sheets to the committee members, Matthews, who never lacked lists, provided additional directions. For the board he provided points that "need your careful consideration" in preparing reports on the books under consideration. Publishers' representatives could not, he reminded the committee members, visit them after October 18, which left five days uninterrupted by lobbying efforts. Calling for a completed evaluation form for each book, he urged them to select carefully only books "*suitable for the areas or subject in which they are proposed.*" Each rater could recommend "one to eight—or none—in each area." Matthews pointed out that in some instances a book "may be excellent but not appropriate for the area proposed." Alternates could be chosen for "the slow learner because of its reading level" but not for the "average or above student or [as] supplementary material." Finally, he directed, "Remember that these books shall become one-third of the knowledge diet of the boys and girls of Mississippi for the next six years. Will your selections give them a balance for your portion of the diet?" The board wanted to receive all evaluations by October 23, 1974.[18]

Despite the board's detailed instructions, rating committee members had to make individual judgments about each textbook's quality and suitability, about its role, as Matthews said, in a balanced knowledge diet. For books outside a rater's expertise, assessments derived necessarily from something other than deep knowledge of the subject; few would have expertise in career development, civics, world history, American history, and Mississippi history. As a result, what made a book suitable or stimulating often remained a very personal decision. In Mississippi, as in states across the country, each appraiser necessarily applied subjective, often unstated, sometimes even subconscious standards, in addition to the formal and official guidelines. Particularly in the humanities and social sciences, for example, a textbook involved not just facts and formulas but interpretations and emphases. A book that shared the values, outlook, and approach of a rating committee member might have quite naturally received a more positive evaluation than one that contradicted the evaluator's views.

As an experienced educator, each selection committee member had also likely developed views or ideas about the role of education in Mississippi society. Under the "closed society," which had not yet fully opened by the 1970s, the public schools continued to reflect the prevailing conservative orthodoxy in politics, economics, government, and especially race relations, with white supremacy a dominant force. In defending the status quo, the rating committee member discovered, or merely quickly sensed, whether a textbook's ideology met the needs of the state's schools. In making the decision, the rating committees necessarily could work only with the books offered to them by publishers.[19]

More experienced with the approval system than the temporary rating committees, publishers tried to work the process to their advantage. After meeting the basic, objective publishing standards, they crafted books to meet the reviewers' expectations and preferences. They routinely aimed to produce safe texts that avoided controversies, blunted conflicting ideas, and supported continuity. When a publisher could not evade a difficult topic, the textbook sought to conform to the evaluators' prejudices. Schools generally resisted change, and publishers wanted to avoid costly investments in developing and testing innovative new textbooks. As a result of the public's lack of interest in schoolbooks, according to one critic, textbooks "receive less public criticism than any other form of writing." Publishers also realized that in the selection process the substance of a typically bland textbook usually held less importance than other peripheral factors.[20]

With so many books to evaluate, each textbook could hardly receive a thorough examination by every committee member. As one expert concluded, "Sales are influenced more by adoption committee's impressions than by facts. These impressions are usually formed in a minuscule time span." Even a book's elaborate design or a publisher's "catchy slogan" could make a difference. Often the key to an adoption appeared in the person of the publisher's local salesman who presented a "familiar face" to the selection committee, and the local representative knew from experience what would sell in his area and how to present it. If, according to one report, "The three magic words in selling a textbook are 'easy—new—free.' In that order," the savvy salesman knew how to apply the magic to the local circumstances. Editors worked hard to develop products that their salesmen could use to meet the preferences of adoption committees because they sought corporate profits, not educational reform. Evidence of the publisher's stress on marketability more than intellectual content appeared in the important role of the salesman rather than the textbook author in meeting with rating committee members.[21]

When Mississippi rating committee members evaluated textbooks, they employed an evaluation form and a rating report furnished by the Textbook Purchasing Board. The form used a combination of a checklist or scorecard and several open-ended, more subjective tasks. First, the form required the rater to assess the textbook's "ability level" as high, average, or low. The choices appeared on one line with four blanks, one before and after each option; a check could ambiguously have applied to either the ranking that came before or after the mark. Next, the form asked the evaluator to use a five-point scale (from 5 [excellent] to 1 [very low] or "not applicable") to grade each textbook on five suggested criteria.[22]

Though vaguely worded, each category paralleled the suggested criteria for books in social studies and the humanities, particularly in Mississippi history. The first simply dealt with the "special nature of submission," that is, whether the book pertained directly to the required course topic. Second, the "desired [topical] approach of content" referred to the approach sought by the board; the directions apparently disallowed any other design. Next, the form called for a determination whether the book covered the "major emphasis" expected in Mississippi history, such as the colonial era, the formation and growth of state government, and economic development. Fourth, the rater judged a book's appropriateness for the ninth grade. Last, the form wanted to ensure the availability of a good and free teacher's manual. The numerical ratings for the five topics made the decisions appear objective, but each called for a very impressionistic judgment, which the rater had to translate into a numerical score for each book.[23]

After the five-part checklist, three open-ended assignments sought "specific objections to the submission." The first asked the evaluator to identify, by "page and line if applicable," any "content considered objectionable." Though the instruction left for the respondent to decide what made something objectionable, use of "objectionable" seemed to assume that the reader might take some personal offense at the book or have an emotional reaction more than an academic or intellectual critique. Second, the form called for the committee member to speculate about "the effect that the objectionable content" might have on ninth grade students. Last, for factual errors found in the text, the board requested sources that provided accurate information. The form provided only three lines for each response.[24]

By structuring the rating committee member's consideration of a book, the evaluation form provided helpful preparation and background for the rating committee report itself, but the directions made no explicit connection between the two documents. On a separate sheet, the report form listed all the books under consideration in a subject area and asked for each individual to rank the books in priority order from first through eighth. The directions added, "If sufficient information is available," but the form did not explain if sufficient material referred to the number of books, the information about a book, or the quality of a book. The reporting form also did not indicate how an evaluator could reject a book as unacceptable. It also did not call for any discussion of the books or any explanation for the rater's rankings.[25]

The seven members of the committee considering ninth-grade Mississippi history books completed their work and submitted their reports by the October 23 deadline. On the summary evaluation form Virginia McElhaney rated Bettersworth's *Your Mississippi* "excellent" on all five criteria and judged its ability level as average and offered no objections to it. For *Conflict and Change,* she considered its ability level high and marked all five criteria as "not applicable." Although she pointed out no specific objections to the book's content, McElhaney did comment, "I do not feel that the ideas concentrated on in this text are expressed in the terms of the junior high student. Perhaps for college level and mature adult." Without identifying the inappropriate ideas, she did not explain what was unsuitable for less mature junior high students. She further stated, "I do not feel that the overall content presents a true picture of the history of Miss. in terms of the course pre-requisites." In her overall ranking, McElhaney awarded Bettersworth's text first place and declined to rank Loewen and Sallis's book.[26]

Mary Kyle also gave the top place to Bettersworth's *Your Mississippi* and ignored *Conflict and Change.* She also judged the ability levels average and high respectively. Like McElhaney, Kyle gave Bettersworth's book all fives and refrained from grading Loewen and Sallis, but she added no critical comments on the latter. In fact, she wrote no words of evaluation on her two forms. Evelyn Wilder also judged *Your Mississippi* the better book and did not rank its new competitor. She differed from her two women colleagues by calling the ability level of each book average. For the five criteria, she gave Bettersworth all above average marks while Loewen and Sallis received an unexplained "not applicable."[27]

John Turnipseed joined the three women in giving Bettersworth an overall number one rating and in leaving the space beside Loewen and Sallis blank. In Turnipseed's opinion *Your Mississippi* had an average ability level, and on the five criteria he checked two excellent and three above average. He made no other additional comment on Bettersworth's book. On the Summary Evaluation Form for *Conflict and Change*, Turnipseed did not even bother to check the ability level or to fill in the blanks asking for the course title and the publisher, or to mark the five criteria on the 1–5 scale. In his only comment, written in big bold letters, he declared, "It is my professional opinion that this book is *'unsuitable'* for classroom use, therefore I cannot recommend it in any manner."[28]

In the only typed report, Howard Railes labeled the ability level in *Your Mississippi* "high" and considered it excellent or above average on the five criteria for evaluation. For *Conflict and Change*, he provided no judgment of the ability level or on the five criteria. In response to the three open-ended assignments, however, he provided the most thorough, if still brief, explanations. He said that he objected to "Page 96—Last Paragraph" in a section on slave "Discipline." The challenged paragraph said,

> When the slaveowner or overseer felt that a slave had done wrong, he sometimes punished the offender severely—usually with a whipping. One slave recalled a whipping that he had witnessed: "I saw old Master get mad at Truman, and he buckled him down across a barrel and whipped him until he cut the blood out of him, and then he rubbed salt and pepper in the raw places. It looked like Truman would die, it hurt so bad."

Railes also took offense at "Page 178—Picture at the bottom of the page" where a caption described "A Mississippi lynching, captured by the camera." The photograph depicted a crowd of twenty whites—all apparently men in coats and ties except for one woman and a youngster—standing around as a black corpse burned. Under the next subject on the effects of the objectionable content, Railes continued, "This is only two examples of many in the book. Continuous coverage of isolated incidents of mis-treatment of slaves and blacks by whites could easily lead the reader to believe that all slaves and blacks were treated in the same manner."

In his overall rating, Railes judged Bettersworth's book the better and refused to put a number beside *Conflict and Change*. Instead Railes placed an asterisk beside the title of Loewen and Sallis's book, and a note below explained, "I feel that this book contains too many controversial issues to fit properly into the curriculum of schools in Mississippi."[29]

James Wash, one of the committee's two black members, found the two textbooks on the same average ability level. While he judged *Your Mississippi* above average on all criteria except for excellent on its approach to the content, Wash found *Conflict and Change* above average except for only average on its coverage of the subject and on its teacher's manual. In response to the evaluation form's query about objectionable content, Wash reported, "On page 178 the topic concerning lynching should not be mentioned." In explaining the effect of the lynching material, he suggested, "I think the 9th grade black student would probably resent hearing about the lynching topic." As a result of his reservations, Wash gave Bettersworth's book the number one rating, but unlike all of his white fellow committee members, he awarded Loewen and Sallis's text the second place.[30]

Conflict and Change received its most positive appraisal from the committee's other black member and its youngest member, Benjamin Burney. The two textbooks were written on the same ability level, according to Burney, and he found each acceptable. Though Loewen and Sallis's teacher's manual received his worst rating of very low, he considered the textbook's topical approach excellent and on the other criteria gave the textbook average or above average marks. Wash rated Bettersworth's coverage excellent but on the other criteria awarded it average or below average grades. In his final report, *Conflict and Change* received the number one rating and Bettersworth came in second. Wash made no narrative comments about either book.[31]

At the regularly scheduled meeting on November 4, 1974, the State Textbook Purchasing Board considered the reports from the rating committees. Each committee could rate eight books from which the board could select five. The board unanimously adopted a proposal that the "top five rated books by the rating committees be accepted unless found not to be acceptable." With five abstentions and only two votes accepting *Conflict and Change* the unusual action of the social studies rating committee may have appeared ambiguous because a majority neither approved nor disapproved the book. To clarify the adoption, the board approved unanimously a proposal "to accept only Steck-Vaughn's book, [Bettersworth's] *Your Mississippi*, in Mississippi history." The board rejected Loewen and Sallis's book.[32]

Loewen and Sallis's book had met the fate that had concerned the authors from the beginning. In their original proposal, the authors expressed confidence that "we can persuade or force [by a lawsuit] the Mississippi Textbook Purchasing Committee to approve these texts for classroom use." At the same time they acknowledged that "we're going to have trouble getting our book accepted!" Expecting to "face a difficult uphill battle to win acceptance by the state textbook board," they conceded "we'll probably have to take the Commission to court." A representative of the Jackson public schools had even told Loewen that the Textbook Purchasing Board would never accept the book unless a court ordered it, and Loewen replied that they would go to court if necessary.[33]

When Loewen and Sallis heard the Textbook Purchasing Board's decision, they did not, despite their earlier comments, immediately choose to sue the state of Mississippi but instead pursued more informal solutions. Within days they sent letters of inquiry to Governor William Waller, state superintendent of education Garvin Johnston, and board official W. A. Matthews. Loewen and Sallis wrote to the governor, ex officio chairman of the Textbook Purchasing Board, to express their disappointment and to ask for his help. Quoting the governor's remarks at the time of his appointment of the 1972 board, they reminded him that he had told the new members, "You are not selected to speak for a tradition of twenty years ago" but instead for "a new era of progressivism." The board nonetheless had rejected *Conflict and Change* and approved Bettersworth's *Your Mississippi* even though the latter violated, according to Loewen and Sallis, the criterion that required that "the contributions of all ethnic groups at different socio-economic levels receive fair and equitable treatment." After hearing that the board objected to their treatment of the Civil War and Reconstruction, the authors said, "We therefore reluctantly conclude that this unusual decision to deny any consideration to our book was motivated by the traditional racial attitudes of Mississippi's past. The progressive spirit you invoked apparently did not prevail." The spurned authors asked for Waller's help in obtaining a rehearing and a reversal.[34]

The day after the decision Loewen expressed to Matthews, the board's executive secretary, his and Sallis's surprise at the rejection of their textbook. "Could you inform of us of the decision in writing," he asked, "since we have not heard it except through unofficial news reports? And could you inform us of the reasons for the decision?" Loewen sent a copy of the letter to Garvin Johnston, the state superintendent, because most of what they had heard about the decision came from Johnston's statements to the press. Johnston claimed not to know why the board had rejected the book and denied the board had "proscribed" its use if the schools wanted to purchase it with their own funds. Praising Bettersworth's book as objective and without "undue emphasis" on any part of the state, the superintendent declared that the board had "adopted a good book for the students." Though he argued that a textbook "shouldn't be a propaganda agent" or "cause division among people," Johnston admitted that "I do not know that the rejected book would have done that." A similarly "surprised" Matthews responded that all communications by the board went through the publisher, and he assured Loewen that a Random

House representative attended the board meeting when it made its decision. "Please work through your publishing company representatives concerning your book," Matthews suggested. Loewen then asked Pantheon to send a letter to Matthews much like the letter he had sent.[35]

Within a week, as news of the Textbook Purchasing Board's decision spread, Matthews, Johnston, and Waller began receiving letters from citizens who protested the rejection of *Conflict and Change*. One black woman from Tougaloo recalled the early 1960s when she "suffered through an almost intolerably dull semester of Mississippi history with the Bettersworth text" at Jackson's Chastain Junior High School. She called her old text "bland" and "uninspiring" because in "a grave error" it "cheated" students of "whole chunks of history," especially black history. In contrast, she characterized Loewen and Sallis's book as "fair," "fully rounded," and "responsible." She decided that the Textbook Purchasing Board "wishes to continue to attempt to convey that Mississippi is an unremarkable state, trouble-free, completely white dominated state. I can only conclude that the members who voted the rejection want to perpetuate their prejudices by censoring facts or ideas which do not fall into line with these biases."[36]

A former teacher in Jackson protested that the board's decision deprived students and teachers of the right to study *Conflict and Change*. Though she had hoped that Governor Waller's promise of golden years ahead for the state included education and living cooperatively, she took the decision as proof of the still "closed society." Arguing that the "enlightened, lively, up-to-date history would have been like a fresh air breeze blowing through innumerable dull, listless classrooms," she called for "objectivity and fair-mindedness" in choosing textbooks. Another Jackson teacher called the rejected book "well researched, very readable" and declared that nothing in the book made it "pedagogically unfit for classroom use." While recognizing that *Conflict and Change* "does present some of the grimmer aspects of Mississippi's history," he contended it would help students "develop positive self-images and mutual respect for one another." He urged the board to reconsider. An Ocean Springs resident called it "a thoughtful book carefully documented" and told the governor, "There was a great *need* for a book of this nature; something NEW." The Rev. Msgr. Paul V. Canonici, director of education services for the Natchez-Jackson Catholic diocese, expressed the "dismay" of 13,000 students at the board's decision because they wanted to be able to use the Loewen and Sallis volume.[37]

In Biloxi, the *Sun-Herald* praised the new textbook as "refreshing." According to Hank Klibanoff, *Conflict and Change* dealt with "substantive, current and vital" topics that since 1959 Bettersworth's textbooks had "ignored or glossed over." The young reporter called *Mississippi: Yesterday and Today* a "well-worn (some would say worn out) history textbook," and he quoted Loewen as having "suggested that it should be called Mississippi[:] The Day Before Yesterday and Yesterday." If the board did not yield, Klibanoff predicted that "the state's tradition of stubborness [sic] to change will end up where it always seems to end up: in the courts," and the resulting fight "might make an interesting closing chapter in an updated version of *Mississippi: Conflict and Change*."[38]

Loewen and Sallis also spoke publicly against the Textbook Purchasing Board's ruling. Three days after the board rejected their book, Loewen and Sallis made the local news on WJDX radio. On the same day they appeared on the evening and late night news on WLBT-TV to charge a racial motive behind their textbook's rejection. The following Sunday they participated in WJDX's two-hour talk show "Point/Counterpoint" moderated by John Quincy Adams, a Millsaps College professor. Callers to the radio show included both listeners who suggested *Conflict and Change* was part of a communist plot and others who praised their book and criticized Bettersworth's.[39]

In an interview with the Millsaps student newspaper, Sallis expressed both his frustration and his determination. "This is not a new interpretation of Mississippi history," he explained. "This is the established point of view as far as southern historians are concerned. . . . But this is not the view of the man in the street and apparently not the view of the Mississippi Rating Committee Board of the State Textbook Commission." The rating committee, however, "won't even talk to us." To try to achieve a compromise, the authors planned to meet with the governor and the board secretary. Sallis insisted on their limited objective. "What we are really asking for," he explained, "is for freedom of choice. We would like to give the teachers a choice—our book or Bettersworth's book or both of them." If they could not achieve a compromise, Sallis favored "legal action" because "I don't want to wait until 1980 to get a new review."[40]

A few weeks later Loewen and Sallis appeared on WJTV's community affairs program "Speculation," hosted by a black commentator. They disputed Governor Waller's contention of a few days earlier that nothing could be done about the board decision because Loewen and Sallis had waited too long to object. The next day, in an attempt to defend the governor and defuse the controversy, Waller's educational spokesman told the television station that the rating committee, not the board, had rejected the textbook, that both books were excellent, and that Loewen and Sallis's book contained no historical errors. His comments failed to mollify the authors. At the Textbook Purchasing Board's next meeting, the board rejected an invitation from WJTV to appear on "Speculation" because "the law and Board policy specified that all actions of the Board be addressed to the publisher and their official representatives and not the authors."[41]

Loewen renewed his quest for information about the board's action in a December 19 letter to Matthews, with a copy sent to William Allain in the state attorney general's office. He asked Matthews for information on four points. He wanted the name, address, race, and credentials of each member of the rating committee. He also requested the name of every book reviewed by the committee and each member's recommendation. He sought also the board's appraisals of the books and any dissenting opinions. Finally, he asked Matthews to send him the minutes of the board's November 4 meeting. Loewen informed Matthews, and Allain, that he and others were considering filing a lawsuit to gain approval for the textbook. He believed that the information that he requested was part of the public record or would be obtainable if they filed a lawsuit.[42]

Early in 1975 Loewen and Sallis met with Governor Waller. As ex officio chairman of the Textbook Purchasing Board he might, they hoped, arrange for the board to reconsider their textbook. Sallis explained to the governor *Conflict and Change*'s strengths and why they thought the board should have approved it. When Waller inquired if they had asked for a hearing before the board, Loewen recounted his exchange with Matthews and the board's insistence that it would communicate only with the publisher. The governor then directed his education adviser to ask the board to hold a hearing to entertain the two authors' request. Before leaving, Loewen and Sallis autographed a copy of their book for the governor. Sallis later told a reporter, "The meeting went well and we got what we wanted."[43]

At the Textbook Purchasing Board's next meeting, however, the members heard a report on, as the minutes indicated, "the activities, publicity, and communications concerning the textbook *Conflict and Change*." Without taking any further action, the board "restated its policy as prescribed by law that it not get involved in the merits of the book." The rating committee had simply found the book unacceptable. The board's policies allowed it to deal only with publishers, and, according to reports to the board, Random House and its representatives "are satisfied with the action of the Board."[44]

Heeding Governor Waller's request, however, the board did modify its procedures to hear a presentation on behalf of *Conflict and Change* by Charles Sallis and Jeanne Middleton. Random House's educational division vice president and its regional manager also attended the meeting, as did a representative from the state attorney general's office. With a prepared six-page, single-spaced statement, Sallis made a full presentation. He expressed shock that the board action did not reflect the governor's announced commitment to a new progressive spirit in the state. When it could have accepted as many as five textbooks in Mississippi history, the board adopted only one and rejected Loewen and Sallis's book. According to reports that Sallis had received, the rating committee disapproved their book's treatment of slavery, lynching, Reconstruction, and the civil rights movement "despite the fact that our treatment is historically accurate and well-informed." Proud that the book was "not traditional in its approach," Sallis observed that the state had changed and that "a new approach to history . . . is needed." The Mississippi native told the board, "We reluctantly have concluded that the decision to deny consideration to our book was motivated by the traditional attitudes of Mississippi's past."[45]

For the board members who had had no obligation to look at the book, much less evaluate it, Sallis highlighted a few specific chapters and reviewed the strengths of *Conflict and Change*. It "invites students to investigate historical issues for themselves and shows the impact of history upon current events." Referring to chapters on folklore and Indians, Sallis stressed that the book contained "responsible treatment of *all* segments of Mississippi society." The chapters on music and folklore demonstrated the text's innovative "interdisciplinary inquiry." The book also covered the recent past. Finally, Sallis wanted the board to realize that the new textbook kept "the readers' attention, not only through a vivid narrative, but also through innovative graphs, telling photographs, marginal notes, and other special material and projects."[46]

In his presentation Sallis moved beyond the book's specific contents. Calling the textbook "pedagogically effective," he mentioned that pretesting the book with black and white students had demonstrated its effectiveness. He emphasized the unique diversity of the authors as northerner and southerner, black and white, male and female, student and teacher. In his attempt to persuade the board of the book's merits, he also referred to comments and reviews of the book. In the end, however, Sallis reminded the board that he did "not seek to displace the text by Dr. Bettersworth, but only to have a plural adoption, so that those schools which wish to use our book may do so."

According to Sallis, Mississippi "could assume a role of leadership" in state histories by accepting *Conflict and Change*. If it continued to reject the book, however, it would "put Mississippi on public notice that only through the courts is progress made." He hoped the board would instruct the rating committee to meet with him and Loewen and to reconsider its decision.[47]

As soon as Sallis and Middleton left the meeting, the board refused to change its decision or to refer the matter back to the rating committee for its further consideration. The members concluded that it "had no authority to conduct a formal hearing, no power to redirect the committees to re-evaluate their ratings of textbooks, and no power to receive petitions relating thereto." Even under the implied threat of a lawsuit, the board directed its executive secretary to tell the authors of its decision to take no further action.[48]

A possible lawsuit did not intimidate the Textbook Purchasing Board, perhaps because it had for the past few years already defended itself in federal court against another challenge to its authority. Calvin Norwood, on behalf of his daughter Dolores, and other black parents of Tunica County public school students sued in U.S. District Court to stop the state's provision of free textbooks for private, all-white segregated schools. A three-judge court heard the case. Represented by Melvyn Leventhal of the NAACP Legal Defense Fund, the plaintiffs did not object to the existence of private schools or to the 1940 state free textbook law. They also recognized that the Mississippi Supreme Court had in 1941 approved the distribution of free textbooks to private schools. After 1964, however, when court-ordered school desegregation began in Mississippi, whites began to create many private, all-white segregated schools to avoid desegregation. For example, in 1963–64, before desegregation, 17 non-Catholic private schools enrolled only 2,362 students, including 916 blacks, but by 1970 after *Alexander v. Holmes* the numbers had increased dramatically to 155 private schools that enrolled more than 42,000 students, nearly all white. More important, 34,000 students at 107 all-white private schools received free textbooks from the state at a cost of almost one-half million dollars.[49]

At the same time control over the distribution of books to private schools changed. Under the original free textbook law in 1940, the Textbook Purchasing Board gave each county superintendent authority over the free textbook program in the county; after school desegregation began, however, the Textbook Purchasing Board in 1970 took responsibility for the distribution of free textbooks to all private schools. In the lawsuit against the board, the plaintiffs contended that such assistance amounted to state support of racially segregated schools and that it violated their right to equal protection of the laws. Instead, the state had an obligation to do whatever necessary to eliminate racial discrimination in public education. Leventhal compared the free textbooks to the previously ruled unconstitutional state tuition grants to students attending private segregated schools and the provision of federal tax-exempt status to segregated private schools.[50]

In April 1972, Judges J. P. Coleman, William Keady, and Orma Smith found that the 1940 law "began without racial motivation" and the textbook program had been administered in "a benevolent and racially neutral" manner. The program issued books to the individual student and not to the schools. According to the judges, "There is no showing that any child enrolled in a private school, if deprived of free textbooks, would withdraw from private school and subsequently enroll in the public schools." They similarly held that free textbooks did not constitute a direct or indirect "financial benefit" for the private schools. As a result the court found "it wholly illogical to require an alteration in the state's textbook program simply because of the advent of more private schools following the desegregation of the public school system." The judges also doubted that the "plaintiffs are threatened with irreparable injury" because of the free textbooks provided the private schools. "Lurking behind all this," the three judges observed, "is the principle that two wrongs do not make a right. Punitive action against the children now receiving free textbooks in the private schools will do nothing to cure acts committed by others (not children) in the years now dead and gone." The court, therefore, found Mississippi's free textbook program that included private segregated schools "not constitutionally invalid."[51]

Leventhal and the plaintiffs appealed the lower court decision to the U.S. Supreme Court, and in November 1972 the Court agreed to hear the case. The U.S. Department of Justice filed an amicus brief in support of the plaintiffs. In considering the arguments, the justices did not accept that equal protection of the law meant that private schools had to "share with public schools in state largesse," such as the free textbook program. To the Court the textbook program "is not legally distinguishable from" the outlawed tuition-grant system. Calling textbooks "a basic educational tool" and an "inescapable educational cost for students," the justices saw free textbooks for students as "a form of financial assistance inuring to the benefit of the private schools themselves." If a school practiced racial discrimination, the "tangible aid in the form of textbooks thereby gives support to such discrimination." The Court distinguished between textbooks and "such necessities of life as electricity, water and police and fire protection," and it rejected textbooks or any state financial aid that "has a tendency to facilitate, reinforce, and support private discrimination."[52]

Arguing that "a permissible purpose cannot sustain an action that has an impermissible effect," the Court showed that in Tunica County a dual school system had emerged. After Court-ordered desegregation all white students left the public schools for a local private, all-white academy. The justices saw that the free textbook program "significantly aided the organization and continuation of a separate system of private schools," while the state had an obligation not to aid "institutions that practice racial or other invidious discrimination." The Court could not separate the private schools from their unacceptable racial practices. In June 1973 a unanimous Court ruled in favor of the plaintiffs but to avoid an unwarranted "blanket condemnation" did not imply that all private schools "are in fact practicing restrictive admissions policies." Instead it asked the district court to develop a certification process to determine "school-by-school" which had nondiscriminatory policies and thereby had qualified for the free textbook program.[53]

Mel Leventhal exulted, "It means we won the lawsuit." He predicted the decision would have "a great impact throughout the nation . . . as it means . . . any tangible aid to racism and segregation is unconstitutional." A still-hopeful attorney general A. F. Summer said, "We had a lot of heart and a lot of hope riding on this case. We will apparently have another day in court." The day would be in Judge Keady's court because he had responsibility for implementing the Supreme Court's decision. In the meantime, the Textbook Purchasing Board with the help of the attorney general's office had to devise a procedure to certify the eligibility of private schools. In July 1974 Judge Keady approved the board's methods and decided that two schools qualified for free books but four others did not. While the board continued to review requests for free textbooks, the court case dragged on. Finally, in March 1976, Judge Keady declared, "Today we write a postlude to this protracted litigation." The last immediate issue involved attorney fees, and the judge ruled the board had to pay for the plaintiffs' lawyers. Despite Keady's efforts, the defendants three times appealed his ruling to the Fifth Circuit Court of Appeals, but in 1977, 1978, and 1981 they lost.[54]

While the board and the state fought the *Norwood* case, the controversy over *Conflict and Change* grew. In reactions to the revisionist text, race played a significant part because the book rejected a segregationist interpretation of the state's past in favor of a history that fully included its black citizens. Clashes over the ninth-grade history books also implicitly involved other perennial issues common to American education, such as who wrote textbooks and who chose them—scholarly experts, laypeople, classroom teachers, other professional educators, or politicians. Debate over the Loewen and Sallis book also encompassed larger crucial constitutional concerns that courts had long considered. Multiple, often overlapping and intertwined questions related to conflicting beliefs about the functions of public education in American society, the competing interests of groups and the individual, and the rights of parents, students, teachers, and communities. The debates became more complicated depending on the age of the student—elementary or secondary—and the relevant community—small town, city, state, or nation. In every case Loewen and Sallis's revisionist textbook reflected nontraditional ideas and values.

As Jim Loewen and Charles Sallis repeatedly said, they wanted their textbook to encourage students "to think critically and analytically," not to memorize the conventional dates and facts of the state's history. Their approach to teaching Mississippi history, and by extension to teaching generally, represented a challenge to established educational approaches and to traditional Mississippi society. According to a prescriptive view of education, schools should inculcate what the prevailing society considered proper values. Public schools transmitted the official knowledge as sanctioned by the educational and political leadership, and students passively absorbed the important social values and the accepted truths. To convey the desired ideas, the state chose appropriate books and teachers. The courts had barred states from enforcing an orthodoxy or homogeneity of ideas; the federal courts opposed indoctrination of students and had declared that "state supported schools may not be enclaves of totalitarianism." States could, however, guard students from inappropriate, offensive, or harmful materials that advocated ideas "manifestly inimical to the public welfare." During the Cold War, for example, some Mississippians wanted to use the schools to promote patriotism and to teach the evils of communism. Citizens objected to books that favorably mentioned socialism or criticized capitalism. In 1962 a member of the state legislature proposed a bill explicitly "to protect the youth of the State of Mississippi by declaring certain books and publications to be unfit for their consumption through the public school system." A member of the state senate proposed in 1974 to restrict teaching about the origin of man. The prescriptive approach to education inherently stressed civic virtues, community order, social stability, and cultural continuity, but it also involved suspicion of new or unusual ideas.[55]

A competing conception of education saw the school as a free market of ideas. In the classroom as marketplace, the teacher exposed students to a wide variety of conflicting ideas about all kinds of subjects. With the teacher's guidance, students engaged the new ideas. In discussing different viewpoints, students learned from the exchange of ideas how to evaluate them and in the process developed the analytical reasoning skills that they could later apply to other topics. The free market welcomed competing new ideas, and teachers, instead of protecting the students from the ideas, used them to stimulate student thinking. The free market ran the risk, of course, that students would adopt ideas disapproved by their parents or other authorities. As the title *Mississippi: Conflict and Change* implied, Loewen and Sallis endorsed the concept of the school as an intellectual marketplace.

Related to the tension between the prescriptive and free-market views of education was the conflict between the interests of the group and the individual. The group usually took the form of a local community or a state, or a combination of the two. A homogeneous small community may have reached a consensus on prescriptive education more easily than a larger heterogeneous state, but even many Mississippi communities encompassed important class and racial divisions. Whether in the form of the community or the state, the group wanted schools to promote the smooth functioning of society. To support the schools, the state set curricular standards, required attendance, certified teachers, and determined other general educational policies. The state and local community also funded public education. In turn, schools assumed the responsibility to train students in the basic citizenship skills, to guarantee academic competency, and to promote student socialization through a set of shared values and ideas. The resulting social harmony would ensure a strong, peaceful, and prosperous community. Though the authors of *Conflict and Change* did not deny the community's interests, they recognized multiple communities, including the black community that earlier texts had largely ignored. Loewen and Sallis also contended that greater academic rights for the individual served the group's larger interests by leading to improvements in society.

The community's desire for self-preservation often clashed with the rights of the individual, and parents, teachers, and students often had competing interests in the classroom. All three recognized the need for classroom discipline and for studying relevant subjects. Though parents, teachers, and students did not deny the state's role in public education, each wanted their rights honored also. Parents claimed the right to determine what their children learned in school as part of their basic right to raise their children as they saw fit. Teachers thought that they had academic freedom and the First Amendment right to free speech in the classroom. Already compelled to attend school, students wanted the right to read and hear all information. Their varying ages complicated the contests over rights because pupils in the primary grades had different needs and more limited rights than high school students. With younger children, educational experts, teachers, and parents recognized a greater need both for parental involvement and for prescriptive education. As the children grew older, the disagreements over greater freedom for students and teachers increased. Loewen and Sallis believed the white community's desire for self-preservation clashed with the rights of black students to learn their own history, and the authors rejected the narrow white history in favor of a comprehensive history of all Mississippians. Confident that well-trained teachers could present the material effectively, the authors believed that ninth-grade students had sufficient knowledge and maturity to handle complicated subjects and unorthodox interpretations in their history lessons. For advocates of prescriptive education, however, the heterodox subjects in *Conflict and Change* would have remained unacceptable for the public school classroom.[56]

To keep the wrong ideas out of the schools, defenders of prescriptive education wanted to prevent the adoption of textbooks with controversial or inappropriate ideas. As censorship battles during the Cold War showed, targets often included political or economic ideas deemed unpatriotic; earlier taboos had involved evolution and religion. After the 1960s, protestors increasingly focused on what they saw as vulgar language, offensive racial and ethnic stereotypes, and immoral sex or sex education. Conservatives often attacked books in general for their alleged immorality, while leftists challenged textbooks for their stereotypes of racial and ethnic minorities. In describing the two sides in censorship struggles, one historian has suggested, "Censors of the right aim to restore an idealized vision of the past. . . . Censors of the left believe in an idealized vision of the future, a utopia in which egalitarianism prevails in all social relations." Partisans on each side assumed they represented the virtuous view and that the textbooks supported by the opposing philosophy would corrupt children. Most bland textbooks attempted to avoid all controversy, and teachers must have sometimes wondered if textbooks had any effect at all.[57]

Avoiding unacceptable schoolbooks required textbook buyers to choose carefully only books that they deemed appropriate, and the selection process involved subjective judgments about content, as well as more objective decisions about contractual factors related to cost, availability, and durability. The buyers worked to eliminate controversy by keeping objectionable books out of schoolchildren's hands. With the line between exclusion and indoctrination often blurred, critics claimed that prior restraint exercised on textbooks amounted to censorship or pre-censorship. Libraries were a slightly different case. While the evaluation and selection process could seek to keep books from the classroom, it did not necessarily call for removing books from school libraries or banning their use entirely. Using a book as a required classroom textbook appeared to give official approval to its contents while merely making it available on the library's shelves avoided such a direct implication. Loewen and Sallis's book, for example, appeared in many Mississippi public school libraries. A challenge to the rejection of their history book as a textbook had the potential to raise complex questions about censorship as well as the rival purposes of education and the competing rights and interests of students, parents, teachers, and the state.

The controversy over *Conflict and Change* had many causes. In opposing the textbook, many professional educators pointed directly and explicitly to the book's emphasis on race relations, civil rights, and black history. They contended that it presented an unbalanced and unfair history of the state, and they worried that it might anger students and disrupt classrooms. Loewen and Sallis believed that their revisionist book's multicultural approach represented the best and latest historical scholarship, not a distortion of the past. They did not want to hide from students their state's true past that included workers and women, as well as class divisions and political conflicts; they specifically wanted to provide the state's black students with an accurate view of their own past. Career educators may have implicitly, even subconsciously, objected to *Conflict and Change*'s revisionist pedagogy. In a still largely closed society, white Mississippians could not welcome, much less appreciate or endorse, a free market of ideas; they did not encourage an uncontrolled debate among clashing opinions over issues of race, class, and gender. Orthodoxy, even if it had to be enforced, must prevail. As a hierarchical, even authoritarian culture, Mississippi did not stress individual rights. Social order and stability took precedence over any First Amendment claims. Whites in authority intuitively understood that a marketplace of ideas protected by free speech would undermine the Mississippi way of life, which still rested on white supremacy even after the civil rights movement. Loewen and Sallis appreciated that conflicting ideas might well produce social change, and, in fact, they wanted to stimulate such change. Both sides in the clash over *Conflict and Change* understood each other and rejected their opponents' values. The courts would have a chance to settle their disagreement over *Conflict and Change* if not the larger cultural and pedagogical questions.

CHAPTER EIGHT

Case

Preparing the Legal Challenge

Soon after the Textbook Purchasing Board refused to reconsider its ruling against *Conflict and Change*, the authors began to develop the legal challenge that they had from the beginning anticipated but had hoped to avoid. Represented by Melvyn Leventhal of the NAACP's Legal Defense Fund (LDF), Loewen and Sallis started by recruiting plaintiffs to join them in the lawsuit. Leventhal offered no assistance because he could not solicit clients, but he did assure Loewen that the plaintiffs would not have to contribute financially to the case because the LDF would cover the costs but that they would have to submit to depositions by the lawyers and would have to attend the trial. Eager to battle the Textbook Purchasing Board, Loewen volunteered to be the lead plaintiff. "I always was a glory hound," he told Leventhal. "And I am more up for the 'risk' than anybody else, even Sallis, I believe," even though Loewen's own risk had recently decreased with his decision to resign from Tougaloo in 1975 and to move to the University of Vermont. Leventhal tried to tamp down Loewen's enthusiasm before it affected the case. Warning Loewen not to try to use the case to publicize the textbook, he worried that the court might as a result "view the lawsuit as a business enterprise." The lawyer explained, "Don't ever lose sight of the fact that the children, parents and educators are the lead plaintiffs. . . . Curb—dear friend—your tendency to feel personally aggrieved; you just wrote the book; Pantheon just published the book; I'm just a lawyer representing clients." He urged Loewen to let the ordinary citizens who become plaintiffs "present *their* case to the media" because they "are the ones really out on a limb."[1]

To present an array of plaintiffs beyond themselves, the authors approached groups and individuals friendly to the textbook. They soon contacted Bishop Duncan M. Gray Jr. of the Episcopal Church. Despite the relatively few Mississippi Episcopalians, Loewen considered Gray's commitment vital because it would make easier the cooperation of others. As the father of an eighth-grade daughter, not officially as bishop or the apparent head of the state's Episcopal schools, Gray agreed to participate as a plaintiff. His action spurred the search for others, especially Catholics.[2]

After the Greenville parochial school had successfully tested the book, the Catholic Church seemed a likely source of support because the parochial schools in Mississippi had desegregated in September 1964. Loewen courted the head of the Catholic school in Canton, just north of Jackson, but the priest waited for the Diocese to act first. Monsignor Paul V. Canonici, the director of the state's Catholic schools, played a key role in the church's involvement. A native of the Delta though a son of Italian immigrants, Canonici had taught social studies and served as a high school principal in integrated parochial schools. In 1970 he received a doctorate in sociology from Mississippi State University where he studied the characteristics of successful middle-class blacks in Jackson. Supporting a textbook that told the full story of the state's history, Canonici by the early summer of 1975 had agreed to join the lawsuit; he did not ask permission to become a plaintiff because he knew the bishop would support the lawsuit too. From Canton's Holy Child Jesus Elementary and High School, Father Luke Mikschl, the superintendent, became a plaintiff, as did Sister Maureen Sullivan, a teacher. Represented by two mothers, seven black students at the Canton Catholic schools also joined the lawsuit.[3]

A mother of three daughters, Mamie Chinn of Canton agreed to join the plaintiffs. As a youth Chinn had converted to Catholicism and in the late 1950s graduated from Holy Child Jesus; in 1975 her daughters attended the fourth, eighth, and ninth grades at the school. Except for several years with an older sister in Detroit, Chinn had grown up in Canton. She married into the prominent African-American Chinn family (the Chinns acknowledged the family's roots among the Mississippi Chinese). Mamie Chinn's father-in-law, C. O. Chinn, operated a successful restaurant and other businesses in Canton, and in the 1960s he emerged as the powerful leader of the local civil rights movement. Like her legendary father-in-law and her husband, Mamie Chinn participated in the movement through the Congress of Racial Equality. Chinn's part in the textbook lawsuit grew out of her Catholicism and her civil rights activism.[4]

To demonstrate wider support, the plaintiffs also wanted a school or an entire school district to support a lawsuit. For wider diversity, the authors also tried to recruit Indians and blacks. Clarice Campbell, a white Rust College professor who had taught at Tougaloo, tried unsuccessfully to arrange for blacks at Rust or in Holly Springs to join the suit. Seeking black plaintiffs, Loewen visited school officials in Mound Bayou, Claiborne County, Holmes County, and Jefferson County, as well as the private Piney Woods School. Loewen spoke to the school board in Jefferson County, where Charles Evers served as mayor of Fayette near Alcorn A&M College. As a result the Jefferson County school board, the superintendent, the assistant superintendent, and two history teachers became plaintiffs; through their mother and father, two black students in the southwestern Mississippi county also signed onto the lawsuit. Though Loewen failed to persuade the Choctaw Indians' tribal chief, by the end of the summer of 1975 the diverse plaintiffs included the two authors, the head of the state's Catholic schools, the Bishop of the Episcopal Church acting as a private citizen, one county school district and its officers, three school teachers, and ten students.[5]

On November 5, 1975, Mel Leventhal and others at the LDF, with the assistance of Fred L. Banks Jr., a black Jackson lawyer, filed a class-action lawsuit in U.S. District Court in Greenville. Naming the members of the history rating committee, the members of the Textbook Purchasing Board, and W. A. Matthews, its executive secretary, as defendants, the lawsuit called for "enjoining the defendants to forthwith approve for use in eligible schools in the State, at state expense, the textbook, *Conflict and Change*." More than four years of motions, written interrogatories, oral depositions, and sworn testimony would elapse before the court handed down its decision in *Loewen v. Turnipseed*.[6]

For strategic reasons Leventhal chose to file the lawsuit against the Textbook Purchasing Board in federal court in Greenville. With the board located in the state capital and members of the board and the Rating Committee from towns scattered across the state, the plaintiffs could have justified filing their suit in almost any town where federal court met. In 1975 Mississippi had two federal judicial districts. The southern district had three judges and the northern district two. In choosing the location, Leventhal considered the judges who might hear his case. In 1961, when the southern district gained a second judge, President John F. Kennedy had appointed William Harold Cox. He soon became notorious for his racism and his hostility to the civil rights movement; he had even referred to black plaintiffs as a "bunch of niggers ... acting like a bunch of chimpanzees." Leventhal, who knew Cox and had tried cases in his court, wanted to avoid any chance of drawing Judge Cox in the textbook case.[7]

The two northern district judges, William C. Keady and Orma R. Smith, had far more progressive reputations. One civil rights lawyer in Jackson later wrote that Judges Keady and Smith, "in contrast to their Southern District brethren, were strongly committed to upholding constitutional principles of equal civil rights." They were "fair-minded judges who gave civil rights plaintiffs a fair hearing." The attorney thought that "much of the racial progress that has occurred in Mississippi stems from their judicial rulings." Judge Keady, a native of Greenville, still lived in the Delta town on the Mississippi River. Judge Smith lived in his native northeastern corner of the state. They held court in Greenville, Clarksdale, Oxford, and Aberdeen.[8]

Though the Textbook Purchasing Board's Jackson office made the southern district a logical location for the case, Leventhal engaged in what lawyers call "forum shopping" to find the most receptive court for his clients. John M. Turnipseed, a member of the Rating Committee, lived in Avon, a small Delta town half a dozen miles south of Greenville. Just as Leventhal agreed to make Loewen the lead plaintiff by listing him first, he selected Turnipseed as the lead defendant by ordering the defendants so that Turnipseed appeared first. Turnipseed's Avon residence provided a rationale for filing the lawsuit in Greenville in the more friendly northern district.

Assisted by other LDF attorneys and by Fred Banks in Jackson, Leventhal led the plaintiffs. A native of Brooklyn, New York, Melvyn Rosenman Leventhal had attended New York University and had graduated from its law school in 1967. He had worked in Mississippi as an intern with the Law Student's Civil Rights Research Council in the summer of 1965, when he met black writer Alice Walker, and the next summer he had interned with the LDF. After law school and marriage, Leventhal and Walker returned to Jackson where he worked as a civil rights lawyer and she taught as a writer in residence at Jackson State University and Tougaloo College. As Mississippi's first legally married interracial couple, they endured steady segregationist harassment. In Jackson's small liberal activist community, they knew Loewen and had met Sallis.[9]

Leventhal joined the LDF's Jackson office that Marian Wright (later Edelman) established in 1964. When Wright left Jackson in 1968, Leventhal and Reuben V. Anderson became the local LDF staff attorneys. Like Leventhal, Anderson had graduated from law school in 1967, but he had the distinction of being the University of Mississippi law school's first black graduate. Their office conducted almost all of the LDF work in Mississippi, with some help from the national office in appellate courts. In 1970 Leventhal and Anderson, with Fred L. Banks Jr., and John A. Nichols, started a private firm, Anderson, Banks, Nichols, and Leventhal, the state's first integrated law firm. Banks had a law degree from Howard University and Nichols from Emory University. While a partner in the firm, Leventhal continued to handle cases for the LDF.[10]

Attorney General A. F. Summer and Assistant Attorney General Ed Davis Noble Jr. initially responded for the state's defendants, but Peter M. Stockett Jr., a special Assistant Attorney General, quickly assumed the state's responsibilities in the case. Born in 1932 in the southwestern Mississippi community of Woodville, Stockett graduated from Washington and Lee University in 1955 and received his law degree in 1960 from the University of Mississippi. After six years in the attorney general's office fighting dozens of civil rights cases, he moved to Washington, D.C., and joined the staff of the Senate Judiciary Committee chaired by Senator James Eastland. In 1973 he became the committee's chief counsel and staff director. By early 1976 he had returned to Mississippi and directed the state's opposition in *Loewen v. Turnipseed*.[11]

Filed almost exactly one year after the Textbook Purchasing Board rejected the Loewen and Sallis book, the complaint asked the federal court to direct the board to approve *Mississippi: Conflict and Change* for use in the state's schools. As factual background, it explained the textbook program, the purchasing procedures, and the state requirement of ninth-grade Mississippi history. The plaintiffs alleged that Loewen and Sallis's text met "all standards–procedural and technical," but the Rating Committee refused to approve the textbook. The Rating Committee also denied the authors' request for a hearing to present the case for their book, refused to discuss the decision, and withheld the committee's actual vote. The board did allow Sallis to address the group but immediately claimed it had no authority to act. Instead the committee and the board approved only one textbook, even though they could have adopted as many as five and did adopt that many in nearly every other subject area.[12]

As the plaintiffs explained to the court, "custom, policy and practice" meant that all previously adopted Mississippi history textbooks "minimize[d], ignore[d] or denigrate[d] the role of blacks and other minorities" and discussed historical events "in a manner sympathetic to principles of racial segregation and discrimination, black inferiority and 'white supremacy.'" According to the plaintiffs, "Solely to obtain approval from defendant textbook authorities," writers, editors, and publishers conformed to the prejudices of the state board. "The Bettersworth text and its predecessors all espouse[d] the required prejudice" and views of minorities and had, therefore, "been approved by the defendants." The rejected Loewen and Sallis book, however, "acknowledge[d] but question[ed] these prejudices," recognized the historical contributions of blacks, and discussed ideas "antithetical to 'white supremacy' and 'black inferiority.'"[13]

On four specific points the plaintiffs argued that the defendants had violated the law and their constitutional rights. First, the complaint protested the defendants' "failure to adopt and implement regulations establishing hearing procedures" for parents, teachers, authors, and publishers to support or oppose a schoolbook. They also did not require written appraisals by the Rating Committee, and the board did not make any textbook appraisals readily available to the public. The six-year interval between adoptions also drew the plaintiff's criticism as excessively long. The defendants' failures violated the plaintiffs' rights to due process and equal protection of the law under the Fourteenth Amendment and under Section 1983 of federal law. Enacted as part of the Civil Rights Act of 1871 to combat abuses by the Ku Klux Klan, Section 1983 prohibited any person acting under state authority from violating another citizen's rights, privileges, and immunities guaranteed by the Constitution or federal law.[14]

Second, the plaintiffs claimed that the Rating Committee and the Textbook Purchasing Board approved only Mississippi history books that "espouse notions of 'white supremacy' and/or minimize the role of blacks in the history of Mississippi." As a result, according to the complaint, the officials refused to approve Loewen and Sallis's *Conflict and Change* simply "because that text questions notions of 'white supremacy,' and records the role of all Mississippians, black and white, in the State's history." In addition to the Fourteenth Amendment's Equal Protection Clause and Section 1983, the plaintiffs argued that the defendants had violated their rights under the Thirteenth Amendment, which abolished slavery and involuntary servitude, and under Section 1981, which originated in the Civil Rights Act of 1866. As interpreted by the U.S. Supreme Court, Section 1981 prohibited racial discrimination in the creation and enforcement of public contracts or contracts made by individuals with state authority.[15]

Third, in a different application of the Equal Protection Clause, the plaintiffs contended the rejection of *Conflict and Change* violated the rights of school children. The Fourteenth Amendment and Section 1983 guaranteed them a public school system that did not discriminate based on race. The facts of the case presented by the plaintiffs explicitly accused the defendant board and committee of acting according to their racial prejudices. Support for white supremacy, black inferiority, racial segregation, and racial discrimination caused the rejection of the Loewen and Sallis book.[16]

Finally, the plaintiffs contended that the refusal to adopt *Conflict and Change* violated their rights under the First and Fourteenth Amendments. As citizens, they claimed that the textbook adoption procedure denied their right of access to proper textbooks because the law allowed the committee and the board to reject textbooks that contained unorthodox ideas. Students and teachers had a First Amendment right to the free exchange of ideas and information without state restrictions.[17]

To achieve their goals, the plaintiffs specifically asked the U.S. District Court to act on four issues. They wanted the court to direct the Textbook Purchasing Board and the Rating Committee to establish procedures for holding hearings on textbooks submitted for adoption. Authors, publishers, educators, students, and parents had no way to participate in the existing adoption process, and they had no means to appeal a decision. Dissatisfied with the six-year textbook adoption cycle, the plaintiffs also asked the court to prohibit "the defendants from limiting the submission and appraisal for textbooks to intervals longer than one year." In addition to a demand for the approval of the Loewen and Sallis textbook for use in the schools, the complaint called for an end to "policies or practices which discriminate against textbooks containing perspectives on history at odds with those traditionally acceptable in Mississippi."[18]

When filed in Greenville, the lawsuit came before Judge Orma Rinehart "Hack" Smith. The seventy-one-year-old had been born in Booneville and in the 1920s had earned his undergraduate and law degrees from the University of Mississippi, where he played football and was a classmate of Senator James O. Eastland. He practiced law in Corinth for forty years and served as president of the state bar and of the university's alumni association before President Lyndon B. Johnson nominated him for the Northern District Court judgeship in 1968. Four years after *Loewen v. Turnipseed* came before his court, Smith entered senior status, the judiciary's partial retirement, but he continued to oversee the case until he finally handed down his decision in April of 1980.[19]

In the period between the fall of 1975 and the spring of 1980, lawyers engaged in lengthy legal wrangling. During the discovery process, each side sought from the other all relevant information that it could use in a trial. For example, the plaintiffs gathered and developed supportive evidence by submitting to the defense written questions, to which the defense sometimes objected but more frequently supplied written responses. Later, by taking sworn personal statements from defense participants, the plaintiffs' lawyers tried to discern weaknesses in the defense's position. In addition, attorneys for each side also took a variety of issues and objections before the court for rulings by Judge Smith.

Jockeying for advantage began immediately when the defense responded to the plaintiffs' original complaint and questions for the defendants by seeking a typical delay in the proceedings. Three weeks after the plaintiffs filed suit, three defendants had yet to receive an official copy of the complaint, so the defense requested from Judge Smith a delay until the court had served the last defendant. The defense then wanted another ten days to respond to the complaint and thirty days to answer the interrogatories. Frustrated by the "inordinate delays," Leventhal sought and received a timetable from the judge. At the same time Leventhal successfully asked the court to certify the case as a class action for groups that shared with the plaintiffs a common set of interests. He wanted the lawsuit to include all of the state's school districts and schools that received free textbooks, all school superintendents and Mississippi history teachers who selected the textbooks, all students who received the textbooks, and all authors who submitted textbooks and were denied a hearing regarding their books.[20]

Two months later, in response to the plaintiffs, Peter Stockett routinely denied all the claims. The special assistant attorney general argued that the court did not have jurisdiction in the case, that the defendants lacked standing to bring the case, and that it could not be a class action. On numerous facts the defendants corrected the plaintiffs. The complaint erroneously listed one deceased member of the Textbook Purchasing Board and mistakenly identified another, and in two instances it cited the Mississippi Code incorrectly. According to the defendants, the board's customary contract period lasted four years with a possible extension to six. The defendants also denied that Loewen and Sallis had "made any formal request for any type of hearing" as the board's rules required. Finally, Stockett denied "any policy and practice of recommending and adopting only those history textbooks which espouse notions of 'white supremacy' and/or which minimize the role of blacks in the history of Mississippi."[21]

Continuing the pretrial maneuvering, the plaintiffs' first set of questions for the defendants asked for background information on each Rating Committee member and for their votes in the 1974 Mississippi history adoption. In a sweeping search for evidence, the plaintiffs sought detailed data on each Mississippi history textbook submitted for adoption since 1942 and for similar information about textbooks in American history and world history. The plaintiffs also requested comparable facts for every "textbook rejected in any subject" by a Rating Committee or the Textbook Purchasing Board and for every textbook currently approved. They also asked for "a list all regulations and policies" of the board since 1942. Finally, they sought copies of the board's formal or informal written statements about *Conflict and Change*.[22]

For the defense Stockett responded that the case applied only to actions taken in considering the Loewen and Sallis textbook and the procedures followed by the defendants, though the defense accepted that a broad interpretation might include all Mississippi history textbooks adopted since 1940. The defense objected, therefore, to questions about American history and world history textbooks, about all rejected textbooks, and about all books currently being used. Executive secretary Matthews provided the requested information about the board members and Mississippi history textbooks. For additional information, he referred the plaintiffs to the "Textbook Administration—Rules and Regulations" and to the board's minutes.[23]

Aware of the potential impact of Leventhal's success in securing a friendly court in Greenville, Stockett countered in February 1976 with an attempt to have Judge Smith change the trial's location. In asking for a transfer to Jackson in the Southern District, Stockett pointed out that none of the plaintiffs resided in the Northern District and that only three of thirteen defendants lived in the Northern District. He further argued that the plaintiffs' out-of-town counsel would have to fly into either Jackson or Memphis to travel to Greenville, that half of the plaintiffs lived in Jackson or nearby Madison County, and that all of the defendants' lawyers worked in the capital. Reminding the court of the board's office in Jackson, the special assistant attorney general told the judge that moving the case to the capital would "greatly minimize the inconvenience and disruption" of the board's office. If the court did not dismiss the case, Stockett proposed that it should for the "convenience of the parties, the witnesses and justice" transfer it to federal court in Jackson. More than four months later, Judge Smith, noting the lawsuit's statewide implications and minimizing any possible disruption to the board, denied any justification for "disturbing plaintiff's selection of a forum."[24]

While the case proceeded slowly in the spring of 1976, Loewen, Sallis, and their supporters did not waiver but remained on the offensive. Frank R. Parker, a civil rights movement lawyer in Jackson, worked sometimes with Leventhal and knew Loewen and Sallis. For his wife and their two daughters, Parker in February wrote to state superintendent of education Charles Holladay to apply more pressure on behalf of *Conflict and Change*. The Parkers' ninth-grade daughter took Mississippi history, and her sister would take it the following year. Ending school segregation, Parker observed, required "insuring that the curriculum is racially neutral and provides equal opportunities to blacks and whites alike." An undergraduate history major who had since college read widely in southern and Mississippi history, he expressed his "shock" at Bettersworth's discussion of race relations; he found it "not history but simple white racist propaganda which can only have the effect of poisoning the minds of Mississippi's 9th graders, if indeed they take it seriously."[25]

On slavery Parker found in Bettersworth "no real discussion of the evils of slavery," of slave revolts, or of the debate over the slave trade. A student essay assignment to explain "your Southern point of view on slavery" failed to provide an option for "attacking slavery or the slave trade." And according to Parker, "The chapter on Reconstruction is even worse." Later discussions of the Ku Klux Klan's founding gave the impression of "honoring and memorializing them" and provided no similar treatment for the NAACP. Modern Mississippi history also came from "the white racist viewpoint" with no attention to the courageous civil rights activists or to whites' violent resistance. Bettersworth's book, Parker concluded, was "regressive, a reflection of a past, discredited viewpoint," and he urged the superintendent to collect all the books and destroy them.[26]

While Parker pushed the textbook with the state superintendent, other friends prodded the Mississippi Historical Society to endorse the new textbook. At the society's annual meeting, Clarice Campbell and Ken Lawrence submitted to the resolutions committee a proposal to support *Conflict and Change*, but the committee rejected the idea. Though Richard A. McLemore explained to Campbell that it violated the society's established policy not to endorse one book over another, he encouraged her to introduce it from the floor of the general meeting. After mentioning the "rare, perhaps unique," praise received by the Loewen and Sallis textbook, Campbell's resolution reminded the society that the Textbook Purchasing Board had not authorized it. She declared, "We hope that the decision of the rating committee of the Textbook Purchasing Board will be reconsidered, and that *Conflict and Change* will be approved" for use with Bettersworth's book or as the sole text.[27]

After Campbell spoke, McLemore explained the committee's reasons for opposing her resolution. When Ken Lawrence rose in support of the resolution, William D. McCain, historian and president of the University of Southern Mississippi, reportedly attempted to start a walkout by leaving the room as he muttered "I'm going to throw up." When few followed him, he returned and spoke against the resolution as "stupid." Glover Moore of Mississippi State University warned that if the resolution passed publishers would lobby the society for endorsements. Only two people voted for Campbell's resolution. Nannie Pitts McLemore later expressed sympathy for the resolution but could not vote for it because she had not read the book. John Bettersworth stressed that his new textbook was better than the 1959 edition because it included more blacks, yet he spoke well of Loewen and Sallis. Though the resolution failed, keeping the issue alive forced people to think about the textbook and the process that had rejected it.[28]

Action in *Loewen v. Turnipseed* stalled over the summer of 1976, but the pace picked up in September with plans for oral depositions in addition to exchanges of further written questions. By early September, Leventhal expected Judge Smith to fix deadlines for the discovery process and to set a tentative trial date for April or May 1977. As he prepared for trial, Leventhal worked to develop his arguments and his evidence. The First Amendment would increasingly provide the basis for the case. The plaintiffs expected to argue that "exposure of our citizenry, especially young adults, to a full range of ideas is fundamental to our development and security. Protecting and assuring such exposure is the objective and burden of the First Amendment; it is given the 'highest priority.'" Conceding that the state could prohibit books that contained obscenities, distorted facts, or omitted facts, Leventhal prepared to contend that "such screening must be narrowly circumscribed and subject to the most careful judicial scrutiny to protect against infringement of First Amendment objectives." Mississippi's excluding textbooks "on the basis of whether they respond to entrenched biases offends the First Amendment." According to Leventhal, Mississippi's actions not only excluded *Conflict and Change* but had a "chilling effect" because they "led to a reluctance by publishers to issue texts which are at odds with local dogma."[29]

To marshal evidence, Leventhal asked Random House's general counsel to provide data on the cost of producing a history text, the sales needed for the publisher to break even, and the effects of local bias. Leventhal suggested gathering information from publishers who refused to publish the Loewen and Sallis book. At the same time, Leventhal wanted Loewen and Sallis to secure expert analysis of all the ninth-grade Mississippi history textbooks used since 1940. He also asked Sallis to determine why the Textbook Purchasing Board rejected Pearl Guyton's textbook in 1949 and the McLemores' elementary school textbook in 1974. Leventhal had special interest in Nannie Pitts McLemore because she had reportedly called her own book "hopelessly outdated," and he wanted to know if either she or Guyton would testify in the trial. Expecting Bettersworth to testify, Leventhal asked Sallis to arrange for a meeting with Bettersworth so the attorney could determine what the author might say under oath.[30]

At the same time, the plaintiffs submitted a second set of questions to the defendants for information about the board's executive secretaries. In reply, the plaintiffs explained that only one previous executive secretary, James B. Baxter, who served briefly in 1960–61, survived. The interrogatory further asked for the number of copies of Bettersworth's 1964 book purchased by the state, and the defendants listed purchases of between five and ten thousand copies for each year between 1964 and 1975. As of October 1, 1976, the state had bought almost seventeen thousand copies of Bettersworth's new textbook. In reply to the interrogatory, the board's executive secretary agreed to make available the 1974 rating reports in Mississippi history, the board's selection criteria, and the board's rules and regulations.[31]

For the second week of October the plaintiffs scheduled depositions with W. A. Matthews and the seven members of the Mississippi history Rating Committee. Delayed for two weeks by conflicts in scheduling, the depositions varied in intensity, friendliness, comprehensiveness, and depth. Matthews in his Textbook Purchasing Board's office provided the first and longest deposition. Questioned by Leventhal, Matthews described the textbook selection process and the rules that governed it. If the Rating Committee rejected a book, the board could on its own ignore the committee's recommendations, wait for its term to expire, and, in effect, call for the appointment of a new board and a repetition of the submission and review process. The board secretary also explained that textbooks went to the board and that curriculum specialists in the Department of Education reviewed them and passed their comments to the superintendent; as a member of the Textbook Purchasing Board he could bring his staff's concerns to the attention of the board.[32]

Matthews also said that the board had in April 1964 and July 1973 adopted procedures for dealing with protests about books "offered for use." Leventhal then presented Matthews with his response to Sallis in which he said "the board has no authority to conduct a formal hearing, no power to redirect committees to re-evaluate their ratings of textbooks, and no power to receive petitions relating thereto." Leventhal asked Matthews to explain how the statement fit with his description of the board's power to balk at the Rating Committee's recommendation and thereby require a repeat of the process and how it conformed to the protest procedures. Pointing out that the board communicated with publishers, not authors, Matthews said that Sallis and Loewen had only asked for the results of the board's work and never filed a written request for a hearing. As good public relations and at the governor's urging, the board agreed to meet with Sallis after he made a verbal request to the governor.[33]

When Leventhal pressed, Matthews admitted that he never told Loewen and Sallis that they lacked standing to protest the Rating Committee's work and that only the publisher could lodge a protest with the board. To Leventhal's suggestion that the policies only allowed for protests against a book, Matthews disagreed and suggested protests could be in favor of a book. He also conceded the protest procedures did not appear in any public documents except the minutes of the board, but he said that the next year's publication of the rules and regulations would contain the 1964 and 1973 provisions for protests.[34]

Leventhal also quizzed Matthews about the reasons the board rejected textbooks approved by a rating committee. One junior high school humanities book, according to Matthews, "was more a moral issues study" than a general humanities book, and a minority on the committee challenged the book's appropriateness. Matthews reported that another rejected humanities book had "[s]hady stories I would say, somewhat profanity in some instance." A high school humanities book that dealt with art, music, and literature contained nude art forms that the board found unacceptable, while another humanities book that focused on religion fell outside the scope of the humanities. Stockett objected to the interrogation outside history, but he did not question Matthews.[35]

In the afternoon after Matthews's deposition, Leventhal and Stockett deposed James Earl Wash, one of the Rating Committee's two black members. As Matthews did for all the Rating Committee members, he attended Wash's deposition. Leventhal suggested, but Wash could not confirm, that he was the first black appointed to a Rating Committee. He taught social studies, including Mississippi history at least once, in the Union County public schools. Though the board and the plaintiffs had interpreted Wash's ratings as approving both textbooks, with Bettersworth ranked above Loewen and Sallis, Wash's sometimes confusing statements seemed to suggest that he had not actually approved *Conflict and Change*. His giving it a "2" may have meant not that he had ranked it second but had instead ranked it last and would have given it a "3" or "4" if the committee had considered additional books. Leaving the confusing ranking aside, the plaintiff's lawyer struggled to elicit negative comments about Bettersworth's *Your Mississippi*. The polite and agreeable Wash refused to follow Leventhal's leads. He did not object to Bettersworth's treatment of women, did not know that Bettersworth was wrong about the absence of slave revolts, and did not get upset over Bettersworth's treatment of the KKK.[36]

Wash had objected to the lynching photograph in Loewen and Sallis, so Leventhal tried to compare it to a Bettersworth photograph showing a plantation mistress teaching blacks to read. Leventhal: "Do you think blacks kids might be insulted by that?" Wash: "No, not at all." Leventhal: "Do you find it objectionable?" Wash: "No, not at all; not at all." Wash also did not object to Bettersworth's failure to report that state law prohibited teaching blacks to read and write. Later, under redirect, he told Leventhal that Bettersworth's book had not caused any objections when he used it because the class in the 1960s was entirely segregated. Especially in an integrated group, the picture of a lynching could make blacks "feel inferior" and cause some whites to feel superior.[37]

When Leventhal questioned Wash about black governments and politicians after the Civil War, Wash agreed that teaching that black officials were corrupt could damage children, but Wash did not know if they were corrupt or not. He did volunteer, "The only thing I know, there were a lot of maybe unqualified blacks probably in office in this particular time." In regard to the KKK, Wash observed, "The blacks know. They don't want to hear it, hear about the Klan, really, not at all. This is something they want to forget." Teaching about the KKK "would serve as a regression for the whole integration of the school in the State of Mississippi." Blacks, according to Wash, knew that "the Klan meant terror for the blacks," and they did not need to hear more. When Leventhal pointedly asked, "So, if history is to be distorted, you prefer Bettersworth—you prefer distortion to protect the children," Wash replied, "The children come first." The witness admitted that he had not made any analytical comparisons of the two textbooks' handling of particular issues or subjects.[38]

In cross-examination Peter Stockett asked Wash if the lynching picture "would be objectionable" to his students, and Wash replied, "Definitely, right. Black students, yes." When Stockett asked if "conflict is a positive virtue in the educational process," Wash disagreed. He believed that teaching *Conflict and Change* would produce conflict and racial animosity in his classroom. He explained that "blacks just resent anything that I would say would carry them back to times of slavery, anything. Then anything to do with the Klan or terrorizing blacks or something of this nature, right, it would definitely bring conflict." If the plaintiffs had expected support from Wash, they miscalculated; he offered more criticisms of Loewen and Sallis than of Bettersworth.[39]

The next day the lawyers took depositions from Virginia McElhaney and Mary Kyle. As the most experienced Mississippi history teacher among the deponents, McElhaney had great confidence in answering questions. As the most talkative and contentious deponent, she provided responses that gave Leventhal many topics to pursue. Though McElhaney claimed that she primarily objected to the Loewen and Sallis book's lack of instructional materials, such as a teacher's manual, from the outset of her testimony she provided a long list of pages that overemphasized racial issues. Most important she complained that *Conflict and Change* put exaggerated stress on race. Often referring to race as "ethnicity," she claimed that it would "blow the minds of junior high school students" and did not present a "true picture" of the state's history. In regard to the book's discussion of segregation, for example, McElhaney told Leventhal that "the question in my mind is why dwell on this?" Questioned about the KKK, she asked again, "Why is this important?"

She stressed that she did not object to it personally but that she found it too mature for ninth graders. Instead she wanted students to "take pride in our state history."[40]

McElhaney also did not consider *Conflict and Change* a textbook, but she did think Bettersworth's was. In response to a question from Peter Stockett, for example, she said that Loewen and Sallis gave a "distorted picture" by leaving out sixteen of the state's governors. She also contended that they placed "so much emphasis on the type of ethnic type thing that there wasn't as much room" for economic, social, and religious history that a textbook should have. The explanatory and suggestive material that Loewen and Sallis placed in their textbook's margins made the pages appear "cluttered" to McElhaney. In her only positive comment after carefully reading *Conflict and Change*, she appreciated their map of Mississippi that outlined the counties.[41]

Later in the afternoon in Jackson, Mary Kyle gave a deposition. A social studies teacher at Jackson's Bailey Middle School, Kyle had taught the Sallis children and tested a manuscript version of *Conflict and Change*. She explained that she placed only a question mark beside the Loewen and Sallis volume on her rating report because she "questioned whether it would be suitable as a textbook" and "did not rate it as a textbook." She left blank the sheet exclusively for their textbook because she thought "if it's not suitable for a textbook there is no point in my even marking it." She objected to the unappealing cover, to the absence of teaching aids for the book, to the photographs' lack of colorful appeal, and to the book's high level of difficulty. When she had used the early manuscript version as a supplement in her Mississippi history class, the students disliked it, and, as a result of her experience, she believed teachers would find it "difficult to follow and to teach."[42]

When pressed by Leventhal, Kyle suggested that Loewen and Sallis failed to keep events in proper perspective, and she pointed to the treatment of Medgar Evers's death and the civil rights movement in general. According to Kyle, Bettersworth mentioned the contributions of blacks in a more positive way than Loewen and Sallis did. Bettersworth also provided better coverage of economics, agriculture, education, and culture. Though she criticized and rejected Loewen and Sallis's book as a textbook, she did not criticize it as a book.[43]

On the third day of a whirlwind of depositions, Leventhal and Stockett deposed Howard E. Railes and John M. Turnipseed at the U.S. Court House in Clarksdale, one hundred and fifty miles north of Jackson. Though Railes had taught Mississippi history for only nine weeks as a practice teacher, he had thoroughly prepared and brought to the deposition a typed detailed summary of his original review of *Conflict and Change*, and he referred to it as he answered Leventhal's questions. To support his objection that the text gave too much coverage to whites' mistreatment of blacks, he offered a list of citations. In regard to the lynching photograph, Railes did not deny the accuracy but argued that "black students would feel that this portrays them as a second class or inferior race." Speaking confidently about the wishes of black Mississippians, the white educator claimed, "I think this is something they would not like to remember." He further suggested that the lynching photograph might cause tensions and conflicts between whites and blacks. Though he challenged the textbook's accuracy about the number of lynchings in Mississippi, he expressed more misgivings about the "continuous pointing" to slavery, race riots, beatings, violence, lynchings, and civil rights. He estimated that 75 percent of the book dealt with slavery, the Civil War, and civil rights. Railes found no bias in Bettersworth's textbook. As an author, Bettersworth had stronger academic credentials in Mississippi history, according to Railes, than did Loewen and Sallis. He also appreciated the teaching and study aids, the slightly lower reading level, the pronunciation guides, and the better organization in Bettersworth's book. Publishers' representatives' visits had no effect on his decisions. At the end of Leventhal's interrogation of Railes, the lawyer told the witness, "I wish I had you for a teacher. You would be wonderful. You are very thorough." Stockett had no questions for Railes.[44]

John Turnipseed, an elementary school teacher and principal, had taught Mississippi history once, more than ten years earlier. Referring to his prepared notes, Turnipseed explained why he had judged *Conflict and Change* "*unsuitable.*" As an example, he offered the picture of a lynching that "would incite hard feelings between the black and white students," and he expressed doubt about the accuracy of lynching statistics. With ready page references to pictures of "white" and "colored" restrooms, segregation at a drag raceway, and a policeman beating a black student, he protested the pictures "would cause resentment" and had "no place in the classroom." He agreed that Bettersworth's treatment of the KKK might cause conflict, but not as much as the material presented by Loewen and Sallis. The latter "harped on" or "dwell[ed] on the issue . . . the white's treatment of blacks; and it just makes it seem like the two were constantly in a clash." Though Turnipseed also complained that Loewen and Sallis did not provide a teacher's edition, he conceded that even with a good one he would have "reservations" about their textbook. Examined by Stockett, Turnipseed stressed that pictures had a greater effect on students than words.[45]

One week later, back at the Textbook Purchasing Board's Jackson office, lawyers deposed Evelyn Harvey Wilder. In the most combative interrogation,

Leventhal and Wilder frequently interrupted each other, showed irritation, bristled at questions and answers, and refused to concede much to the other side. Leventhal first established that the governor had appointed her to the social studies Rating Committee even though she taught at Jackson Preparatory School, a segregated private school without tax-exempt status that could not use state-provided textbooks. He next confirmed that she had never taught history or social studies. Wilder acknowledged that the Loewen and Sallis text should be used as a resource or reference book but not as a textbook. She admitted that as an English teacher "I'm not fully qualified" to evaluate its historical content yet she judged the book's style, sentence structure, and vocabulary unsuitable for ninth-grade students, and she criticized the uneven writing style caused by multiple authors. In pointing out grammatical errors she mentioned the authors' use of "we" as "a shift in persons from third to first, and this is not good writing." She declared, "You do not do that."[46]

When Wilder insisted that *Conflict and Change* was too advanced for average students, Leventhal asked about the above-average student. She insisted that in making her assessment she had to consider the average student. When Leventhal tried to remind her that the Rating Committee and the board could have approved both books, one for average students and one for above average students, and let the local districts choose, Wilder responded, "I didn't know—are several books approved? I thought they were allowed one textbook. Are they allowed two?" When pressed, she continued, "That was my idea; that one textbook would be suitable for the children of Mississippi." She believed that all others would be excluded. Even if she could have approved two, she continued to insist that she would not have approved *Conflict and Change*. She refused to recognize that it contained extensive suggested readings, numerous maps, and definitions for words. The Bettersworth bibliography, according to Wilder, surpassed the one in Loewen and Sallis.[47]

On one matter of content Wilder did express her opinion. Bettersworth provided a "more rounded" treatment of all ethnic groups, while "*Conflict and Change* definitely emphasized the more liberal attitude than Bettersworth does." When Leventhal asked what she meant, she said, "I think racism is pointed up to some extent, in these, and I am not particularly conscious of racism." She found unnecessary a picture of James Meredith after he had been shot on his 1966 march, and she accused Loewen and Sallis of not providing "the other side." An incredulous Leventhal asked, "The other side? . . . What would be the other side of that?" Wilder could only muster, "I don't know." Unyielding, she continued to criticize Loewen and Sallis's book because it focused on and overemphasized "the black viewpoint." In Bettersworth she found no similar bias. She claimed that the excessive attention to race constituted only a minor factor in her decision against the book.[48]

Equally insistent, Leventhal asked why she had not criticized Bettersworth's text when she came prepared to criticize Loewen and Sallis, and she replied, "I did not come prepared to criticize." He then asked if the defendants' attorney and Matthews had cautioned her to "avoid any reference to race or sexism in the Loewen-Sallis text." After declaring that they had only discussed procedures, she digressed to say how she "loved the children of Mississippi and I have worked with them for many years, and it disturbs me when you assume a responsibility to help the children of Mississippi that your integrity is questioned." Leventhal ignored the remark. When he moved on to ask about other suggested criteria, Wilder brought up the sixteenth criterion's demand that a book meet "all the legal requirements related to textbook selection," and she mentioned that she "presumed that those [criteria] were legal requirements." Leventhal tried to explain that the "document is headed 'Suggested Criteria.' You weren't required to follow any of these criteria, in fact." The English teacher could only respond, "Well, that was my understanding; that I was to follow this criteria [sic]."[49]

Peter Stockett asked Wilder to examine several pages at the end of Bettersworth's book. She told him, "These are the references for the students to use to further their reading," and she judged them "an excellent list of reading material for the student." Moments later, when his turn came, Leventhal challenged Wilder: "How do you know if it's excellent? You don't know anything about outside reading in Mississippi history." Determined to charge on, she said it was a long list and seemed "to be broad in scope." When he asked how she knew anything about its breadth, she answered, "I'm just looking at titles and authors quickly." Leventhal asked how the list could be broad in scope when it had only two sections, "General" and "Local History." Wilder confidently opined that it was broad compared to Loewen and Sallis, to which Leventhal pointed out the end of each chapter listed about ten titles. Wilder admitted that she had "not tried to compare those two at this point," but she refused to rate Loewen and Sallis as superior to Bettersworth.[50]

In a final exchange, Leventhal attempted once again to have Wilder say that Loewen and Sallis's book should have been approved for use by superior students, but she would not budge. Finally the frustrated lawyer confessed, "Well, I might as well tell you now—your lawyers will tell you as soon as this deposition ends—you could have approved up to five books for this course.

You could have approved both Loewen-Sallis and Bettersworth. That comes as a shock to you doesn't it?" Wilder agreed, "I was not aware of that." The intense, contentious session had lasted little more than an hour.[51]

A few minutes later, in the last deposition, lawyers calmly questioned Benjamin Burney, the only member of the Rating Committee to give *Conflict and Change* the top ranking. A black public school teacher from the Gulf Coast, Burney tried to give a balanced assessment of the textbooks. In a mechanical process, Leventhal used the suggested evaluation criteria to have Burney compare the books, and he judged Loewen and Sallis better on six, Bettersworth better on four, and the two tied on the others. He liked Bettersworth's teacher's manual and supplementary materials, its summaries and exercises for students, and its table of contents, preface, glossary, and index. Regarding coverage of ethnic groups, illustrations, accuracy, coverage of religion, and format, Burney preferred Loewen and Sallis. He doubted, however, that the below average student could handle their textbook as well as they could Bettersworth's.[52]

Responding to Leventhal's queries, Burney stressed the unusual and detailed coverage provided by Loewen and Sallis, their unwillingness to gloss over the state's history, and their excellent maps (he also taught geography). In regard to the KKK, Burney liked Loewen and Sallis's treatment and thought it would not offend his students, but he admitted that in some classes it might "cause friction." Black students who "feel that this type thing will still go on" might speak up and cause some controversy. As a result, he "admit[ted] that there are some places in some cases that I am sure that the Bettersworth book would be the best one" to avoid a "disturbance." When Peter Stockett asked if Loewen and Sallis's description of a Reconstruction riot in Vicksburg in which two whites and twenty-nine blacks died could, in Stockett's words, "produce a reaction of rage among some black students and on the part of white students, either guilt or anger," Burney agreed.[53]

Depositions from the Rating Committee members demonstrated that racial concerns mattered most in their reactions to *Conflict and Change*. More than its reading level, more than its lack of a teacher's edition, more than its unusual design, more than its historiographical arguments, more than anything else, Loewen and Sallis's full inclusion of blacks and their thorough attention to race relations disturbed the textbook raters. Each candidly complained about the textbook, and three offered specific examples of the book's offending passages. Even one of the black members voiced objections to the textbook. Worries that *Conflict and Change* would cause controversy in classrooms may have reflected the conflicts that some committee members

believed threatened their state's stability and social peace. To bring the disagreements up in class would risk exacerbating conflicts in the state. The committee members expressed their discomfort with or even opposition to the
assumptions of conflict and change that lay behind Loewen and Sallis's work.

While the plaintiffs deposed the members of the Rating Committee, the
defendants in early November 1976 submitted their first interrogatories about
the authors of *Conflict and Change*, their backgrounds and qualifications,
when they worked on the book, and the "nature and scope of the work done."
During the first few months of 1977, the two sides exchanged more interrogatories
and requests for documents. For example, the plaintiffs wanted detailed information on books adopted and copies of the Rating Committee reports.
On the other side, the defendants asked for the guidelines controlling the
contributors to the textbook and for an explanation of the writers' and editors' roles. On the last point, the defendants pressed about whether Loewen
and Sallis actually were the "authors or writers" of the book, "why were they
not designated or named as such on the title page of the book?" The plaintiffs
eventually explained that Loewen and Sallis "were not the only authors or
writers who participated in writing the textbook. All those listed as authors
participated in writing parts of the book. Those listed as editors were responsible for overall editing of the written materials submitted by the various authors and for writing parts of the textbook themselves." In private Loewen
said that the listed authors wrote parts of the chapters, and he and Sallis
"wanted correctly to credit their effort." At the same time, he and Sallis edited
each chapter and made sure it had coherence, and they wrote more than half
the book themselves. Accepting the defendants' challenge, he advised Leventhal, "Bettersworth is also vulnerable to this type of questions. Note his many
errors. Did he really rewrite his book?" He suggested that Leventhal ask Bettersworth in his deposition.[54]

In late May 1977, Leventhal outlined for Loewen and Sallis upcoming
events in their case. While Leventhal inspected all the documents received
from the defendants, Loewen and Sallis needed to arrange for expert readings
of the textbooks. All the plaintiffs would discuss their roles in the trial and
should review their expected testimony. Leventhal anticipated a two- or
three-day trial in Greenville, and an opinion from Judge Smith within six
months. Counsel expected the defendants to appeal if they lost in the District
Court; an appeal, perhaps to the U.S. Supreme Court, could take eighteen
months for a resolution. To speed the pretrial process along, Leventhal asked
Judge Smith for a set of deadlines. A schedule would also allow Loewen, who
had moved to the University of Vermont, and expert witnesses as well as the

defendants time to make travel plans. Leventhal also announced that he would file an amended complaint. Peter Stockett agreed to "expedite the disposition of this case," but he wanted time for a few depositions and to respond to the amended complaint. Judge Smith complied by setting an August 15, 1977, deadline for the end of the discovery phase, but he set no court date.[55]

The plaintiffs' amended complaint made two important changes. First, it asked to add to the class action "all textbook authors whose textbooks have been denied or may in the future be denied approval by the defendants." Second, and more important, it significantly shifted the constitutional arguments and the relief sought. The new complaint declared that the state's "statutory scheme for the screening and adoption of textbooks included three levels of censorship any one of which can be interposed to deny a teacher and his (her) students the use of textbooks at state expense." The Rating Committee, the Textbook Purchasing Board, and the local district could each reject a textbook. The law provided for "unreviewable and unfettered multi-phased censorship of textbook submissions." The complaint argued that the censorship "violates the rights of named plaintiffs and all class members . . . assured by the First Amendment to the Constitution of the United States." Instead of just seeking approval of *Conflict and Change* and institution of an appeal process before the board, the plaintiffs asked for the court to find the textbook purchasing law unconstitutional and to issue an injunction preventing the state from denying approval to a textbook that met minimal scholarly standards, fulfilled basic curricular requirements, and had the support of a local school board and its Rating Committee. The amended complaint called not for modifying the textbook approval process but for throwing it out as unconstitutional. What had been a lawsuit based primarily on civil rights law and on the Thirteenth and Fourteenth Amendments had turned into a censorship case based on the First Amendment.[56]

In early August, before Judge Smith's deadline, the plaintiffs conducted one final deposition with John Bettersworth, and the defendants deposed both Loewen and Sallis. When Leventhal notified Bettersworth of his interest in deposing him, Bettersworth asked his publisher for legal advice. After consulting with the officials at Steck-Vaughan, Bettersworth informed Leventhal that the author and his publisher had "no reason to become involved with either side of the suit." As a result, at Leventhal's request, the court subpoenaed Bettersworth to appear in Starkville at the Oktibbeha County Court House on August 4. The deposition occurred in the grand jury room, with Charles Sallis, Bettersworth's former student, also present.

Questioning of Bettersworth began in a friendly manner, as he recounted his personal and professional background. When Leventhal began to press him on his treatment of slavery in the original 1959 version of the Mississippi history textbook, Stockett objected. Arguing that Bettersworth was not a hostile witness, Stockett protested Leventhal's use of leading questions, his attempts to discredit the witness professionally, and his insistent interrogation. Stockett maintained that many of Leventhal's questions lacked relevance because the lawsuit sought to make *Conflict and Change* available to teachers and students, not to eliminate Bettersworth's book from the schools. Even more, in Stockett's opinion, Bettersworth's earlier textbooks lacked relevance. As the deposition proceeded, though Stockett repeatedly lodged his objections, Leventhal persisted in criticizing Bettersworth's work. He wanted to show that the Textbook Purchasing Board had consistently approved biased books, including Bettersworth's. When Leventhal focused on specific word choices, such as "massacre" in regard to Indians, and on the omission of certain topics, such as the illegal slave trade, Bettersworth often had to confess, "I have no idea" or "I haven't the faintest idea" why he had chosen the words or written exactly as he did. The university vice chancellor could not remember details from eighteen years earlier. Throughout Bettersworth maintained his composure and replied in an agreeable and professional manner, and he spoke warmly of his friendships with Sallis and Bishop Gray.[57]

In many instances Leventhal wanted Bettersworth to account for differences among the various editions of his textbook, and Bettersworth could not. He explained that editors played a significant role in shaping the books to fit changing public attitudes, particularly on racial subjects. Early in the deposition he argued that between his original textbook in 1959 and the latest edition in 1974, popular attitudes had changed "tremendously," especially in regard to black history, and the changes allowed him to completely rewrite the textbook with "no holes [holds] barred." When Leventhal tried to get Bettersworth to tell how his work conformed to the contemporary prejudices, the author did not remember any pressures on him in 1959 and was not aware of "any conscious effort" on his part to satisfy them in his discussions of slavery or Reconstruction. Bettersworth also told Leventhal that he "couldn't be sure which was which now" among what he wrote, what the editors cut or changed, and what finally appeared in the book. Though he did not "remember what I wrote and what they [his editors] did," he told Leventhal, "I am willing to accept responsibility for what changes were made." While the plaintiffs' attorney tried to establish the biases in Bettersworth's books, particularly the 1959 edition, the author repeatedly wanted to steer the discussion to his 1974 book, but Leventhal kept asking about the earlier versions. Stockett continually objected.[58]

When Leventhal asked Bettersworth why "you don't mention lynching at all" in his textbook, the author replied, "I don't recall that I didn't." When Leventhal expressed surprise, Bettersworth inscrutably said, "No. It certainly was not an intention to pretend that it didn't exist. It may have been a desire to forget that it ever existed." Later Leventhal asked Bettersworth if students could be exposed to the statistics on lynching that appeared in *Conflict and Change,* and he replied, "Oh, of course. No problem . . . there is no point in trying to cover up the fact of lynching." He also agreed with Leventhal that studying lynching can "help the kids understand the past." On a related point, Peter Stockett asked Bettersworth about Loewen and Sallis's use of the word "massacre" in relation to Nathan Bedford Forrest. After mentioning the word's "dramatic" effects, the professor commented that the word applied to others than Indians, and he did not object to its use in relation to Forrest and judged that Forrest's actions "belonged in the same class" as the Indians. He also did not object to its use in a ninth-grade textbook: "I don't think you can protect them from the knowledge of violence . . . from the bloodiest things."[59]

In one of his final exchanges with the witness, Leventhal reminded him that he had said school desegregation was a major change in Mississippi's history and then asked why he "devoted only two sentences to school desegregation." Once again Stockett objected but Bettersworth answered. "I don't know how many sentences were devoted to it," said the professor. "But the total tenure [tenor] of the text, I think, was designed to be a textbook following the days when desegregation was achieved. After you do it," he explained, "you don't talk about it as much as you do before it starts, but it is an obvious fact."[60]

The plaintiffs had pointed out Bettersworth's errors, omissions, and inconsistencies in writing his textbooks, but Leventhal had not elicited any admission from Bettersworth that he had deliberately shaped his text to fit white Mississippians' prejudices. A careful and elusive witness, Bettersworth claimed not to remember many of the details in his various textbooks. When Leventhal confronted him with specific examples, Bettersworth brushed them aside with references to editorial control, dismissed them as unimportant, or refused to recognize the point. Throughout the interrogation, Bettersworth politely never criticized Loewen, Sallis, or their book.

For more than six months after the Bettersworth deposition, progress in *Loewen v. Turnipseed* slowed, but significant changes did occur. The plaintiffs' request for designation of their lawsuit as a class action remained unsettled even though the court had directed each side to submit briefs on the motion by August 12, 1977. After the court extended the deadline to September 12, the new deadline passed without any briefs and without court action. Maintained by the clerk of court, the case's docket sheet showed no activity between Bettersworth's deposition and April 1978 when the court set another new deadline of July 28 for the end of discovery.

In the spring of 1978 the plaintiffs experienced a significant change when Leventhal left the NAACP Legal Defense Fund to join President Jimmy Carter's administration as deputy director of the Office of Civil Rights in the Department of Health, Education, and Welfare. When he departed Jackson, Leventhal asked his friend Frank R. Parker to take over as plaintiffs' counsel in the textbook case. In April the court recognized the thirty-seven-year-old lawyer as the new lead counsel. Parker practiced law with the Lawyers' Committee for Civil Rights Under Law, which had started in the summer of 1963 at the suggestion of President John F. Kennedy. More than two hundred lawyers established the committee to promote civil rights within the bar and among the public, to encourage lawyers to serve as negotiators and mediators, and to represent pro bono plaintiffs in civil rights cases.[61]

Under Parker's direction, activity accelerated. Parker found "some unfinished business in the case which goes way back" and moved to clear up matters. First, and most urgent, the plaintiffs had to respond to the defendants' request for documents and to their second and third set of interrogatories from the previous May and July. In answer to the defendants' questions, the plaintiffs sent a list of twenty-nine people who read all or parts of the textbook manuscripts for the authors; readers included more than a dozen Mississippi scholars and journalists, authors Alvin Toffler and Milton Meltzer, and a Greenville photographer. As requested, Parker provided two documents that guided the works of all the textbook's writers. The plaintiffs' reply also explained that Loewen and Sallis decided to list themselves as editors and the other contributors as writers. From funds provided by the Southern Education Foundation, the Project had paid the other six contributors a total of $9,025 for research and writing. *Conflict and Change* had sold 1,461 hardcover copies and 1,647 paperback copies (royalties had not yet covered the $2,500 advance to Loewen and Sallis).[62]

Second, Parker continued to press for having the court certify the lawsuit as a class action. In a supplemental memorandum he called the lawsuit "a civil rights case" that challenged the defendants' actions. Repeating Leventhal's arguments for including the state's school districts, the districts' personnel, children enrolled in Mississippi history classes, and authors who have been or will be denied approval by the Textbook Purchasing Board, Parker claimed the groups met the requirements for inclusion because they were large in number, they did not have conflicting interests, and the defendants' actions affected each group. As evidence the plaintiffs listed 152 school districts, an additional 12 other state schools, and 21 private schools; the public schools alone enrolled 502,025 students, with 45,452 in the ninth grade. In his pleading Parker stressed the allegation of censorship that Leventhal had first emphasized in his complaint. Parker bluntly declared, "Here we have book censorship by a state agency" and "exclusion and censorship of controversial subject matter and ideas." He also mentioned racial discrimination, teachers' academic freedom, and students' right to learn, but censorship came first and last in his list of violations by the state.[63]

With Parker's direction the plaintiffs shifted further away from an attack on Bettersworth and his book and toward a criticism of the Rating Committee and its actions. Sallis, who had studied with Bettersworth and considered him a friend, preferred the new approach. Under Parker's influence the plaintiffs would also soon drop their attempt to have the entire textbook law ruled unconstitutional and opt instead for court-mandated guarantees of nondiscrimination. The case increasingly revolved around claims of state censorship and violations of the plaintiffs' civil rights.[64]

While the court considered the claim for certification as a class action, the defendants took depositions from Loewen and Sallis in the morning of June 12, 1978. Held in the attorney general's office, Loewen's lasted longer and had more intensity than Sallis's. Without any introductory or background questions, Stockett pursued copies of Loewen's writings, published and unpublished, as part of his effort to discredit Loewen by exposing his ideas as radical. Stockett especially expressed interest in a 185-page draft entitled "School Desegregation in Mississippi." Loewen denied the relevance of many of his works, and he and Parker resisted producing the incomplete desegregation study. Even after Stockett reminded Loewen that he had circulated *Conflict and Change* in draft form, Loewen refused to make it available. Stockett returned to the topic at the end of the deposition, and Loewen replied that "it's not ready for showing." He volunteered copies of prepublication pieces, and Stockett agreed to accept the offer if the case had not already ended.[65]

For more insights into Loewen's ideas, Stockett turned to the textbook itself. Starting with the discussion of ideology in the textbook's first chapter, which Loewen wrote, Stockett probed for Loewen's personal ideology. As a confident teacher, Loewen used the occasion to teach; as a trained sociologist, he came to his exchanges with Stockett far better prepared than the attorney. He offered long, well-crafted answers to broad questions. The defense lawyer asked the professor to describe his ideology. To the "complex question" about his beliefs about how society operates, Loewen offered a "quick summary" in three parts. First, he saw society as "a system of competing and coalescing institutions and groups," which ranged from the family to the church and to corporations. Second, he believed "society is stratified" or divided along lines of "class, status, and power." Third, he mentioned the process of socialization through which an individual learns the "basic social roles" to become "a functioning member of society."[66]

Stockett next awkwardly asked for Loewen's "value judgment . . . upon these facts." Drawing on Gunnar Myrdal's analysis of American race relations, the professor saw "conflict between values related to equalitarianism . . . and values connected to stratification." The "basic dynamic or conflict between these two values," Loewen observed, "characterizes much of American society and underlies much of our political and social issues." He volunteered that he preferred expanding opportunities to people who under past stratification had fewer opportunities. When asked by Stockett, Loewen identified written history as a force that supported stratification. In Loewen's opinion, history usually emphasized the actions of powerful white male leaders from the upper class and left others out. The exclusion of some types of people taught young people that the groups had accomplished nothing, so the students could not either, and the resulting process of socialization made them passive and alienated. Loewen advocated a more inclusive history to encourage all to participate and strive for achievement. He also told Stockett that "wealth and income are certainly stratified," but he refused to prescribe a cure for economic differences.[67]

The defense attorney then asked about any "ideological significance or content" in the textbook's title, and Loewen readily declared that each history had a viewpoint. Calling *Your Mississippi, Mississippi: The Magnolia State,* and *Our Mississippi* "public relations titles," he said *Conflict and Change* sought to tell students that "change usually does involve conflict." Referring to recent conflict involved in ending racially segregated education, he conceded, "That conflict was unfortunate, but the change that it brought about was fortunate." When asked about conflict in the classroom, the professor thought "intellectual conflict . . . could be an exciting learning experience."[68]

With questions about Loewen's scholarship, Stockett continued his quest for evidence of radicalism. Quoting Loewen's description of a book as having "many excellent chapters" even though it had an "[a]nti-Marxist" perspective, Stockett sensed a defense of Marxism and asked why anti-Marxist had pejorative connotations. Maintaining that sociologists consider Marx a "major social theorist," Loewen explained that they studied Marxist theory. Declaring "I am not a Marxist," Loewen criticized the book because it failed even to mention Marx in its more than five hundred pages, and he said that he also mentioned the text in his "Action and Sociology" exchange with Philip Hauser. Prepared to discuss the article, Stockett quizzed the witness about his dissident views within the sociological profession, especially his opposition to an "oligarchy" that ostensibly controlled the American Sociological Association. Loewen repeated that the society's elite frequently chose leaders without substantial intellectual achievement, while neglecting giant sociologists such as Thorstein Veblen, W. E. B. Du Bois, C. Wright Mills, and Paul Goodman. Stockett latched onto Du Bois and Mills and elicited from Loewen that as an older man Du Bois had been a communist and Mills was a "left-wing Democrat." Referring again to the article, Stockett asked why Loewen had called E. A. Ross a "Little League racist," and Loewen obliged with a discussion of Ross's fears fifty years earlier of the "yellow peril," a massive influx of "Mongolians." Stockett next quoted Hauser's charge about Loewen's espousal of a "New Left catechism." Denying knowledge of any such catechism, Loewen described a "splintered" New Left and maintained his views were his own. Once again Loewen rebuffed repeated attempts to make him a menacing Marxist, radical, or New Leftist.[69]

Stockett also pressed the professor on the book's bibliographies. First, he targeted a reference to books by Bettersworth and the McLemores as "prerevisionist." Though a sociologist, Loewen explained that historical revisionism occurred largely after 1940 and that it tried to include the actions and viewpoints of "the so-called lower strata as well as the upper strata," which the books mentioned did not do. When Stockett also highlighted a comment calling a book "sympathetic to the Confederate cause," Loewen suggested that the description tried to alert potential readers to the book's lack of objectivity. In the last in the line of questions, Stockett asked about the ideology of Herbert Aptheker because the textbook cited two of his books. Loewen acknowledged Aptheker's Marxism but did not know if he belonged to the Communist Party. According to Loewen, the annotations did not recommend Aptheker but parts of his books, and his politics had no relevance just as did the views of other writers such as Bettersworth. To provide perspective, Loewen pointed to the textbook's praise for Bettersworth's *Confederate Mississippi* as "an excellent account" but criticism of its neglect of blacks, a neglect that Aptheker and James McPherson corrected. In Aptheker's case, and in Bettersworth's, Loewen said, "I think the book stands for itself."[70]

Loewen finally defended himself against Stockett's suggestion that sociology did not prepare him to write a history textbook. He argued not only that his *Mississippi Chinese* was "essentially historical" but that "no clear distinction [existed] between sociology and history." He proposed that his sociological background, when combined with Sallis's historical training, added "a strength to the book." When Stockett supposed that a sociologist brought "a different viewpoint," Loewen rejected the idea and claimed that a sociologist brought "different methodological skills" and not a particular viewpoint. He also denied Stockett's suggestion that sociologists "minimize the importance of facts in the study of history" in favor of "broad trends" because statistics could sometimes demonstrate trends more effectively than facts could reconstruct particular events. On questions about the academic disciplines and their methodologies, the lawyer proved no problem for the professor.[71]

Soon after the conclusion of Loewen's deposition, Charles Sallis entered the room, and Loewen remained to observe his coauthor's deposition. In the interrogation, Stockett started by asking how the authors "verified and affirmed facts and interpretation." As an example, he quoted from the textbook about the "tragedy of Reconstruction." Sallis explained his familiarity with the literature in southern history, cited several books, and mentioned his own extensive research. When Stockett still wanted to know how he knew the statements were "true" and "other reasonable interpretations" were false, Sallis acknowledged an "older, more traditional interpretation" but argued that it had "been discredited since about 1930." Stockett sought clarification of the "tragedy," and Sallis pointed to "the failure of the Nation to live up to its commitment of equality," not the general suffering of the South after the war. To a question from Parker, Sallis proposed both that the war caused the South's suffering, not Reconstruction, and that historians had exaggerated the degree of suffering during Reconstruction. The history professor also discounted Reconstruction's severity in Mississippi by pointing out that federal forces in the state numbered fewer than a thousand and Democrats controlled a majority of the counties. Less confrontational, more unproductive for the defense, and far shorter, Sallis's deposition wrapped up before lunch.[72]

In questioning Loewen and Sallis, Stockett repeatedly and unwisely focused on subjects about which the witnesses knew far more than the assistant attorney general. In discussing Loewen's scholarship, the professor had greater competence, and confidence, than Stockett did, especially about Loewen's unpublished work. Apparently without realizing his own weaknesses, the defendants' attorney had little chance of eliciting from the sociologist anything embarrassing about Marxism, ideology, and radical sociology. Instead of exposing Loewen's vulnerabilities, the state's attorney succeeded only in revealing his own. In questioning Sallis, Stockett similarly mistakenly asked about Sallis's own specialty, Reconstruction. During the depositions Stockett seemed ill-prepared and inept, and perhaps not totally committed to the case. In fact, his lack of preparation meant that he, like everyone else in the case, missed one important mistake in the book.

Many objections to *Conflict and Change* focused on the photograph of "A Mississippi lynching." Rating Committee members found it offensive and worried that it would upset students and disrupt classes using the textbook. With the caption "White mob exulting over its dead victim. Burned to death in Mississippi," the photograph had in 1929 appeared in Scott Nearing's *Black America*, where forty-five years later Loewen and Sallis found it. Nearing had claimed to have taken the pictures in his book during a tour of the South in the fall of 1928 while he was also the Communist Party candidate for governor of New Jersey. Trusting the radical Nearing, Loewen and Sallis reproduced the picture in their own book without verifying its accuracy. The authors did not realize, the Rating Committee did not know, and Stockett did not discover that the picture did not depict a Mississippi lynching. The incendiary photograph actually came from a riot in Omaha, Nebraska, in September 1919 and appeared in the Chicago *Tribune* on October 1, 1919. Four months later the NAACP used the same photograph in a pamphlet entitled "An Appeal to the Conscience of the World."[73] Disclosure of the egregious error would have greatly embarrassed the plaintiffs and undermined their case for having written an authoritative textbook, but everyone involved in the case missed the mistake.

With the depositions completed, the discovery phase of the case ended. The court had yet to resolve the plaintiffs' application to certify the case as a class action and the defense's request for summary judgment. After hearing from each side, the U.S. magistrate judge for the District Court recommended denial of class action status. The magistrate believed that any relief provided the plaintiffs "will inure to the benefit of all persons similarly situated and that class action is therefore not necessary." In his opinion, the plaintiffs failed to make a convincing argument for class action. The plaintiffs objected to the magistrate's recommendations, especially as they applied to the student plaintiffs. If the case lasted much longer the individual plaintiffs might not be affected by what happens in the ninth grade, and for them the case would become moot. Including all students in a class action would preserve their arguments for students in general not just for themselves as individuals; otherwise, as students finished the ninth grade, the plaintiffs would have to add a new set of students. The defendants denied the plaintiffs' concern about mootness.

When Judge Orma Smith finally ruled September 29, he accepted the plaintiffs' concern and denied class action certification except for "children presently enrolled or who soon may be enrolled in Mississippi History courses of study in schools eligible to receive state owned textbooks."[74]

The court also had to respond to the defense's technical legal arguments that the court should summarily dismiss the case. The defendants claimed that the federal court did not have jurisdiction in the state matter and the remedy sought would constitute an unwarranted intrusion in the actions of a state agency. The state also argued that only the plaintiffs' publisher (not the plaintiffs themselves) had contract rights regarding textbooks under Section 1981 of the Civil Rights Act of 1867. Pointing out that the Rating Committee was not a person, the state maintained that Section 1983 of the Civil Rights Act of 1871 pertaining to racial discrimination by a state official (a person) did not apply. The plaintiffs responded that Sections 1981 and 1983 did apply because of the "policy and practice of approving only racist history textbooks." Quoting from the Rating Committee reports, the plaintiffs argued that the rejection "was unreasonable, arbitrary, capricious, and based on race." The plaintiffs filed affidavits from Jim Loewen and Jan Hilegas, a Jackson activist and paid researcher, that showed the state used the Rating Committee "as an instrument of state propaganda and for the censorship of ideas" and, "in particular, to censor school textbooks advocating equality of the races and racial integration." Rebutting the plaintiffs' contentions, the defense repeated its arguments and accused the plaintiffs of quoting the Rating Committee reports out of context, and the defense rejected the "inference of racial motivation or bias." Instead the defense claimed the rating committee "objected to the pervasive theme of . . . extreme White violence and oppression directed against Blacks." In support the defense cited Matthews's affidavit that reported on his study of the indexes in *Conflict and Change* and *Your Mississippi*. According to the defense, "the Rating Committee was not racist, but was anti-racist." After all the pleadings, the court rejected the defense's call for a summary judgment against the plaintiffs and allowed the case to proceed.[75]

Early in 1979, the clerk of the U.S. District Court called a pre-trial conference for February 26 before the magistrate in Greenville. At the conference a lawyer for each side would present a set of facts established in the case, a compilation of the contested legal and factual issues, a list of documents to be offered at the trial, and a roster of witnesses expected to be called. The notice of the pre-trial hearing also announced that the trial would probably take place in April. Four and a half years after the plaintiffs filed their complaint, a judge might finally hear the case.[76]

CHAPTER NINE

Trial

Loewen v. Turnipseed *in Federal Court*

The trial in *Loewen v. Turnipseed* opened on August 27, 1979. For five days in Greenville, the U.S. District Court heard testimony presented by the plaintiffs. After a break for Labor Day weekend, the trial resumed in the Oxford federal courthouse, and for three days the defense presented its case. Thirty witnesses testified. After hearing the testimony, Judge Orma R. Smith deliberated for seven months before rendering his decision, but wrangling between the two sides continued for four months after his ruling.

Intense preparation for the trial began months before court convened in Greenville. In the weeks leading up to a pre-trial conference for February 26, counsel considered a possible settlement. Frank Parker discussed with Peter Stockett possible revisions to *Mississippi: Conflict and Change* to satisfy the Textbook Purchasing Board. Stockett assumed that if the board approved a revised textbook, the plaintiffs would withdraw their complaint. Though Stockett expressed skepticism that the law permitted a compromise, he discussed it with the board at its regular meeting on February 13, and the board decided a settlement would not comply with the law. When Stockett reported the decision to Parker, the defense attorney reiterated his openness to further discussions if they could achieve an agreement compatible with state law. For guidance on the board's possible expectations, Stockett referred Parker to an affidavit from Matthews that highlighted six objectionable passages from *Conflict and Change*.[1]

As the Textbook Purchasing Board's executive secretary, Matthews coordinated its work but had no official role in evaluating the textbooks, a responsibility of the board and its Rating Committee. In an October 1978 affidavit, Matthews nevertheless appeared to step out of his bureaucratic role to speak for the board. His statement suggested that he had opinions about the Mississippi history texts and that he wanted to affect the decision. Without explanation for his statement, Matthews listed objectionable passages in *Conflict and Change*: part of a sketch of Nathan Bedford Forrest that included the quotation "Kill all the niggers," an account of the 1874 Vicksburg riot in which whites killed twenty-nine blacks, 1875 violence in Clinton that killed at least a score of blacks, a discussion of the "tragedy of Reconstruction," the infamous lynching photograph, and a section on "Violence Against Blacks" in 1959. He also mentioned the marginal remark about "racial murders in 1955." In Stockett's judgment, the material identified by Matthews "would be at the core of the material which the members of the State Textbook Purchasing Board would wish to change." The plaintiffs refused such drastic alterations, and negotiations ceased.[2]

At the February 26 pretrial conference with U.S. Magistrate J. David Orlansky, each side detailed what it expected to do at the trial. The magistrate had directed the lawyers to "prepare for the final pretrial conference with the same thoroughness as for the trial." The resulting Pre-Trial Order served as a blueprint for the trial. From separate perspectives each party summarized the facts in the case, outlined the contested facts, explained the relevant legal issues, listed the exhibits to be offered, and described the expected witnesses. The plaintiffs claimed *Conflict and Change* met all criteria for adoption but was rejected "because it fails to present erroneous traditional Mississippi viewpoints regarding race" and because it was too "controversial." The rejection fit a "pattern and practice" of selecting books that "perpetuate white stereotypes" and "minimize and denigrate the roles of black people." The Textbook Purchasing Board's action "influences the racial attitudes of students, causes psychological damage to students, and contributes to the negative evaluation of blacks" by both whites and blacks. According to the plaintiffs, the selection process "has been an instrument of state propaganda to exclude controversial viewpoints, operates as a state instrument of unconstitutional censorship, and fails to provide due process of law."[3]

In denying the plaintiffs' allegations, the defense argued that the board based its rejection of *Conflict and Change* "on valid educational and academic standards and criteria" and not on "any impermissible discriminatory purpose or intent." It did not engage in "unconstitutional censorship," and it had not had, and did not have, a policy of approving only books that advocated white supremacy or that disparaged blacks. Contested factual issues involved, therefore, the board's general policy and practice, the reasons for the board's action, and the psychological effects of textbooks on black and white students. The most pointed disagreement occurred over whether a "textbook with a recurring theme of racial violence and racial oppression depicted graphically in words and pictures create[d] such hostility, strife and discord among the students using such a textbook as to impede the educational process." Disputes over the law dealt with the protection of rights under the First Amendment, the Thirteenth Amendment, the Due Process and Equal Protection clauses of the Fourteenth Amendment, and Section 1983 of the Civil Rights Act of 1871.[4]

The plaintiffs listed seventy-eight exhibits that they planned to introduce at the trial, and the defendants anticipated objecting to nearly half of them. The defendants proposed presenting twenty-one exhibits, and the plaintiffs intended to object to three. Parker provided information on nearly fifty witnesses he wanted to call, while Peter Stockett listed fewer than a dozen. Though the notice of the pre-trial hearing announced that the trial would probably take place in April, the court later accommodated school officials and students by delaying the trial until late in the summer.[5]

One month after the pre-trial conference, each side submitted its "proposed findings of facts and conclusions of law." The proposals allowed each side to develop its legal argument and to provide the court with references to supporting court decisions. In effect, presented in the form of a proposed final ruling for the judge, each side provided arguments for a ruling in its favor. As part of a fifty-page brief, Parker recounted the history of free textbooks, of censorship during the Red Scare, and of the submission and rejection of *Conflict and Change*. He also described the textbook's special strengths and presented its "extensive critical acclaim and favorable reviews." Using the board's criteria to compare Loewen and Sallis's text to Bettersworth's *Your Mississippi*, the plaintiffs' brief argued that Bettersworth's book "minimizes, ignores, and degrades the roles of blacks and other minorities in Mississippi history and presents historical events in a manner sympathetic to principles of racial segregation, and discrimination, black inferiority, and 'white supremacy.'" With abundant quotations from *Your Mississippi*, the plaintiffs castigated the textbook's treatments of slavery, Reconstruction, the post-Reconstruction period, and the modern civil rights era. The Bettersworth book, they charged, rendered blacks invisible.[6]

The plaintiffs' "proposed conclusions of law" demonstrated their shift in emphasis from a civil rights case to a First Amendment one. An initial eleven pages contended that the First Amendment protected academic freedom, the right to learn, the right to teach, the right to free inquiry, and the right to read. According to the brief, the "defendants are merely asserting an interest in their own unbridled discretion to suppress a textbook it considers 'too controversial.' This distinguishes defendants' actions from the realm of book selection into censorship." The defendants had acted arbitrarily and capriciously without "any valid educational rationale" or even "any coherent explanation" in rejecting *Conflict and Change*. An additional four pages detailed the plaintiffs' original contention that rejection of the textbook violated the Thirteenth and Fourteenth Amendments and Section 1983 of the Civil Rights Act of 1871. From the enactment of the textbook law in 1940 to the decisions by the Rating Committee and board in 1974, the plaintiffs saw "a racially discrim-

inatory purpose." The selection of only *Your Mississippi* "unlawfully perpetuates racial discrimination" in the state's schools and violated the guarantee of
equal protection of the laws. Finally, the plaintiffs claimed the lack of an appeal process in the selection of textbooks failed to provide the plaintiffs with
due process as guaranteed by the Fourteenth Amendment.[7]

In a far shorter document, the defense argued that the "evidence fails to
show that said Rating Committee defendants were motivated or actuated by
racial discrimination in making their decisions." After recounting the Rating
Committee members' explanations, the brief concluded that their testimony
and other evidence "completely negates any inference of racial or impermissible discrimination" in the rejection of *Conflict and Change*. In regard to the
application of the law, the defense called for dismissing the case against the
Textbook Purchasing Board because it was not a "person" but a government
agency. The brief also argued that the defendants had not engaged in censorship and "in no way interfered with the publication, sale, or distribution,
of the book"; indeed the book appeared on the shelves of school libraries and
teachers used it as supplementary material. The defense also denied that the
Thirteenth Amendment applied to local or state control of education. As for
violations of the plaintiff's contract rights, the defense maintained that no
plaintiff had the right to make a contract with the state for textbooks, only
a publisher could; if the defendants had no contract rights, their rights to due
process could not have been violated. Finally, if, as the brief claimed, the defendants did not act in a racially discriminatory way, they did not abridge the
Equal Protection of the Laws guarantee of the Fourteenth Amendment. According to the defense, "the Complaint should be dismissed with prejudice,
with costs to be borne by the plaintiffs."[8]

After submitting their proposed findings, each side had to wait five months
for the trial's start. In the interval, though the defendants planned to call no
experts to testify, the plaintiffs continued preparing their expert witnesses for
the trial. From the beginning, a score of scholars in a variety of disciplines had
advised the authors and critiqued their work, and from the group the plaintiffs
identified several authorities they could use in court. The plaintiffs' potential
witnesses consisted of more than a dozen scholars in history, anthropology, literature, and psychology, including Paul Gaston, Robert Coles, and Alvin Pous-
saint. After considerable discussions, Parker, Loewen, and Sallis decided to
call anthropologist John Peterson, literature professors Evans Harrington and
Margaret Walker Alexander, and historians Neil R. McMillen and John A.
Scott. They could testify to the scholarly accuracy and importance of *Conflict
and Change*.[9]

With concerns extending beyond their book's historical integrity, Loewen and Sallis enlisted experts to defend *Conflict and Change*. Aware of the need to aim the textbook at the appropriate reading level, they had early on secured Maryellen Hains Clampit's assistance. While the textbook developed, she divorced and moved to teach at Western Michigan University. Clampit informed Loewen in 1979 that she could not travel to Mississippi to testify, but she arranged to have a colleague in education help with the case. Professor Ted K. Kilty, a specialist in reading, agreed to appear for the plaintiffs. Loewen and Sallis also knew that they would need a comparative analysis of the treatments of minorities and women in Bettersworth's book and their own. In 1971, through Philip Stone at Harvard University, Loewen contacted Stanford University education professor Thomas E. Fox who helped with preliminary analysis of the two textbooks. Later Stone conducted his own examination, and when the trial approached, the professor of psychology and social relations agreed to serve as an expert witness about the textbooks' treatments of blacks. The plaintiffs also secured the service of Robert B. Moore, the coordinator of the Racism/Sexism Resource Center for Teachers in New York City. Moore had several years earlier written a lengthy comparative review of the two Mississippi history textbooks, but until he heard from Loewen in 1979 he had "assumed the case to be dead."[10]

Other plaintiffs' witnesses included black parents and school officials who had joined the lawsuit. Barbara Phillips, a young black attorney with the Lawyers' Committee, contacted the other plaintiffs. After telling them the trial's expected dates, she explained that Parker wanted each of them present throughout. She realized that some might have difficulty missing work that long, so she volunteered to have them subpoenaed if a court order would convince their employers. For most of them the trial would be their first court experience, especially in a federal court away from their own communities. To allay any apprehension among the inexperienced witnesses, Phillips asked to meet with them in Greenville after the trial began to discuss their testimony. She described the trial process, explained what the lawyers might ask them, and suggested how they might respond.[11]

After lunch on Monday, August 27, the U.S. District Court finally convened in Greenville to hear the case of *Loewen v. Turnipseed*. Located in the heart of the fertile Delta, 150 miles south of Memphis and eighty miles north of Vicksburg, Greenville was the region's largest town. According to one scholar, it had a reputation as "the most open and tolerant community in the Delta and perhaps in all of Mississippi as well." The head of the state NAACP had in the mid-1960s once called Greenville "the heaven of Mississippi."

Home to William Alexander Percy, David Cohn, Hodding Carter, and Shelby Foote, the town ostensibly had "more writers per square foot than any other city of its size." The federal courthouse, a four-story building completed in 1960, sat on the southwest side of Main Street in the middle of downtown. Only a few blocks separated it from Lake Ferguson, an oxbow in the Mississippi River, where the river itself had once flowed. Judge Orma Smith presided over Courtroom 2 on the third floor.[12]

Judge Smith opened the case by calling on Frank Parker to make his opening statement. Born in Pennsylvania in 1940 and raised in Ohio, Parker had graduated from Oberlin College, studied at Oxford University, and received his law degree from Harvard. After working in Washington for two years as a staff attorney with the U.S. Commission on Civil Rights, he moved to Jackson in 1968 and joined the five-year-old office of the Lawyers' Committee for Civil Rights Under Law. For thirteen years the cigar-smoking, bushy-haired, red-bearded lawyer litigated cases involving racial segregation, voting rights, reapportionment, and public employment discrimination. Though he clashed with Judge Harold Cox in the Southern District, Parker won repeatedly in the Northern District. Hailed by one political commentator as a "legal dynamo," "virtually a one-man legal army," and a "genius in accomplishing some amazing results," Parker fought successfully for the underdog. According to the analyst, Parker influenced the state's history more than any public official in the 1970s.[13]

For the twenty-nine plaintiffs—Loewen and Sallis, the Jefferson County schools, the state's Catholic schools, teachers, parents, and students—Parker summarized their case against the Textbook Purchasing Board and the Rating Committee. Calling *Mississippi: Conflict and Change* probably the nation's best state history, he argued that the Textbook Purchasing Board refused to approve it because its views on race and blacks did not conform to traditional white Mississippi attitudes. The plaintiffs claimed that the book not only met the board's criteria but exemplified sound historical evidence and interpretation. The rejection of *Conflict and Change* violated the plaintiff's protection from censorship under the First Amendment, their constitutional rights to due process and equal protection of the law, and their right to nondiscriminatory public schools.[14]

Peter Stockett responded for the defense. The special assistant attorney general's opening statement contended the Rating Committee applied "valid academic standards and criteria" in finding *Conflict and Change* unacceptable. The raters did not engage in any racial discrimination and had no policy of supporting racial discrimination or white supremacy. Stockett maintained the committee and the board did not undertake or practice any form of censorship. As a result he refuted the alleged violations of the plaintiffs' constitutional rights. The Rating Committee and the Purchasing Board simply fulfilled their legitimate educational responsibilities by approving Bettersworth's *Your Mississippi* and rejecting *Conflict and Change*.[15]

The plaintiffs called as their first witness Charles Sallis. The gentle, modest Mississippi native took the stand on his forty-fifth birthday. At the outset Sallis established his credentials as a teacher, scholar, and historian. Under friendly questioning by Parker, he described the previous Mississippi history textbooks. The works by Pearl Guyton, Aubrey and Nannie McLemore, and John Bettersworth confirmed the dominant whites' attitudes toward slavery, the Civil War, and Reconstruction; their books merely reflected the racism of the 1940s and 1950s. Sallis explained that he and Loewen wanted to write a textbook that would serve "as an antidote or remedy to correct the racial imbalance in traditional Mississippi texts." In considerable detail, Sallis explained how they wrote the textbook with the help of Millsaps and Tougaloo students. He also described the book's submission to the Textbook Purchasing Board and, after its rejection, his appearance before the board. Sallis's testimony continued the next day. When Stockett cross-examined Sallis, he failed to elicit anything significant.[16]

The second day of the trial fell on Tuesday, August 28, the same day as the state Democratic primary election. With political news to cover, the Jackson newspapers did not have reporters at the Greenville courthouse, but the morning's *Jackson Clarion-Ledger* did feature a half-page article on the lawsuit. The bulk of the article provided "examples of disparities" between the two books. It juxtaposed excerpts from *Conflict and Change* and *Your Mississippi* on slavery, Reconstruction, the 1960s, and the Sovereignty Commission. In the election that day, William F. Winter defeated Evelyn Gandy to win the Democratic nomination and, therefore, the governorship. The political story overwhelmed reporting on the Greenville trial.[17]

After Sallis's cross examination ended on the second day, Parker called James Loewen as the second witness. As Sallis had, Loewen presented his scholarly credentials. He then described the textbook's positive reviews and explained his involvement in writing, editing, and pretesting the textbook. The sociologist came prepared with facts and statistics. He presented the findings of his recent survey of the state's 150 school superintendents. Of the 96 responding, nearly half had spent no local money on textbooks in the last year, and 48.9 percent had not in the last three years. If they expended local funds, only 11.5 percent spent local funds on regular textbooks, and 81.2 percent spent less than $1,000 in a year; only 2.1 percent spent more than $5,000. The

mean expenditure came to only $622. Even if financing presented no prob-
lem, 72.8 percent of the responding superintendents acknowledged they
would choose only from the state approved list. According to Loewen's survey, most school districts could not buy copies of *Conflict and Change* with
local revenue because they did not have the money, so rejection by the Textbook Purchasing Board meant students would not have access to the book.[18]

Loewen also offered data on the treatment of blacks in *Conflict and Change*
and *Your Mississippi*. In Loewen and Sallis, 74 percent of index references
were to whites, 23 percent to blacks, and 3 percent to Indians, but in Bettersworth the comparable figures were 91 percent white and 7 percent black. He
also testified that 25.6 percent of photographs in *Conflict and Change* portrayed blacks, 37 percent showed whites, and the remainder members of both
races; in *Your Mississippi* only 5 percent contained blacks, 65 percent presented whites, and the rest portrayed both races. Accusing Bettersworth of
incorporating white prejudice into his history, Loewen declared that research
on textbooks showed that texts with few blacks reinforced white prejudice
and undermined blacks' self-image. He pointed to Bettersworth's treatment
of Reconstruction as a prime example of support for white bias. Loewen concluded, "The student who reads our book sees visual evidence that blacks
played a significant role in Mississippi history. The student who reads Bettersworth does not."[19]

In his testimony Loewen took responsibility for choosing *Conflict and
Change*'s photographs and writing the captions. Though he had tried to verify
every picture and caption, he acknowledged two errors in the textbook. According to Loewen a printer's error mixed up the names of three Reconstruction congressmen. He also had no explanation for misidentifying the state
capitol as the Canton courthouse. He knew of no other mistakes. Stockett's
cross-examination of more than two and a half hours failed to weaken Loew-
en's presentation, just as it had in his deposition.[20] Unlike at the deposition,
Stockett made no effort to portray Loewen as a radical, and he did not have
the information to challenge the erroneous lynching photograph.

In one late-afternoon hour, the court heard testimony from four more witnesses. First came the Right Reverend Duncan M. Gray Jr., bishop of the
Episcopal Diocese of Mississippi, a resident of Jackson, and one of the plaintiffs. Gray had initially heard about the textbook from his son Lloyd, a student of Charles Sallis at Millsaps. When the bishop first read *Conflict and
Change* in the fall of 1974 soon after its publication, he liked its engaging format, style, and writing, and he found that it "provides a necessary corrective
to the past." He joined the lawsuit on behalf of his daughter because he hoped

she would be able to use it when she reached the ninth grade. Gray especially appreciated the opening chapter, "The Uses of History," but also praised the section on Indians. According to the bishop, the chapter on Reconstruction corrected the errors in previous textbooks. The textbook would, according to Gray, help students understand the historical roots of contemporary problems, and the coverage of recent history would show their state's progress but also how much remained to be done. Though he believed the textbook would challenge students, he found "nothing too hard or controversial for ninth graders." After St. Andrew's Episcopal School started using *Conflict and Change* in 1976, other schools in the diocese had also used it without any problems.[21]

Catherine Gray, the bishop's daughter, followed him to the witness stand. In the spring of 1977 as a ninth grader at St. Andrew's Episcopal School, she had used *Conflict and Change* in her Mississippi history course, the first class at St. Andrew's to use the book. Though a private school, St. Andrew's qualified for state-funded textbooks, but it could not use state money to purchase a book rejected by the Textbook Purchasing Board. In the summer of 1976 Headmaster Allen W. Becker had, with the advice of Bishop Duncan Gray and history teacher Jerry McBride, selected the Loewen and Sallis textbook. Gray reported that she and her fellow ninth graders had enjoyed the textbook because it explained why events happened. While older students who had not used *Conflict and Change* considered Mississippi history boring, Gray and her classmates found it interesting and wanted to discuss what they had read, and they did so without upsetting anyone. Though the picture of a lynching startled some students, it made them realize for the first time that such events had occurred in their state. Stockett's cross examination yielded from Gray that her class at the expensive private school numbered only fifteen students, of whom two were black.[22]

Monsignor Paul V. Canonici, who served as director of educational services for the Catholic Diocese of Natchez-Jackson, testified next for the plaintiffs. He told the court that three schools in the diocese used *Conflict and Change*. Like St. Andrew's Episcopal School, St. Joseph's in Greenville, Holy Child Jesus in Canton, and Immaculate Conception in Clarksdale had to buy the books with their own money because they could not use state funds. According to Canonici, three other Catholic schools would like to use the textbook but could not afford it. He believed Loewen and Sallis did a better job than other books depicting the contributions of Mississippi blacks, and their inclusion helped white children as well as black appreciate what blacks had done in the state. According to Canonici, using the book caused no problems for the teachers or the students.[23]

The final witness on the trial's second day, the superintendent of Jefferson County schools, agreed with the monsignor. In southwestern Mississippi just north of Natchez, Jefferson County had the highest percentage of black citizens of any county in the nation, and in 1969 Charles Evers had won election as mayor of its county seat, Fayette. Superintendent Marion L. Hayes wanted his schools to use *Conflict and Change*, but they could not afford it without state funding. Coming from a black county, Hayes wanted textbooks that related to his students and their history. Bettersworth's textbook, according to Hayes, "treated blacks somewhat like an invisible type of people in the historical narrative." When his teachers supplemented *Your Mississippi* with information from *Conflict and Change*, student interest increased. The former social studies teacher had no reservations about using the Loewen and Sallis textbook except for its cost. He had no local funds to buy the book, so his students could have access to it only if the state board approved it for purchase with state money. If anything, he wanted even more material on black history.[24]

When court reconvened on Wednesday morning, the plaintiffs presented testimony by residents of Jefferson County and of Canton. The first witness, Julius Heidelberg, Jefferson County's black assistant superintendent of schools, testified that students showed little interest in Mississippi history when studying Bettersworth's textbook because of its bias for white supremacy. He observed that it omitted many events that all children needed to know about, while *Conflict and Change*'s more complete coverage would provide black children with information that promoted racial pride. Two Mississippi history teachers from Jefferson County, Hennie B. Taylor and Willie B. Harding, explained why they found *Conflict and Change* superior. It contained more detail about the lives of free blacks, especially William Johnson, "the barber of Natchez," and students found it interesting and easy to read. The inclusion of minorities gave students models and heroes. Dr. Charles Humphrey, the county coroner and father of two black girls in the county schools, claimed that leaving a group of people out of history constituted suppression that deprived them of motivation. The former teacher explained that his daughters considered Bettersworth's book dull, and he believed Loewen and Sallis would stimulate further study. After a mother from Canton testified in favor of *Conflict and Change*, Gregory Coleman, a black student from Canton, criticized Bettersworth, "We are just completely left out."[25]

In the afternoon court session, the plaintiffs offered expert testimony by two historians. Educated at Oxford University and Columbia University, John Anthony Scott taught half time at Rutgers University law school and half time at the Ethical Culture School in New York. In addition to writing more than a dozen books, he glowingly reviewed *Conflict and Change* in 1974 for "The Committee on History in the Classroom Newsletter." He had also written about the textbook adoption case for professional publications. According to Scott, *Your Mississippi* followed an outmoded white-oriented approach to history. Viewing slavery from the slaveowner's perspective, it saw the institution as benign and paid little attention to its horrors. Bettersworth wrote a "traditional history that has failed to keep up with the pace of historical research." On the other hand, the pioneering work by Loewen and Sallis treated slavery objectively by discussing the treatment of slaves and their resistance to bondage. Scott declared that *Conflict and Change*'s "first great strength is its courage" in presenting a "remarkably more human picture of life" that would be "more inspiring to students." And the book came from Mississippi. "Since state history is also national history in microcosm," Scott argued, "this book makes Mississippi the nation's pioneer in human history." He worried that the state's rejection would discourage others from writing similar books.[26]

Expert testimony also came from a history professor at the University of Southern Mississippi. Neil R. McMillen, a native of Michigan, had been educated at Southern Mississippi and Vanderbilt University, where he received his doctorate in 1968. His dissertation and first book examined the segregationist Citizens' Councils and "organized resistance" to the civil rights movement. McMillen contended that Bettersworth avoided the central themes of race and class in Mississippi history, but Loewen and Sallis dealt with them directly. "We're guilty of distorting the past," McMillen declared, "if we portray Mississippi's race history as one of mutual respect and advantage." Reflecting the latest scholarship, *Conflict and Change* provided "remarkably complete" coverage of Reconstruction, Jim Crow, and the civil rights movement. Though race provided a major theme, McMillen claimed that overemphasizing it would be difficult, and Loewen and Sallis did not. They told the truth in a candid and lively way.[27]

To the court McMillen brought unusual judgment because he had a decade of experience writing American history textbooks. Based on his expertise, he praised *Conflict and Change* for its handling of abstractions and blamed textbooks like *Your Mississippi* for not preparing the state's students to work with ideas. When in cross-examination Stockett pressed for an explanation, McMillen said Loewen and Sallis dealt with "complex and difficult issues like ideologies, like questions of public morality, official lawlessness, questions that are very often, in fact, not generally treated in texts for high school students." When an unsatisfied Stockett asked what he meant by official lawlessness, McMillen responded, "From 1890 until 1965 Mississippi defied the

15th Amendment [extending the vote to blacks] as an official policy of the state. That's an act of contempt for the Constitution of the United States." As a further example he mentioned Governor Ross Barnett's breaking of federal law in attempting to keep James Meredith out of the University of Mississippi.[28]

When Stockett also asked McMillen if the books mentioned in the bibliographies would be available to a student in an average high school library, McMillen replied, "The pertinent question is would these works be useful. His teacher or librarian would know how to find them." In an attempt to discredit McMillen, the assistant attorney general supposed that the professor had not been in a school library since his days as a high school student, but McMillen quickly corrected Stockett by telling him that he went into one nearly every afternoon because his wife worked as a school librarian. Stockett also tried to discredit McMillen's testimony as coming from a Michigan native who disliked Mississippi. The witness told the defense attorney that the description would surprise McMillen's Mississippi-born wife and their two Mississippi children.[29] Stockett's weak challenges to McMillen displayed his inadequate trial preparation because he did not know the answers to his own questions, and as a result McMillen's replies made the lawyer look foolish.

On the trial's fourth day, the plaintiffs called three more experts. Robert B. Moore of the Council on Interracial Books for Children had extensive experience studying stereotypes and racism in books. Educated at the University of Massachusetts where he earned a doctorate in education, Moore had worked for four years as resource coordinator for the Council's Racism/Sexism Resource Center for Educators. In 1976 he wrote "Two History Texts: A Study in Contrast," that compared *Your Mississippi* and *Conflict and Change*. In his court appearance, Moore repeated many of the points in his article. He saw the former as biased and the latter as unbiased. He called the Bettersworth book "an exemplary text" for racial omissions, distortions, and stereotypes. In regard to slavery, Moore said Bettersworth mistook the exceptional slave owner for the typical. By adopting the Confederates' point of view, Bettersworth also presented a negative interpretation of Reconstruction and ignored segregation, Jim Crow, lynching, and sharecropping in the late nineteenth century. He also omitted the civil rights movement because *Your Mississippi* glossed over social problems. Calling *Conflict and Change* "a unique text," he praised its honest treatment of slavery, Native Americans, the Ku Klux Klan, women, and desegregation. Adoption of Bettersworth would, he believed, deny the existence of problems and deprive students of the opportunity to understand society and to function as a citizen.[30]

Longtime newspaper reporter W. F. Minor followed Moore to the stand. From his thirty years' experience covering Mississippi for the New Orleans *Times-Picayune*, Minor had expertise in recent Mississippi history. Based on his own reporting, he explained previous attempts in the 1950s and under Governor Barnett to censor "alien influences" in the state's textbooks. He faulted Bettersworth's text for its "skimpy" coverage of the civil rights movement and for its failure to explain the meaning of events. Minor also disparaged its shallow discussions of recent politics. He judged *Conflict and Change* the better book, and better written too.[31]

Perhaps the plaintiffs' star witness was Margaret Walker Alexander, the acclaimed black author of *Jubilee*. Her ten years of historical research for the novel and her long teaching career at Jackson State University made her an expert on nineteenth-century history and education. To teach blacks and whites about black heritage, she had established at Jackson State the Institute for the Study of the Life, History, and Culture of Black People. Referring to *Your Mississippi* she charged, "It talks about black people as if he [Bettersworth] suddenly thought about it in passing." She pointed out that "Bettersworth is a scholar of the Confederacy. That is what he espouses. It is hard for him to change when he comes to *Your Mississippi*." If critics had alleged that *Conflict and Change* stressed race so much that the textbook became black history, Alexander denied the charge. No good history could exclude blacks, and, she proposed, "I doubt any scholar of black history would say this is black history. This is Mississippi history." She especially celebrated the book because it "throws light on the three races [white, black, Indian] involved in Mississippi." Alexander defended the photograph of a lynching, "They are atrocities that are a part of our history. I doubt seriously that it would cause any problem in anybody's classroom. Black people have always been aware of this kind of thing happening in the black community and black children knew it when it happened." Endorsing *Conflict and Change* as "especially good for the young mind," she declared that it "helps overcome alienation between the races and in general inspires the young person with a love for his homeland and some knowledge of it."[32]

The day's last witness, Jeanne Middleton, brought both her experience as a contributor to *Conflict and Change* and her subsequent training in education. After graduating from Millsaps in 1971, Middleton studied at Harvard University where she received her doctorate in 1978. Her dissertation examined school desegregation in Jackson. She worked in the Jackson public schools for three years before she became a professor of education at her alma mater. She defended *Conflict and Change* as better than *Your Mississippi* on at least five of the sixteen criteria used to evaluate textbooks: equitable treatment of all ethnic groups, suitable vocabulary and sentence structure, illustrations and graphics, exercises and activities for students, and stimulation of original thinking. Middleton especially defended the photographs, including the lynching picture. If *Conflict and Change* promoted controversy in the classroom, Middleton approved because learning required some controversy to prompt a student to want to learn more.[33]

On the trial's final day in Greenville, four more experts appeared before the court session ended at lunchtime. The plaintiffs first called Ted Kilty, a Western Michigan University professor of education and an expert on reading. A former middle school teacher with a decade of experience, Kilty received his doctorate from the University of Michigan in 1970 and studied on a postdoctoral fellowship at Harvard where he knew professor Jeanne S. Chall. To evaluate the reading levels of the two Mississippi history textbooks, Kilty used the Dale-Chall Readability Formula. After selecting ten samples of at least one hundred words in each textbook, he examined them for sentence length and unfamiliar vocabulary. *Your Mississippi* sentences averaged 14 words, and *Conflict and Change* 18 words. Bettersworth's sentences contained an average of 13 unfamiliar words in every 100, while Loewen and Sallis had 15. According to Kilty, no significant difference in readability existed between the two texts. When Stockett cross examined Kilty, he told the witness that the Rating Committee had applied the Frye readability formula to determine *Conflict and Change* unacceptable. Kilty dismissed the unscientific Frye test as one "used by people not concerned about the intellectual honesty of the score."[34]

The next witness for the plaintiffs brought a quite different analysis of the two textbooks. Professor Philip J. Stone, a Harvard psychologist, used research from the 1964 Watts riots on "black invisibility." Content analysis of newspapers had shown that the rioting resulted in part from the lack of black visibility in Los Angeles. Even as the black population grew, the news devoted to blacks had remained disproportionately low. Stone measured the degree of black invisibility in the textbooks. References to "Mississippians" or "Mississippian" that did not apply to blacks rendered blacks invisible. He found 148 instances of the words in Bettersworth and 114 in Loewen and Sallis. In Bettersworth, 43 cases did not include blacks, and one in Loewen and Sallis did not. When Stone searched for references to "black Mississippians" that recognized their separate identity, he found one in Bettersworth and eighteen in Loewen and Sallis. Similarly for "white Mississippians," he found three in Bettersworth and thirty in Loewen and Sallis. Though Stone carefully avoided saying that the state should reject *Your Mississippi*, he did observe, "A black student reading this book would gain the notion that when they talk about Mississippians, blacks are not among them. They're something external." He contended that a good textbook needed to stress that "blacks are not just in Mississippi like trees and cotton plants. They're in Mississippi as Mississippians. It is important for white students to see that Mississippians are a community of blacks and whites and for blacks to see that they are not just tourists or guest workers passing through the state." Under cross examination by Stockett, however, Stone himself fell into using "Mississippians" when he meant white Mississippians.[35]

John H. Peterson Jr., an anthropologist at Mississippi State University, criticized Bettersworth's *Your Mississippi* for including "almost nothing on Indians except for some information on treaties." As a result the textbook omitted or distorted the Indians' contributions to the state. The Georgia native had written his University of Georgia dissertation on "The Mississippi Band of Choctaw Indians: Their Recent History and Current Social Relations" and, as an expert on the state's Indians, he had advised with Adams and others on the Mississippi History Project. Perhaps as a result of his advice, he believed that *Conflict and Change* had "a better grasp" of Indian history and contemporary conditions. For Indians, Peterson did not consider Bettersworth's book a real history, and he took exception to its use of the term "Indian giving." Though Peterson recognized Bettersworth's attempts to improve the coverage of Indians in his 1974 textbook, he thought "it would be better if some of the treatment he gives them were forgotten rather than published."[36]

The last plaintiffs' witness was Evans Harrington, University of Mississippi professor of English. Before joining the English department, Harrington had taught high school social studies and supervised practice teachers in English. He also had published a novel and more than a dozen short stories, in addition to his scholarship. A number of Harrington's works dealt with William Faulkner, and for five years he had directed an annual conference on Faulkner. He testified to literature's importance in Mississippi and explained that history, society, and culture produced the state's literature, which he considered the most important in the nation. Calling *Conflict and Change* "extraordinarily imaginative and effective" in discussing literature, Harrington appreciated that it discussed folklore as an introduction to literature. Unlike *Your Mississippi*, Loewen and Sallis's broad coverage also included playwright Tennessee Williams and novelist Richard Wright.[37]

After Harrington's testimony, Parker and the plaintiffs rested their case. Stockett immediately moved to have the court dismiss some of the plaintiffs, but Judge Smith overruled the motion and adjourned court until the Tuesday after Labor Day. The trial would continue in Oxford in the north-central part of the state, 130 miles northeast of Greenville. The U.S. District Court's Oxford division met just a block off the town square in the four-story federal building, constructed a few years earlier. Oxford was also the home of the University of Mississippi.

Starting when Judge Smith reconvened court, the defendants brought eight witnesses forward to testify. The defense called six members of the Rating Committee, all except for Benjamin Burney who had approved *Conflict and Change*. In response to Stockett's questions, each repeated objections made at the time of the ratings. Evelyn H. Wilder had married since the filing of the case, so she took the stand as Evelyn H. Kennington. She again criticized *Conflict and Change*'s inappropriate reading level and its coverage of race relations. When she started to give other reasons for rejecting *Conflict and Change*, Parker objected because she tried to give reasons that she had not submitted in writing to the Textbook Purchasing Board. Judge Smith sustained the objection. Kennington then provided a list of the book's errors and shortcomings and criticized the book's negative, unbalanced approach. The Jackson Preparatory Academy English teacher also pointed out pronouns with incorrect or vague antecedents, the use of the word "myth" instead of "legend," inadequate bibliographies, and insufficient student activities. She also opposed the textbook because it did not have a teacher's edition. On cross examination, she admitted that neither the laws nor the criteria required a teacher's edition. Parker also established that Kennington had no expertise in Mississippi history and had read no books on Mississippi history.[38]

One of the two blacks on the Rating Committee, James Wash of Forest, testified next. He repeated his worries that the lynching photograph would damage black self-esteem and cause trouble in the classroom. The judge again sustained an objection when he started to offer other reasons for downgrading *Conflict and Change*. On cross examination by Parker, Wash did concede that a textbook should not hide lynching, and he admitted that the Loewen and Sallis book was better than the textbook currently used, which was Bettersworth's.[39]

As the day's last witness, Howard Railes followed Wash to the stand. The Tate County administrator came fully prepared to explain, in response to Stockett's questions, why he rejected *Conflict and Change*. In objecting to the textbook's coverage of racial incidents, he alleged, "The continuous coverage of isolated incidents is misleading." Railes mentioned more than a half dozen specific examples that ranged from slave revolts to whitecapping (white-on-black extralegal violence) to a 1960 Biloxi beach demonstration, and he estimated that 70 to 80 percent of the text dealt with slavery, the Civil War, and civil rights. Railes also identified many places where the authors expressed their opinions. For example, he objected to the first chapter's discussion of the mistakes of the past, their later effects, and the necessity to learn from them and change. He also disliked the insertion of opinions in the explanation of lynching and even the inclusion of lynching statistics. Railes complained about what individual chapters included and the book's general organization, the relevance of specific pictures, the lack of color in maps, the small print, and the lack of a teacher's edition. Citing more than twenty examples, Railes also criticized the authors' questions sprinkled throughout the text, usually after an inserted document or graphic.[40]

Under cross examination by Parker, Railes said he had taken Mississippi history as a student at Mississippi State University but had read none of the books listed in the textbooks' bibliographies except James W. Silver's *Mississippi: The Closed Society*. When Parker asked about the student's right to study controversial issues, Railes declared it depended on the effects on the student, the classroom, and the wider community. Judge Smith then interrupted to ask, "Who is to judge?" Railes replied that the teacher would decide. Parker then asked, "Not the Textbook Board?" Railes explained that all of the Rating Committee members were teachers. Referring to the state's instructions to the Rating Committee, Parker declared, "By keeping this book out of the classroom, you are depriving teachers all over Mississippi the use of this book under the free textbook program." Railes maintained that in integrated classes the textbook would cause conflict. Using the lynching picture as an example, he argued that "this type of picture would . . . ally students one against the other."[41]

At the reopening of court on Wednesday, September 5, Judge Smith announced that he reversed his earlier decision and would allow testimony from Rating Committee members about their reasons for rejecting *Conflict and Change* even if the reasons given in court had not appeared in their evaluative reports back in 1974. When cross examination of Railes resumed, Parker asked if the witness thought Loewen and Sallis suggested that all whites treated all blacks harshly. Railes reminded the court that when he voted against *Conflict and Change* "I was thinking about our school situation. This was just four short years after integration." When Parker responded, "What about today?" Railes refused to change his evaluation.[42]

After a recess for lunch, the trial continued with Virginia McElhaney's testimony. The Hattiesburg teacher liked the songs and vignettes in *Conflict and Change* and reported that her school's library contained a copy of the book that she used for supplementary material. The book's high reading level and advanced ideas prompted her negative appraisal. "The students I have taught," she reported, "could read the words but could not understand the implication of the text." The book, especially its treatment of racial issues, "was more mature than the thinking of junior high school students." She also said Loewen and Sallis's overemphasis on race did not provide "a true picture of the history of Mississippi." Though she recognized students might need to know about lynching, she did not think the book should "belabor" it. "I just don't see why they [students] need to know how many lynchings there were," McElhaney explained, "when so many good things happened in our state." Under cross examination, she explained that Mississippi history should promote pride in the state. Instead, Loewen and Sallis's "liberal viewpoint" provided a controversial account of the history.[43]

Mary Kyle from Jackson next took the witness stand. By 1979 she had taught all three of the Sallis children at Bailey Middle School. In her Mississippi history classes she assigned the McLemores' textbook because students found Bettersworth's book too difficult. When she had used the prepublication manuscript version of *Conflict and Change*, the students had complained and would not read it; they had said it did not have any information that the McLemores did not cover. While Kyle had no objection to the interpretations in the McLemores' textbook, she did not want *Conflict and Change* on the approved list. She partly based her opinion on her belief that a textbook should "cover topics objectively without inserting your own opinion." Kyle also considered as a negative factor the lack of a teacher's edition for the textbook. Although acknowledging that she drew on Loewen and Sallis's book for its maps, illustrations, definitions, bibliographies, special projects, and ideas for field trips, she did not "think it was a textbook. It was more sociology and history."[44]

The trial's last day commenced with John Turnipseed as the defense witness. The experienced educator from the Delta declared his "major reason" for voting against *Conflict and Change* was the lack of a teacher's edition, even though the Random House representative told him one would be available soon. He also did not "see the historical value" of the way Loewen and Sallis treated racial conflict, and as a result he considered their textbook "unsuitable for classroom use." In "a racially mixed classroom, the discussion of the material would be improper," Turnipseed declared. "I thought it would be, for lack of a better term, embarrassing." According to Turnipseed, photographs that "would cause harsh feelings in the classroom" included a lynching, an advertisement claiming "All white help!," a protest bumper sticker saying "Don't buy gas where you can't use the rest room," and pictures of restroom signs for "Men," Women," and "Colored." "Quite frankly," Turnipseed declared, "I felt that the book harps on the black vs. white issue." In an important colloquy, perhaps the most revealing of the trial, an incredulous Judge Smith intervened to ask Turnipseed about segregated restrooms and sporting events:

JUDGE SMITH: "You don't think that's a part of Mississippi history?"

TURNIPSEED: "No sir. I can't see that it would be related to a study of history."

JUDGE SMITH: "You don't see any historical value in that kind of situation?"

TURNIPSEED: "No sir, I don't. I feel the contributions made by blacks as well as whites are more important and should not be degraded."

JUDGE SMITH: "The racial situation that existed wouldn't have had any historical significance at all? Where are students to learn the facts if they don't learn them in school?"

TURNIPSEED: "Again, I think in integrated classrooms it would cause resentment."

The judge also pressed Turnipseed about his objection to the lynching photograph:

JUDGE SMITH: "But that happened didn't it? Didn't Mississippi have more lynchings than any other state?"

TURNIPSEED: "Well, yes. But that all happened so long ago. Why dwell on it now?"

JUDGE SMITH: "Well, it is a *history* book!"

At that point, the plaintiffs gained confidence that the judge would rule in their favor. Turnipseed, undaunted, maintained on cross examination that Bettersworth's *Your Mississippi* did not contain anything controversial.[45]

In a tactical change, Peter Stockett next sought to undermine *Conflict and Change* by discrediting one of its illustrations. He called as his next-to-last witness Sam Yarbrough, a school principal from Bruce and former superintendent of the Lafayette County schools. Yarbrough testified about the inaccuracy of one picture caption. Under a photograph showing white children in a classroom, the caption said, "Although progress was made after 1900, this one-room school was still used in Lafayette County in 1962." According to Yarbrough the photograph actually pictured Yokona Vocational High School in Lafayette County built in 1923, and it had had ten rooms before its destruction in the 1960s. Under cross examination Yarbrough explained that he had noticed the error in 1975 when W. A. Matthews telephoned him to ask about the school photograph.[46]

For its final witness the defense called W. A. Matthews. The Textbook Purchasing Board's executive secretary outlined the procedure followed by the board and how it tabulated and considered the Rating Committee reports. He defended the six-year adoption cycle used by the board because it gave publishers the incentive of a long period of sales and because it protected the state by guaranteeing a fixed price for books. Matthews also reported that he compiled the comparisons of the indexes from the two Mississippi history textbooks.[47]

As soon as Matthews's testimony concluded, the defense rested its case. The plaintiffs offered no rebuttal. Judge Smith announced that he "did not feel in a position" to offer a ruling then. Instead he set an eighty-day schedule for each side to submit briefs supporting its side and responding to the other side. He expected to rule soon thereafter.

Led by Peter Stockett, the state appeared to present a superficial defense of the State Textbook Purchasing Board's decision. In addition to inadequate preparation, the assistant attorney general offered few challenges to the plaintiffs' case. His courtroom examination of witnesses lacked the vigor of his interrogations during depositions. Stockett may have simply not cared much about the case because he considered the state's position weak, if not incorrect. At the time of the trial, he said about Loewen and Sallis, "I don't think anybody's saying that what they are portraying in the book is historically wrong or inaccurate. I think it's a question of emphasis." Admitting his respect for *Conflict and Change*, Stockett recognized, "No doubt about it, it's got good reviews, which means to me a lot of knowledgeable people think it has merit as a history book." Offering his own personal evaluation, the defense lawyer conceded, "I've read the thing a number of times and found it enjoyable and interesting. I'd pay $6.95 for it; it's money well spent."[48]

For some commentators, the case had an obvious solution. "History must be truthful," declared the *Biloxi Sun-Herald*. Comparing the state's textbook authorities to Stalin's dictatorship, "on a much smaller scale," the editorial suggested that the textbooks had "glossed over part of this state's history" as Russian history "ignored" the "murders" and "horrors" under Stalin. "History is the record of what happened," and it should not "pretend that we live in an all-white society and that blacks had no part in our history." History textbooks must "give the facts as they were, not as we would have liked them to be." Bill Minor objected to Bettersworth's books that "spoke only of the white exploits in building Mississippi and virtually treated blacks as appendages of white society." By 1979, Minor claimed, blacks could not be "shunted off into their own (and inferior) schools," but whites "didn't change the books that dealt with blacks as virtual non-persons."[49]

On October first, the plaintiffs formally repeated their objectives in the case in their proposed final ruling. First, they wanted the court to order the Textbook Purchasing Board to approve *Conflict and Change*, or a revised edition, for a period of six years. Second, the plaintiffs sought "rules and regulations providing for procedural due process in state textbook selection." Third, they requested shortening the regular textbook approval period to two years. Fourth, they wanted the defendants to create "minimum standards of scholarship and reasonable curriculum requirements by which textbooks shall be evaluated." Last, they expected the defendants to pay plaintiffs' court costs and attorneys' fees.[50]

Two weeks later the defendants responded with their own suggested remedies. If the court gave the plaintiffs any relief, the defense argued that it should be limited to the adoption of *Mississippi: Conflict and Change*, not any "corrected or updated" edition. At a maximum the book should be on the approved list until July 1, 1981, when the next review of Mississippi history textbooks in 1980 would take effect. The defense also recommended that the court follow precedent and not interfere in the operation of a state agency, the Textbook Purchasing Board, as long as the enabling legislation had not been found unconstitutional. On two points the state seemed willing to yield if the court granted the plaintiffs any relief. Any rating committee member who failed or refused to rate a book "must state in writing the specific reason or reasons why he or she failed or refused to give such a book a rating and recommend it for adoption." In a major concession, the defense said that the Textbook Purchasing Board "should be directed to instruct" the members of the Rating Committees "to make their recommendations strictly on the basis of accepted criteria, and not to act on the basis of bias against, or hostility to, the ideology or historical viewpoint of the books being considered." Implicitly recognizing faults in 1974, the state proposed, "This would assure fair and nondiscriminatory action at the 1980 adoption in the course of Mississippi History."[51]

Additional pleadings submitted by each side reached different conclusions based on the evidence and testimony presented at the trial, and their positions mostly repeated their earlier contentions. The defense filed its own proposed final ruling on October 11. As testimony showed, five of the Rating Committee members based their decision partly on the lack of a teacher's edition for *Conflict and Change*. In a new position, the defense argued that the court should dismiss from the case most of the plaintiffs because they presented neither evidence nor testimony that their rights had been violated.

The defense also claimed that a sufficient procedure for review of the Textbook Purchasing Board's decisions existed within the state courts. Even if the defendants had acted in a discriminatory way, "plaintiffs have to show that such action deprived them personally and individually of a legally cognizable right," and the defense denied they had done so. The state proposed "no relief" for the plaintiffs.[52]

In November the plaintiffs replied to the defense's arguments. In regard to a teacher's edition, Frank Parker pointed out that no witness could refer to a law or criterion that required one; criterion six even said one was unnecessary if the textbook had "appropriate suggestions for teachers." More generally the plaintiffs claimed a "First and Fourteenth Amendment prohibition against State-imposed indoctrination and homogeneity of thought" as evidenced by the rejection of *Conflict and Change*. The rating committee's "purported justifications . . . are entirely pretextual, spurious, and designed to cover up an unconstitutional rejection." Parker repeated his objection to allowing Rating Committee members to testify to "purported reasons for rejecting the book other than those committed to writing on the Summary Evaluation forms." The photographs provided examples of trumped up excuses. In his testimony Loewen himself brought up the erroneous captions for two photographs, so the defendants could not have used them five years earlier as reasons for rejection. The mistake in identifying a school revealed by Sam Yarbrough came to the attention of the defendants only in 1975 after Matthews intervened by calling Yarbrough to ask about the caption. As the plaintiffs' pleading noted, the investigation came after the rejection and by executive secretary Matthews, not by a member of the Rating Committee. The evidence showed "beyond doubt that the white majority of the rating committee was racially motivated in its rejection" of *Conflict and Change*. The plaintiffs interpreted the adoption of Bettersworth's *Your Mississippi* as "an 'affront' to all black students" and as "a symbol of resistance to integration in the Mississippi schools." After he submitted the plaintiffs' response, Frank Parker told his clients, "This concludes the briefing in the case, and the ball is now in Judge Smith's court."[53]

Five months later, a decade after Loewen and Sallis began their textbook project, Judge Smith ruled in *Loewen v. Turnipseed*. In a forty-four-page decision, Smith thoroughly reviewed the history of the case. He paid special attention to the reasons for the rejection of *Conflict and Change*. Though he had permitted Rating Committee members to testify to other reasons for their rejection, Smith considered the additional reasons "an after-the-fact judgment." If they "had been substantial and played an important role in the rejection," the judge declared, "such reasons would have been inserted in the summary evaluation forms." Six years later he rejected them as irrelevant. As for the lack of a teacher's edition, Smith noted that the *suggested* criteria did not make one "mandatory." The criteria even allowed for the substitution of "appropriate questions for teachers" instead of a teacher's edition, and Judge Smith found *Conflict and Change* "is filled with questions for class discussions, . . . maps and other illustrations, definitions of terms used, special projects, suggestions for field trips, and, at the end of each chapter, an annotated bibliography." Smith decided the lack of a teacher's edition "did not contribute in a substantial way to its rejection." As a result, the judge concluded that the textbook "was not rejected for any justifiable reason" and "the decision of the rating committee stands without any avenue of challenge."[54]

After reviewing the legislative history of the book selection process, Judge Smith found the legislature sought to give the governor and the superintendent of education "the power to control the destiny of any textbook offered for adoption . . . to eliminate allegedly controversial material from the schools' curriculum, and to insure that only the views of those in authority would be communicated to school children." He found an "adamant intent" that textbooks "reflected the predominant racial attitudes of the day," which he labeled "segregation and discrimination." Smith said that "the avowed purpose of such a scheme [the textbook selection process] was to insure that no unauthorized ideas crept into the classroom." According to Smith, the rejection of *Conflict and Change* "was motivated and influenced by racial issues," and the "controversial treatment of racial issues was not a justifiable reason for rejection by the committee." More generally Judge Smith objected to a selection system that provided no avenue of appeal or review by the parties affected, such as Loewen and Sallis. As the judge wrote, "This procedure is objectionable, not because it regulates, but because it regulates *unreasonably*." Judge Smith decided to intervene in the process because it "implicates constitutional values" and the plaintiffs had no way to "safeguard their First Amendment freedoms."[55]

In more complicated legal reasoning, Judge Smith also affirmed the plaintiffs' right to file their lawsuit in federal court and to claim protection under the First and Fourteenth Amendments and under Sections 1981 and 1983 of the Civil Rights Acts of 1867 and 1871. The plaintiff authors, school administrators, teachers, and students proved that they had been injured by the actions of an agency of the state. The plaintiffs had both demonstrated violations of the rights of freedom of the press and speech, academic freedom, the freedom "to receive useful information," and due process, and they had traced the causes of their injuries to the defendants' actions. "The court concludes, therefore, that the defendants have deprived the plaintiffs, under color of law, of their constitutionally protected rights of freedom of speech and of the press, and of their rights to due process of law under the Fourteenth Amendment" and under the Civil Rights Acts of 1867 and 1871.[56]

As an appropriate remedy, Judge Smith directed the defendants to "approve and place on the approved list . . . *Mississippi: Conflict and Change*, or a revised version thereof, for a period of six years." Plaintiffs had sixty days to submit proposed revisions, and defendants thirty days to accept or reject them "based upon and supported by objective criteria" listed by the Textbook Purchasing Board. The court also "permanently enjoined [the defendants] from denying approval to or rejecting any submitted history textbook for racially discriminatory reasons, or for reasons motivated by racially discriminatory intent." The court wanted the board to follow its own official criteria. Finally, Judge Smith directed the defendants to pay the plaintiffs' costs in bringing the lawsuit and their attorneys fees. At the same time Smith refused the plaintiffs' request "to dictate to the defendants a plan of textbook approval" as part of a broader remedy.[57]

The news "delighted" Jim Loewen. "I think the state of Mississippi and all children in the ninth grade and younger should also be delighted," said Loewen. "What we asked for is what we got," said his "thrilled" co-author. Sallis observed, "This is what we felt all the time. It's something we've worked very hard for." The plaintiffs' attorney, Frank Parker, seeing the verdict's wider implications, said, "The decision strikes a blow for academic freedom, freedom of thought, and freedom to learn nationally, but particularly in the South." Peter Stockett told reporters that he had "no immediate plans to appeal" and would study the ruling and consult with others in the attorney general's office before making a decision. Attorney General William Allain had no comment. At its May meeting, the Textbook Purchasing Board voted not to appeal the decision, and the state did not pursue the case.[58]

Two troublesome issues remained from the lawsuit: agreement on acceptable revisions of *Conflict and Change* and the defendants' payment for plaintiffs' expenses. As Judge Smith directed, Loewen and Sallis submitted proposed textbook revisions that included simple updates of information from 1974 to 1980, corrections to errors in numbering and grammar, movement of content on a page, additions to bibliographies, and responses to defendants' objections and complaints. The authors also rewrote chapter 17 and added a new chapter 18 to bring the history to the present. In response to the revisions, the defendants lodged seventeen specific objections that mentioned, for example, a date for Senator James Eastland's retirement, the location of meetings of the state teachers' association, and a prediction about reapportionment in

1990. The authors generally found the comments "very helpful" and accepted most of them, though they considered some "simply wrong."[59]

Loewen and Sallis rejected as a matter of interpretation the defendants' objection to their mentioning their court victory when they wrote, "Because of *Loewen v. Turnipseed* you have been able to read this book." They refused two other objections where passages had appeared in the first edition and did not represent a change. To a defense objection about use of "exurb" without a definition, the authors simply referred to a definition five pages earlier; the authors promised to rectify a similar objection about "tract houses" with a definition in the teachers' edition. To other suggestions on the revised text, the authors did not comply "because they were simply matters of taste or style, or differences in interpretation," and in every instance they worked to maintain the text's readability. Judge Smith accepted the revisions as satisfactory and announced he would "not undertake the task of editing the textbook or dictating editorial policy to the authors." Except for the financial matter, he declared his ruling of April 2 to be final.[60]

Wrangling over litigation expenses lasted a few weeks longer than discussions over textbook revisions. Plaintiffs originally asked for an award of $74,162.06. In filing the motion, Parker reminded the court that the Lawyers' Committee, a "private charitable civil rights organization," took cases on a non-fee, contingent basis and depended on awards of attorneys' fees. In response the state protested that the plaintiffs asked for as much as one hundred dollars per hour in lawyer's fees and claimed an excessive number of hours. In addition to describing the plaintiffs' request as "unreasonable" and "inappropriate," the defense reminded the court that the plaintiffs won only two of their six forms of relief, so the court should "minimize the attorneys' fee to be awarded." The defense argued that the award should not exceed forty thousand dollars. Judge Smith disregarded the argument over the charitable status of the Legal Defense Fund and the Lawyers' Committee, and he denied expenses that a lawyer would normally absorb and not bill to a client. He specifically rejected Loewen's claim of nearly two thousand dollars in expenses because the record did not show that Loewen "is indigent" or incurred the expenses involuntarily. After dismissing many expenses and reducing the lawyers' hourly fee to fifty dollars, Smith directed the defense to pay $44,761.81 for the plaintiffs' expenses.[61]

In court Loewen and Sallis had won. The next test would come in the marketplace.

CHAPTER TEN

Change
The Book's Effects and the Culture Wars

As directed by the U.S. District Court, the Textbook Purchasing Board in August 1980 added *Conflict and Change* to the approved list for six years and signed a contract with Random House. With the legal contest concluded, the state's schools could adopt it for use in ninth-grade Mississippi history classes. The Loewen and Sallis book joined three others the board had approved for the regular 1980 selection cycle. John Bettersworth had revised his earlier textbook as *Mississippi: The Land and the People.* John Ray Skates, a professor of history at the University of Southern Mississippi, produced *Mississippi's Past and Present;* earlier he had written the Mississippi volume in a bicentennial series published by W. W. Norton. At the University of Southern Mississippi, Skates had taught David G. Sansing as a graduate student. Sansing wrote *Mississippi: Its People and Culture* for the ninth grade. A University of Mississippi professor, Sansing had gained recognition in state history circles with his popular Mississippi history class and with *A History of the Mississippi Governor's Mansion.* In a remarkable coincidence, Sansing, Skates, and Charles Sallis had long-standing personal connections. As youths the three authors had known each other in Greenville, where, though not close friends, Sallis and Skates completed high school in the same class, a year after Sansing. About fifteen years later, Skates and Sallis interviewed for the job at Millsaps College that Sallis accepted. Within a dozen years they had competing ninth grade Mississippi history textbooks vying for adoption.[1]

As a result of Loewen and Sallis's work and the state's changing race relations, the Bettersworth and the Skates textbooks had improved treatments of African Americans and expanded coverage of the civil rights movement, but they fell far short of the avowedly and thoroughly revisionist *Conflict and Change.* In many ways their new textbooks' inclusion of underrepresented Mississippians amounted only to "new levels of tokenism." Bettersworth's new more sympathetic textbook suggested that many white Mississippians had believed slavery was wrong and hoped to find a way out of the slave system, but cotton profitability made them "afraid to give it up." He also conceded, "There were many cases of cruelty to slaves." Though some slaves remained loyal to their masters during the Civil War, after the war the freedmen "roamed the state" because they lacked jobs and homes. In covering the postwar era, Bettersworth acknowledged the antiblack violence perpetrated by the Ku Klux Klan and the 1890 constitution's objective "to limit black voting." He also candidly called Vardaman a demagogue who campaigned primarily on the racial question. Bettersworth again provided limited coverage of the civil rights movement. His discussion of desegregation referred only briefly to resistance to the *Brown* decision, and he devoted only one paragraph each to James Meredith's integration of the university, the assassination of Medgar Evers, and the Neshoba County murders of James Chaney, Andrew Goodman, and Michael Schwerner. He did briefly mention Robert Clark's election to the legislature in 1967 and Charles Evers's as major of Fayette in 1969, as well as the 1970 deaths of two Jackson State College students. He included pictures of Charles Evers and James Meredith.[2] Though lacking the commitment to the white racial orthodoxy that had dominated his earlier textbooks, Bettersworth's 1981 book failed to meet the revisionist standard set by *Conflict and Change*.

John Ray Skates's discussion of antebellum Mississippi barely mentioned slaves in relation to cotton and omitted them entirely from coverage of health, medicine, and cooking. Recognizing that historians "hotly debated" the nature of slave life, he offered a slightly revisionist view of slavery as profitable but as concerned with "social control" as much as economics, and he saw slave discipline as "more lenient in practice" than "in law and theory." Ignoring the black majority, Skates declared, "Given a choice between the abolition of slavery and secession, almost all Mississippians would have chosen secession." After describing the near total wreckage and destruction caused by the Civil War, Skates explained that white Mississippians believed that Congress wanted to "take over and punish Mississippi and protect the freedmen." Whites saw the Freedmen's Bureau as "meddlesome, dishonest, political, and prone to spy on the conduct of the planters." In the late nineteenth century, Skates did find racial, economic, regional, and political "divisions, suspicions, and fears," and he recognized that "blacks suffered from increased violence" in riots, lynchings, and whitecapping. When segregation replaced slavery, the 1890 constitution stripped blacks of the "last remnant of their political independence." The last chapter on the "end of segregation" celebrated a new era "marked by cooperation instead of conflict, by equal opportunity instead of oppression." "The modernization of Mississippi's economy and society," his text concluded, "made it necessary and inevitable that white Mississippians recognize the legal equality of black Mississippians."[3]

If Skates's narrative showed some effects of revisionism, his illustrations lagged. In addition to advertisements for "Negro Blankets," "Negro Brogans," runaway slaves, and "Negroes For Sale!!!" it contained pictures of only five blacks (Hiram Revels, Blanche K. Bruce, J. R. Lynch, Medgar Evers, and Richard Wright). At the same time it devoted nearly a full page to a picture of an elderly Jefferson Davis, complemented by a photograph of his home Beauvoir and three of the Vicksburg National Military Park. Later portraits of white politicians included white supremacists L. Q. C. Lamar, James K. Vardaman, and Theodore G. Bilbo, and also a picture of Bilbo's tomb. Though significantly better than the textbooks of the 1950s, Skates's book fell far short of Loewen and Sallis's full and fair treatment of all Mississippians.[4]

Between the more orthodox books by Bettersworth and Skates and the daringly radical text by Loewen and Sallis appeared Sansing's textbook that deliberately sought to appeal to a broad market. In the interpretive space opened by Lowen and Sallis, Sansing's approach seemed not so threatening, even acceptable, to whites. His more moderate position would, he hoped, offer a liberal interpretation without arousing the ire of segregationists that had a generation earlier doomed Professor James W. Silver. Learning also from the extended battle over *Conflict and Change* and from the state's progress in race relations, Sansing offered a more positive spirit and a less critical tone than Loewen and Sallis; in effect, he de-emphasized the conflict in the state's past. Especially on race relations Sansing's text presented attitudes far different from earlier textbooks but without Loewen and Sallis's crusading spirit. Recognizing the "emotional intensity" involved in studying slavery, Sansing provided an empathetic view of the peculiar institution. He pointed to the "almost total regulation" of slave life and mentioned the many forms of slave resistance, including possible slave revolts. In stressing the importance of family and religion to slaves, Sansing declared, "Mississippi slaves did not give up their humanity and dignity simply because they were slaves." He described most black Reconstruction officials as "conscientious and diligent," while whites "often refused to cooperate with them." When the KKK failed to intimidate blacks, "a criminal element took over the Klan and resorted to violence."[5]

Around the turn of the century, Sansing conceded, the convict lease system "became a public scandal" because the usually white employers "abused, overworked, underfed, ill-clothed, and ill-housed" the mostly black prisoners. According to a similarly candid account, the Constitution of 1890's literacy test and poll tax sought "to make it difficult for Mississippi blacks to register" and "eliminated blacks as a political force in state politics." Sansing also offered a more balanced discussion of demagogue James K. Vardaman. With race the "dominant issue" in his 1903 reelection campaign, Vardaman advocated repeal of the Fourteenth and Fifteenth Amendments, called blacks "lazy, dishonest, and mentally unfit," and claimed they "were more prone to crime" than whites. According to Sansing, however, "Vardaman's racial actions were very different from his racial speeches," and as governor he opposed both the convict lease system and lynching.[6]

Sansing's discussion of the civil rights era included white opponents as well as movement activists. After a straightforward presentation of the *Brown* decision, he mentioned the Citizens' Council, interposition, the State Sovereignty Commission, and constitutional amendments to abolish the public schools and require voters to have "good moral character." He also covered the integration of the University of Mississippi, Freedom Summer, the Neshoba County murders, and Fannie Lou Hamer. In a description far removed from the white supremacist textbooks of the 1950s, and even from Skates's and Bettersworth's 1980 books, Sansing described Hamer as "one of the nation's most admired and beloved civil rights activists." When he compared Reconstruction to the civil rights era, he explained that "it is difficult for people who have been taught to believe something all their lives to change their beliefs. But the vast majority of white Mississippians are law-abiding and peaceful people. And many of them were willing to change their traditions and customs even if they did not change their beliefs, in the interest of peace and order." As an example, he described the progress in school desegregation. In an approving tone Sansing decided, "Within a decade Mississippi's long-standing racial traditions were significantly modified . . . . Mississippi adjusted to these changes with less difficulty than most people would have believed possible."[7]

In its careful attention to black Mississippians, Sansing's textbook included photographs of William Johnson (the Barber of Natchez), Hiram Revels and Blanche K. Bruce, Isaiah T. Montgomery, James Meredith, Fannie Lou Hamer, Medgar Evers, and Dr. Walter Washington, longtime president of Alcorn State University. It also included a paragraph on the Piney Woods Country Life School, a private Christian boarding school for black high school students. Unlike Bettersworth and Skates, Sansing dealt with what he called the "most significant population trend in Mississippi in the twentieth century," the great migration of blacks and whites out of the state. With a more balanced, even, and comprehensive coverage of black Mississippians and race relations than other Mississippi history textbooks, except for Loewen and Sallis, Sansing positioned his book as a comfortable alternative. As a graduate of Mississippi College and the University of Southern Mississippi, a veteran of ten years' teaching at Perkinston Junior College on the Gulf coast, and a professor at the university in Oxford, the native of the Delta had ties across the state.[8]

Before the Textbook Purchasing Board formally signed a contract with Random House, Frank Parker urged several school superintendents to adopt *Conflict and Change*. Saying that Bettersworth "attempts to brainwash students with the most outrageous white supremacist propaganda," Parker declared the Loewen and Sallis book would provide "the most honest and best information about the past history of Mississippi." After the Textbook Purchasing Board approved *Conflict and Change*, Parker sent to black school superintendents a newspaper article about the board action and Robert Moore's pamphlet comparing the two textbooks. In 1981 Parker moved to Washington to continue his work with the Lawyers' Committee, and from his new position he could not effectively continue promoting the textbook. At about the same time, Loewen's ability to influence adoptions also diminished because he moved to Australia for a visiting teaching appointment. Still in Mississippi, Charles Sallis and Jeanne Middleton lobbied the Jackson area junior high schools, and a local activist and advocate for Random House, Gordon D. Gibson, also pushed the book.[9]

Each individual school district had to choose among the four approved textbooks. As the state's largest, the Jackson school district had great practical importance; as the capital and as home to Loewen and Sallis when they wrote the book, Jackson also held symbolic significance. Each public junior high school sent one teacher as a delegate to the Districtwide Selection Committee for Mississippi history. Public school officials had heard little concern about *Conflict and Change* because principals had received no negative comments and PTAs had not discussed it. At its March meeting, the district committee of thirty teachers found Loewen and Sallis the least biased in its treatment of blacks, Indians, and women, but Pantheon and Random House neglected to send a representative to make the case before the committee. A month later the committee passed over *Conflict and Change* and chose Sansing's textbook because of its easy-to-read sixth-grade level, its maps and graphs of politics, and its portraits of famous Mississippians. When he heard about the decision, Sallis said, "I am very disappointed and saddened."[10]

By early summer all of the state's school districts had made their choices. With seventy-two adoptions, Sansing's textbook edged out Bettersworth's as the most popular. Twenty districts had chosen *Conflict and Change*, but eleven of them also approved at least one of the other books. Skates trailed with only fourteen selections. In a report to Pantheon, Gordon Gibson concluded, "Looked at from the angle of our having gotten started late in the campaign, maybe we didn't do too badly. Looked at from the angle of how well a book of this quality *should* have done, we got miserable results." In two places, according to Gibson, just a couple of telephone calls made the difference in the selection of Loewen and Sallis's book. The book had its strongest appeal in the heavily black counties of the Delta (Bolivar, Holmes, Jefferson, Leflore, Sharkey, Sunflower) and in towns near the edge of the Delta (Grenada, Canton, Winona, Yazoo City). In a few places with comparatively low black populations (Pontotoc, Richton, Starkville), the adoptions encouraged Gibson because "the selection was made in all likelihood on the basis of sheer merit." Without exception the large districts rejected *Conflict and Change*, but Gibson did not quit.[11]

In a letter to the Jackson school superintendent, Gibson protested the selection of Sansing's book. "The book is, to be charitable, mediocre," he claimed. Saying that he "could see only two possible explanations: residual racism, or an almost criminal stupidity," Gibson asked for a reconsideration so that students could use "the award-winning, educationally innovative, historically complete *Mississippi: Conflict and Change.*" At the superintendent's suggestion, Gibson discussed the selection with several other school officials. In a meeting he suggested the district review its decision, start in-service training for teachers using *Conflict and Change*, and create a process that deemphasizes the role of publishers' sales representatives. His efforts failed.[12]

With private schools *Conflict and Change* had only slightly better success. St. Andrew's Episcopal School continued to use it, but with state funding. The St. Andrew's headmaster called it "more comprehensive" and "thought provoking" than *Your Mississippi*, which he said "is your Mississippi as long as you are white." The schools in the Catholic diocese also continued with Loewen and Sallis or planned to adopt it as soon as they could. Students in a dozen other Jackson area private schools chose to use Bettersworth. Established for whites after school integration, the segregated private schools would likely have had little interest in the themes and perspectives presented in *Conflict and Change*, even if they could have used state funds to purchase it.[13]

Though Loewen and Sallis worked on revising the textbook and creating a teacher's manual, sales of *Conflict and Change* lagged behind Pantheon's expectations. Even districts that had adopted the book did not necessarily immediately buy it. If it was a dual selection, most teachers may have opted for the other book. If it was the sole selection, the district may have decided to use its previous adoption as long as it could get sufficient copies. Pantheon never published a thoroughly revised second edition, and after six years the slightly revised 1980 edition had sold fewer than five thousand copies. In court Loewen and Sallis had won, but in the marketplace they lost. They failed to get their book into many of the state's classrooms.

While school districts in the winter of 1981 prepared to choose among Mississippi history textbooks, a scandal engulfed the Textbook Purchasing Board. In January, revelations of a private profit scheme within the Textbook Purchasing Board rocked the state capital. The state's Performance Evaluation and Expenditure Review Committee (PEER) reported that the state superintendent of education and other members of the board had received thousands of dollars by selling their sample textbooks. From 1976 to 1979, board members had received more than $80,000 (equal to $260,000 in 2016). Publishers had sent them thousands of free books to consider, and the board members then sold the books to the private School Book Supply Company (SBSC). Starting in 1979, the Ethics Commission required reporting of any income over $2,500; failure to do so constituted a misdemeanor punishable by a fine up to $5,000. Three board members who received a total of more than $50,000 escaped an ethics violation because they left the board in 1979 before the allegations. Superintendent Charles E. Holladay, however, received $4,226 in 1976 and $6,125 in 1979, but in 1979 he had returned the money to the SBSC and requested that it instead pay his son who had passed them on to the company. Dave Hamlin, who attended the board meetings for Governor Finch, sold books for $10,201 in 1979; when the SBSC refused to pay him instead of Finch, the governor's other staffers insisted it pay Hamlin. W. A. Matthews, head of the Textbook Purchasing Board, received $20,559 for sample textbooks that he sold to the SBSC. Matthews explained that his payments came from more than forty publishers, not the SBSC, so no one company's payments approached the $2,500 limit, and he also claimed the practice went back as far as 1940. The SBSC's James Campbell said the practice was widespread across the nation.[14] Despite the reformers' best intentions, the creation of a state agency to select textbooks had not eliminated corruption.

Common Cause of Mississippi wanted the state to recover what it called the "unjust enrichment" of public officials. Jere Nash, the state director, claimed that "to use one's public office for private benefit is to make a mockery of the trust and confidence citizens place in their governmental officials." Political reporter Bill Minor alleged the corruption extended to county and local officials who also sold textbooks. The state head of the AFL-CIO called on the superintendent of education, whom the organization had supported in the last election, to resign. The *Jackson Daily News* declared that "40 years of unethical behavior . . . doesn't justify its continuance. It smacks of a scandal and no amount of rationalization can make it look otherwise."[15]

A second PEER report charged that Matthews had received free meals, tours, and other benefits from publishers, booksellers, textbook depositories, and others in the industry. Instead of consulting the state attorney general, Matthews often relied on the publishers' lawyers for advice. Mississippi also paid more for some textbooks than other states did. "The publishing companies," PEER concluded, "appear to have substantial influence over Mr. W. A. Matthews."[16]

Early in February 1981, the attorney general gave the six officials with the Textbook Purchasing Board seven days to work out a plan for repayment; if they did not, he promised to file civil suits to recover the money. The six promptly made arrangements to repay the money, and a Hinds County grand jury declined to indict them. At the same time, the legislature began working on reforming the State Textbook Purchasing Board to make profiting from the sale of sample textbooks illegal.[17]

For W. A. Matthews the season of scandals did not end so easily. In the midst of the allegations of private profiteering, the *Clarion-Ledger* revealed more charges against him. The state's largest newspaper reported that in 1976 a State Highway Patrol officer and a Game and Fish Commission warden had arrested Matthews and Michael Gregg of Jackson in a public restroom at Legion Lake Park south of Mendenhall. The police charged Matthews with committing a homosexual act in public. Matthews pleaded guilty. In 1981 Matthews claimed that he had gone into the restroom to wash his hands and struck up a conversation with Gregg when the police entered and arrested them in what Matthews believed "was a set-up deal." Five years later, he said, "It was my word against [the arresting officers'] and I felt that I had no choice but to plead guilty" because "the publicity of a trial would be more damaging than pleading guilty and letting it go." When the story broke in 1981, Matthews denied that he was a homosexual. At the same time when Governor William F. Winter asked for Matthews's resignation, the governor said that he had not known of the 1976 charges and that they had not affected his decision to oust Matthews.[18]

When Frank Parker heard the news about Matthews, he exulted, "Bill Matthews bites the dust." In a letter to Jim Loewen, the plaintiffs' former counsel said that "I've always considered Matthews to be the real bad guy" in the case. Parker could not "believe that all the rating committee members did it on their own." In particular he recalled Matthews's extraordinary telephone call to the Lafayette County superintendent of schools in an effort to discredit a picture caption in *Conflict and Change*. For Parker, Matthews had an animus against the book and "was just interested in saying bad things" about it. Parker regretted that Leventhal had not asked Matthews during his deposition if he had ever been arrested, because the homosexuality arrest could have proved devastating.[19] Emerging five years later it may have suggested one reason for Matthews's opposition to *Conflict and Change*.

In 1975 Philip J. Stone, the Harvard professor of psychology and social relations, had told Loewen that the textbook "obviously baits the [State Textbook Purchasing] Board" with its revisionism. As an example, Stone pointed to the prominent photograph from a Jackson production of *The Boys in the Band* that depicted gay characters. "Did you have to put in the picture from *Boys in the Band*?" Stone asked. Mart Crowley, a native of Vicksburg, wrote the play that opened off Broadway in 1968 and ran for one thousand performances; in 1968 it became a motion picture. Critics said it "broke the mould" in its depiction of homosexuals by moving from "the old dispensation of homosexual guilt and despair," "sin and cause of stigma," to a positive and approving portrayal of "community [and] sexual self-confidence." Even for Broadway audiences, Crowley provided a "dangerously daring" introduction to Gay Liberation.[20]

In response, Loewen reminded Stone that "we didn't write the book with the Board [or the Rating Committee] in mind, at least not from a 'baiting' standpoint" and that they did not try to "psych out" the board in any way. The author defended including "a photo of the most important Mississippi production of the most important play by Mississippi's most important recent playwright." Loewen expressed amazement that the lynching photograph offended the reviewers because the state led the nation in lynchings and other textbooks routinely contained "much gorier lynching photos." Though also surprised by the reaction to the lynching image, Stone offered another theory. "I still would not discount," Stone told Loewen, "a Freudian model of the Board being unable to express feelings about homosexuality and instead protesting a race picture."[21]

The picture from *Boys in the Band* may have offended Matthews, whether he was a homosexual or not. The son of a Church of God minister, Matthews believed that his conservative religious and social morality contributed to his selection to direct the State Textbook Purchasing Board. State officials trusted him with the responsibility to protect schoolchildren from dangerous ideas that would undermine the orthodox Mississippi way of life by corrupting the students' values. If integration and black equality posed the immediate concern, any change in ideas about sexuality and gender posed an even more radical, if still remote, danger. As Stone suggested, Matthews may have unconsciously shifted his discomfort with references to homosexuality onto lynching because it provided a more acceptable, less threatening, less controversial rationale and because it would have been more persuasive to the members of

the Rating Committee and the board. In 1974 Mississippi, race had more sa-
lience than sexuality, though the two issues could hardly be separated (most
lynching, after all, resulted from accusations of rape). Inclusion of any explicit
reference to homosexuality would have concerned many Mississippians who
considered the textbook. Combined with *Conflict and Change*'s racial egalitarianism, any apparent approval of gay rights would have certainly marked
the textbook as unacceptably extreme.

Loewen and Sallis encouraged their ninth-grade readers to question
traditional authorities and challenge orthodoxies, whether in race relations,
historical interpretations, or, by implication, all other areas presented in their
textbook, even sexuality. They introduced students to new ways of thinking
by discussing the diversity of Mississippians, including the too-often-ignored
racial and ethnic minorities, workers, dissenters, artists, and women. *Conflict
and Change* wanted readers to exercise their intellectual autonomy by thinking freely about their society and its problems. Students' critical discussions
and debates could promote social changes that Mississippi needed. As Frank
Parker observed, "We have been engaged in a long, hard struggle to bring
Mississippi into contemporary America in terms of values."[22]

In many ways the fight over the values expressed by a ninth-grade Mississippi history book grew out of the civil rights movement of the 1960s and
anticipated the culture wars of the 1980s and later. Though the culture wars
involved much more than history—abortion, affirmative action, school prayer,
family values, censorship, and many other issues—history played a key role
because it had a major impact on what students learned about American
identity. *Conflict and Change* made an early attempt to change the definition
of Mississippi just as reformers in the culture wars sought to redefine the
meaning of America. Progressives and conservatives clashed over ideas about
what being a Mississippian or an American meant. By stressing racial equality
as one element of a diverse culture that included women, labor, the poor, and
other groups neglected by Mississippi histories, Loewen and Sallis's textbook
connected the black freedom struggle with the beginnings of a national emphasis on diversity and multiculturalism.

Conflict and Change wanted students to recognize and understand their
state's complicated history that told of struggle and failure by all kinds of Mississippians, not just continual progress by whites. The authors valued critical
analysis over celebration, conflict over consensus, change over custom. Instead of defending an oppressive, traditional past, they wanted students to
appreciate their flawed past and embrace a creative, modern future. By challenging readers to examine and question assumed truths, Loewen and Sallis,

in effect, emphasized new ways of thinking while conservatives, in the still-closed society of 1970s Mississippi, stressed the preservation of a traditional, unified cultural identity dominated by whites. The needs of students' individual self-esteem conflicted with the requirements of state identity. Not only did black history and accounts of racial oppression violate the white orthodoxy, but the slightest suggestion about gay and lesbian equality, for example, threatened fundamental ideas about gender and sexuality. Alarmed by potential instability and uncertainty, traditionalists resisted anyone who wanted to disturb students' thinking about established standards of race, gender, and even history itself. For Loewen and Sallis history could be a "tool for social change"; for conservatives history should "inculcate a love" of the state.[23]

Similar to the 1970s controversy over Loewen and Sallis's textbook, two events in the national culture wars demonstrated the importance of American history. To commemorate the fiftieth anniversary of the end of World War II, the Smithsonian's National Air and Space Museum in 1994 planned an exhibit around the *Enola Gay*, the plane that dropped the first atomic bomb on Japan. Museum curators, using their historical expertise, wanted to investigate the full historical context of the event, and, as a result, the planned exhibit raised questions about American policy that involved the first wartime use of nuclear weapons. The experts' efforts challenged the "sacred historical narrative" that celebrated the use of the bomb in ending the "Good War." Though endorsed by professional historians, the museum exhibit ran into strenuous opposition from veterans, the American Legion, congressmen, and conservative commentators who called instead for a commemoration that honored the veterans and the nation's collective memory. They objected to any denigration of the heroism and honor crucial to the veterans' identity and to the national memory.[24]

One major issue in the dispute involved disagreement over how many American lives the bomb had saved. The traditional view, part of the national memory, celebrated the dropping of the bomb because it made an invasion unnecessary and saved as many as one million American and Japanese lives. Recent scholarship used by the curators estimated, however, that fewer than one hundred thousand would have perished. The different views pitted historical memory versus historical research. Veterans also clashed with historians because scholars had questioned American motives in using the bomb, had considered Japanese interests and opinions, and had connected the first nuclear weapon to the development of the Cold War. Conservative critics argued that the *Enola Gay* exhibit represented "America as arrogant, oppressive, racist and destructive" and sought "to inculcate into American youth a revulsion toward America's past." As Rush Limbaugh argued, revisionist history portrayed the nation as "inherently evil" and "corrupt." Veterans and their supporters expected a positive view of the nation's past that would build patriotism and pride. Wanting to analyze controversial historical issues directly, liberals pushed for a historically accurate exhibit even if it portrayed the United States as less than "a righteous and innocent nation." After months of protests and negotiations, the Smithsonian gave in to critics and cancelled the exhibit. As one scholar observed, by defeating an enemy perceived as "political correctness, multiculturalism, postmodernism, or historical revisionism," conservatives had won a battle in the culture wars.[25]

Just as *Conflict and Change* two decades earlier had encountered opposition because it revised Mississippi's history, the *Enola Gay* exhibit provoked protests because it violated the usual understanding of Hiroshima. Representing the latest scholarship, a new interpretation threatened the collective memory and civic identity by raising uncomfortable questions. The textbook and the museum exhibit each wanted to debate a complicated historical reality, not celebrate a heroic, patriotic narrative. Instead of seeing the United States as an exceptionally united and honorable nation, the revisionists saw their country's flaws, diversity, and complexity. Controversial new views of American history extended beyond textbooks and museum exhibits when the culture wars entered history classrooms across the nation.

In 1994 the teaching of American history exploded in controversy over the *National History Standards*. The "battle over the *National History Standards*," according to one scholar of the culture wars, became "one of the archetypal skirmishes in the war for the soul of America." The controversy grew out of a 1989 action by the National Governors' Association, at President George H. W. Bush's urging, to establish National Education Goals. With congressional support and the Bush administration's continued backing, the move for national standards grew. In 1992, funding from the National Endowment for the Humanities (NEH) and the Department of Education supported the development of national history standards by the National Center for History in the Schools at the University of California at Los Angeles (UCLA). Under Lynne Cheney the NEH had in the 1980s also funded and helped start the UCLA center. Gary B. Nash, an established scholar of early American history, and Charlotte Crabtree, an expert on curriculum development, directed the history standards project. With the advice and cooperation of task forces, councils, committees, and focus groups composed of professional historians, school teachers, other educators, and private citizens, the UCLA center created standards for teaching history.[26]

In October 1994, just before the public release of the new standards, Lynne Cheney, the former director of the NEH, lashed out in the *Wall Street Journal*. Cheney's essay, "The End of History," protested that "those pursuing their revisionist agenda no longer bother to conceal their great hatred of traditional history" and "save their unqualified admiration for people, places, and events that are politically correct." The standards, according to Cheney, presented a "grim and gloomy" history that overemphasized the Ku Klux Klan and McCarthyism while they neglected Daniel Webster and denigrated John D. Rockefeller; they mentioned Harriet Tubman, an African-American abolitionist, more than Paul Revere, Thomas Edison, the Wright brothers, and Jonas Salk. As a result of the biased standards, Cheney feared, "Much that is significant in our past will begin to disappear from our schools."[27]

What Cheney began, Rush Limbaugh and other conservatives continued. Limbaugh ranted that the standards effectively said "our country is inherently evil" and "American is a rotten place," and he demanded flushing the "bastardization of American history" represented by the standards "down the sewer of multiculturalism." Columnist John Leo objected, "U.S. history is now being written from the counter-cultural perspective by oppression-minded people who trashed the dean's office in the 1960s (or wished they had.)." U.S. Senator Slade Gorton (R-Wash.) complained that "these standards are ideology masquerading as history" and called on Congress to "repudiate" their "perverted" view of history. Conservative historian John Diggins argued that revisionist historians rejected as elitist the importance of great men in history so that they could instead write about and speak for "workers, slaves, and other subalterns of the past who have no voice." Also ruing the virtual disappearance of the great figures in the revisionist American history, Cheney declared, "I think our kids need heroes. I think they need models of greatness to help them aspire."[28]

Gary Nash and many other historians defended the history standards. They maintained that the standards represented the scholarly findings of modern historians who examined the lives of people neglected in early histories— blacks, women, workers, ethnic minorities, and other ordinary Americans. Telling history "from the bottom up" meant, as one historian commented, that historians had "thrown open the historical tent flaps and embraced the experience of a far broader range of Americans than had ever before been represented" in history textbooks. The new approach stressed the importance of race, class, and gender, and as a result "the American past is as crowded and diverse and contentious and fascinating as is the American present." The new history standards represented a view of the past that displaced the traditional history dominated by a white male elite.[29]

Early in 1995 the U.S. Senate voted 99 to 1 to reject the history standards, and soon the controversy abated. The Council for Basic Education sponsored a revision of the history standards, and Gary Nash and his colleagues cooperated with the process. After many meetings and conferences, after intense negotiations and compromises, a set of revised standards appeared in the spring of 1996. The new standards edited wording that struck critics as "politically biased" and eliminated more than two thousand suggested classroom activities for teaching American history (critics had often focused on the teaching suggestions more than the standards). On May 3, 1996, a letter in the *Wall Street Journal* signaled an end to the history standards debate. Diane Ravitch and Arthur Schlesinger Jr., two critics of the original standards, declared the revised standards were "rigorous, honest, and as nearly accurate as any group of historians could make them. They do not take sides, and they pose the most fundamental questions about our nation's history. In our judgment, they will make a solid contribution to the improvement of history education in American schools." If the original standards had stressed diversity too much, the revision retained a multicultural emphasis but also explained what united the nation. As one mollified critic suggested, the standards brought *e pluribus* and *unum* back into balance. A year and a half after publication of the original standards and Cheney's attack, "the guns of this history war," according to Gary Nash, "nearly fell silent."[30]

Though "largely a 'media event' fought by elite politicians, journalists, and professors" without widespread popular clamor, according to one historian, the battle over the history standards represented another round in the culture wars and in many ways echoed the fight over *Mississippi: Conflict and Change* nearly two decades earlier. The new standards, like the Mississippi textbook, diversified American history to include blacks, women, workers, and others left out of conventional histories. Following the new interest in "history from the bottom up," the standards actually acknowledged the bottom, the left out, and the ignored. Loewen and Sallis had incorporated the same approach. According to critics, new subjects such as Harriet Tubman resulted in insufficient appreciation for white heroes, just as members of the Mississippi textbook rating committee had complained that *Conflict and Change* had discussed minor black politicians but had not mentioned all the governors. Attention to marginalized groups and people, to others than the dominant winning whites, meant that the new histories presented a broader history that discussed less attractive aspects of the past—what Rush Limbaugh had damned as evil and rotten—such as racial segregation and the KKK. Instead of portraying a heroic story of a united nation or state that only experienced progress, success, and consensus, the revisionists inserted conflict, dissent, and oppression into what Gary Nash referred to as the conventional "happy-face history."[31]

Like the larger culture wars, the 1994 controversies over American history dealt with Americans' ideas about themselves. History as presented in museums and as taught in the schools played a major role in defining the nation because it described the American people and explained their common experiences and their shared values. By telling Americans how to perceive themselves, history described a national culture and provided a national identity. In times of crisis like the Cold War, the importance of national unity increased, and history had a responsibility to instill patriotism by teaching a positive, heroic view of America and its past. According to one historian of the culture wars, the end of the Cold War resulted in a "loss of national purpose" and caused a "crisis in national identity." In a period of cultural uncertainty and instability, history's role "to inculcate a love of country" became "more paramount than ever." At the same time, the revisionists' disruptive demand for diversity and debate brought a strong reaction from conservatives because the push to expand the nation's story to include a multitude of peoples and cultures threatened the conservatives' sense of American identity and shared purpose. As a result of "confusion regarding the nation's role in a post–Cold War world," conservatives initiated the controversies over the *Enola Gay* exhibit and the *National History Standards*, each of which questioned the nation's sacred narrative. Seeking to perpetuate traditional history, conservatives wanted to maintain a love of country by celebrating its superiority and honoring its traditional heroes; revisionists, rejecting "sugar-coated history," wanted to include the "glorious and shameful, extraordinary and mundane."[32]

Similarly, Loewen and Sallis had in the 1970s challenged the state's established sacred narrative. In the wake of the momentous changes brought by the civil rights movement, the state faced an uncertain future without racial segregation, white supremacy, and black subservience. At the very time when Mississippi, especially its white citizens, struggled for a new self-identity, *Mississippi: Conflict and Change* presented an alternative definition for the state and its history by fully incorporating blacks, Native Americans, and other neglected Mississippians into the state's history. So soon after the tumult of the civil rights movement, the textbook's boldness proved too much for the

Textbook Rating Committee to accept. Only an appeal to the federal courts saved the textbook.

The battle over *Conflict and Change* differed in some respects from the well-publicized conflicts in the national culture wars. As a local struggle, it garnered little national attention except for occasional commentaries in professional historical publications; even the state press paid little attention to the case. It also did not involve well-known conservative spokesmen or advocacy organizations. Mel and Norma Gabler, prominent textbook policemen in Texas, failed to enter the debate over the ninth-grade history book. Though the Mississippi DAR and the American Legion had protested controversial textbooks in the late 1950s and early 1960s, they ignored the Loewen and Sallis book. Indeed neither side in the Mississippi case mentioned the contemporaneous and widely publicized textbook protest in West Virginia, they ignored the Gablers' attempts at censorship in Texas, and they failed to refer to the issues in the emerging culture wars.[33]

Charges against *Conflict and Change* came from the almost anonymous members of the obscure Textbook Rating Committee. In assessing a history of their state, they complained not about the questions that stirred national protests, the treatment of communism and capitalism, or religion and morality. Instead the committee's primary objection pertained to the issue particularly pertinent in Mississippi: race. According to the rating panel, the book so exaggerated the historical importance of blacks that *Conflict and Change* became black history, not state history. The textbook's innovations extended beyond race to other neglected groups and topics. Though it reflected contemporary scholarship, committee members expressed discomfort with the textbook's attention to ordinary people and its neglect of the state's leaders, especially some of its governors. For the committee, *Conflict and Change*'s modern inclusive, interdisciplinary approach did not even qualify as history. The book's unconventional design and its radical content may have made the committee members uncomfortable in ways they could not describe. As Philip Stone, the Harvard psychologist, had suggested, the committee may have expressed their inchoate concerns about other cultural issues in the racial language common in the Mississippi political culture. Perhaps most troubling to the rating panel, Loewen and Sallis asked students to go beyond the traditional reverential treatment of the state's past; rather than teach facts to memorize, the book challenged ninth graders to question their history. The initial rejection of *Conflict and Change* resembled the conservative opposition in the national culture wars, even if the Mississippi participants remained isolated from and unaware of the larger national developments.

The larger culture war did soon invade the state with controversies over sexuality, religion, and historic symbols. In the summer of 1981, for example, Congressman Jon Hinson resigned from office amid charges related to homosexuality. Two years later, toward the end of a gubernatorial campaign, conservative Republicans charged the Democratic candidate, Bill Allain, with sexual misconduct with a black male transvestite; Allain, the state's attorney general, survived the charges to win election. Later in the 1980s a group of Mississippians won a lawsuit to stop the display of a Christian cross on the state's Walter Sillers Building in Jackson, and a few years later a woman in Pontotoc successfully sued her local school district over daily devotionals broadcast over the intercom. In a 2001 referendum, the state voted on changing the state flag that incorporated the Confederate battle flag, but voters rejected the change by a margin of nearly two-to-one. Controversies also emerged over abortion, gay marriage, and other cultural issues, and Mississippi conservatives usually won the cultural battles except when, as in the case of *Conflict and Change*, the federal courts could rule.[34]

Though Loewen and Sallis won a significant verdict in federal court, it amounted largely to a moral victory whose effects defy precise measurement, but the controversy over *Conflict and Change* undoubtedly promoted change in other history textbooks. In Mississippi history, David Sansing had responded with a textbook more similar to Loewen and Sallis's than to anything published in the 1950s, and he later credited *Conflict and Change* with a major role in forcing open the closed society. Even Ray Skates's book and John Bettersworth's revised text had demonstrated awareness of the issues raised by *Conflict and Change*. In the larger historical community, the revisionist textbook also had an impact. When a group of progressive historians led by Herbert Gutman planned a revisionist American history textbook, they found an interested editor in Pantheon's Andre Schiffrin. The American Social History Project wanted to tell about the roles of "ordinary men and women" by looking at the "fundamental economic and social conflicts" that challenged the idea of a "broad consensus about the nation's basic values." As the project began, Schiffrin sent the historians copies of *Mississippi: Conflict and Change* as an example of radical history. Although *Who Built America?*, published in 1989, did not follow Loewen and Sallis's model, it did resemble it in general approach and in some of its themes. Other textbooks would gradually also adopt many of the design innovations of *Conflict and Change*. Loewen and Sallis also anticipated Howard Zinn's iconoclastic, extremely popular *A People's History of the United States*, published in 1980, that told the story from the perspective of the common people.[35]

The ninth-grade textbook and the resulting lawsuit did have other positive effects. The American Library Association soon recognized *Loewen v. Turnipseed* as a "notable First Amendment Court Case" for its protection of "the right to read freely" and of "freedom of expression in schools." In the American Historical Association's *Newsletter*, law professor John Anthony Scott hailed it as "a landmark case" that struck "a blow against intellectual monopoly" and "a blow for academic freedom." Most important in Scott's view, the *Loewen* case "lays the axe to the ideological defense of segregation and racism" that had "found a stronghold in the texts not only in the South but nationwide."[36]

The struggle over *Mississippi: Conflict and Change* did not end the culture wars, resolve debates about who should control textbooks, eliminate all discriminatory treatment of minorities from textbooks, settle questions over who determined historical truth, or solve Mississippi's many problems. Too often the state remained near the bottom in the best categories and at the top in the worst characteristics. For example, illiteracy, ill health, unemployment, heavy taxes, poor infrastructure, and poverty persistently plagued the Magnolia State.

As Loewen and Sallis had hoped, their successful conflict with educational authorities promoted change in Mississippi, though in limited and indirect ways. Approval of their textbook ensured that integrated schools would have textbooks that treated blacks and whites more fairly. As Frank Parker said after the ruling in *Loewen v. Turnipseed*, "Desegregation of the public schools in the South is now protected even more by a constitutional prohibition against maintaining racial segregation in the curriculum and in textbooks." Mississippi and other states would no longer dare to make students study books that presented a grossly distorted, white supremacist view of history. From the beginning Loewen and Sallis had recognized the dangers of racist textbooks. They understood that powerful interests used history, especially Mississippi history, "as a tool of social control." As they said in a 1971 discussion of their project, the "theft of the past by the power structure is a crime rather than a mere accident." For too long whites had denied to blacks knowledge of their own history. *Conflict and Change* helped bring blacks, and other neglected groups, into a more accurate version of the state's history and thereby break the white supremacist elite's hold on one aspect of public education. The end of a state-devised and officially enforced ignorance through the control of history textbooks helped to free whites, as well as blacks. By exercising intellectual independence and understanding their past, blacks and whites could be freer to change their state for the better.[37]

Acknowledgments

Jim Loewen and Charles Sallis could not have provided greater cooperation with my research. They readily supported and encouraged my writing about important events in their lives. On numerous occasions each welcomed me into his home and granted lengthy interviews. As scholars they recognized the importance of their own papers and granted me full access. They also understood the necessity of authorial freedom and independence.

Archivists may be a historian's best colleagues, and several offered me important guidance and advice. At the state archive, Anne Webster again spoiled a researcher with her smart, friendly, and efficient service. At the much smaller Millsaps College archive, Deborah McIntosh welcomed a stranger and thoughtfully directed me to many valuable documents. The late Mary Evelyn Tomlin at the National Archives branch in Morrow, Georgia, once again took a special interest in her home state's history and guided me to the official *Loewen v. Turnipseed* case file. Jana Hill with Mississippi State University's archive made photographs of John Bettersworth available. Though not archivists, two others gave me access to crucial complementary collections related to *Loewen v. Turnipseed*. In the state Attorney General's office, Reese Partridge made its copy of the case file and related correspondence available, and in Washington, D.C., Brenda Shum did likewise at the offices of the Lawyers' Committee for Civil Rights Under Law.

Librarians may rank second only to archivists. At the university library, Stan White-horn, Amanda Bennett, Barbara Swindle, and others made working in the library as easy and enjoyable as possible. In the university archive, Jennifer Ford and Leigh McWhite frequently and expertly assisted me. Lisa Harrison, Anne Johnson, and Judy Greenwood in the interlibrary loan department made the library seem big by quickly retrieving sometimes obscure works. In the law school library Kris Gilliland offered expert guidance in legislative and judicial records.

Many fellow historians and friends criticized the manuscript. As he always has, Gaines Foster perceptively commented on the earliest version of the manuscript, and a later one too, and helped improve it. Keri Bradford provided a rigorous review of an early draft, and Paul Anderson made thoughtful suggestions. Though not southern historians, Jeff Adler and Alan Draper each sharpened the manuscript's focus. Drawing on her vast knowledge of lynching photographs, Amy Louise Wood graciously identified the lynching picture in the textbook, and Louis Kyriakoudes introduced me to his friend Robert Proctor. The late Tom Freeland, an Oxford attorney, saved me from many errors in discussing legal matters. Will Hustwit took time from his own work on Mississippi to read several chapters. Ken Rutherford responded to queries about the law, and Andy Mullins answered vital questions related to his alma mater, Millsaps. Hank Klibanoff secured some of his old contributions to the *Boston Globe*. To gain the benefit of their expertise, I asked two scholars whom I have never met to read my work. Michael Apple of the University of Wisconsin and Jonathan Zimmerman of New York University each generously agreed, and their invaluable comments and advice improved my work. Later Mike and Charles Bolton read the manuscript for the University of North Carolina Press and suggested additional revisions. At the press, Jad Adkins, Dino Battista, and many others have eased the publishing process. Chuck Grench again proved just how good an editor can be. Every author should be lucky enough to have an editor like Chuck. At Westchester Publishing Services, Michelle Witkowski displayed considerable patience and understanding in a difficult time. At the university, several individuals provided invaluable help. From the very beginning, Max Williams had confidence in the project. All along Kelly Houston provided essential support. Toward the end Patricia Stewart handled crucial logistical matters, and Jonathan Orange offered important research assistance.

Two great men grace the dedication page. George Brown Tindall, who insisted on using full names, first advised me as a graduate student and later as a friend. Without his faithful support and steady encouragement, not to mention his wit and humor, I would never have finished graduate school. His example showed me how to be a historian and scholar. W. F. Minor, who for good reason keeps his full name confidential (except for a very few of us, and I am not saying), has been a valued friend for more than thirty years. A legendary journalist, Bill has covered Mississippi since Bilbo's funeral in 1947. Knowing him and hearing his stories has been one of the treasured rewards of living in the magnolia jungle. In all things Mississippi, Bill has been a trusted mentor and guide.

Bill Minor's appearance as a plaintiffs' witness in *Loewen v. Turnipseed* raises the unavoidable question of my personal connections to the story about *Conflict and Change*. I first heard about the textbook in the early 1970s from my graduate school friend Joe Herzenberg who was reading a draft for his former Tougaloo colleague Jim Loewen. Over the years Joe and I discussed the textbook case and how someone should tell the book's history. Through Joe I met John Dittmer in the mid-1970s and, not much later, Jim Loewen. Since 1983 I have also known David Sansing as a history department colleague and Neil McMillen as a fellow historian in Hattiesburg. Despite my connections to the plaintiffs in *Loewen v. Turnipseed*, I have aimed for fairness in discussing them and John Bettersworth and the defendants.

My absolute favorite archivist, librarian, and historian, is Brenda. She excels as an editor and critic and as a knowledgeable student of Mississippi history, but even more as a friend, wife, and mother. I thank her and all the others who helped me with this project.

Essay on Sources

The story of *Mississippi: Conflict and Change* begins not with the controversial text-book itself but the important background to the fight over the ninth-grade history book. The prelude examines the national history of textbooks, their importance in education, the methods of publishing and marketing them, and the procedures employed to adopt them. A dry, eclectic list of article titles in old education publications like *School and Society*, references to Mississippi state legislative journals and laws from as early as the nineteenth century, citations to minor cases in Mississippi courts, and occasional newspaper articles would result in many cumbersome and burdensome pages of primary sources with little benefit. The notes should provide a sufficient guide to the specific sources and their immediate pertinence. The 1974 textbook also emerges from the historiographical and historical contexts of earlier Mississippi histories. A similar list of a dozen Mississippi histories from Mary V. Duval's 1892 textbook to *Conflict and Change* eighty years later would serve little use other than pedantry. Instead what follows will highlight the most valuable sources unique to this work.

Specifically on the Mississippi History Project itself, the personal papers of Jim Loewen and Charles Sallis proved essential. Compared to Loewen, Sallis retained a modest number of documents because Loewen apparently saved nearly everything about the creation of *Conflict and Change*. The Mississippi Department of Archives and History contains seven boxes of his rich files, and nearly all relate to *Conflict and Change*. Loewen still has in his possession a large collection of documents related to the textbook. The Mississippi Department of Archives and History also houses the papers of Ernst Borinski, and it maintains numerous subject files that contain invaluable clippings and articles. The file on Nash Burger, for example, clarified the links between Bettersworth, Burger, and the *New York Times*. The state archive also has case files for a number of textbook cases fought in the state courts.

The Mississippi State Textbook Purchasing Board's actions and policies emerge from the Board's minutes and files at its office in the state capital. For *Loewen v. Turnip-seed*, several repositories proved vital. Both the National Archives branch in Morrow, Georgia, and the Mississippi Attorney General's office have, though slightly different, copies of the case file. The file in the Attorney General's office includes some correspondence and documents prepared by the defense. In Washington, the Lawyers' Committee for Civil Rights Under Law also has important correspondence and materials related to the plaintiffs in the lawsuit. Unlike many subjects in recent history, newspapers offered little, because the development of *Conflict and Change* garnered no public attention, and the press largely ignored the controversy over the textbook and the resulting lawsuit. John Bettersworth's dozens of contributions to the *New York Times*

Book Review did, however, add a crucial dimension to understanding his historical views.

Though many of the participants have died (Frank Parker, Bruce Adams, Peter Stockett, Olivia Jones Love, and Judge Orma Smith, for example), interviews yielded important information. Several especially important interviews with Jim Loewen and Charles Sallis (and his wife, Harrylyn) provided personal background, context for events of the 1960s, and details about their project. Others interviewed included contributors to the textbook (Jeanne Middleton Hairston, James Brown, Stephen Immer, Maryellen Clampit, and William R. Ferris) and participants in the legal case and trial (Melvyn Leventhal, Barbara Philips, Paul Canonici, Mamie Chinn, Hennie Taylor, Neil McMillen, Bill Minor, and Catherine Gray). Additional help came from interviews with W. A. Matthews, Peter Bernstein, Robert Bernstein, David Sansing, and Jerry McBride.

Innumerable scholars of Mississippi, education, textbooks, and the culture wars supplied information and insights, and several deserve special recognition. Jonathan Zimmerman's *Whose America: Culture Wars in the Public Schools* and Andrew Hartman's *A War for the Soul of America: A History of the Culture Wars* established the larger context for the battle over *Conflict and Change*. Michael Apple's *Official Knowledge: Democratic Education in a Conservative Age* and *Teachers and Texts: A Political Economy of Class and Gender Relations in Education* explained how the educational system can work. The innovative scholarship of Robert Proctor and his colleagues in *Agnotology: The Making and Unmaking of Ignorance* presented new perspectives on the "closed society" of Mississippi and the function of textbooks Last, Maria R. Lowe's articles made a major contribution to understanding Tougaloo and Millsaps colleges during the civil rights era.

Notes

Abbreviations used in notes

BPMDAH	Ernst Borinski Papers, Mississippi Department of Archives and History, Jackson, Mississippi
DDT	Greenville (Miss.) *Delta Democrat Times*
JCL	Jackson (Miss.) *Clarion-Ledger*
JDN	Jackson (Miss.) *Daily News*
JST	Jackson (Miss.) *State Times*
LCPDC	Papers of the Lawyers Committee for Civil Rights Under Law, Washington, D.C.
LPDC	James Loewen Papers, in Loewen's possession, Washington, D.C.
LPMDAH	James Loewen Papers, Mississippi Department of Archives and History, Jackson, Mississippi
MAGF	Files of the Mississippi Attorney General, Jackson, Mississippi
MCA	*Memphis (Tenn.) Commercial Appeal*
MDAH	Mississippi Department of Archives and History, Jackson, Mississippi
MSTBPB	Mississippi State Textbook Publishing Board, Jackson, Mississippi
NARA	National Archives and Records Administration, Morrow, Georgia
NOTP	*New Orleans Times-Picayune*
NYTBR	*New York Times Book Review*
SPJM	Charles Sallis Papers, in Sallis's possession, Jackson, Mississippi

Conflict

1. James Loewen and Charles Sallis, *Mississippi: Conflict and Change* (New York, Pantheon, 1974). References to the textbook will be to the 1980 edition that is more widely available.

2. James W. Loewen, *Lies My Teacher Told Me: Everything Your American History Textbook Got Wrong* (New York: New Press, 1975). For an attack on the methodology and conclusions of *Lies My Teacher Told Me*, see David Warren Saxe, "Lies and History: Unmasking Academic Complacency," in *The New Social Studies: People, Projects and Perspectives*, ed. Barbara Slater Stern (Charlotte: Information Age Publishing, 2010), 407–32. An education professor at Pennsylvania State University, Saxe alleges that *Lies My Teacher Told Me* contained "errors, exaggeration, and lies" and "egregious fabrications," and he labels it a scholarly failure and "a skillfully conceived piece of propaganda." Calling Loewen "a dedicated leftist" who engages in "polemical rhetoric," he compares Loewen to Howard Zinn and Don Quixote. See 410, 411, 421, 428.

3. Wilbert E. Moore and Melvin M. Tumin, "The Social Functions of Ignorance," *American Sociological Review* 14 (December 1949): 787–95; Jules Henry, "Education for Stupidity," *New York Review of Books*, May 9, 1968, 220–26; Robert N. Proctor and Londa Schiebinger, eds., *Agnotology: The Making and Unmaking of Ignorance* (Stanford: Stanford University Press, 2008). In *Agnotology*, see two particularly helpful essays: Robert N. Proctor, "Agnotology: A Missing Term to Describe the Cultural Production of Ignorance (and Its Study)," 1–33 (quotation appears on 11), and Michael J. Smithson, "Social Theories of Ignorance," 209–29. Herbert N. Foerstel does not discuss the concept of ignorance in his *Studied Ignorance: How Curricular Censorship and Textbook Selection Are Dumbing Down American Education* (Santa Barbara: Praeger, 2013), and he ignores Loewen and Sallis's textbook and the field of agnotology.

4. Charles W. Mills, "White Ignorance," in *Agnotology*, ed. Proctor and Schiebinger, 230–49.

5. Eric Broudy, "The Trouble with Textbooks," *Teachers College Record* 77 (September 1975): 14; Hillel Black, *The American Schoolbook* (New York: William Morrow, 1967), 3, 5, 73; Howard K. Beale, *Are American Teachers Free? An Analysis of Restraints Upon the Freedom of Teaching in American Schools*, part XII, *Report of the Commission on the Social Studies*, American Historical Association (New York: Scribners, 1936), 261; Diane Ravitch, *The Language Police: How Pressure Groups Restrict What Students Learn* (New York: Knopf, 2003), 140; Martin Mayer, "The Trouble with Textbooks," *Harper's* 225 (July 1962): 65–71. In a 1934 survey of antiblack bias in American history textbooks used in the South, Lawrence D. Reddick, a black scholar, observed that "we should remember that to the pupils . . . . these historical representations are the true accounts of 'what has happened.'" See Lawrence D. Reddick, "Racial Attitudes in American History Textbooks of the South," *Journal of Negro History* 19 (July 1934): 265. In a cautionary note, Tulley and Farr commented in 1990 that someone needed to study the influence of textbooks on educational quality, because no study demonstrated texts had a major impact. Michael Tulley and Roger Farr, "Textbook Evaluation Selection," in *Textbooks and Schooling in the United States: Eighty-ninth Yearbook of the National Society for the Study of Education*, ed. David L. Elliott and Arthur Woodward (Chicago: University of Chicago Press, 1990), 168.

6. Broudy, "The Trouble with Textbooks," 13–14.

7. Black, *The American Schoolbook*, 34, 59; Broudy, "The Trouble with Textbooks," 14; John P. Dessauer, "U.S. Book Markets: Where They Have Been, Where They Are Going." *Publishers Weekly* 210 (July 26, 1976): 41; R. B. Edgerton, "Odyssey of a Book: How a Social Studies Text Comes Into Being," *Social Education* 33 (1969): 286; Gerald Giordano, *Twentieth-Century Textbook Wars: A History of Advocacy and Opposition* (New York: Peter Lang, 2003), 21.

8. For discussions of the progressive school, see John Higham, *History: Professional Scholarship in America* (Baltimore: Johns Hopkins University Press, 1965; 2nd ed. 1989); Gene Wise, *American Historical Explanations: A Strategy for Grounded Inquiry* (Homewood, IL: Dorsey Press, 1973); Peter Novick, *That Noble Dream: The "Objectivity Question" in the American Historical Profession* (New York: Cambridge University Press, 1988); Fran-

cis G. Couvares et al., "Introduction to U.S. Historiography," 1–24, in *Interpretations of American History*, vol. 2, *From Reconstruction* (Boston: Bedford/St. Martin's, 2009); Allen F. Davis and Harold D. Woodman, eds., "Introduction: History and Historians," 1–18, in *Conflict and Consensus in American History*, vol. 1 (Boston: Houghton Mifflin, 1997).

9. For discussions of the consensus school, see the sources cited above in note 5.

10. James W. Silver, *Mississippi: The Closed Society* (New York: Harcourt, Brace and World, 1964).

11. Mills, "White Ignorance," 241.

12. See Ronald W. Evans, *The Social Studies Wars: What Should We Teach the Children?* (New York: Teachers College Press, 2004); Michael W. Apple, *Official Knowledge: Democratic Education in a Conservative Age* (New York: Routledge, 1993); Jonathan Zimmerman, *Whose America? Culture Wars in the Public Schools* (Cambridge, MA: Harvard University Press, 2002); Adam Laats, *The Other School Reformers: Conservative Activism in American Education* (Cambridge, MA: Harvard University Press, 2015); Gary Nash, Charlotte Crabtree, and Ross E. Dunn, *History on Trial: Culture Wars and the Teaching of the Past* (New York: Knopf, 1997); Margaret Hartmann, "Why Oklahoma Lawmakers Voted to Ban AP U.S. History," *New York Magazine*, February 18, 2015; Carol Mason, *Reading Appalachia from Left to Right: Conservatives and the 1974 Kanawha County Textbook Controversy* (Ithaca: Cornell University Press, 2009).

13. Andrew Hartman, *A War for the Soul of America: A History of the Culture Wars* (Chicago: University of Chicago Press, 2015), 7; Zimmerman, *Whose America?* 216.

Textbooks

1. *JCL*, February 28, March 1, and April 1, 1960; *JST*, February 25 and 28, and March 24, 1960.

2. *Laws of the State of Mississippi, 1871*, xlvii, 10; *Laws of the States of Mississippi, 1873*, 14; *Laws of the State of Mississippi, 1875*, 97; Aubrey Keith Lucas, "Education in Mississippi from Statehood to the Civil War," in Richard Aubrey McLemore, *A History of Mississippi* (Hattiesburg: University and College Press of Mississippi, 1973), vol. 1, 352–55; Reuben W. Griffith, "The Public School, 1890–1970," in McLemore, *A History of Mississippi*, vol. 2, 392–93.

3. Gerald Giordano, *Twentieth-Century Textbook Wars: A History of Advocacy and Opposition* (New York: Peter Lang, 2003), 13–14; Hillel Black, *The American Schoolbook* (New York: William Morrow, 1967), 81, 127–28; Charles A. Madison, *Book Publishing in America* (New York: McGraw-Hill, 1966) 122; Richard L. Venezky and Carl F. Kaestle, "From McGuffey to Dick and Jane: Reading Textbooks," in *Print in Motion: The Expansion of Publishing and Reading in the United States, 1880–1940*, in *A History of the Book in America*, ed. Carl F. Kaestle and Janice A. Radway (Chapel Hill: University of North Carolina Press, 2009), vol. 4, 421; Ruth Miller Elson, *Guardians of Tradition: American Schoolbooks of the Nineteenth Century* (Lincoln: University of Nebraska Press, 1964).

4. Madison, *Book Publishing in America*, 122–24; Venezky and Kaestle, "From McGuffy to Dick and Jane," 421–22; Lewis A. Coser, Charles Kadushin, and Walter W. Powell,

Books: The Culture and Commerce of Publishing (New York: Basic, 1982), 22; Giordano, *Twentieth-Century Textbook Wars,* 1.

5. Howard K. Beale, *Are American Teachers Free? An Analysis of Restraints Upon the Freedom of Teaching in American Schools,* part XII, *Report of the Commission on the Social Studies,* American Historical Association (New York: Scribners, 1936), 272, 276–80; Black *The American Schoolbook,* 133–36.

6. *Laws of the State of Mississippi, 1892,* 74–75, 897. See also Billy M. Bishop, "Public Education in Mississippi, 1910–1954" (MA thesis, Mississippi State University, 1963).

7. *Laws of the State of Mississippi, 1904,* 116–17, 123, 124.

8. Ibid., 117–21.

9. *Laws of the State of Mississippi, 1912,* 179; *Laws of the State of Mississippi, 1916,* 259–62; *Laws of the State of Mississippi, 1918,* 150; Michael W. Apple, "Regulating the Text: The Socio-historical Roots of State Control," *Educational Policy* 3 (2, 1989): 107–16. On southern progressivism, see Dewey W. Grantham, *Southern Progressivism: The Reconciliation of Progress and Tradition* (Knoxville: University of Tennessee Press, 1983), and William L. Link, *The Paradox of Southern Progressivism, 1880–1930* (Chapel Hill: University of North Carolina Press, 1992).

10. Apple, "Regulating the Text." See also the same essay in *Textbooks in American Society: Politics, Policy, and Pedagogy,* ed. Philip G. Altbach, Gail P. Kelly, Hugh G. Petrie, and Louis Leis (Albany: State University of New York Press, 1991), 7–26; Guy M. Whipple, "The Selection of Textbooks," *The American School Board Journal* 80 (May 1930): 51–53, 158; Nelson B. Henry, "Value of State Textbook Adoption is Debatable," *The Nation's Schools* 12 (December 1933): 19–20.

11. Burnett, "Textbook Provisions in the Several States," *Journal of Educational Research* 43 (January 1950): 365–66; Michael Tulley and Roger Farr, "The Purpose of State Level Textbook Adoption: What Does the Legislation Reveal?" *Journal of Research and Development in Education* 18 (2, 1985): 1–2, 7; Victor R. Durrance, "Public Textbook Selection in Forty-Eight States," *Phi Delta Kappan* 33 (January 1952): 262–64.

12. In addition to the sources cited above in note 11, see Reynolds C. Seitz, "Supervision of Public Elementary and Secondary School Pupils Through State Control Over Curriculum and Textbook Selection," *Law and Contemporary Problems* 20 (1, 1955): 115–16; Durrance, "Public Textbook Selection," 262–64; Tulley and Farr, "The Purpose of State Level Textbook Adoption," 1; W. L. Coffey, "Legislative Agencies for Textbook Adoption," in *The Textbook in American Education, The Thirteenth Yearbook of the National Society for the Study of Education, Part II,* ed. Guy Montrose Whipple (Bloomington, IL: Public School Publishing Co., 1931), 249–50; Giordano, *Twentieth-Century Textbook Wars,* 8–13.

13. Black, *The American Schoolbook,* 136; Venezky and Kaestle, "From McGuffy to Dick and Jane," 421; Beale, *Are American Teachers Free?,* 277; Madison, *Book Publishing in America,* 124–25.

14. Upton Sinclair, *The Goslings: A Study of the American Schools* (Pasadena, CA: Upton Sinclair, 1924), 170, 185–86, 225, 315–26; Beale, *Are American Teachers Free?,* 275.

15. Larry Thomas Balsamo, "Theodore G. Bilbo and Mississippi Politics, 1877–1932." (PhD dissertation, University of Missouri, 1967), 144–50.

16. John Franklin Brown, *State Publication of Schoolbooks* (New York: Macmillan, 1915), 474–85; Coffey, "Legislative Agencies for Textbook Adoption," 249–50; Burnett, "Textbook Provisions in the Several States," 358–61; Burnett, "State Textbook Policies," 258–60; Giordano, *Twentieth-Century Textbook Wars*, xvii, 8–13.

17. Coffey, "Legislative Agencies for Textbook Adoption," 249–50; Burnett, "Textbook Provisions in the Several States," 358–61; Burnett, "State Textbook Policies," *Phi Delta Kappan* 33 (January 1952): 258–60; Giordano, *Twentieth-Century Textbook Wars*, xvii, 8–13.

18. Ibid; John Franklin Brown, "State Publication of School Books," *School and Society* 2 (October 2, 1915): 474–85; T. A. McNeal, "Discussion and Correspondence: The State Publication of School Books," *School and Society* 2 (1915): 669–70.

19. Brown, "State Publication of School Books," 474–85.

20. McNeal, "The State Publication of School Books," 669–70.

21. Balsamo, "Theodore G. Bilbo," 155–62; *Mississippi House Journal*, January 17, 1928, 111–28.

22. Balsamo, "Theodore G. Bilbo," 169, 182–85, 206; *Mississippi House Journal*, October 1, 1928, 38.

23. Balsamo, "Theodore G. Bilbo," 168–69.

24. Publications by the Mississippi Press Association included "Brief by the Mississippi Press Association in the Discussion of the Proposed State Printing Plant" (1927), "Why?" (1928), "What the Newspapers Say" (1928), "Facts and Figures About the Proposed State Printing Plant" (1928), "Leading Educators of California and Kansas Give Reasons for Disapproval of State Printing of School Text-books" (1928), and "Comments on Bilbo's Catechism on the State Printing Plant Bill" (1928), in MDAH.

25. *Laws of the State of Mississippi, 1924*, 441–44.

26. Ibid., 435, 441–44.

27. *JCL*, September 4, 1930.

28. Ibid., November 1; December 20, 21, and 22, 1929; January 2, 24, 26, and 29; February 13 and 16, 1930.

29. Ibid., February 20, 23, and 25; March 2 and 12, 1930.

30. *JDN*, June 22, 1930; *Natchez Democrat*, July 17 and 22, 1930; *Trimble et al. v. John C. Winston Co. et al.*, Chancery Court of Adams County, Mississippi, case file in MDAH. The John C. Winston Company started in 1884, entered the textbook business in 1918, began publishing religious books in 1928, and later issued *Lassie Comes Home* in 1940. It merged in 1959 with Henry Holt to form Holt, Rinehart and Winston. See John Tebbel, *A History of Book Publishing in the United States: Volume IV: The Great Change, 1940–1980* (New York: R. R. Bowker, 1981), 222, 241, and 531. The other defendant publishers were D. C. Heath, Allyn and Bacon, W. S. Benson, Rand McNally, Row-Peterson, and Smith-Hammond.

31. *JDN*, July 22 and 31, and August 10, 1930; *JCL*, August 9, 1930; *Natchez Democrat*, July 23, 1930.

32. *JDN*, August 12, 13, 14, 20, 25, and 26, 1930; *JCL*, August 12, 14, 15, 16, 19, 20, and 25, 1930; February 16 and 17, 1932; *Natchez Democrat*, August 12, 14, 17, 20, and 26, 1930;

February 16 and May 17, 1932; *Trimble v. Winston* 56 F.2d 150; *Winston v. Trimble* 286 U.S. 555; 52 S.Ct. 580. See also Michael Tulley and Roger Farr, "Textbook Evaluation Selection," in *Textbooks and Schooling in the United States: Eight-ninth Yearbook of the National Society for the Study of Education*, ed. David L. Elliott and Arthur Woodward (Chicago: University of Chicago Press, 1990), 162–77.

33. Giordano, *Twentieth-Century Textbook Wars*, 3–7; Burnett, "Textbook Provisions in the Several States," 361–63; Burnett, "State Textbook Policies," 257.

34. Ward W. Keeseker, "[untitled]," *Phi Delta Kappan* 33 (January 1952): 261; Giordano, *Twentieth-Century Textbook Wars*, 7.

35. *JCL*, January 17, 20, and 31, 1940.

36. *JDN*, January 26, 30, and 31, 1940; *JCL*, January 24, 25, 26, 27, and 29, 1940.

37. *JDN*, February 5 and 13, 1940; Bishop Theodore D. Bratton, letter to the editor, *JCL*, February 15, 1940.

38. *JCL*, February 7, 8, 9, 11, and 15; *JDN*, February, 6, 7, and 15, 1940.

39. *JCL*, February 16 and 18, 1940; *JDN*, February 16 and 17, 1940.

40. *JCL*, February 17, 1940; *JDN*, February 17, 1940.

41. *JCL*, February 18, 1940.

42. *Chance et al. v. Mississippi State Textbook Rating and Purchasing Board et al.* 190 Miss. 453; *Laws of the State of Mississippi, 1942*, chapter 152. See also case file in MDAH.

43. Burnett, "Textbook Provisions in the Several States," 358–61, 363–65; Burnett, "State Textbook Policies," 257–58; Tulley and Farr, "The Purpose of State Level Textbook Adoption," 7; Durrance, "Public Textbook Selection," 262–65.

44. Beale, *Are American Teachers Free?*, 205, 296, 298, 554; Jack Nelson and Gene Roberts Jr., *The Censors and the Schools* (Boston: Little, Brown, 1963), 24–25, 27–31; *Laws of the State of Mississippi, 1926*, 435; Jonathan Zimmerman, *Whose America? Culture Wars in the Public Schools* (Cambridge, MA: Harvard University Press, 2002), 14–31.

45. Tebbel, *A History of Book Publishing*, 78–79; Nelson and Roberts, *The Censors*, 34–39; Diane Ravitch, *The Troubled Crusade: American Education, 1945–1980* (New York: Basic Books, 1983), 90–91; Zimmerman, *Whose America?*, 55–80; Evans, *The Social Studies Wars: What Should We Teach the Children?* (New York: Teachers College Press, 2004), 37–39, 59–65.

46. Nelson and Roberts, *The Censors*, 54–57; Zimmerman, *Whose America?*, 81–105; E. Merrill Root, *Brainwashing in the High Schools: An Examination of Eleven American History Textbooks* (New York: Devin-Adair, 1958), 48, 178, 232.

47. Nelson and Roberts, *The Censors*, 54–55, 71–72; Erling M. Hunt, review of *Brainwashing in the High Schools* by E. Merrill Root, in *Social Education* (March 1959): 138–39; William Cartwright, review of *Brainwashing in the High Schools* by E. Merrill Root, in *Scholastic Teacher* (February 6, 1959), quoted in "A Printed Copy of the Remarks Made by Mr. D. C. Leach In Connection with a Panel Discussion, March 1, 1961, at the YWCA in Jackson, Mississippi," in MDAH. Hunt was a professor at Teachers College, Columbia University, and a leader in the National Council for the Social Studies. Cartwright was chairman of the Department of Education at Duke University and a former president of the Southern Council on Teacher Education. Later Ronald W. Evans summarized Root's

errors as "incomplete quotations taken out of context, reasoning from false premises, and employing other dubious tricks." See Evans, *Social Studies Wars*, 117.

48. Hunt, review of *Brainwashing in the High Schools*, 139; Nelson and Roberts, *The Censors*, 75, 85–86; Zimmerman, *Whose America?*, 105.

49. JCL, September 6 and October 8, 1959; JST, October 7, 1959; JDN October 7, 1959. Ronald W. Evans observed that the attacks on textbooks appeared to have local origins but really had been "orchestrated and supported by national pressure groups." See Evans, *Social Studies Wars*, 101.

50. For examples of advertisements, see JCL, August 2, 1959.

51. JCL, September 6 and October 8 and 11, 1959; JDN, October 7, 1959; JST, October 7, 1959. Nelson and Roberts provide a summary of the Mississippi controversy in *The Censors*, 90–96.

52. DDT, October 8, 1959; JST, November 18 and 20 and December 22, 1959; JCL, November, 18, 19, 20, and 24, 1959; JDN, November 18, 19, and 20, 1959; General Legislative Investigating Committee to Governor and the Legislature, April 1960, in Mississippi State Sovereignty Commission Papers, MDAH.

53. General Legislative Investigating Committee to Governor and the Legislature, January 1960, in Sovereignty Commission Papers; JCL, MCA, and NOTP, all for January 6, 1960.

54. JCL, January 6, 9, 1, 18, 22, 24, 25, 27, and 30, and February 2, 3, 4, 5, and 6, 1960; JST, January 14, 1960.

55. JCL, February 28, March 1, and April 1, 1960; JST, February 25 and 28 and March 24, 1960.

56. JCL, April 8, 10, and 12, 1960; JST, April 6, 7, and 10, 1960; DDT, April 10, 1960.

57. JCL, April 10, 18, 19, and 27, 1960; DDT, April 27 and 28, 1960; JST, April 14, 15, 17, and 28, 1960.

58. JCL, April 29 and May 1, 4, and 6, 1960; JST, May 1, 3, 4, and 15.

59. JST, September 18, 1960; JDN, September 18, 1960; DDT, September 18, 1960, and July 29, 1962; JCL, May 31, 1962. For examples of later stirrings of controversy, see JCL, March 18 and April 1, 1962; January 4, 1963; DDT, October 14, 1960; MCA, March 9, 1962, and December 2, 1963; NOTP, October 13, 1963.

Histories

1. Frances Fitzgerald, *America Revised: History Schoolbooks in the Twentieth Century* (New York: Atlantic Monthly Press, 1979), 47n19; Michael W. Apple, *Official Knowledge: Democratic Education in a Conservative Age* (New York: Routledge, 1993), 43–44, and especially chapter 3, "Cultural Politics and the Text," 42–60; George Orwell, *1984: A Novel* (New York: Harcourt Brace Jovanovich, 1949). A different view of textbooks and education will appear later, in chapter 6.

2. Fitzgerald, *America Revised*, 47n19.

3. *Laws of the State of Mississippi, 1873*, 13; *Laws of the State of Mississippi, 1878*, 89–115; *Laws of the State of Mississippi, 1890*, 89; *Annotated Code of the General Statute Laws of the*

State of Mississippi, 1892, 889. The law only indirectly required a course on state history; it first declared that the areas for examining teachers constituted the school curriculum and then listed Mississippi history as one of the subject areas for examining teachers. The provision in the *Code, 1892* could not be located in earlier editions of the *Laws of the State of Mississippi*. Michael Apple argues, "Since schools are *state* apparatuses, we should expect them to be under intense pressure to act in certain ways, especially in times of both fiscal and ideological crisis." See Apple, *Teachers and Texts: A Political Economy of Class and Gender Relations in Education* (New York: Routledge and Kegan Paul, 1986), 38.

4. *Laws of the State of Mississippi, 1904*, 116; *Laws of the State of Mississippi, 1924*, 492; *Laws of the State of Mississippi, 1958*, 484. State history also appeared in legislative requirements for state teacher's license, but only for examinations for the highest grade of license; the second-grade license called for testing on U.S. history only. See *Laws of Mississippi, 1890*, 88–89.

5. Two essays by Fred Bailey proved helpful for the next several paragraphs. All quotations from primary sources are as cited in his work. See Fred Arthur Bailey, "The Textbooks of the 'Lost Cause': Censorship and the Creation of Southern State Histories," *Georgia Historical Quarterly* 75 (Fall, 1991): 507–33; Fred A. Bailey, "How Heritage Became Hate: Mississippi's Quest for a Suitable Past, 1890 the Present," the Walter M. and Evalynn Burress Lecture Series, Howard Payne University, Brentwood, Texas, October 2005 (rough draft), MDAH. For other relevant background, see Karen L. Cox, *Dixie's Daughters: The United Daughters of the Confederacy and the Preservation of Confederate Culture* (Gainesville: University of Florida Press, 2003); Caroline E. Janney, *Remembering the Civil War: Reunions and the Limits of Reconciliation* (Chapel Hill: University of North Carolina Press, 2013); and Sally Leigh McWhite, "Echoes of the Lost Cause: Civil War Reverberations in Mississippi from 1865 to 2001," (PhD dissertation, University of Mississippi, 2003).

6. Bailey, "The Textbooks of the 'Lost Cause'"; Bailey, "How Heritage Became Hate."

7. Bailey, "The Textbooks of the 'Lost Cause'"; Bailey, "How Heritage Became Hate."

8. Bailey, "The Textbooks of the 'Lost Cause'"; Bailey, "How Heritage Became Hate."

9. Bailey, "The Textbooks of the 'Lost Cause'"; Bailey, "How Heritage Became Hate."

10. Bailey, "The Textbooks of the 'Lost Cause'"; Bailey, "How Heritage Became Hate"; quotation from Meridian UDC found in McWhite, "Echoes of the Lost Cause," 104.

11. Bailey, "The Textbooks of the 'Lost Cause'"; Bailey, "How Heritage Became Hate"; McWhite, "Echoes of the Lost Cause," 70.

12. Bailey, "How Heritage Became Hate."

13. Mary V. Duval, *History of Mississippi and Civil Government* (Louisville, KY: Courier-Journal Job Printing Co., 1892), 145, 156, 161, 168, 169, 201–2; Mary V. Duval, subject file, MDAH. The recommendations appear in the book after the table of contents and the author's introduction.

14. Daval, *History of Mississippi*, 220, 221, 222, 223, 258, 293. In ten additional chapters on "civil government" (293–345), Duval discussed most aspects of the U.S. Constitution, but she jumbled the Reconstruction amendments (348–49). In an appendix (351–87), she reprinted the Mississippi Constitution of 1890.

15. Robert Lowry and William H. McCardle, *A History of Mississippi for Use in Schools* (New York and New Orleans: University Publishing Co., 1892), 3; Robert Lowry and William H. McCardle, subject files, MDAH. See also Lowry and McCardle, *A History of Mississippi: From the Discovery of the Great River by Hernando DeSoto . . . to the Death of Jefferson Davis* (Jackson: R. H. Henry and Co., 1891). On the major habeas corpus case, *Ex parte McCardle* 74 U.S. 506 (1869), see Sever L. Eubank, "The McCardle Case: A Challenge to Radical Reconstruction," *Journal of Mississippi History* 18 (April 1956): 111–27; and Stanley I. Kutler, "*Ex parte McCardle*: Judicial Impotency: The Supreme Court and Reconstruction Reconsidered," *American Historical Review* 72 (April 1967): 835–51.

16. Lowry and McCardle, *A History of Mississippi*, 175, 215, 216, 219, 234, 235, 251.

17. Lowry, subject file, MDAH.

18. Franklin L. Riley, *School History of Mississippi for Use in Public and Private Schools* (Richmond: B. F. Johnson Publishing Co., 1900); Franklin Lafayette Riley, subject file, MDAH. For background on Riley, see Howard D. Southwood, "Riley of Mississippi," *Journal of Mississippi History* 13 (October 1951): 193–211; W. Conrad Gass, "Franklin L. Riley and the Historical Renaissance in Mississippi, 1897–1914," *Journal of Mississippi History* 32 (August 1970): 195–228; Roger D. Tate, "Franklin L. Riley and the University of Mississippi (1897–1914)," *Journal of Mississippi History* 42 (May 1980): 99–112.

19. Sanford W. Higginbotham, "The Writing of Mississippi History: A Brief Survey," *Journal of Mississippi History* 20 (July 1958): 162; Richard Aubrey McLemore and Nannie Pitts McLemore, "Histories of Mississippi," *Journal of Mississippi History* 9 (October 1947): 262; Riley, *School History*, 7.

20. Riley, *School History*, vii, 160, 161, 163, 164, 218, 229, 230, 233.

21. Ibid., 271, 280, 282, 283, 285, 305.

22. Ibid., 295, 315, 317, 319, 324, 325.

23. Ibid., 340.

24. Claude Bennett and Charles Sackett Sydnor, subject files, MDAH. On Sydnor, see also Fred Arthur Bailey, "Charles S. Sydnor's Quest for a Suitable Past," in *Reading Southern History: Essays on Interpreters and Interpretation*, ed. Glenn Feldman (Tuscaloosa: University of Alabama Press, 2001), 88–111.

25. Charles S. Sydnor and Claude Bennett, *Mississippi History* (New York: Rand McNally, 1930), vii, viii, 173, 178. Sydnor's treatment of slavery undoubtedly drew from his research that led to *Slavery in Mississippi* (New York: D. Appleton-Century, 1933). He had by 1930 published "The Free Negro in Mississippi Before the Civil War," *American Historical Review* 32 (July 1927): 769–88, and "The Life Span of Mississippi Slaves," *American Historical Review* 35 (April 1930): 566–74. See also John David Smith, introduction to *Slavery in Mississippi* (1933; Columbia: University of South Carolina Press, 2013), xi–xxxix.

26. Sydnor and Bennett, *Mississippi History* 188, 203.

27. Ibid., 207, 214, 216, 218, 222.

28. Ibid., 229, 248, 249. Though Fred Bailey seems to gloss over differences among the books, he sees the Sydnor-Bennett volume as typical of "Lost Cause" textbooks

and groups it with the textbooks by Lowry and McCardle and by Duval. See Bailey, "Sydnor's Quest," 97, and Bailey, "How Heritage Became Hate." Two odd chapters in Sydnor-Bennett discussed "some eminent Mississippians" and "Mississippians prominent since 1900," all of whom were white. See 252–63 and 343–55. Another chapter on "Mississippi soldiers" discussed the treatment of veterans of the Civil War, the Spanish-American War, and World War I. See 300–314.

29. David E. Guyton, foreword to *The History of Mississippi* by Pearl Vivian Guyton (Syracuse: Iroquois Publishing, 1935), v–vi; Pearl Vivian Guyton, subject file, MDAH.

30. Guyton, *History of Mississippi*, 155, 157, 163, 171, 174.

31. Ibid., 180, 184, 186, 192, 193, 195, 217.

32. Richard Aubrey McLemore and Nannie Pitts McLemore, subject files, MDAH.

33. Richard Aubrey McLemore and Nannie Pitts McLemore, *Mississippi Through Four Centuries* (Chicago: Laidlaw Brothers, 1945), 143, 150, 152, 153, 154, 169.

34. Ibid., 170, 178.

35. Ibid., 234, 235, 241, 248, 249.

36. Ibid., 253, 260, 261.

37. Minutes, MSTPB, July 3, 1940; September 18, 1942; June 8, 1944; January 22, 30, 31, 1945; December 8, 1947; November 17, 1949. Records of the earlier board have not survived, but the 1940 minutes indicated that the board was re-adopting the Sydnor-Bennett text. The board routinely extended contracts for an additional year or two.

38. Pearl Vivian Guyton, *Our Mississippi* (Austin: Steck, 1952), 154–55.

39. Minutes, MSTPB, November 22, 1952; September 30, 1954; May 4, 1956.

40. Minutes, MSTPB, October 3, 1952; October 26, 1954; September 21, 1960.

41. *Laws of the State of Mississippi, Extraordinary Session, 1953*, 120; *Laws of the State of Mississippi, 1958*, 484; *Laws of the State of Mississippi, 1962*, 856–57; *Laws of the State of Mississippi, 1970*, 430–31.

42. Minutes, MSTPB, May 9, September 8, and December 9, 1958; March 18, 1959.

43. John Knox Bettersworth, subject file, MDAH; William L. Giles, "John Knox Bettersworth: A Tribute," *Mississippi Quarterly* 45 (Winter 1991–92): 3–7.

44. John K. Bettersworth, *Confederate Mississippi: The People and Policies of a Cotton State in Wartime* (Baton Rouge: Louisiana State University, 1943), 2, 5, 6, 164, 165, 305; Bettersworth, *People's College: A History of Mississippi State* (University, Alabama: University of Alabama Press, 1953). Bettersworth's coverage of slave revolts prompted an addendum by Herbert Aptheker in "Notes on Slave Conspiracies in Confederate Mississippi," *Journal of Negro History* 29 (January 1944): 75–79.

45. For the Burger-Bettersworth connection, see Nash K. Burger with Pearl A. McHaney, *The Road to West 43rd Street* (Jackson: University Press of Mississippi, 1995); Nash K. Burger, subject file, MDAH.

46. Bettersworth, review of *Last Train from Atlanta* by A. A. Hoehling and *The Battle of Atlanta and the Georgia Campaign* by William Key, in *NYTBR*, October 26, 1958, 42.

For examples of the works of other scholars in the same edition as Bettersworth's reviews, see the following editions of the *NYTBR*: December 5, 1954, 26 (Williams); March 18, 1856, 7 (Donald); September 23, 1956, 3 (Woodward); October 28, 1956, 4 (Wiley); November 24, 1957, 6 (Commager); July 20, 1958, 6–7 (Handlin).

47. Bettersworth, review of *The Peculiar Institution: Slavery in the Ante-Bellum South* by Kenneth M. Stampp, in *NYTBR*, September 23, 1956, 3. On the radical origins and nature of Stampp's work, see James Oakes, "Kenneth Stampp's Peculiar Reputation," in *Reading Southern History: Essays on Interpreters and Interpretation*, ed. Glenn Feldman (Tuscaloosa: University of Alabama Press, 2001), 202–11.

48. Bettersworth, review of *Ploughshares into Swords: Josiah Gorgas and Confederate Ordinance* by Frank E. Vandiver, in *NYTBR*, April 27, 1952, 23; Bettersworth, review of *Victory Rode the Rails: The Strategic Place of Railroads in the Civil War* by George Edwin Turner, *NYTBR*, November 8, 1953, 22; Bettersworth, review of *Last Train from Atlanta* by A. A. Hoehling and *The Battle of Atlanta and the Georgia Campaign* by William Key, in *NYTBR*, October 26, 1958, 42; Bettersworth, review of *The Plantation South* by Katherine M. Jones, in *NYTBR*, December 22, 1957, 11; Bettersworth, review of *Seeds of Time: The Background of Southern Thinking* by Henry Savage Jr., in *NYTBR*, May 31, 1959, 6; Bettersworth review of *Southern Yankees* by Helen R. Speicher and Kathryn K. Borland," *NYTBR*, May 14, 1961, 6; Bettersworth, review of *Jefferson Davis: Confederate President* by Hudson Strode, in *NYTBR*, October 18, 1959, 7; Bettersworth, review of *The Night the War Was Lost* by Charles L. Dufour, in *NYTBR*, December 4, 1960, 54. Bettersworth's comments could be cutting. He concluded his review of Vandiver's book by saying, "One may wish that the author, who by-passed high school and college to enter graduate school, had not by-passed freshman composition, for grammatical lapses occasionally mar otherwise brilliant writing."

49. Bettersworth, review of *Grierson's Raid* by D. Alexander Brown, in *NYTBR*, December 5, 1954, 26; Bettersworth, review of *Gray Ghosts and Rebel Raiders* by Virgil Carrington Jones and *Reminiscences of Big I* by Lieut. William Nathaniel Wood, edited by Bell Irwin Wiley, in *NYTBR*, October 28, 1956, 4, 22.

50. Bettersworth, review of *Prince of the Carpetbaggers* by Jonathan Daniels, in *NYTBR*, July 20, 1958, 6; Bettersworth review of *Reconstruction: The Great Experiment* by Allen W. Trelease," in *NYTBR*, July 25, 1971, 8.

51. Bettersworth, review of *Seeds of Time: The Background of Southern Thinking* by Henry Savage Jr., in *NYTBR*, May 31, 1959, 6; Bettersworth review of *Southern Yankees* by Helen R. Speicher and Kathryn K. Borland," *NYTBR*, May 14, 1961, 6.

52. Giles, "Bettersworth," 4.

53. Burger and Bettersworth, *South of Appomattox* (New York: Harcourt, Brace and Company, 1959), 10, 11, 16; Burger, *The Road to West 43rd Street*, 163–64. Burger and Bettersworth also justified Southern slave owners as no "less moral or humanitarian than the Yankee traders and shipowners who sold" slaves, and they described postwar race relations as, "on the whole, remarkably good." See pages 7 and 15.

54. T. Harry Williams, review of *South of Appomattox* by Burger and Bettersworth, in *North Carolina Historical Review* 37 (January 1960): 105; Rembert W. Patrick, review

of *South of Appomattox* by Burger and Bettersworth, in *Journal of Southern History* 26 (February 1960): 128; C. Vann Woodward, review of *South of Appomattox* by Burger and Bettersworth, in *NYTBR*, September 20, 1959, 46; Burger, *The Road to West 43rd Street*, 164. More generally see also Dewey W. Grantham, "The Southern Bourbons Revisited," *South Atlantic Quarterly* 60 (Summer 1961): 286–95. Woodward, a proponent of discontinuity in Southern history, did not criticize Burger and Bettersworth's argument for continuity. See "Origin of *Origins [of the New South, 1877–1913]*" in Woodward, *Thinking Back: The Perils of Writing History* (Baton Rouge: Louisiana State University Press, 1986), 59–79.

55. Bettersworth, *Mississippi: A History* (Austin: Steck, 1959); Giles, "Bettersworth," 4.

56. Deposition of John K. Bettersworth, August 4, 1977, and deposition of W. A. Matthews, October 26, 1976, both in *Loewen v. Turnipseed* case file, MAGF; John K. Bettersworth, "Mississippi Historiography: Research Materials and Researchers," *Mississippi Quarterly* 10 (Summer 1957): 143–44; Minutes, MSTPB, March 18, 1959. Matthews suggested that the board "might have been" involved in persuading Bettersworth to write his textbook, but at the time Matthews did not work with the board. The National Archives and Records Administration branch in Morrow, Georgia, has the official case file (NARA), but the files of the Mississippi Attorney General also contain nearly all of the same documents (MAGF) and some not in NARA.

57. Answer of Defendants to Plaintiffs First Request for Admissions, and Second Set of Interrogatories or in Alternate Request for Production of Documents, October 25, 1976, in *Loewen v. Turnipseed* case file, MAGF; Apple, *Official Knowledge*, 38, 44.

58. Bettersworth, *Mississippi*, 191, 192, 193, 194, 251, 313, 333, 339. For an assessment of textbook treatment of slavery in American history textbooks in the 1950s, see Leah H. Wasburn, "Accounts of Slavery: An Analysis of United States History Textbooks from 1900 to 1992," *Theory and Research in Social Education* 25 (Fall 1997): 47–91, especially 77–81.

59. Bettersworth, *Mississippi*, 437, 438, 484.

60. A more detailed and comprehensive analysis of a later edition of Bettersworth's text appears in chapter 5.

Writers

1. Millsaps's eastern boundary is North State Street; five miles north, Tougaloo College lies a few blocks west of North State Street.

2. On Ernst Borinski, see Gabrielle Simon Edgcomb, "Ernst Borinski: 'Positive Marginality' 'I Decided to Engage in Stigma Management,'" in *From Swastika to Jim Crow: Refugee Scholars at Black Colleges*, 117–29 (Malabar, Florida: Krieger, 1993); Donald Cunnigen, "The Legacy of Ernst Borinski: The Production of an African American Sociological Tradition," *Teaching Sociology* 31 (October 2003): 397–411; Maria Lowe, "An Unseen Hand: The Role of Sociology Professor Ernst Borinski in Mississippi's Struggle for Racial Integration in the 1950s and 1960s," *Leadership* 27 (4,

2008): 27–47; Maria Lowe, "'Sowing the Seeds of Discontent': Touglaoo College's Social Science Forums as a Prefigurative Movement Free Space, 1952–1964," *Journal of Black Studies* 39 (July 2009): 865–87; Maria Lowe, "An 'Oasis of Freedom' in a 'Closed Society': The Development of Tougaloo College as a Free Space in Mississippi's Civil Rights Movement, 1960–1964," *Journal of Historical Sociology* 20 (December 2007): 486–520; and from Zack J. Van Landingham to Director, October 9, 1958, Mississippi State Sovereignty Commission Papers, MDAH, which derived from University of Chicago records.

3. Biographical information about Borinski derives from sources listed above in note 2.

4. Vernon Lane Wharton, *The Negro in Mississippi, 1865–1890* (Chapel Hill: University of North Carolina Press, 1947), 255. For the history of Tougaloo College, see Clarice T. Campbell and Oscar Allan Rogers Jr., *Mississippi: The View from Tougaloo* (Jackson: University Press of Mississippi, 1979). Unless otherwise noted, the subsequent account of Tougaloo's history comes from Campbell and Rogers's work.

5. Paul Luebke quoted in Edgcomb, "Ernst Borinski," 122; Zack J. Van Landingham to Director, October 9, 1958, Mississippi State Sovereignty Commission Papers, MDAH. See also sources cited above in note 2.

6. Ernst Borinski, "The Social Science Laboratory at Tougaloo College," *Journal of Educational Sociology* 22 (December 1948): 276–86; Lowe, "'Sowing the Seeds of Discontent,'" 869–72.

7. Lowe, "'Sowing the Seeds of Discontent,'" 869–72, 874; Cunnigen, "The Legacy of Ernst Borinski," 404; Lowe, "An Unseen Hand," 37–40; Lowe, "'Oasis of Freedom,'" 500.

8. W. A. Bender, "Desegregation in the Public Schools of Mississippi," *Journal of Negro Education* 24 (Summer 1955): 287–92.

9. *JCL*, December 2, 1955.

10. Ibid., December 5, 1955.

11. Ibid., March 5, 7, 10, 1958; clipping from *Morton Progress-Herald*, March 20, 1958, and Zack J. Van Landingham to Director, October 9, 1958, Mississippi State Sovereignty Commission Papers, MDAH; Joy Ann Williamson, *Radicalizing the Ebony Tower: Black Colleges and the Black Freedom Struggle in Mississippi* (New York: Teachers College Press, 2008), 72–73.

12. Lowe, "'Oasis of Freedom,'" 498–502; John Dittmer, *Local People: The Struggle for Civil Rights in Mississippi* (Urbana: University of Illinois Press, 1994), 2–3.

13. Lowe, "'Oasis of Freedom,'" 503–5; Lowe, "Unseen Hand," 41; Williamson, *Radicalizing the Ebony Tower*, 99; Dittmer, *Local People*, 87–89.

14. Lowe, "'Oasis of Freedom,'" 508–9; Dittmer, *Local People*, 234–36; Campbell and Rogers, *View from Tougaloo*, 215–17; Williamson, *Radicalizing the Ebony Tower*, 97–102.

15. David M. Key, "Historical Sketch of Millsaps College," *Mississippi College Bulletin* 30 (December 1946): 1–25 (reprinted from *Southern Association Quarterly*); Ross Moore, "Millsaps According to Ross Moore," *Major Notes* 23 (December 1982): 1, 5; George M. Harmon, "Millsaps College: Determining the Agenda," Newcomen [Society of the United States] Publication Number 1244 (Jackson: Millsaps, 1985); Frances Lucas-Tauchar,

"The Inaugural Acceptance," *Millsaps Magazine* (Summer 2001): 10–17; Wharton, *The Negro in Mississippi, 1865–1890*, 157.

16. Harmon, "Determining the Agenda," 11; Lucas-Tauchar, "The Inaugural Acceptance," 11.

17. Harmon, "Determining the Agenda," 11–12; Lucas-Tauchar, "The Inaugural Acceptance," 11; Campbell and Rogers, *View from Tougaloo*, 170.

18. Campbell and Rogers, *View from Tougaloo*, 171; Lucas-Tauchar, "The Inaugural Acceptance," 11.

19. Maria R. Lowe and J. Clint Morris, "Civil Rights Advocates in the Academy: White Pro-integrationist Faculty at Millsaps College, *Journal of Mississippi History* 69 (2, 2007): 127–29; Campbell and Rogers, *View from Tougaloo*, 171–72.

20. Lowe and Morris, "Civil Rights Advocates in the Academy," 129–30.

21. *JCL*, March 9, 1958; Lowe and Morris, 130–32; Lucas-Tauchar, "The Inaugural Acceptance," 11–12.

22. Lowe and Morris, "Civil Rights Advocates," 132–35.

23. Ibid.; Lucas-Tauchar, "The Inaugural Acceptance," 11–12; Charles C. Bolton, *The Hardest Deal of All: The Battle over School Integration in Mississippi, 1870–1980* (Jackson: University Press of Mississippi, 2005), 141–42. In the spring of 1964 Millsaps leaders at first agreed to allow integrated groups to take the Scholastic Aptitude Test on its campus only to change their mind in response to public pressure. See Jan Bates Wheeler, *A Campaign of Quiet Persuasion: How the College Board Desegregated SAT Test Centers in the Deep South, 1960–1965* (Baton Rouge: Louisiana State University Press, 2013), 149–51 and 153–56.

24. Lowe and Morris, "Civil Rights Advocates," 140; Harmon, "Determining the Agenda," 13; Lucas-Tauchar, "The Inaugural Acceptance," 13.

25. Report of Student Symposium Committee Meetings, no date, June 20 and 27, and July 6, 1967; Ernst Borinski to John A. Griffin, September 17 and October 1, 1970, all in BPMDAH.

26. Lowe and Morris, "Civil Rights Advocates," 141–42; interview with Charles and Harrylyn Sallis.

27. Lowe, Morris, and Pizzo, "Academic Agitators"; interview with Charles and Harrylyn Sallis.

28. Interview with Charles and Harrylyn Sallis; Sallis's curriculum vita, *Loewen v. Turnipseed* case file, NARA; William Charles Sallis, "A Study of the Life and Times of Leroy Percy" (MA thesis, Mississippi State College, 1957).

29. Sallis, "A Study of the Life and Times of Leroy Percy," 11, 14, 16, 22, 39, 53; interview with Charles and Harrylyn Sallis. Sallis's curriculum vita, *Loewen v. Turnipseed* case file, NARA.

30. Interview with Charles and Harrylyn Sallis; Wharton, *The Negro in Mississippi, 1865–1890*.

31. Interview with Charles and Harrylyn Sallis.

32. Ibid.

33. Ibid; Millsaps *Purple and White*, September 4, 1968.

34. Sallis, "The Color Line in Mississippi Politics, 1865–1915" (PhD dissertation, University of Kentucky, 1967), 2, 4, 6, 15, 55, 59, 66; interview with Charles and Harrylyn Sallis.

35. Sallis, "The Color Line," 153, 155, 237, 238, 337, 344.

36. Ibid., 437–38.

37. Interview with Charles and Harrylyn Sallis.

38. Ibid.; Alliance Against Racism, Newsletter #2, July 11, 1970, and *JCL*, January 31, 1971, both in Mississippi State Sovereignty Commission Papers, MDAH.

39. Interview with Charles and Harrylyn Sallis; Millsaps *Purple and White*, October 24, 1973; Sallis's curriculum vita, *Loewen v. Turnipseed* case file, NARA.

40. Interview with Charles and Harrylyn Sallis; Millsaps *Purple and White*, April 5, 1973.

41. Mary Frances Derfner, "Perpetuation of a Myth: The Nature of State History as Taught in Mississippi Schools"; James Loewen, "The Writing of *Mississippi: Conflict and Change*," January 1975, both in LPMDAH.

42. James Loewen, "The Writing of *Mississippi: Conflict and Change*"; interview with James Loewen. The date of Loewen's class appears as 1969 in Loewen, *Teaching What Really Happened: How to Avoid the Tyranny of Textbooks and Get Students Excited About Doing History* (New York: Columbia University, Teachers College Press, 2010), 2, and as 1970 in Loewen, *Lies My Teacher Told Me: Everything Your American History Textbook Got Wrong* (New York: New Press, 1975), 149. The earlier date fits better with the chronology of the textbook's development.

43. The circumstances surrounding Loewen and Sallis's first meeting remain unclear. Differing stories appear in the sources.

44. Interview with James Loewen; Loewen, *Teaching What Really Happened*, 111. In the post-war years, sociologists often described Decatur as a typical American town. See John H. Summers, "Perpetual Revelations: C. Wright Mills and Paul Lazarsfeld," *Annals of the American Academy of Political and Social Science* 608 (November 2006): 25–40.

45. Interview with James Loewen.

46. Ibid. See John Dollard, *Caste and Class in a Southern Town* (New Haven: Yale University Press, 1937).

47. Interview with James Loewen; James Loewen, "1978–79 White House Fellowship Application," in LPMDAH.

48. Interview with James Loewen; Loewen to Peter Loewen, June 26, 1966, in LPMDAH. See Loewen, *The Mississippi Chinese: Between Black and White* (Cambridge, MA: Harvard University Press, 1971).

49. Loewen, "1978–79 White House Fellowship Application," in LPMDAH; interview with James Loewen.

50. Loewen to Clifton H. Johnson, February 15, 1970, in BPMDAH; Loewen to Griffin, October 18, 1971; "Caste, Class, and Commerce in Mound Bayou, Mississippi," March 1971; "Report on School Involvement Project," 1972–73; Mary Artilee Evans, "Caste, Class, and Commerce in Mound Bayou, Mississippi," March 1971; School Involvement Project, Final

Report for 1972–73 [working draft], no date; all in LPMDAH; interview with James Loewen.

51. Robert Perrucci, "In the Service of Man: Radical Movements in the Professions," in *Professionalization and Social Change*, ed. Paul Halmos (Keele: University of Keele, 1973), 179–94; Abigail A. Fuller, "Producing Radical Scholarship: The Radical Sociology Movement, 1967–1975," *Sociological Imagination* 33 (Fall 1996): 37–54; J. David Colfax, and Jack L. Roach, "Introduction," *Radical Sociology* (New York: Basic Books, 1971), 3–27. For the parallel movement in history, see John Higham, *History: Professional Scholarship in America* (updated ed.; Baltimore: Johns Hopkins University Press, 1989), 235–39; Peter Novick, *That Nobel Dream: The "Objectivity Question" and the American Historical Profession* (Cambridge: Cambridge University Press, 1988), 415–68; interview with James Loewen.

52. Philip M. Hauser, "On Actionism in the Craft of Sociology," *Sociological Inquiry* 39 (Spring 1969): 139–47 (quotations on 140, 142, and 147); interview with James Loewen. For evidence of the revolt within sociology see the articles that appeared in the next issue of the journal, along with Loewen's critique: Albert Szymanski, "Toward a Radical Sociology," 3–12; Carol Brown, "A History and Analysis of Radical Activism in Sociology, 1967–1969, with Special Reference to the Sociology Liberation Movement, the Black Caucus, the Executive Council, the War in Vietnam and a Few Other Things," 27–33; and Steven E. Deutsch, "The Radical Perspective in Sociology," 73–83, all in *Sociological Inquiry* 40 (Winter 1970).

53. Loewen, "Action and Sociology," *Sociological Inquiry* 40 (Winter 1970): 105–9; Hauser, "On 'Action and Sociology' by James W. Loewen," *Sociological Inquiry* 40 (Winter 1970): 109.

54. Loewen, *Mississippi Chinese*; interview with James Loewen.

55. Loewen, *Mississippi Chinese*, 2, 26, 98; interview with James Loewen.

56. Loewen, *Mississippi Chinese*, 110, 158.

57. Ibid., 23, 101.

58. Interviews with Loewen and with Charles and Harrylyn Sallis; Answers to First Set of Interrogatories to Plaintiffs, May 5, 1977, *Loewen v. Turnipseed* case file, NARA; "Mississippi History Project: A Prospectus," no date, and Syllabus for Sociology 43, Statistics and Methods of Social Research, both in LPMDAH; Loewen to Mel Leventhal, November 8, 1976, in SPJM. The syllabus suggests that Adams took Loewen's class.

59. Interview with Jeanne Middleton.

60. Interviews with James A. Brown and with Stephen C. Immer.

61. Interviews with William R. Ferris and with Maryellen Hains.

Project

1. James Loewen to Bruce Adams, June 30, 1970; Loewen to Arthur S. Nichols and Anna Ochs, March 16, 1972; "Mississippi History Project: A Prospectus," no date;

Loewen to John A. Griffin, May 22 and June 23, 1970; all in LPMDAH; interviews with James Loewen and with Charles and Harrylyn Sallis.

2. *Alexander v. Holmes County Board of Education* 396 U.S. 1218 (1969).

3. Loewen, "The Writing of *Mississippi: Conflict and Change*," January 1975; Loewen to Griffin, May 22, 1970, Southern Education Foundation, Inc., Annual Report, 1970–71, 5; "Proposal for Support of New Textbooks in Mississippi History," [May 1970], all in LPMDAH; Borinski to Griffin, September 15, 1969, in BPMDAH; interview with James Loewen.

4. Loewen to Griffin, May 22, 1970, with a two-page description of the Project, in LPMDAH; Borinski to Griffin, May 26, 1970, in BPMDAH.

5. Griffin to Loewen, June 30 and July 28, 1970, and February 2, 1971; Loewen to Griffin, October 6 and December 10, 1970, and February 4, 1971; Southern Education Foundation, Inc., Annual Report, 1970–71, 7, 12–13, all in LPMDAH; Hodding Carter to Loewen, no date, and Loewen to M. J. Roussant, director, Twentieth Century Fund, December 2, 1970, both in LPDC. Loewen later reported to Griffin library purchases under the grant gave the Tougaloo library "the most complete collection of this newspaper [*New York Times*] in the greater Jackson area." Loewen to Griffin, May 31, 1971, in LPMDAH.

6. Jack E. Cousins, "State History: The Reign of Provincialism," in *Social Studies in the United States*, ed. C. Benjamin Cox and Byron G. Massialas (New York: Harcourt, Brace and World, 1967), 80–104 (quotations on 83, 92, 100); John Robert Moore, "State History Textbooks: Essays in Ethnocentrism," *Social Education* 33 (March 1969): 267–76 (quotations on 267, 268); Jeffrey J. Blaga and Lynn E. Nielsen, "The Status of State History Instruction," *Journal of Social Studies Research* 7 (Spring 1983): 45–57; R. W. Cordier, "The Study of History Through State and Local Studies," *Social Studies* 60 (March 1969): 99–104; Charles E. Dabbert, "State History Requirements and Our Mobile Population," *Social Education* 30 (May 1966): 338–40; Thomas Steven Peet, "A Selective History of Social Studies Scope and Sequence Patterns, 1916–1984" (PhD dissertation, Ohio State University, 1984); C. P. Smith and J. L. Hupp, "The Teaching of State History in the United States," *Educational Research Bulletin* 5 (February 17, 1926): 67–70.

7. D. D. Draves, "What's Wrong with the Teaching of History in the High School?" *Social Studies* 56 (March 1965): 103–06 (quotation on 103); Steven M. Terry, Sr., and W. Bruce Wingo, "State Studies: Is It Really Worth the Time?" *Georgia Social Science Journal* 19 (Fall 1989): 17–19 (quotation on 17); John Alexander Williams, "A New Look at an Old Field," *Western Historical Quarterly* 9 (July 1978): 281–96 (quotation on 292); Russell R. Elliott, "On the Writing of State History," *Western Historical Quarterly* 9 (July 1978): 323–32; William B. Fink, "A Comment on 'State History Textbooks: Essays in Ethnocentrism,'" *Social Education* 33 (March 1969): 276–78; Lawrence Elmer Giles, "The Teaching of State History in the Public Schools of the United State: A Survey and Analysis of the Prevalence, Placement, and Content of State History Courses and Units" (PhD dissertation, University of Minnesota, 1950).

8. Franklin L. Riley, "Is State History Worth While?" *The History Teacher's Magazine* 2 (1911): 156–57; Richard Aubrey McLemore and Nannie Pitts McLemore, "Suggestion for the Teaching of Mississippi History," *Mississippi Educational Advance* 37 (November 1945): 14; McLemore and McLemore, "The Historical Tour," *Mississippi Educational Advance* 38 (April 1947): 12.

9. Charlotte Capers, "Highlights of Mississippi History" in seven parts, *Mississippi Educational Advance* 48 (October 1956): 17, 37–38; 48 (November 1956): 20, 45–46; 48 (December 1956): 18, 35–36; 49 (January 1957): 19, 22; 49 (February 1957): 19, 30; 49 (April 1957): 20–21; 49 (May 1957): 17, 27; John K. Bettersworth, "Mississippi Historiography: Research Materials and Researchers," *Mississippi Quarterly* 10 (Summer 1957): 138–45; "Tips on Teaching Mississippi History," *Mississippi Educational Advance* 51 (November 1959): 36–37.

10. "Mississippi History: A Prospectus," no date, in LPMDAH.

11. Fred M. Hechinger, "History Texts Take a New Look at Slavery," *New York Times*, June 14, 1970; Loewen to Griffin, June 23, 1970, and Jeanne Middleton to Loewen, April 11, 1972, both in LPMDAH; Mark M. Krug, "Freedom and Racial Equality: A Study of 'Revised' High School History Texts," *School Review* 78 (May 1970): 297–354.

12. Jonathan Zimmerman, *Whose America? Culture Wars in the Public Schools* (Cambridge, MA: Harvard University Press, 2002), 32–34, 42–48; Lawrence D. Reddick, "Racial Attitudes in American History Textbooks of the South," *Journal of Negro History* 19 (July 1934): 264. Other than Zimmerman's statement, no evidence appeared about black history courses in Mississippi in the 1930s.

13. Mary Elizabeth Carpenter, "The Treatment of the Negro in American History Textbooks: A Comparison of Changing Textbook Content, 1926–1939, with Developing Scholarship in the History of the Negro in the United States" (PhD dissertation, Columbia University, 1941); Committee on the Study of Teaching Materials in Intergroup Relations, *Intergroup Relations in Teaching Materials: A Survey and Appraisal* (Washington: American Council on Education, 1949), 117, 120, 121, 132.

14. L. Marcus, *Treatment of Minorities in Secondary School Textbooks* (New York: B'nai B'rith, 1961), 38; Emily Fuller Gibson, "The Three D's: Distortion, Deletion, and Denial," *Social Education* 33 (April 1969): 405; Nancy Larrick, "The All-WHITE World of Children's Books," *Saturday Review* September 11, 1965, 63; Lerone Bennett Jr., "Reading, 'Riting, and Racism," *Ebony*, March 1967, 130, 132; Zimmerman, *Whose America?*, 107–19; "Books for Schools and the Treatment of Minorities," Hearings before the *Ad Hoc* Subcommittee on Defacto School Segregation of the Committee on Education and Labor, House of Representatives, 89th Congress, 2nd Session (Washington, D.C.: U.S. Government Printing Office, 1966), 3, 68.

15. *Wall Street Journal*, March 24, 1965; Zimmerman, *Whose America?*, 107–19.

16. Kenneth M. Stampp, Winthrop D. Jordan, Lawrence W. Levine, Robert L. Middlekauf, Charles G. Sellers, and George W. Stocking Jr., "The Negro in American History Textbooks," *Integrated Education*, October–November 1964, 9–10; Mark M. Krug, "Freedom and Racial Equality: A Study of 'Revised' High School History Texts," *School Review* (May 1970): 297–354 (quotations on 299).

17. Melton McLaurin, "Images of Negroes in Deep South Public School State History Texts," *Phylon* 32 (1971): 237–46; Melton A. McLaurin to Loewen, June 2, 1971, in LPMDAH. For other examples, see S. M. Elkin, "Minorities in Textbooks: The Latest Chapter." *Teachers College Record* 66 (March 1965): 502–8; I. A. Newby, "Historians and Negroes," *Journal of Negro History* 54 (January 1969): 32–47; Irving Sloan, *The Negro in Modern American History Textbooks* (Chicago: American Federation of Teachers, AFL-CIO, October 1966).

18. The teachers on the Rating Committee and the members of the Textbook Purchasing Board also did not refer to Loewen and Sallis's precursors, and neither the plaintiffs nor the defendants nor the judge in the case cited them.

19. Mrs. Charles C. [Jessie Bryant] Mosley, *The Negro in Mississippi* (Jackson: Hederman Brothers, 1950), 5–6. Mosley was a community activist. In the mid-1960s she participated in the interracial Wednesdays in Mississippi program, and in the 1980s she cofounded the Smith Robertson Museum and Cultural Center in Jackson; it was located in the former Smith Robertson School, the first public school in Jackson for blacks. For her promotion of Black History Month, the National Education Association and the Association of the Study of African American Life and History in 1987 presented her the Carter G. Woodson Memorial Award. See *JCL*, June 30, 1991, and June 12 and 15, 2003; Debbie Z. Harwell, *Wednesdays in Mississippi: Proper Ladies Working for Radical Change, Freedom Summer 1964* (Jackson: University Press of Mississippi, 2014).

20. Mosley, *The Negro in Mississippi*, 17, 31, 42, 48, 53, 56, 131, and 132.

21. Ibid., 30, 33, 40, 48.

22. On Freedom Schools, see Doug McAdam, *Freedom Summer* (New York: Oxford University Press, 1988); Daniel Perlstein, "Teaching Freedom: SNCC and the Creation of the Mississippi Freedom Schools," *History of Education Quarterly*, 30 (Fall 1990): 297–324; George W. Chilcoat and Jerry A. Ligon, "Developing Democratic Citizens: The Mississippi Freedom Schools as a Model for Social Studies Instruction," *Theory and Research in Social Education* 22 (Spring 1994): 128–75; Joe Street, *The Culture War in the Civil Rights Movement* (Gainesville: University Press of Florida, 2007); Charles Cobb, "Organizing the Freedom Schools," in *Freedom Is a Constant Struggle: An Anthology of the Mississippi Civil Rights Movement*, ed. Susie Erenrich (Montgomery, AL: Black Belt Press, 1999), 134; Florence Howe, "Mississippi's Freedom Schools: The Politics of Education," *Harvard Educational Review* 35 (Summer 1965): 144–60; *Freedom School Curriculum: Mississippi Freedom Summer, 1964*, edited and introduced by Kathy Emery, Sylvia Braselmann, and Linda Gold (67). The last was a collection of documents related to the Freedom Schools with a lengthy introduction by the editors. It was found at *http://educationanddemocracy.org/ED_FSC.html.*

23. Emery et al., *Freedom School Curriculum*, 14; Howe, "Mississippi's Freedom Schools," 144. Emery et al. include the *Guide to Negro History* on 212–26.

24. Street, *Culture War*, 280.

25. Loewen and Sallis, *Mississippi: Conflict and Change*, 2. Note: all quotations from *Mississippi: Conflict and Change* represent the final published product as edited and

often rewritten by Loewen and Sallis. Though attributed to the writers originally responsible for chapters, the quotations may more accurately reflect the words and thoughts of the two main editors. With few preliminary drafts available, no effort was made to distinguish the contributions of writers and editors, and their collaborative effort lessens the importance of such distinctions.

26. Loewen and Sallis, *Conflict and Change*, 6, 7, 9, 10, 11.

27. Ibid., 13. Despite the suggestion in the text, Loewen and Sallis provided no biographical information about the authors to help the reader evaluate the possible effect of the authors' ideology on their textbook.

28. Ibid., 17.

29. Ibid., 139, 141, 142, 147, 149, 155, 160, 165, 167.

30. Ibid., 165, 168, 171, 178, 179, 181, 186–87.

31. Loewen to Bruce Adams, June 30, 1970; Answers to First Set of Interrogatories to Plaintiffs, May 5, 1977, *Loewen v. Turnipseed* case file, NARA. The MHP apparently expected weekly report from Adams, Jones, and Middleton, the non-faculty contributors. The regularity and detail of the reports varied widely.

32. Bruce Adams, Progress Reports, July 6 to August 24, 1970; August 25 to 31, 1970; September 21 to 25, 1970; and October 12 to 16, 1970; handwritten note to Adams at bottom of Loewen to Maryellen Clampit, October 16, 1970, all in LPMDAH.

33. Bruce Adams, Progress Reports, September 1 to 8, 14 to 18, and 21 to 25, 1970; October 19 to 23, 1970; Loewen to Adams, no date; Adams to John Peterson, May 25, 1971; John [Peterson?] to Loewen, December 7, 1971; Loewen to John Ferguson, June 3, 1972, all in LPMDAH.

34. Loewen and Sallis, *Mississippi: Conflict and Change*, 27, 33, 37, 38, 43–44, 59.

35. Ibid., 46, 47, 55, 62.

36. Ibid., 116, 129, 134, 136, 137. The chapter's "Further Reading" included Marxist scholar Herbert Aptheker's *Essays in the History of the American Negro* (New York: International Publishers, 1964) but also John K. Bettersworth's *Confederate Mississippi*, described as "an excellent account of the period." See 137.

37. Olivia Jones, Progress Reports, September 10 to 14, 14 to 21, 1970; October 6 to 13, 13 to 19, and 27 to November 2, 1970; March 29 to April 3, 1971, all in LPMDAH; Answers to First Set of Interrogatories to Plaintiffs, May 5, 1977, *Loewen v. Turnipseed* case file, NARA. See also Charles S. Sydnor, *Slavery in Mississippi* (New York: D. Appleton-Century, 1933); Kenneth M. Stampp, *The Peculiar Institution: Slavery in the Ante-bellum South* (New York, Knopf, 1956); Herbert Aptheker, *Negro Slave Revolts in the United States, 1526–1860* (New York: International Publishers, 1939); Allen Weinstein and Frank Otto Gatell, eds., *American Negro Slavery: A Modern Reader* (New York: Oxford University Press, 1968); Gilberto Freyre, *The Masters and the Slaves: A Study in the Development of Brazilian Civilization* (New York: Knopf, 1946); Joseph G. Baldwin, *The Flush Times of Alabama and Mississippi* (New York: D. Appleton and Company, 1856); Percy Lee Rainwater, *Mississippi: Storm Center of Secession, 1856–1861* (Baton Rouge: O. Claitor, 1938).

38. Loewen and Sallis, *Mississippi: Conflict and Change*, 103–5.

39. Loewen and Sallis, *Mississippi: Conflict and Change*, 93, 96, 97, 98, 99.

40. Ibid., 101, 102, 103, 104, 106.

41. Olivia Jones, Progress Reports, February 2 to 8, 9 to 15, and 16 to 21, 1971; Jones to Loewen, July 18, September 14, 1972; October 26, 1973; Loewen to Jones, March 18 and July 21, 1972, all in LPMDAH; Answers to First Set of Interrogatories to Plaintiffs, May 5, 1977, *Loewen v. Turnipseed* case file, NARA.

42. Jeanne Middleton, Progress Reports, September 7 to 12, 14 to 19, 22 to 29, 29 to October 5, 1970; October 13 to 20, 27 to November 3, 1970; January 31 to February 7, 1971; February 14 to 20, 21 to 27, and 28 to March 6, 1971, all in LPMDAH; Answers to First Set of Interrogatories to Plaintiffs, May 5, 1977, *Loewen v. Turnipseed* case file, NARA.

43. Jeanne Middleton, Progress Reports, February 14 to March 13, 1971; May 18 to 22, 22 to 29, 18 to 30, 1971; Loewen to Middleton, March 29, May 26, and October 6, 1971; Middleton to Loewen, January 28, [1972], and April 11, 1972, all in LPMDAH; Answers to First Set of Interrogatories to Plaintiffs, May 5, 1977, and curriculum vita of Middleton, in *Loewen v. Turnipseed* case file, NARA.; interview with Jeanne Middleton.

44. Loewen and Sallis, *Mississippi: Conflict and Change*, 203, 207, 208, 210, 213, 217, 247.

45. Ibid., 238, 239, 246.

46. Loewen to Jeanne Middleton, no date; Olivia Jones, Progress Report, April 5 to May 20, 1971; Loewen, "Bibliography format for Mississippi history project," March 6, 1971, all in LPMDAH; Loewen to Mel Leventhal, June 6, 1977, in LPDC.

47. Loewen to Jeanne Middleton, no date; two unsigned and undated comments on chapter 14, all in LPMDAH.

48. Loewen to Bruce Adams, no date; Loewen comments on partial draft of chapter 3, no date; "Criticisms of Olivia Jones's Chapters, As Revealed on 7 July 1971," all in LPMDAH.

49. Loewen to Maryellen Hains Clampit, October 16, 1970, and Clampit to Loewen, March 19, 1971, both in LPMDAH; Answers to First Set of Interrogatories to Plaintiffs, May 5, 1977, *Loewen v. Turnipseed* case file, NARA; interview with Mary Ellen Hains (Clampit).

50. Maryellen Hains Clampit to Loewen, March 19, 1971, in LPMDAH; *Principles and Practices in the Teaching of the Social Sciences: Concepts and Values* (New York: Harcourt Brace Jovanovich, 1970).

51. Loewen to Mississippi History Project Workers re Format, no date [1971], in LPDC; Kevin Lynch, *The Image of the City* (Cambridge: MIT Press, 1960).

52. Loewen to "all Members of the Mississippi History Project," no date [March 1971]; Loewen to F. Louis Friedman, Ira Peck, et al., March 6, 1971, both in LPMDAH.

53. Bruce Adams to Maryellen Hains Clampit, May 17, 1971; Loewen to Clampit, May 27, June 9, and October 6, 1971; Clampit to Loewen, June 7, 1971; Clampit to Olivia Jones, August 4, 1971; Clampit, Comments on Chapter 16, undated, all in LPMDAH; interview with Mary Ellen Hains.

54. Loewen, "Questions to Ask of Each Chapter in Mississippi: Conflict and Change," January 1972, in SPJM.

55. "How to Evaluate Textbooks for Sex and Ethnic Biases," no date, unknown origin, in LPMDAH.

56. Ibid.

57. Loewen and Sallis, *Mississippi: Conflict and Change*, 184–85, 290, 292.

58. Ibid., 165–66.

59. Interview with James Loewen; interview with Charles and Harrylyn Sallis.

60. Loewen to John A. Griffin, December 10, 1970; January 16, and May 31, 1971; Loewen to Jeanne Middleton, March 29 and May 26, 1971; Loewen to Maryellen Hains Clampit, May 27, 1971; Bruce Adams to Maryellen Hains Clampit, May 17, 1971, all in LPMDAH.

61. Bruce Adams, Progress Report, February 15 to 17, 1971; Adams to Maryellen Hains Clampit, May 17, 1971, both in LPMDAH.

62. Loewen to Stephen C. Immer, September 28, 1971; Immer to Loewen, October 6, 1971; and Immer to Loewen, November 11, 1973, all in LPMDAH; Answers to First Set of Interrogatories to Plaintiffs, May 5, 1977, *Loewen v. Turnipseed* case file, NARA; interview with Stephen Immer. In the interview Immer remembered his experience with the MHP quite fondly as an experience important to him personally, and he gave no indication of disappointment or frustration.

63. Loewen to James Brown, February 16, 1972, in LPMDAH; Answers to First Set of Interrogatories to Plaintiffs, May 5, 1977, *Loewen v. Turnipseed* case file, NARA; interviews with James Loewen and with James Brown.

64. Loewen and Sallis, *Mississippi: Conflict and Change*, chapter 15, 249–85, especially 257–58, 277–78.

65. Loewen to Bill Ferris, August 2, September 29, 1972; Loewen to [apparently memo to file], September 29, 1971; Bill Ferris to Loewen, October 5, 1971, all in LPMDAH; interview with Bill Ferris. In the interview Ferris recalled no major conflict or disagreement with Loewen, just that his involvement did not work out. He praised *Conflict and Change*.

66. Loewen to Bill Ferris, October 11, 1971, and January 14, April 5, and July 17, 1972; Loewen to [apparently memo to file], September 29, 1971; Loewen to Charles Sallis, James Brown, and Mel Leventhal, January 3, 1972; Bill Ferris to Loewen, April 13 and August 21, 1972, all in LPMDAH.; interview with Bill Ferris. Ferris published a version of his work as "Black and White Folklore in Mississippi: A Resume," *Mississippi Folklore Registry* 6 (Winter 1972): 121–37.

67. Loewen to John A. Griffin, July 17, 1971; Loewen to Maryellen Hains Clampit, October 6, 1971; Loewen to Jeanne Middleton, October 6, 1971; John A. Griffin to Loewen, February 9, 1972; Loewen to Olivia Jones, April 18 and July 21, 1972, all in LPMDAH.

68. Loewen to Griffin, October 18, 1971, in LPMDAH.

Reception

1. Loewen to possible publishers, May 11, 1971, in LPMDAH. The articles appeared in the *New York Times* on May 10 and June 14, 1970. See James W. Loewen, *The Mississippi Chinese: Between Black and White* (Cambridge, MA: Harvard University Press, 1971).

2. "Economic argument re *Mississippi: Conflict and Change*," no date, in LPMDAH.

3. Martin Mayer, "The Trouble with Textbooks," *Harper's*, July 1962, 69; Marjory R. Kline, "Social Influences in Textbook Publishing," *Educational Forum* 48 (Winter 1984): 223; R. B. Edgerton, "Odyssey of a Book: How a Social Studies Text Comes Into Being," *Social Education* 33 (March 1969): 280–81; Eric Broudy, "The Trouble with Textbooks," *Teachers College Record* 77 (September 1975): 16–17; Paul Goldstein, *Changing the American Schoolbook* (Lexington, MA: Lexington Books, 1978), 56–57. For Loewen's own later devastating critique of American history textbook production, see Loewen, *Lies My Teacher Told Me: Everything Your American History Textbook Got Wrong* (New York: Touchstone, 2007), rev. ed., especially chapter 12, "Why Is History Taught Like This?" 301–39.

4. Broudy, "The Trouble with Textbooks," 16, 24; Goldstein, *Changing the American Schoolbook*, 4, 23, 57; Mayer, "The Trouble with Textbooks," 70.

5. Mayer, "The Trouble with Textbooks," 67–69.

6. Albert Alexander, "Does the American History Textbook Still Wear a Gray Flannel Cover?" *Social Education* 33 (March 1969): 300–301; Mayer, "The Trouble with Textbooks," 67; Broudy, "The Trouble with Textbooks," 24.

7. Broudy, "The Trouble with Textbooks," 8; Loewen to John A. Griffin, May 31, July 17, and October 18, 1971; Loewen to Jerry Matthews, October 27, 1971; Loewen to Richard W. DeBruin, November 23, 1971; Loewen, "The Writing of *Mississippi: Conflict and Change*," January 1975, all in LPMDAH.

8. "Summary of Pilot Study of *Mississippi: Conflict and Change*" [spring 1972], in LPDC

9. Ibid.

10. Ibid.

11. Loewen, "Reactions to *Mississippi: Conflict and Change*, from Various New York and Mississippi Organizations as of 12–5–71," in LPDC; Loewen to John A. Griffin, October 18, 1971, and Loewen to Brandon Sparkman, December 30, 1972, in LPMDAH.

12. Paul McArdle, "A Review of *Mississippi Conflict and Change* Edited by James W. Loewen and Charles Sallis," in LPMDAH.

13. Ibid.

14. Ibid.

15. Brandon B. Sparkman to Melvyn R. Leventhal, February 29, 1972; Leventhal to Sparkman, March 6, 1972; Loewen and Sallis to Sparkman, no date [after March 6, 1972], in LPDC.

16. Leventhal to Sparkman, March 6, 1972; Loewen and Sallis to Sparkman, no date [after March 6, 1972], in LPDC.

17. Deposition of Mary Kyle, October 27, 1976, *Loewen v. Turnipseed* case file, NARA; interview with Charles and Harrylyn Sallis.

18. Loewen to Brother Egan Hunter, October 27, 1971; Kenneth M. Stampp to Loewen, November 23, 1971; John Hope Franklin to Loewen, December 9, 1971; August Meier to Loewen, May 18, [?], all in LPDC. Franklin later agreed to look at the manuscript but said he could not get to it for several months. See Franklin to Loewen, January 25, 1972, in LPDC. For lists of individuals who offered comments, see untitled, undated document, LPDC; Plaintiff's Answers to Defendants' Second Set of Interrogatories

to Plaintiffs, April 27, 1978, *Loewen v. Turnipseed* case file, MAGF. Loewen's papers do not contain responses from many of the individuals asked to comment on the manuscript. No record exists of who actually responded with significant commentaries, and some certainly did not.

19. Larry Goodwin to Loewen, April 22, 1972, in LPDC.

20. C. Vann Woodward to Loewen, November 24, 1971; Milton Meltzer to Loewen, January 21, 1972; Wilfrid C. Bailey to Phillip Martin, May 2, 1972; James R. Richburg to Phillip Martin, May 2, 1972; Loewen to Phillip Martin, May 17, 1972, all in LPDC.

21. Walter Hurn and Robert Walker to Loewen, February [?], 1972, in LPDC.

22. John Dittmer to Loewen, Tuesday p. m. [no date], in LPDC; Dittmer to Loewen, [no date], in LPMDAH.

23. John Dittmer to Loewen, Tuesday p. m. [no date], in LPDC.

24. Ken Lawrence to Loewen, March 16, 1973, in LPDC.

25. Ibid.

26. Loewen to Ken Lawrence, March 16, 1973, in LPDC.

27. Eugene R. Mechelke, "Some Observations on Mississippi's Reconstruction Historiography," *Journal of Mississippi History* 33 (February 1971): 21–38; Loewen, "Mississippi's Reconstruction and Its Histories: A Reply to Mechelke," March 23, 1971; Loewen to John Edmund Gonzales, March 24, 1971, in LPMDAH.

28. John Edmund Gonzales to Loewen, May 4, 1971, in LPMDAH; Mechelke, "Some Observations on Mississippi's Reconstruction Historiography," 21, unnumbered note.

29. Bruce Adams, Progress Report, October 19 to 23, 1970; Loewen to John A. Griffin, December 10, 1970; Loewen to Leventhal and Frank Parker, August 8, 1971, all in LPMDAH. By 1975, Loewen had extended his complaints to the "inherently racist" historical markers erected all over the state by the Department of Archives and History. See Loewen memo to file in re MDAH, April 15, 1975, in LPDC.

30. List of people asked to comment on textbook, December 5, 1971; Pat Watters to Loewen, October 14, 1971; Verne Moberg to Loewen, October 11, 1971, all in LPDC; Pat Watters and Reese Cleghorn, *Climbing Jacob's Ladder: The Arrival of Negroes in Southern Politics* (New York: Harcourt, Brace and World, 1967); Pat Watters, *Down to Now: Reflections on the Southern Civil Rights Movement* (New York: Pantheon Books, 1971).

31. Andre Schiffrin, *The Business of Books: How International Conglomerates Took Over Publishing and Changed the Way We Read* (London: Verso, 2000), 58–59; Loewen, "The Writing of *Mississippi: Conflict and Change*," January 1975, in LPMDAH; Loewen to Andre Schiffrin, December 5, 1971, in LPDC; interview with James Loewen.

32. For Andre Schiffrin's background, see Schiffrin, *A Political Education: Coming of Age in Paris and New York* (Hoboken, NJ: Melhouse House, 2007). On his political activism, see Schiffrin, "The Student Movement in the 1950s: A Reminiscence." *Radical America* 2 (May–June 1968): 26–41, and Maurice Isserman, *If I had a Hammer . . . : The Death of the Old Left and the Birth of the New Left* (New York: Basic Books, 1987). See also his obituary, *New York Times*, December 1, 2013.

33. John A. Tebbel, *A History of Book Publishing in the United States: Volume IV: The Great Change 1940–1980* (New York: R. R. Bowker, 1981), 74, 291; Jacob Burkhardt,

Force and Freedom: An Interpretation of History (New York: Pantheon, 1943); Zoe Oldenbourg, *The World Is Not Enough* (New York: Pantheon, 1948); *The I Ching: Or, Book of Changes*, trans. Richard Wilhelm and Cary F. Baynes (New York: Pantheon, 1950); Boris Pasternak, *Dr. Zhivago* (New York: Pantheon, 1957); Schiffrin, *Business of Books*, 16.

34. Schiffrin, *Political Education*, 203; Schiffrin, *Business of Books*, 41; E. P. Thompson, *The Making of the English Working Class* (New York: Pantheon, 1964); Eugene D. Genovese, *The Political Economy of Slavery: Studies in the Economy and Society of the Slave South* (New York: Pantheon, 1967); Staughton Lynd, *Intellectual Origins of the American Radicalism* (New York: Pantheon, 1968); Frances Piven Fox and Richard A. Cloward, *Regulating the Poor: The Functions of Public Welfare* (New York: Pantheon, 1971).

35. Schiffrin, *Political Education*, 203, 210; Schiffrin, *Business of Books*, 57–58; James M. McPherson, *The Negro's Civil War: How American Negroes Felt and Acted During the War for the Union* (New York: Pantheon, 1965); Loren Miller, *The Petitioners: The Story of the Supreme Court of the United States and the Negro* (New York: Pantheon, 1966); Watters, *Down to Now*.

36. "Suit to Win State Textbook Adoption—In Mississippi," *Publishers Weekly*, November 24, 1975, 18–19; Loewen, "The Writing of *Mississippi: Conflict and Change*," January 1975, in LPMDAH; Milly Daniels to Loewen, March 8, 1972, in LPDC.

37. Milly Daniel to Loewen, March 8, August 8, and October 20, 1972; Loewen to Daniel, May 17 and June 14, 1972; Loewen and Sallis contract with Pantheon, May 10, 1973, all; in LPDC.

38. Loewen to Milly Daniel, June 1, 1973; Daniel to Loewen, June 28, 1973; Loewen to Daniel, July 6, 1973, all in LPDC.

39. Milly Daniel to Loewen, August 29, 1973; Loewen to Daniel, September 1, 1973, in LPDC.

40. Loewen to Milly Daniel, September 12, 1973, in LPDC.

41. Loewen to Andre Schiffrin, September 12, 1973, in LPDC; *Berkeley Wire*, November 27, 2012.

42. Loewen to Allen Graubard, November 29, 1973, and March 14, 1974; Graubard to Loewen, February 28, 1974, all in LPDC.

43. Loewen to Allen Graubard, April 14, 1974; Loewen to Kathleen Macomber, August 6 and September 1, 1974, all in LPDC.

44. Richard Aubrey McLemore, ed., *A History of Mississippi* (Hattiesburg: University and College Press of Mississippi, 1973); David Herbert Donald, review of *A History of Mississippi*, edited by Richard Aubrey McLemore, *American Historical Review* 78 (December 1973): 1523–25. For another critical review see Monroe Billington, *Journal of American History* 60 (December 1973): 801–3, and for a more positive assessment see Aaron M. Boom, *Journal of Mississippi History* 35 (November 1973): 626–27.

45. Donald, review of *A History of Mississippi*, *American Historical Review* 78 (December 1973): 1523–25.

46. Ibid.

47. Loewen to David Herbert Donald, January 1, 1974; Janet Hearne to Loewen, May 9, 1974; Loewen to Janet Hearne, July 25, 1974, all in LPDC; Loewen to the editor, *American Historical Review* 80 (February 1975): 206–7. Hearne was an assistant editor at the journal. Loewen gave her permission to edit his letter to fit the journal's length requirement. In a related development, when Loewen and John Dittmer heard that James W. Silver, formerly at the University of Mississippi, had the *New York Times Book Review*'s assignment to review McLemore's two-volume history, they sent Silver their criticisms of the book. Loewen's comments closely resembled his letter nine months later to David Donald. See Loewen to James W. Silver, March 8, 1973, and John Dittmer to Silver, March 19, 1973, both in LPDC. The *New York Times Book Review* never published a review of McLemore. Silver had a review in the *Greenville Delta Democrat Times*, August 3, 1975, in which he called the history a "ponderous" and "well-laundered." According to Silver, "The mythology of the Old South, the Confederacy and Reconstruction has scarcely been disturbed." He concluded, "I must sadly confess indignation that the recorded history of Mississippi has changed more slowly than the state itself."

48. Loewen to David Herbert Donald, January 1, 1974, in LPDC; Loewen to the editor, *American Historical Review* 80 (February 1975): 206–7.

49. Victor Wilson, review of *Mississippi: Conflict and Change*, in *NOTP*, September 22, 1974. Apparently distributed by a wire service, Wilson's review also appeared on the same day in the *Newark (NJ) Star-Telegram*.

50. Bob Casey, review of *Mississippi: Conflict and Change*, in *JCL*, October 20, 1974.

51. Jason Berry, "Speaking Directly to the Young," *Nation*, April 12, 1975, 441–42.

52. Reviews of *Mississippi: Conflict and Change*, in *Journal of American History* 52 (June 1975): 210; in *Journal of Southern History* 41 (May 1975): 286; in *Equity and Excellence in Education* 13 (2, 1975).

53. W. F. Minor, "Conflict and Change in Mississippi," *Harvard Educational Review* 45 (February 1975): 114–19. Minor's review came after the state rejected the textbook but before the resulting lawsuit and court decision.

54. Robert Coles, "Much More Than A Textbook," *Virginia Quarterly Review* 52 (Spring 1976): 314–21.

55. Ibid.

56. John Anthony Scott, review of *Mississippi: Conflict and Change*, in Committee on History in the Classroom Newsletter, December 1974.

57. Robert B. Moore, "Two History Textbooks: A Study in Contrast. A Study Guide and Lesson Plan." New York: Racism/Sexism Resource Center, 1977, 21. Moore's quotations, while substantively true, sometimes lacked precise accuracy. For example, Loewen and Sallis's actual words regarding the desegregation of the Highway Patrol were "Owing to a 1971 court order, the Mississippi Highway Patrol finally began to hire blacks as patrolmen." See *Conflict and Change*, 314.

58. Moore, "Two History Textbooks," 4, 6, 10.

59. Ibid., 3, 12.

60. Jimmie Lee Franklin, review of *Mississippi: Conflict and Change*, in *Red River Valley Historical Review* 42 (2, 1979): 94–95.

61. [Loewen's?] notes on Lillian Smith ceremony, January, 1976, in LPDC; H. J. Geiger, review of *All God's Dangers: The Life of Nate Shaw*, ed. by Theodore Rosengarten, in *New York Times Book Review*, October 20, 1974, 20; Norman Lederer, review of *Roll, Jordan, Roll: The World the Slaves Made* by Eugene D. Genovese, in *Library Journal*, September 1, 1972, 2064; Orlando Patterson, review of *Roll, Jordan, Roll: The World the Slaves Made* by Eugene D. Genovese, in *New Republic*, November 9, 1974, 37. Another blockbuster history book in 1974 was Robert William Fogel and Stanley L. Engerman, *Time on the Cross* (Boston: Little, Brown, 1974). For a recent appreciation of *All God's Dangers*, see Dwight Garner, "Lost in Literary History: A Tale of Courage in the South," *New York Times*, April 19, 2014. The earlier non-fiction winners were George Brown Tindall, *The Emergence of the New South, 1913–1945* (Baton Rouge: Louisiana State University Press, 1967); Dan T. Carter, *Scottsboro: A Tragedy of the American South* (Baton Rouge: Louisiana State University Press, 1969); Paul M. Gaston, *The New South Creed: A Study in Southern Mythmaking* (New York: Knopf, 1970); Anthony Dunbar, *Our Land Too* (New York: Pantheon, 1971); Robert Coles, *Children of Crisis*, vol. II: *Migrants, Sharecroppers, and Mountaineers*, and vol. IV: *The South Goes North* (Boston: Little, Brown, 1971); Harold *Martin, Ralph McGill: Reporter* (Boston: Little, Brown, 1973); C. Vann Woodward, *The Strange Career of Jim Crow* (New York: Oxford University Press, 1974), 3rd rev. ed. The SRC apparently made no awards in 1975. In 1973 the SRC began making an award for fiction, and the first two went to Alice Walker, for *Revolutionary Petunias and Other Poems* (New York: Harcourt Brace and Jovanovich, 1973), and Albert Murray, for *Train Whistle Guitar* (New York: McGraw-Hill, 1974). The 1976 award went to Reynolds Price for *The Surface of Earth* (New York: Atheneum, 1975).

62. George H. Esser to Loewen, December 15, 1975; [Loewen's?] notes on Lillian Smith ceremony, January, 1976, both in LPDC.

Controversy

1. James Loewen to Kathleen Macomber, September 1, 1974, in LPDC; Loewen to John A. Griffin, September 6, 1974, in LPMDAH; Millsaps *Purple and White*, April 5, 1973.

2. Mississippi Textbook Adoption, August 28, 1974–October 30, 1974, no date [1974]; Mississippi State Textbook Purchasing Board, "Textbook Administration: Rules and Regulations," July 1973, both in *Loewen v. Turnipseed* case file, NARA. Sources do not indicate which members the governor named and which the superintendent.

3. Mississippi Textbook Adoption, August 28, 1974–October 30, 1974, no date [1974]; Mississippi State Textbook Purchasing Board, "Textbook Administration: Rules and Regulations," July 1973, both in *Loewen v. Turnipseed* case file, NARA.

4. *JCL*, August 29, 1974; *Biloxi Sun-Herald*, November 10, 1974. *JCL* staff writer Josie Tullos provided a lively feature story on the meeting rather than a dry news account.

5. Statement of Publisher Submitting Books for Adoption and Warranty of Publisher, both in *Loewen v. Turnipseed* case file, NARA.

6. Mississippi Textbook Adoption, *Loewen v. Turnipseed* case file, NARA.

7. Deposition of Virginia W. McElhaney, October 27, 1976, *Loewen v. Turnipseed* case file, NARA; Answer of Certain Defendants to First Set of Interrogatories to Defendants, January 30, 1976, *Loewen v. Turnipseed* case file, MAGF. See obituary in *Hattiesburg American*, February 21, 2014. McElhaney could have been a student in one of Bettersworth's high school classes.

8. Answer of Certain Defendants to First Set of Interrogatories to Defendants, January 30, 1976, *Loewen v. Turnipseed* case file, MAGF; deposition of Mary Kyle, October 27, 1976, *Loewen v. Turnipseed* case file, NARA.

9. Answer of Certain Defendants to First Set of Interrogatories to Defendants, January 30, 1976; Deposition of Mary Harvey Wilder, December 3, 1976, both in *Loewen v. Turnipseed* case file, MAGF. See also obituary in *JCL*, October 17, 2006; Deposition of Mary Kyle, October 27, 1976, *Loewen v. Turnipseed* case file, NARA.

10. Answer of Certain Defendants to First Set of Interrogatories to Defendants, January 30, 1976; Deposition of John M. Turnipseed, October 28, 1976; John M. Turnipseed to W. A. Matthews, December 1, 1975; all in *Loewen v. Turnipseed* case file, MAGF. See obituary in *DDT*, February 28, 1993.

11. Answer of Certain Defendants to First Set of Interrogatories to Defendants, January 30, 1976; Deposition of Howard E. Railes, October 28, 1976, both in *Loewen v. Turnipseed* case file, MAGF; Deposition of John M. Turnipseed, October 28, 1976, *Loewen v. Turnipseed* case file, NARA.

12. Answer of Certain Defendants to First Set of Interrogatories to Defendants, January 30, 1976; Deposition of Benjamin Berry Burney Jr., December 3, 1976, both in *Loewen v. Turnipseed* case file, MAGF; Deposition of James Earl Wash, October 26, 1976, *Loewen v. Turnipseed* case file, NARA. See obituaries for Burney in the *Biloxi Sun-Herald*, May 27 and June 2, 1989.

13. Deposition of W. A. Matthews, October 26, 1976, *Loewen v. Turnipseed* case file, MAGF; Minutes, MSTPB, July 12, 1972.

14. Depositions by rating committee members discuss the operation of the committee. See, for example, Deposition of John M. Turnipseed, October 28, 1976; Deposition of Virginia W. McElhaney, October 27, 1976, both *Loewen v. Turnipseed* case file, MAGF. McElhaney did describe a slight acquaintance with Kyle.

15. Mississippi Textbook Adoption, and Suggested Criteria for Textbooks Selection, both in *Loewen v. Turnipseed* case file, NARA; Deposition of W. A. Matthews, October 26, 1976, *Loewen v. Turnipseed* case file, MAGF.

16. Suggested Criteria for Textbooks Selection, Criteria for the Selection of Textbooks in All Areas, *Loewen v. Turnipseed* case file, NARA.

17. Ibid.

18. Instructions for Rating Books, Mississippi State Textbook Purchasing Board to Rating Committee Members, no date [1974], *Loewen v. Turnipseed* case file, NARA.

19. The competing views on higher education are developed more fully later in the chapter.

20. R. Follett, "The School Textbook Adoption Process," *Book Research Quarterly* 1 (Summer 1985): 21–22; Paul Goldstein, *Changing the American Schoolbook* (Lexington,

MA: Lexington Books, 1978), 5, 51; Martin Mayer, "The Trouble with Textbooks," *Harper's* 225 (July 1962): 65.

21. Follett, "The School Textbook Adoption Process," 19–20; Mayer, "The Trouble with Textbooks," 67–68.

22. Mississippi State Textbook Purchasing Board, Summary Evaluation Form, *Loewen v. Turnipseed* case file, NARA. For examples of textbook evaluation procedures, see Arthur S. Nichols and Anna Ochoa, "Evaluating Textbooks for Elementary Social Studies: Criteria for the Seventies," *Social Education* 35, no. 3 (March 1971): 290–94, 304; Willard B. Spalding, "The Selection and Distribution of Printed Materials," in *Text Materials in Modern Education: A Comprehensive Theory and Platform for Research*, ed. Lee J. Cronbach (Urbana: University of Illinois Press, 1955), 166–87, 177–78.

23. Mississippi State Textbook Purchasing Board, Summary Evaluation Form, *Loewen v. Turnipseed* case file, NARA.

24. Ibid.

25. Rating Committee Report (Individual), *Loewen v. Turnipseed* case file, NARA.

26. Virginia McElhaney, Summary Evaluation Form and Rating Committee Report, October 22, 1974, *Loewen v. Turnipseed* case file, MAGF.

27. Mary Kyle, Summary Evaluation Form and Rating Committee Report, October 21, 1974; Evelyn H. Wilder, Summary Evaluation Form and Rating Committee Report, October 20, 1974, both in *Loewen v. Turnipseed* case file, MAGF.

28. John M. Turnipseed, Summary Evaluation Form and Rating Committee Report, October 22, 1974, *Loewen v. Turnipseed* case file, MAGF.

29. Howard E. Railes, Summary Evaluation Form and Rating Committee Report, October 21, 1974, *Loewen v. Turnipseed* case file, MAGF; Loewen and Sallis, *Mississippi: Conflict and Change*, 96 and 178.

30. James E. Wash, Summary Evaluation Form and Rating Committee Report, October 18, 1974, *Loewen v. Turnipseed* case file, MAGF.

31. Benjamin F. Burney, Summary Evaluation Form and Rating Committee Report, October 21, 1974, *Loewen v. Turnipseed* case file, MAGF.

32. Minutes, MSTPB, September 9, 1966, and November 4, 1974.

33. Loewen Proposal for Support of New Textbooks in Mississippi History, no date; Loewen to Arthur S. Nichols and Anna Ochoa, March 16, 1972; Loewen to John A. Griffin, September 11, 1972, all in LPMDAH; Loewen to Phil Stone, July 28, 1971; Loewen and Sallis to Brandon Sparkman, no date [after March 6, 1972], both in LPDC.

34. Loewen and Sallis to William L. Waller, November 7, 1974, in LPDC.

35. Loewen to W. A. Matthews, November 8, 1975; Loewen to Garvin Johnston, November 8, 1974; W. A. Matthews to Loewen, November 15, 1975; Loewen to Pantheon, Melvyn Leventhal, Ben Snyder, and George A. Owens, December 3, 1974; all in LPDC; *New York Times*, November 10, 1974; *JCL*, November 8, 1974. The more than two-week delay in Loewen's forwarding Matthews's suggestion to Pantheon may be partly attributed to the Thanksgiving interruption.

36. Carol Cox to W. A. Matthews, November 11, 1974, in LPDC.

37. Mrs. Caroline H. Moore, to W. A. Matthews, November 15, 1974; Ben E. Bailey to W. A. Matthews, November 15, 1974; Ronald A. Pook to William Waller, November 22, 1974; Rev. Msgr. Paul V. Canonici to Garvin H. Johnston, November 19, 1974; all in LPDC.

38. *Biloxi Sun-Herald*, November 10, 1974.

39. Loewen to Melvyn Leventhal, November 11, 1974; John Quincy Adams to Loewen, November 23, 1974; Loewen to Pantheon, Melvyn Leventhal, Ben Snyder, and George A. Owens, December 3, 1974; all in LPDC.

40. Millsaps *Purple and White*, December 6, 1974.

41. Loewen to Pantheon, Melvyn Leventhal, Ben Snyder, and George A. Owens, December 3, 1974; all in LPDC; Minutes, MSTPB, December 10, 1974.

42. Loewen to W. A. Matthews, December 19, 1974, in LPDC.

43. Loewen, memo to file, undated [after January 2, 1975], in LPDC; Millsaps *Purple and White*, January 29, 1975.

44. Minutes, MSTPB, January 14, 1975.

45. Charles Sallis, "To the Board Members of the Mississippi State Textbook Purchasing Board," February 11, 1975, in LPDC; Millsaps *Purple and White*, February 27, 1975.

46. Charles Sallis, "To the Board Members of the Mississippi State Textbook Purchasing Board," February 11, 1975, in LPDC.

47. Ibid.

48. Minutes, MSTPB, February 11, 1975; W. A. Matthews to Charles Sallis and Jean Middleton, February 11, 1975, in LPDC.

49. *Norwood v. Harrison*, F.Supp. 1003 (ND Miss. 1972).

50. Ibid.

51. Ibid.

52. *Norwood v. Harrison*, 413 U.S. 455; 93 S. Ct. 2804; *JCL*, February 20, 1973.

53. *Norwood v. Harrison*, 413 U.S. 455; 93 S. Ct. 2804.

54. *JCL*, June 26, 1973; *Norwood v. Harrison*, 382 F.Supp. 921 (1974); 410 F.Supp. 133 (1976); 563 F.Supp. 722 (1977); 581 F.2d 518 (1978); 643 F.2d 348 (1981); Minutes, MSTPB, July 11 and 31, August 29, September 5, and October 10, 1973.

55. Several essays especially shaped and informed the discussion of issues in education in the following half dozen paragraphs. See David M. Bieber, "Textbook Adoption Laws, Precensorship, and the First Amendment: The Case Against Statewide Selection of Classroom Materials," *John Marshall Law Review* 17 (Winter 1984): 167–94; Julia T. Bradley, "Censoring the School Library: Do Students Have the Right to Read?" *Connecticut Law Review* 10 (Spring 1978): 747–74; Miranda E. Fritz, "What Will We Tell the Children? A Discussion of Current Judicial Opinion on the Scope of Ideas Acceptable for Presentation in Primary and Secondary Education," *Tulane Law Review* 56 (April 1982): 960–1005; Reynolds C. Seitz, "Supervision of Public Elementary and Secondary School Pupils Through State Control Over Curriculum and Textbook Selection," *Law and Contemporary Problems* 20 (1, 1955): 104–24; Nat Stern, "Challenging Ideological Exclusion of Curriculum Material: Rights of Students and Parents," *Harvard Civil Rights-Civil Liberties*

Law Review 14 (Summer 1979): 485–528; unsigned, "School Boards, Schoolbooks and the Freedom to Learn," *Yale Law Journal* 59 (April 1950) 928–54. See also Jack Nelson and Gene Roberts Jr., *The Censors and the Schools* (Boston: Little, Brown, 1963), and Diane Ravitch, *The Language Police: How Pressure Groups Restrict What Students Learn* (New York: Knopf, 2003). For the specific examples, see *Mississippi Senate Journal*, March 8, 1962, Senate Bill 1857, 315; January 8, 1974, Senate Bill 1781, 29; *Mississippi House Journal*, March 16, 1964, House Bill 459, 318. See also the discussion above in chapter 1.

56. If Loewen and Sallis had not dropped their idea to produce a Mississippi history text for fifth-graders, writing it would have forced them to consider the differences between ten-year-old and fourteen-year-old students and, therefore, the validity of the marketplace of ideas and the applicability of student rights to elementary school pupils.

57. Ravitch, *The Language Police*, 63.

Case

1. Melvyn R. Leventhal to Loewen March 18 and July 25, 1975; Loewen to Leventhal, June 7, 1975, in LPDC.

2. Loewen to Mr. and Mrs. Duncan M. Gray Jr., March 31, 1975; Loewen to Leventhal, June 7, 1975, in LPDC.

3. Loewen to Rev. Msgr. Paul V. Canonici, March 24, 1975; Loewen to Father Luke Mikschl, March 24, 1975; Father Luke Mikschl to Loewen, April 17, 1975; Most Rev. Joseph Howze to Loewen, May 1, 1975; Loewen to Melvyn R. Leventhal, July 31, 1975; all in LPDC; interview with Paul V. Canonici.

4. Interview with Mamie Chinn. On C. O. Chinn, see John Dittmer, *Local People: The Struggle for Civil Rights in Mississippi* (Urbana: University of Illinois, 1994), 188; Charles E. Cobb Jr., *This Nonviolent Stuff'll Get You Killed: How Guns Made the Civil Rights Movement Possible* (New York: Basic Books, 2014), 187–91.

5. Clarice Campbell to Loewen, May 23, 1975; Loewen to Clarice Campbell, May 27, 1975; Loewen to Melvyn R. Leventhal, June 7, 1975; Loewen to Calvin Isaac, July 10, 1975; Loewen to Marion L. Hayes, July 21, 1975, all in LPDC.

6. Complaint, November 5, 1975, in case file for *Loewen v. Turnipseed*, MAGF.

7. Nick Bryant, *The Bystander: John F. Kennedy and the Struggle for Black Equality* (New York: Basic Books, 2006), 286–88; Jack Bass, *Unlikely Heroes* (New York: Simon and Schuster, 1981), 164–68. Cox had a close friendship with Sen. James O. Eastland, chairman of the Senate Judiciary Committee. Bryant tells the story that Eastland agreed to approve Thurgood Marshall as federal judge in New York in exchange for Cox's appointment. The senator told Attorney General Robert Kennedy, "Tell your brother that if you give me Harold Cox, I will give him the nigger." Bryant, 288.

8. Frank Parker, *Black Votes Count: Political Empowerment in Mississippi after 1965* (Chapel Hill: University of North Carolina Press, 1990), 161, 220 n. 9.

9. Fred L. Banks Jr., "The United State Court of Appeals for the Fifth Circuit: A Personal Perspective," *Mississippi College Law Review* 16 (1996): 275–88, especially n.14 on 277; Evelyn C. White, *Alice Walker* (New York: Norton, 2004), 135–36.

10. *Ibid.*

11. *JDN*, November 9, 1973. Woodville was also the home of Anne Moody, author of *Coming of Age in Mississippi* (New York: Doubleday, 1968).

12. Complaint, November 5, 1975, *Loewen v. Turnipseed* case file, MAGF.

13. Ibid.

14. Ibid.

15. Ibid.

16. Ibid.

17. Ibid. The plaintiffs would later drop their First Amendment claim.

18. Complaint, November 5, 1975, *Loewen v. Turnipseed* case file, MAGF. A fifth point called for "awarding plaintiffs costs and reasonable attorneys' fees."

19. *JCL*, July 7, 1982; Presentation of Portrait of the Honorable Orma R. Smith to the United States District Court, Northern District of Mississippi, Eastern Division, by the Bar of the Northern District in Mississippi, July 11, 1980, in U.S. Fed. Suppl. lxxii–lxxiv.

20. Motion for Stay, November 18, 1975; Judge Smith, Orders, December 11 and 30, 1975, both in *Loewen v. Turnipseed* case file, NARA; Leventhal to Loewen, Sallis, and Andre Schiffrin, January 5, 1976, in SPJM.

21. Answer and Other Defenses of Defendants, January 9, 1976, *Loewen v. Turnipseed* case file, MAGF. On one odd "fact," the two sides agreed because each said the Textbook Purchasing Board rejected the Loewen and Sallis book at its November 6, 1974, meeting; the board's minutes clearly state, however, that the board met and acted on November 4, 1974. Minutes, MSTPB, November 4, 1974.

22. First Set of Interrogatories to Defendants, November 5, 1975, *Loewen v. Turnipseed* case file, NARA.

23. Objection to Interrogatories, January 30, 1976, *Loewen v. Turnipseed* case file, NARA; Answer of Certain Defendants to First Set of Interrogatories to Defendants, January 30, 1976, *Loewen v. Turnipseed* case file, MAGF.

24. Motion of the Defendants for Change of Venue, February 6, 1976; Order, June 21, 1976, *Loewen v. Turnipseed* case file, NARA.

25. Frank R. Parker to Charles Holladay, February 17, 1976, in LPDC.

26. Ibid.

27. Ken Lawrence to Loewen, March 5–7, 1976; Proposed Resolution by Clarice T. Campbell and Robert M. Walker, March 1976, both in LPDC.

28. Ibid; Ken Lawrence to Loewen, March 5–7, 1976, in LPDC.

29. Melvyn R. Leventhal to R. Hollingsworth, September 10, 1976; Leventhal to Loewen and Sallis, September 13, 1976, in SPJM.

30. Melvyn R. Leventhal to R. Hollingsworth, September 10, 1976; Leventhal to Loewen and Sallis, September 13, 1976, in SPJM.

31. Plaintiffs First Request for Admissions, and Second Set of Interrogatories or in Alternate Request for Production of Documents, September 8, 1976, and Answer of Defendants to Plaintiffs First Request for Admissions, and Second Set of Interrogatories or in Alternate Request for Production of Documents, October 25, 1976, *Loewen v. Turnipseed* case file, NARA.

32. Notice of Depositions Upon Oral Examination, September 9, 1976, and Deposition of W. A. Matthews, October 26, 1976, *Loewen v. Turnipseed* case file, MAGF.

33. Deposition of W. A. Matthews, October 26, 1976, *Loewen v. Turnipseed* case file, MAGF.

34. Ibid.

35. Ibid.

36. Deposition of James Earl Wash, October 26, 1976, *Loewen v. Turnipseed* case file, NARA.

37. Ibid.

38. Ibid.

39. Ibid.

40. Deposition of Virginia W. McElhaney, October 27, 1976, *Loewen v. Turnipseed* case file, NARA.

41. Ibid.

42. Deposition of Mary Kyle, October 27, 1976, *Loewen v. Turnipseed* case file, NARA.

43. Ibid. Stockett asked no questions of Kyle.

44. Deposition of Howard E. Railes, October 28, 1974, *Loewen v. Turnipseed* case file, MAGF.

45. Deposition of John M. Turnipseed, October 28, 1976, *Loewen v. Turnipseed* case file, NARA.

46. Deposition of Mary Evelyn Wilder, December 3, 1976, *Loewen v. Turnipseed* case file, MAGF.

47. Ibid.

48. Ibid.

49. Ibid.

50. Ibid.

51. Ibid. The Wilder deposition began at 10:00 a.m., and the Burney deposition began at 11:40 the same morning.

52. Deposition of Benjamin Berry Burney Jr., December 3, 1976, *Loewen v. Turnipseed* case file, MAGF.

53. Ibid.

54. Plaintiffs' Third Interrogatories and Second Request for Inspection of Documents to Defendants, March 8, 1977, *Loewen v. Turnipseed* case file, NARA; Defendants' First Set of Interrogatories to Plaintiffs, November 2, 1976; Answers to First Set of Interrogatories to Plaintiffs, May 5, 1977; Answer of Defendants to Plaintiffs' Third Interrogatories and Second Request for Inspection of Documents, May 25, 1977; Defendants' Second Set of Interrogatories to Plaintiffs, May 26, 1977; Plaintiffs' Answers to Defendants' Second Set of Interrogatories to Plaintiffs, April 27, 1978; all in *Loewen v. Turnipseed* case file, MAGF; Loewen to Leventhal, June 6, 1977, in LPCD.

55. Leventhal to Loewen and Sallis, May 27, 1977, in LPCD; Leventhal to Judge Orma R. Smith, May 31, 1977; Peter M. Stockett to Judge Orma R. Smith, June 3, 1977; Order, June 7, 1977, *Loewen v. Turnipseed* case file, MAGF.

56. Amendment to Complaint, [June 12, 1977], *Loewen v. Turnipseed* case file, NARA. See David M. Bieber, "Textbook Adoption Laws, Precensorship, and the First Amendment: The Case Against Statewide Selection of Classroom Materials," *John Marshall Law Review* 17 (1984): 183 n. 112, where Bieber observes, "The *Loewen* plaintiffs abandoned their original request for a judgment declaring the Mississippi adoption law unconstitutional."

57. Amendment to Complaint [June 12, 1977], *Loewen v. Turnipseed* case file, NARA; Leventhal to Loewen and Sallis, May 27, 1977, in LPDC. In a deposition, an attorney could object to a question, but the witness usually had to answer it. The judge would later review the transcript and decide the legitimacy of the objection and whether the answer could be used in the trial.

58. Deposition of John K. Bettersworth, August 4, 1977, *Loewen v. Turnipseed* case file, MAGF. The court reporter recorded "no holes barred," and the obvious error has been translated here into "no holds barred."

59. Deposition of John K. Bettersworth, August 4, 1977, *Loewen v. Turnipseed* case file, MAGF.

60. Ibid.

61. Docket Sheet, *Loewen v. Turnipseed* case file, NARA; Frank R. Parker to Charles Sallis, April 21, 1978; Order on Discovery Deadlines, March 28, 1978, MAGF.

62. Frank R. Parker to Charles Sallis, April 21, 1978; Plaintiffs' Answers to Defendants' Third Set of Interrogatories and Request for Production of Documents, June 9, 1978, both in *Loewen v. Turnipseed* case file, MAGF; Plaintiffs' Answers to Defendants' Second Set of Interrogatories to Plaintiffs, April 27, 1978, *Loewen v. Turnipseed* case file, NARA.

63. Plaintiffs' Supplemental Memorandum of Law in Support of Motion to Certify Class Action, April 25, 1978, *Loewen v. Turnipseed* case file, MAGF. The original complaint contained the word "censor" only once, and it appeared in the last alleged violations of the law. The next time it or a variant form appeared in the legal documents came when the word "censorship" appeared twice in the amended appeal.

64. Vincent Clark, "Mississippi Book Burning: A Review of *Loewen v. Turnipseed*," Paper submitted to Paul Gaston, University of Virginia, Spring 1993.

65. Deposition of James W. Loewen, June 12, 1978, *Loewen v. Turnipseed* case file, MAGF.

66. Ibid.

67. Ibid.

68. Ibid.

69. Ibid.

70. Ibid.

71. Ibid.

72. Deposition of William Charles Sallis, June 12, 1978, *Loewen v. Turnipseed* case file, MAGF.

73. Scott Nearing, *Black America* (New York: Vanguard Press, 1929), 195 (picture #13); John A. Saltmarsh, *Scott Nearing: An Intellectual Biography* (Philadelphia: Temple University Press, 1991), 224–29; Amy Louise Wood, *Lynching and Spectacle: Witnessing*

Racial Violence in America, 1890–1940 (Chapel Hill: University of North Carolina Press, 2009), 212–13; Amy Louise Wood to author, May 24, 2015. Based on her own extensive research, Amy Wood, the expert on lynching photographs, offered "pretty definitive evidence" that the photograph came from the Omaha riot of 1919.

74. Report and Recommendations of the United States Magistrate, August 15, 1978; Plaintiffs' Objections to Report and Recommendations of United States Magistrate, September 5, 1978; Defendants' Response to Plaintiffs' Objections to Report and Recommendations of United States Magistrate, September 21, 1978; Judge Orma R. Smith, Order, September 26, 1978, all in *Loewen v. Turnipseed* case file, NARA.

75. Plaintiffs' Memorandum in Opposition to Defendants' Motion for Summary Judgment, October 4, 1978; Affidavit of W. A. Matthews, October 26, 1978, both in *Loewen v. Turnipseed* case file, MAGF; Defendants' Rebuttal to Plaintiffs' Memorandum in Opposition to Defendants' Motion for Summary Judgment, October 26, 1978; Affidavit of Jan Hilegas, October 4, 1978; Affidavit of James W. Loewen, October 4, 1978, *Loewen v. Turnipseed* case file, NARA. The case files did not include the defendants' original motion (ca. August 28, 1978) or the judge's ruling (January 2, 1979).

76. Notice of Pretrial Conference, January 10, 1979, *Loewen v. Turnipseed* case file, NARA.

Trial

1. Peter M. Stockett Jr. to Frank R. Parker, February 19, 1979, MAGF; Minutes, MSTPB, February 13, 1979; Affidavit of W. A. Matthews, October 26, 1978, *Loewen v. Turnipseed* case file, NARA.

2. Peter M. Stockett Jr. to Frank R. Parker, February 19, 1979, MAGF; Minutes, MSTPB, February 13, 1979; Affidavit of W. A. Matthews, October 26, 1978, *Loewen v. Turnipseed* case file, NARA. No evidence exists for Matthews's affecting the decisions of either the Rating Committee or the Textbook Purchasing Board, but Loewen suspected his involvement. Interview with James Loewen.

3. Pre-Trial Order, February 26, 1979, and revised June 28, 1978 [*sic*], *Loewen v. Turnipseed* case file, NARA.

4. Ibid.

5. Ibid.

6. Plaintiffs' Proposed Findings of Fact and Conclusions of Law, March 26, 1979, *Loewen v. Turnipseed* case file, MAGF.

7. Ibid.

8. Defendants' Proposed Pre-Trail Findings of Fact and Conclusions of Law, [March 27, 1979?], *Loewen v. Turnipseed* case file, NARA.

9. Pre-Trial Order, February 26, 1979, and revised June 28, 1978 [*sic*]; Civil Minutes—Trial, both in *Loewen v. Turnipseed* case file, NARA.

10. Maryellen Hains to Frank Parker, April 9, 1979; Parker to Ted Kilty, June 27, 1979; Kilty to Parker, July 12, 1979; Loewen to Phil Stone, July 28, 1971; February 28, 1975, and January 16, 1979; Stone to Loewen, May 5, 1975, and February 5 and 7, 1979; Thomas E.

Fox to Loewen, February 10, 1972; Loewen to Fox, February 14, 1972, all in LPDC; Robert D. Hess to Loewen, September 2, 1971; Loewen to Hess [undated reply to letter of September 2, 1971]; Hess to Loewen, September 14, 1971, and October 13, 1971, all in LPMDAH.

11. Barbara Y. Phillips to plaintiffs, August 6, 1979, in LCPDC.

12. James C. Cobb, *The Most Southern Place on Earth: The Mississippi Delta and the Roots of Regional Identity* (New York: Oxford University Press, 1992), 306.

13. *Capital Reporter*, February 19, 1981; *JCL*, February 15, 1981, and July 11 and 20, 1997.

14. No transcript for the trial exists because the defendants did not appeal the verdict. As a result, no permanent official record of what happened in the trial was made. The civil minutes for the trial provide only opening and closing times for each day, the location, and a list of witnesses. Newspapers did not cover the trial fully. The best existing and, of course, unofficial record comes from Jim Loewen's twenty-two-page handwritten Diary of Trial, which is far from a verbatim account; his notes are uneven (nothing appears when he testified) and undoubtedly contain errors (he somehow misdated every session). When Loewen's notes and newspaper accounts overlapped, the newspaper stories confirmed the accuracy of Loewen's work, even his occasional direct quotations. Some testimony can be pieced together from the Defendants' Proposed Post-Trial Findings of Fact and Conclusions of Law, October 11, 1979, and the Plaintiffs' Response, November 9, 1979, both in *Loewen v. Turnipseed* case file, NARA. Other sources include newspaper accounts, depositions, and interviews. Much of the testimony must have covered information presented here in earlier chapters (e.g., Charles Sallis's background or the process of writing *Mississippi: Conflict and Change*), and no effort will be made to repeat it.

15. *DDT*, August 29, 1979.

16. Ibid.; Loewen's Diary of Trial, in LPDC; Defendants' Proposed Post-Trial Findings of Fact and Conclusions of Law, October 11, 1979, and the Plaintiffs' Response, November 9, 1979, *Loewen v. Turnipseed* case file, NARA.

17. *JCL*, August 28 and 29, 1979.

18. *DDT*, August 29, 1979; "Survey of Mississippi School Superintendents, March 25 to July 1, 1979," in LCPDC; Defendants' Proposed Post-Trial Findings of Fact and Conclusions of Law, October 11, 1979, and the Plaintiffs' Response, November 9, 1979, *Loewen v. Turnipseed* case file, NARA.

19. *DDT*, August 29, 1979; Index of Last Names, *Mississippi: Conflict and Change*, with Racial Identifications; Index of Last Names, *Your Mississippi*, with Racial Identifications; Summary of Photographs, *Your Mississippi*, with Racial Identifications; Summary of Photographs, *Mississippi: Conflict and Change*, with Racial Identifications; all in *Loewen v. Turnipseed* case file, NARA.

20. Defendants' Proposed Post-Trial Findings of Fact and Conclusions of Law, October 11, 1979, and the Plaintiffs' Response, November 9, 1979, *Loewen v. Turnipseed* case file, MAGF.

21. *DDT*, August 29, 1979; Loewen's Diary of Trial, in LPDC; Defendants' Proposed Post-Trial Findings of Fact and Conclusions of Law, October 11, 1979, and the Plaintiffs'

Response, November 9, 1979, *Loewen v. Turnipseed* case file, MAGF; interviews with Catherine Gray Clark and with Jerry McBride.

22. Loewen's Diary of Trial, in LPDC; Defendants' Proposed Post-Trial Findings of Fact and Conclusions of Law, October 11, 1979, *Loewen v. Turnipseed* case file, MAGF; interviews with Catherine Gray Clark and with Jerry McBride.

23. *DDT*, August 29, 1979; Loewen's Diary of Trial, in LPDC; Defendants' Proposed Post-Trial Findings of Fact and Conclusions of Law, October 11, 1979, and the Plaintiffs' Response, November 9, 1979, *Loewen v. Turnipseed* case file, MAGF.

24. *DDT*, August 29, 1979; Loewen's Diary of Trial, in LPDC; Defendants' Proposed Post-Trial Findings of Fact and Conclusions of Law, October 11, 1979, and the Plaintiffs' Response, November 9, 1979, *Loewen v. Turnipseed* case file, MAGF.

25. *DDT*, August 29 and 30, 1979; *DDT*, August 29, 1979; Loewen's Diary of Trial, in LPDC; Defendants' Proposed Post-Trial Findings of Fact and Conclusions of Law, October 11, 1979, and the Plaintiffs' Response, November 9, 1979, *Loewen v. Turnipseed* case file, MAGF. On William Johnson, see Edwin Adams Davis and William R. Hogan, *The Barber of Natchez* (Baton Rouge: Louisiana State University Press, 1973).

26. *DDT*, August 30, 1979; Loewen's Diary of Trial, in LPDC; Defendants' Proposed Post-Trial Findings of Fact and Conclusions of Law, October 11, 1979, and the Plaintiffs' Response, November 9, 1979; vita of John Anthony Scott, *Loewen v. Turnipseed* case file, NARA; Frank R. Parker to Scott, September 20, 1976, in LCPDC. See also John Anthony Scott, review of *Mississippi: Conflict and Change, The Committee on History in the Classroom Newsletter*, December 1974; "Textbooks: History Textbook Adoption Procedure Challenged in Mississippi," *Inequality in Education* 22 (July 1977): 129–32; "*Loewen v. Turnipseed*—A landmark case for historians of American state and national history," *Committee on History in the Classroom Newsletter*, February 1977, 1–3.

27. *DDT*, August 30, 1979; Loewen's Diary of Trial, in LPDC; Defendants' Proposed Post-Trial Findings of Fact and Conclusions of Law, October 11, 1979, and the Plaintiffs' Response, November 9, 1979, *Loewen v. Turnipseed* case file, NARA; vita of Neil R. McMillen, *Loewen v. Turnipseed* case file, NARA; Frank R. Parker to McMillen, September 21, 1976, in LCPDC. See Neil R. McMillen, *The Citizen's Council: A History of Organized Southern White Resistance to the Second Reconstruction, 1954–1964* (Urbana: University of Illinois Press, 1971).

28. *DDT*, August 30, 1979; Loewen's Diary of Trial, in LPDC; Defendants' Proposed Post-Trial Findings of Fact and Conclusions of Law, October 11, 1979, and the Plaintiffs' Response, November 9, 1979, *Loewen v. Turnipseed* case file, NARA.

29. *DDT*, August 30, 1979; Loewen's Diary of Trial, in LPDC; Defendants' Proposed Post-Trial Findings of Fact and Conclusions of Law, October 11, 1979, and the Plaintiffs' Response, November 9, 1979, *Loewen v. Turnipseed* case file, NARA; interview with Neil R. McMillen.

30. *DDT*, August 30, 1979; Loewen's Diary of Trial, in LPDC; Plaintiffs' Response, November 9, 1979; vita of Robert B. Moore, *Loewen v. Turnipseed* case file, MAGF.

31. *DDT*, August 31, 1979; Loewen's Diary of Trial; Frank R. Parker to Moore, September 20, 1976, both in LPDC; Defendants' Proposed Post-Trial Findings of Fact and

Conclusions of Law, October 11, 1979, and the Plaintiffs' Response, November 9, 1979; vita of Jeanne Middleton, *Loewen v. Turnipseed* case file, MAGF.

32. *DDT*, August 31, 1979; Loewen's Diary of Trial, in LPDC; Defendants' Proposed Post-Trial Findings of Fact and Conclusions of Law, October 11, 1979, and the Plaintiffs' Response, November 9, 1979, *Loewen v. Turnipseed* case file, MAGF.

33. Loewen's Diary of Trial, in LPDC; vita of Jeanne Middleton; Defendants' Proposed Post-Trial Findings of Fact and Conclusions of Law, October 11, 1979, and the Plaintiffs' Response, November 9, 1979, all in *Loewen v. Turnipseed* case file, MAGF.

34. *DDT*, September 31, 1979; Ted Kilty to Frank R. Parker, June 12, 1979; Parker to Kilty, September 20, 1979; vita of Ted K. Kilty; Loewen's Diary of Trial, all in LPDC; Defendants' Proposed Post-Trial Findings of Fact and Conclusions of Law, October 11, 1979, and the Plaintiffs' Response, November 9, 1979, all in *Loewen v. Turnipseed* case file, MAGF. Howard Railes had said that his wife had applied the Frye test to the two books, and the court ruled the information inadmissible because he had not done it himself.

35. *DDT*, August 31 and September 2, 1979; Philip J. Stone to Loewen, February 2, 1979; Stone to Loewen, Frank R. Parker, and Steve Williamson, February 5, 1979; Loewen's Diary of Trial, all in LPDC; Defendants' Proposed Post-Trial Findings of Fact and Conclusions of Law, October 11, 1979, and the Plaintiffs' Response, November 9, 1979, all in *Loewen v. Turnipseed* case file, MAGF; vita of Philip J. Stone, *Loewen v. Turnipseed* case file, NARA. Stone later suggested "not just counting mentions of Blacks, but to show that there is a difference on such things as active-passive dimensions." He apparently did not conduct such an analysis and did not present it in court. See Stone to Loewen, May 16, 1979, in LPDC.

36. *DDT*, September 2, 1979; Loewen's Diary of Trial, in LPDC; vita of John H. Peterson Jr.; Defendants' Proposed Post-Trial Findings of Fact and Conclusions of Law, October 11, 1979, and the Plaintiffs' Response, November 9, 1979, all in *Loewen v. Turnipseed* case file, MAGF.

37. *DDT*, September 2, 1979; Loewen's Diary of Trial, in LPDC; vita of Evans Harrington; Defendants' Proposed Post-Trial Findings of Fact and Conclusions of Law, October 11, 1979, and the Plaintiffs' Response, November 9, 1979, all in *Loewen v. Turnipseed* case file, MAGF.

38. Loewen's Diary of Trial, in LPDC.

39. *JDN*, September 5, 1979; Loewen's Diary of Trial, in LPDC.

40. *JCL*, September 6, 1979; Loewen's Diary of Trial, in LPDC; Defendants' Proposed Post-Trial Findings of Fact and Conclusions of Law, October 11, 1979, and the Plaintiffs' Response, November 9, 1979, all in *Loewen v. Turnipseed* case file, MAGF.

41. *JDN*, September 5, 1979; *DDT*, September 6, 1979; Loewen's Diary of Trial, in LPDC; Defendants' Proposed Post-Trial Findings of Fact and Conclusions of Law, October 11, 1979, and the Plaintiffs' Response, November 9, 1979, all in *Loewen v. Turnipseed* case file, MAGF.

42. Loewen's Diary of Trial, in LPDC.

43. *JDN*, September 6, 1979; *DDT*, September 6, 1979; *JCL*, September 6, 1979; Loewen's Diary of Trial, in LPDC; Defendants' Proposed Post-Trial Findings of Fact

and Conclusions of Law, October 11, 1979, and the Plaintiffs' Response, November 9, 1979, all in *Loewen v. Turnipseed* case file, MAGF.

44. *JCL*, September 6, 1979; *DDT*, September 6, 1979; Loewen's Diary of Trial, in LPDC; Defendants' Proposed Post-Trial Findings of Fact and Conclusions of Law, October 11, 1979, and the Plaintiffs' Response, November 9, 1979, all in *Loewen v. Turnipseed* case file, MAGF.

45. *JCL*, September 7, 1979; *DDT*, September 7, 1979; *MCA*, September 7, 1979; Loewen's Diary of Trial, in LPDC; Defendants' Proposed Post-Trial Findings of Fact and Conclusions of Law, October 11, 1979, and the Plaintiffs' Response, November 9, 1979, all in *Loewen v. Turnipseed* case file, MAGF; James W. Loewen, *Teaching What Really Happened: How to Avoid the Tyranny of Textbooks and Get Students Excited About Doing History* (New York: Teachers College Press, 2010), 6. The exchange between Judge Smith and Turnipseed appears only in Loewen's *Lies My Teacher Told Me: Everything Your American History Textbook Got Wrong* (New York: The New Press, 1995), 160, and in his 2010 book.

46. Loewen's Diary of Trial, in LPDC; Defendants' Proposed Post-Trial Findings of Fact and Conclusions of Law, October 11, 1979, and the Plaintiffs' Response, November 9, 1979, *Loewen v. Turnipseed* case file, MAGF. In his dairy of the trial, Loewen noted, "(I erred. Not a one-room school.)."

47. *MCA*, September 7, 1979; Tupelo *Northeast Mississippi Journal*, September 7, 1979; Loewen's Diary of Trial, in LPDC; Defendants' Proposed Post-Trial Findings of Fact and Conclusions of Law, October 11, 1979; Defendants' Memorandum on Appropriate Relief, October 15, 1979, *Loewen v. Turnipseed* case file, MAGF.

48. *Boston Globe*, September 3, 1979. Hank Klibanoff wrote the article.

49. *Biloxi Sun-Herald*, September 9, 1979; *Capital Reporter*, September 6, 1979.

50. Plaintiffs' Memorandum on Appropriate Relief and Proposed Judgment for Appropriate Relief, October 1, 1979, *Loewen v. Turnipseed* case file, MAGF.

51. Defendants' Memorandum on Appropriate Relief, October 15, 1979, *Loewen v. Turnipseed* case file, NARA.

52. Defendants' Proposed Post-Trial Findings of Fact and Conclusions of Law, October 11, 1979, *Loewen v. Turnipseed* case file, MAGF.

53. Plaintiffs' Response to Defendants' Proposed Post-Trial Findings of Fact and Conclusions of Law, November 9, 1979; Frank R. Parker to James W. Loewen, et al., November 13, 1979, MAGF.

54. Memorandum of Decision, April 2, 1980, *Loewen v. Turnipseed* case file, NARA. Actually the defense filed a short Rebuttal to the Plaintiffs' Response (December 18, 1979), and counsel on each sided sent additional materials to Judge Smith. See Peter M. Stockett to Orma R. Smith, November 11, 1979, and February 26, 1980; Frank R. Parker to Orma R. Smith, November 26, 1979, and February 22, 1980, all in LCPDC.

55. Memorandum of Decision, April 2, 1980, *Loewen v. Turnipseed* case file, NARA.

56. Ibid.

57. Ibid.; Order and Permanent Injunction, April 2, 1980, *Loewen v. Turnipseed* case file, NARA.

58. *JCL*, April 3, 1980; *DDT*, April 3, 1980; *Oxford Eagle*, April 3, 1980; Frank R. Parker to John Anthony Scott, April 7, 1980, in LCPDC; Minutes, MSTPB, May 13, 1980.

59. Defendants' Objections to Proposed Revisions to the Textbook, *Mississippi: Conflict and Change*," [July 2, 1980], *Loewen v. Turnipseed* case file, MAGF.

60. Plaintiffs' Response to Defendants' Objections to Proposed Textbook Revisions, July 25, 1980; Final Judgment, August 5, 1980, *Loewen v. Turnipseed* case file, NARA.

61. Motion for an Award of Attorneys' Fees and Litigation Expenses, May 12, 1980; Defendants' Response to Plaintiffs' Motion for an Award of Attorneys' Fees and Litigation Expenses, July 22, 1980; Memorandum of Decision, August 21, 1980, *Loewen v. Turnipseed* case file, NARA.

Change

1. Minutes, MSTPB, December 17, 1980; John K. Bettersworth, *Mississippi: The Land and the People* (Austin, TX: Steck-Vaughn, 1981); John Ray Skates, *Mississippi's Past and Present* (Jackson, MS: International Geographic, 1973); Skates, *Mississippi, A Bicentennial History* (New York: Norton, 1979); Skates with David G. Sansing, *Mississippi: Its People and Culture* (Minneapolis: T. S. Denison, 1981); Sansing, *Mississippi: Its People and Culture* (Minneapolis: T. S. Denison, 1980); Sansing and Carroll Waller, *A History of the Mississippi Governor's Mansion* (Jackson: University Press of Mississippi, 1977); interviews with Sallis and with David Sansing. A story in the *JCL* incorrectly reported the board had approved *Conflict and Change* at the December 17 meeting. See *JCL*, December 18, 1980.

2. Arthur Woodward and David L. Elliot, "Textbooks: Consensus and Controversy," *Textbooks and Schooling in the United States: Eight-ninth Yearbook of the National Society for the Study of Education*, ed. David L. Elliott and Arthur Woodward (Chicago: University of Chicago Press, 1990), 155; Bettersworth, *Mississippi: The Land and the People*, 137, 201, 212, 218, 250, 260, 300–3.

3. Skates, *Mississippi's Past and Present*, 84–86, 90–93, 101, 105, 110, 123, 139, 141, 149, 150, 183, 184, 185, 222, 228.

4. Ibid., 107, 109, 110, 113, 121, 122, 134, 137, 138, 142, 149, 151, 152, 172, 193, 194, 226, 233.

5. Sansing, *Mississippi: Its People and Culture*, 152, 157, 158–59, 207, 213; interview with David Sansing.

6. Sansing, *Mississippi: Its People and Culture*, 233–34, 251, 261, 263–34.

7. Ibid., 308–14, 315–18, 321–22, 323, 324–25.

8. Ibid., 161, 210, 251, 315, 322, 323, 339, 357; interview with David Sansing.

9. Frank R. Parker to Reecy Dickson, September 3, 1980; Parker to Black School Superintendents, December 31, 1980, in LCPDC; Parker to Loewen, February 9, 1981; Loewen to Parker, May 20, 1981, in LPDC.

10. *JCL*, January 28–29, March 25–26, April 22–23, and May 23, 1981. The double dates for some issues of the *JCL* refer to a "Focus North" weekly supplement that appeared in the paper.

11. *JCL*, July 24, 1981; *DDT*, July 24, 1981; Mississippi State Textbook Purchasing Board, Local Selection of Multiple Texts, July 1, 1981; Gordon D. Gibson to Robin Stevens, May 18, 1981, both in LPDC.

12. Robert N. Fortenberry to Gordon D. Gibson, June 5, 1981; Gibson to Fortenberry, July 8, 1981; Gibson to David Teague, July 8, 1981, all in LPDC.

13. *JCL*, January 21–22, 1981.

14. Ibid., January 14 and 28, 1981; *JDN*, January 14, 26, 28, and 29, 1981.

15. *JCL* January 15, 1981; *Capital Reporter*, January 22 and February 19, 1981; *JDN*, January 27, 1981.

16. *JCL*, January 28, 1981.

17. Ibid., February 6 and 10, 1981.

18. Ibid., February 6, 1981. Matthews later had no recollection of the incident. Interview with W. A. Matthews.

19. Frank Parker to Loewen, February 9, 1981, in LCPDC.

20. Nicholas de Jongh, *Not in Front of the Audience: Homosexuality on Stage* (London: Routledge. 1992), 91, 119, 133. See also John Howard, *Men Like That: A Southern Queer History* (Chicago: University of Chicago Press, 1999), 226, 354 n. 150.

21. Philip J. Stone to Loewen, May 5, 1975, and May 16, 1975; Loewen to Stone, May 14, 1975, all in LPDC.

22. Frank Parker to John Anthony Scott, September 20, 1979, LCPDC; interview with W. A. Matthews. Parker went on to suggest, "All they can do is respond the same way a white Alabama legislator responded to a friend of mine (working for the American Friends Service Committee): 'Please don't send me any more information.'"

23. Andrew Hartman, *A War for the Soul of America: A History of the Culture Wars* (Chicago: University of Chicago Press, 2015), 254, 276.

24. Edward T. Linenthal and Tom Engelhardt, eds. *History Wars: The Enola Gay and Other Battles for the American Past* (New York: Henry Holt, 1996); Linenthal and Engelhardt, "Introduction: History Under Siege," in *History Wars*, 6; Michael J. Hogan, "The *Enola Gay* Controversy: History, Memory, and the Politics of Presentation," in *Hiroshima in History and Memory*, ed. Michael J. Hogan (New York: Cambridge University Press, 1996), 200–232; Hartman, *A War for the Soul of America*, 276–83.

25. Linenthal, "Anatomy of a Controversy," in *History Wars*, 60, 61; Mike Wallace, "Culture War, History Front," in *History Wars*, 175; Hogan, "The *Enola Gay* Controversy," 229–30.

26. Hartman, *A War for the Soul of America*, 267. For discussions of the battle over the National History Standards, see also Gary B. Nash, Charlotte Crabtree, and Ross E. Dunn, *History on Trial: Culture Wars and the Teaching of the Past* (New York: Knopf, 1997; New York: Vintage, 2000); Diane Ravitch, "The Controversy over National History Standards," *Bulletin of the National Academy of Arts and Sciences* 51 (Jan.–Feb. 1998), 14–28; Ronald W. Evans, *The Social Studies Wars: What Should We Teach the Children?* (New York: Teachers College Press, 2004), 166–69; Wallace, "Culture War," 171–98.

27. Lynne Cheney, "The End of History," *Wall Street Journal*, October 20, 1994.

28. Hartman, *A War for the Soul of America*, 272–75; Evans, *The Social Studies Wars*, 165–66; Nash, Crabtree, Dunn, *History on Trial*, 3–6; Ravitch, "The Controversy over National History Standards," 16–17; Wallace, "Culture War," 192.

29. Nash, Crabtree, and Dunn, *History on Trial*, 193 *passim* (a section entitled "Answering the Critics"); Wallace, "Culture War," 187.

30. Nash, Crabtree, and Dunn, *History on Trial*, 248–55; Ravitch, "The Controversy over National History Standards," 18–20; Diane Ravitch and Arthur M. Schlesinger Jr., "The New, Improved History Standards," *Wall Street Journal*, April 3, 1966.

31. Jonathan Zimmerman, *Whose America? Culture Wars in the Public* (Cambridge, MA: Harvard University Press, 2002), 217; Gary B. Nash, "The History Standards Controversy and Social History," *Journal of Social History* 29 (Special issue, Fall 1995): 46.

32. Hartman, *A War for the Soul of America*, 276, 283; Nash, Crabtree, and Dunn, *History Trial*, 15, xxi.

33. Edward B. Jenkinson, *Censors in the Classroom: The Mind Benders: 40 Questions and Answers* (Carbondale: Southern Illinois University Press, 1979) and *The Schoolbook Protest Movement* (Bloomington: Phi Delta Kappa Educational Foundation, 1986); Carol Mason, *Reading Appalachia from Left to Right: Conservatives and the 1974 Kanawha County Textbook Controversy* (Ithaca: Cornell University Press, 2009).

34. Howard, *Men Like That*, 257–78 and 280–90; *ACLU of Mississippi v. Mississippi State General Services Administration*, 652 F.Supp. 380 (1987); *Herdahl v. Pontotoc County School District*, 887 F.Supp. 902 (1995).

35. Bruce Levine, et al., *Who Built America? Working People and the Nation's Economy, Politics, Culture, and Society* (New York: Pantheon, 1989), xvii; Joshua Brown to author, November 20, 2014; Howard Zinn, *A People's History of the United States* (New York: Harper and Row, 1980); interview with David Sansing. The textbook's impact on state histories of other states remains unknown. One examination of state history textbooks assessed the effect of Loewen's *Lies My Teacher Told Me* but not the more relevant *Conflict and Change*. The article indirectly referred to the Loewen and Sallis book only when it mentioned the "issues he [Loewen] underwent while writing a textbook for a Mississippi history course. Some of these challenges led to his decision to file a discrimination lawsuit . . . a suit that Loewen won." Loewen had provided "advice, feedback, critique, and suggestions" and had "graciously agreed to read a draft" of the article. See Scott Roberts, "'Georgia on My Mind': Writing the 'New' State History Textbook in the Post-Loewen World," *History Teacher* 47 (November 2013): 42, 43, 57 n. 1.

36. John Anthony Scott, "*Loewen v. Turnipseed*: A Landmark Case," *American Historical Association Newsletter* (October 1980): 7–8.

37. Frank Parker to John Anthony Scott, April 7, 1980, LCPDC; Outline of Social Sciences Forum, Tougaloo College, September 15, 1971, in LPDC; interview with David Sansing. On the uses of ignorance, see Robert N. Proctor and Londa Schiebinger, eds., *Agnotology: The Making and Unmaking of Ignorance* (Stanford: Stanford University Press, 2008).

Index